THE GUINNESS

BOOK OF

SPORTS

RECORDS,

1992

THE GUINNESS
BOOK OF
SPORTS
RECORDS,
1992

EDITOR
MARK YOUNG

Facts On File
New York • Oxford

THE GUINNESS BOOK OF SPORTS RECORDS, 1992

Copyright © 1992 by Guinness Publishing Ltd

Facts On File, Inc.
460 Park Avenue South
New York NY 10016
USA

This book is taken in part from *The Guinness Book of Records* © 1991

Facts On File books are available at special discounts when purchased in bulk quantities for businesses, associations, institutions or sales promotions. Please contact the Special Sales Department of our New York office at 212/683-2244 (dial 800/322-8755 except in NY, AK or HI).

ISBN 0-8160-2651-3 (hardcover)
ISBN 0-8160-2652-1 (paperback)
ISSN 1054-4178

Text design by Ron Monteleone
Jacket design by Ron Monteleone and Sam Moore
Composition by Ron Monteleone/Facts On File, Inc.
Production by Michael Braunschweiger
Manufactured by R. R. Donnelley & Sons, Inc.
Printed in the United States of America

10 9 8 7 6 5 4 3 2 1

This book is printed on acid-free paper.

CONTENTS

ILLUSTRATION CREDITS

Dale Williams: 65, 112, 210, 211

PHOTOGRAPH CREDITS

t=top b=bottom m=middle l=left r=right

Advantage International: 190t
American Horse Shows Association: 68b
American Amateur Racquetball Association: 168b
Amateur Softball Association: 183t
AP/Wide World Photos: 16t, 20tr, 32t, 42tl, 51b, 57t, 149bl, 149br, 153b, 154b, 155t, 156b, 161b, 162t, 167tl, 167br, 172b, 174t, 180t, 182t, 187b, 205tr, 207tl, 207tr, 218t, 219t, 231m, 241t
Arkansas Gazette: 93b
Association of Volleyball Professionals: 215b
ATP Tour: 198t, 203t

Vernon J. Biever: 74b
The Blood-Horse: 142bl, 140br
Tim Boggan: 191t
Boston Celtics: 38t
Boston Red Sox: 19tr
Surfing Magazine/Peter Brouillet: 185t

Canadian Football League Hall of Fame and Museum: 100b
Chicago Bears: 73t
Chicago Bulls: 39t
Bob Coglianese: 139t
Rich Cruse/RC Photo: 214 (all)

Detroit Pistons: 41tl
Duke University: 228m

Fay Foto, Boston: 210b, 211b
Furman University: 42bl

Robert F. George: 62b
Golden Bear International: 113bl

Sports File/Tony Henshaw: 159t

Hockey Hall of Fame and Museum: 127t, 129tl, 129tr, 131t
Stan Honda: 212b
Houston Rockets: 41tr

Mark Jenkins: 64 (all)

Kansas City Chiefs: 77b
Kansas City Royals: 28tl

Ladies' Professional Golf Association: 116t, 118bl, 118tr
Los Angeles Lakers: 36b, 36t
Louisiana State University: 42tl

Major Soccer League: 182b
Sports File/Scott Markewitz: 177tl, 177ml, 178t
Jeff McBride/PGA Tour: 113tl
Milwaukee Bucks: 34t
Minnesota Vikings: 77tr
Montreal Expos: 18b

National Association for Stock Car Auto Racing: 9t
National Hot Rod Association/ Les Lovett: 11tl, 11tr
New York Giants: 87t
New York Mets: 28tr

Ohio State University: 99t
Oklahoma State University: 88t
Orienteering North America: 164bl, 164br
Orlando Magic: 34b

Pennsylvania State University: 47b
PGA World Gold Hall of Fame: 112tr
PGA Tour Archives: 112br, 113tl
Photography Inc: 128t, 134b
Pittsburgh Penguins: 135t
Professional Bowlers Association: 53t, 54b
Professional Rodeo Cowboys Association: 170b

Williams S. Romano: 114b, 119b
"©Rosenfeld Collection, Mystic Seaport Museum, Inc., James Burton photographer.": 220t
Louis Ross: 12t

San Francisco 49ers: 84t
Seattle Seahawks: 77tl
Sports File/Ski Racing Magazine Archives 177tr
Sports File/Sporting Pictures 186b
Brian Spurlock: 6tl, 6tr, 7t, 67t, 121b, 205tl
St. Louis Cardinals: 20tl

Len Taylor: 171b
Texas Christian University: 88b
Texas Rangers: 19tl

United States Archery Association: 3t
United States Speedskating Association: 184t
United States Trotting Association Photo: 124t
University of California at Los Angeles: 46bl, 46tr
University of Michigan: 233b
University of Notre Dame: 71t, 94 (all), 95 (all)

Cor Vos: 63b

Sports File/Lee Wardle 179t
Washington Redskins: 87b
Western Michigan University: 93t
Wham-O/Jeff Colick: 106bl, 106br
Sports File/Ski Raching Association/Kirk Williamson: 176b
Winnipeg Jets: 127b
Women's International Bowling Congress: 55b
Women's Tennis Association: 193t, 200b

ACKNOWLEDGMENTS

The goal of this book is to provide the most comprehensive and accurate account possible of the records established in the world of sports. Accumulating such a vast and disparate array of information has required the cooperation, patience and expertise of many organizations and individuals. I would like to thank the media representatives, librarians and historians of the following organizations for their help: U.S. National Archery Assoc., Championship Auto Racing Teams, Indianapolis Motor Speedway, National Assoc. for Stock Car Auto Racing, National Hot Rod Association, U.S. Badminton Assoc., International Badminton Federation, Major League Baseball, The National Baseball Hall of Fame and Museum, Elias Sports Bureau, Little League Baseball, National Collegiate Athletic Assoc., Naismith Memorial Basketball Hall of Fame, National Basketball Assoc., U.S. Biathlon Assoc., U.S. Bobsled and Skeleton Fed., Professional Bowling Assoc., Ladies' Professional Bowling Tour, American Bowling Congress, Women's Int'l Bowling Congress, USA Boxing, U.S. Canoe and Kayak Team, U.S. Croquet Assoc., U.S. Curling Assoc., U.S. Cycling Assoc., Ultra Marathon Cycling Assoc., U.S. Diving, American Horse Shows Assoc., U.S. Fencing Assoc., U.S. Field Hockey Assoc., U.S. Figure Skating Assoc., National Football League, University of Notre Dame, Arena Football League, Canadian Football League, World Flying Disc Federation, Professional Golfers' Assoc., Ladies' Professional Golfers Assoc., European PGA Tour, U.S. Gymnastics Fed., U.S. Hang Gliding Assoc., U.S. Trotting Assoc., National Hockey League, Daily Racing Form, Churchill Downs, Breeders' Cup, New York Racing Assoc., Maryland Jockey Club, National Horseshoe Pitchers Assoc., U.S. Judo, USA Karate Fed., U.S. Modern Pentathlon Assoc., U.S. Olympic Committee, U.S. Orienteering Fed., U.S. Polo Assoc., Billiard Congress of America, American Powerboat Assoc., American Amateur Racquetball Assoc., Professional Rodeo Cowboys Assoc., U.S. Amateur Confederation of Roller Skating, U.S. Rowing Assoc., National Rifle Assoc., U.S. Skiing, Iditarod Trail Committee, Major Soccer League, Amateur Softball Assoc., U.S. Int'l. Speedskating Assoc., Assoc. of Surfing Professionals, U.S. Swimming, U.S. Synchronized Swimming, U.S. Table Tennis Assoc., U.S. Taekwondo Union, U.S. Team Handball Fed., Women's Tennis Assoc., I.B.M./A.P.T Tour, The Athletics Congress, New York Road Runners Club, Boston Athletic Assoc., American Trampoline and Tumbling Assoc., Triathlon Fed. USA, Assoc. of Volleyball Professionals, U.S. Water Polo, American Water Ski Assoc., U.S. Weightlifting, USA Wrestling, America's Cup Organizing Committee.

Regrettably, space prevents me from mentioning all the individuals who have helped me compile this book; however, I must mention certain people whose contributions have added immensely to this project: at Guinness Publishing in Enfield, England, Peter Matthews, Michelle Dunkley McCarthy, Stewart Newport and Debbie Collings. Thanks to Mark Jenkins for his help on the Siberian Passage feature, and to Bill Inglish for his contribution to the Masters feature. Several members of the staff of the *Facts On File World News Digest* have contributed their "clippings," but special thanks is extended to Ken Park for being on the cutting edge of sports records! I must also thank my brother, Andrew Young, who as an ex-B.B.C. Brain of Sport Champion is an invaluable research source for any sports trivia editor.

As I wrote in this space last year, publishing, like sports, requires the efforts of many people to produce the on-field performance. I am once again indebted to the talented and professional team of people who have assisted me in producing this book: Jo Stein, Ron Monteleone, Grace M. Ferrara, Dale Williams, Scott Wight, Joe Reilly, Virginia Rubens, Marjorie Bank, John W. Hansen, Linda Palamara . . . and *"danke schön"* to Michael Braunschweiger, who overcame Swiss soccer depression and an unexpected trip to Hong Kong (which is now the official cure for Swiss soccer depression) to make sure the book was "on schedule."

Mark Young
New York City

ARCHERY

ORIGINS The invention of the bow is ranked as one of the three most important advances in human history, next to the development of language and the art of making fire, since it provided humankind with an enhanced means of subsistence. The exact date of its invention is unknown, but historians agree that it was at least 50,000 years ago. The origins of archery as a competitive sport are also unclear. It is believed that the ancient Olympic Games (776 B.C. to 393 A.D.) featured archery, using tethered doves as targets. The legends of Robin Hood and William Tell indicate that archery prowess was highly regarded in Europe by the 13th century. Archery became an official event in the modern Olympics in 1900. In 1931, the *Fédération Internationale de Tir à l'Arc* (FITA) was founded as the world governing body of the sport.

United States The date of the first use of the bow as a weapon in North America is unknown; however, it is believed that Native American tribes in the eastern part of North America were familiar with the bow by the 11th century. The National Archery Association was founded in 1879 in Crawfordsville, Ind. and is the oldest amateur sports organization in continuous existence in the United States.

TARGET ARCHERY

The most widely practiced discipline in archery is Olympic-style target archery (also known as FITA style). Olympic-style target archery competition is based on the Single FITA round system of scoring. A Single FITA round consists of 36 arrows shot from four distances: 90, 70, 50 and 30 meters for men; 70, 60, 50 and 30 for women, for a total of 144 arrows. Scoring ranges from 10 in the center gold circle to 1 in the outer white ring. The maximum possible score for a Single FITA round is 1,440 points. Competition varies from accumulated scores based on two or more Single FITA rounds to single elimination rounds in which each archer's score reverts to zero at each stage of the tournament.

WORLD RECORDS (Single FITA Rounds)

Men

Event	Archer	Country	Points	Year
FITA	Vladimir Esheev	USSR	1,352	1990
90 m	Vladimir Esheev	USSR	330	1990
70 m	Hiroshi Yamamoto	Japan	344	1990
50 m	Rick McKinney	U.S.	345	1982
30 m	Takayoshi Matsushita	Japan	357	1986
Final	Vladimir Esheev	USSR	345	1989

Women

Event	Archer	Country	Points	Year
FITA	Lee Eun-Kyung	S. Korea	1,370	1990
70 m	Kim Soo-nyung	S. Korea	336	1989
60 m	Kim Soo-nyung	S. Korea	347	1989
60 m	Lee Eun-Kyung	S. Korea	347	1990
50 m	Lee Eun-Kyung	S. Korea	337	1990
30 m	Joanne Edens	Great Britain	357	1990
Final	Kim Soo-nyung	S. Korea	346	1990

Source: U.S. National Archery Association

FLIGHT SHOOTING WORLD RECORDS

The object in flight shooting is to fire the arrow the greatest distance possible. There are two flight shooting classifications: regular flight and broadhead flight.

Regular Flight

Men

Bow Type	Distance	Archer	Date
Crossbow	2,047 yds 0 ft 2 in	Harry Drake	July 30, 1988
Unlimited Footbow	2,028 yds 0 ft 0 in	Harry Drake	Oct. 24, 1971
Conventional Footbow	1,542 yds 2 ft 10 in	Harry Drake	Oct. 6, 1979
Recurve Bow	1,336 yds 1 ft 3 in	Don Brown	Aug. 2, 1987
Compound Bow	1,159 yds 2 ft 6 in	Bert McCune Jr.	Aug. 2, 1987
Longbow	304 yds 1 ft 8 in	Don Brown	June 25, 1988
Primitive Bow	244 yds 2 ft 1 in	Daniel Perry	June 24, 1990

Women

Bow Type	Distance	Archer	Date
Recurve Bow	1,039 yds 1 ft 3 in	April Moon	Sept. 13, 1981
Conventional Footbow	1,113 yds 2 ft 6 in	Arlyne Rhode	Sept. 10, 1978
Compound Bow (25kg)	904 yds 0 ft 4 in	April Moon	Oct. 5, 1989

Broadhead Flight

All records listed are for the "unlimited" bow classification.

Men

Bow Type	Distance	Archer	Date
Compound Bow	742 yds 0 ft 2 in	Jesse Morehead	June 24, 1990
Recurve Bow	526 yds 0 ft 5 in	Don Brown	June 26, 1988
Longbow	304 yds 1 ft 8 in	Don Brown	June 25, 1988
Primitive Bow	244 yds 2 ft 7 in	Daniel Perry	June 24, 1990

Women

Bow Type	Distance	Archer	Date
Compound Bow	481 yds 0 ft 7 in	April Moon	June 24, 1989
Recurve Bow	364 yds 0 ft 4 in	April Moon	June 28, 1987
Longbow	205 yds 1 ft 5 in	April Moon	June 28, 1987
Primitive Bow	107 yds 1 ft 5 in	Gwen Perry	June 24, 1990

Source: U.S. National Archery Association

OLYMPIC GAMES Archery made its first appearance in the 1900 Games in Paris, France. It was also featured in 1904, 1908 and 1920, but then was omitted until 1972, when enough countries had adopted FITA standardized rules to allow for a meaningful international competition.

Most gold medals Hubert van Innis (Belgium) has won six gold medals (au cordon dore—33 meters, au chapelet—33 meters, 1900; moving bird target 28 meters, 33 meters, moving bird target [team] 33 meters, 50 meters, 1920).

Most medals Hubert van Innis has won nine medals in all: six gold (see above), and three silver (au cordon dore—50 meters, 1900; moving bird target 50 meters, moving bird target [team] 28 meters, 1920).

Most medals (country) The United States has won 27 medals: seven gold, five silver and four bronze in men's events; five gold, three silver and three bronze in women's.

United States The most successful American archer at the Olympic Games has been Darrell Pace, who won gold medals in 1976 and 1984. Lida Howell (née Scott) won two gold medals in individual events in 1904; however, only American archers competed in the women's events that year.

WORLD CHAMPIONSHIPS Target archery world championships were first held in 1931 in Lwow, Poland. The championships are staged biennially.

Most titles (archer) The most titles won is seven, by Janina Spychajowa-Kurkowska (Poland) in 1931–34, 1936, 1939 and 1947. The most titles won by a man is four, by Hans Deutgen (Sweden) in 1947–50.

Most titles (country) The United States has a record 14 men's and eight women's team titles.

United States The most individual world titles won by a U.S. archer is three, by Rick McKinney: 1977, 1983 and 1985. Jean Lee, 1950 and 1952, is the only U.S. woman to have won two individual world titles.

UNITED STATES NATIONAL CHAMPIONSHIPS The U.S. national championships were first held in Chicago, Ill. from August 12–14, 1879, and are staged annually.

ON TARGET ■ RICK MCKINNEY HAS WON THREE WORLD ARCHERY TITLES AND NINE U.S. TITLES, AND HOLDS THE WORLD RECORD IN THE 50 METER SINGLE FITA ROUND CLASS.

Most titles The most archery titles won is 17, by Lida Howell between 1883 and 1907. The most men's titles is nine (three individual, six pairs), by Rick McKinney, 1977, 1979–83, and 1985–87.

AUTO RACING

The nationality of the competitors in this section is U.S. unless noted otherwise.

ORIGINS The site of the first automobile race is open to debate. There is a claim that the first race was held in the United States in 1878, from Green Bay to Madison, Wis., won by an Oshkosh steamer. However, France discounts this, claiming that *La Velocipede*, a 19.3-mile race in Paris on April 20, 1887, was the first race. The first organized race did take place in France: 732 miles from

Paris to Bordeaux and back, on June 11–14, 1895. The first closed-circuit race was held over five laps of a one-mile dirt track at Narragansett Park, Cranston, R.I. on September 7, 1896. Grand Prix racing started in 1906, also in France. The Indianapolis 500 was first run on May 30, 1911 (see below).

INDIANAPOLIS 500

The first Indianapolis 500 was held on May 30, 1911 at the Indianapolis Motor Speedway, where the event is still run. The Speedway was opened on August 19, 1909. The original track surface was crushed stone and tar, but several accidents during its initial races convinced the owners to install a paved surface, a project that required 3.2 million bricks and was completed by December 1909. In 1937, parts of the track were resurfaced with asphalt, and the track was completely resurfaced in 1976. The race track is a 2½ mile square oval that has two straightaways of 3,300 feet and two of 660 feet, all 50 feet wide. The four turns are each 1,320 feet, all 60 feet wide and banked 9 degrees, 12 minutes. A 36-inch strip of original brick marks the start–finish line.

VICTORY LANE

Most wins Three drivers have won the race four times: A. J. Foyt Jr., in 1961, 1964, 1967 and 1977; Al Unser, in 1970–71, 1978 and 1987; and Rick Mears, in 1979, 1984, 1988 and 1991.

Fastest win The record time is 2 hours 41 minutes 18.404 seconds (185.981 mph) by Arie Luyendyk (Netherlands) driving a 1990 Lola-Chevrolet on May 27, 1990.

INDIANAPOLIS 500 WINNERS (1911–1952)

Year	Driver	Av. Speed (mph)	Year	Driver	Av. Speed (mph)
1911	Ray Harroun	74.602	1932	Fred Frame	104.144
1912	Joe Dawson	78.719	1933	Louis Meyer	104.162
1913	Jules Goux	75.933	1934	William Cummings	104.863
1914	Rene Thomas	82.474	1935	Kelly Petillo	106.240
1915	Ralph DePalma	89.840	1936	Louis Meyer	109.069
1916	Dario Resta	84.001	1937	Wilbur Shaw	113.580
1917	(not held)		1938	Floyd Roberts	117.200
1918	(not held)		1939	Wilbur Shaw	115.035
1919	Howard Wilcox	88.050	1940	Wilbur Shaw	114.277
1920	Gaston Chevrolet	88.618	1941	Floyd Davis & Mauri Rose	115.117
1921	Tommy Milton	89.621	1942	(not held)	
1922	Jimmy Murphy	94.484	1943	(not held)	
1923	Tommy Milton	90.954	1944	(not held)	
1924	L.L. Corum & Joe Boyer	98.234	1945	(not held)	
1925	Peter DePaolo	101.127	1946	George Robson	114.820
1926	Frank Lockhart	95.904	1947	Mauri Rose	116.338
1927	George Souders	97.545	1948	Mauri Rose	119.814
1928	Louis Meyer	99.482	1949	Bill Holland	121.327
1929	Ray Keech	97.585	1950	Johnnie Parsons	124.002
1930	Billy Arnold	100.448	1951	Lee Wallard	126.244
1931	Louis Schneider	96.629	1952	Troy Ruttman	128.922

Slowest win The slowest time is 6 hours 42 minutes 8 seconds (74.602 mph) by Ray Harroun in the inaugural race in 1911.

Consecutive wins Four drivers have won the race in consecutive years: Wilbur Shaw, 1939–40; Mauri Rose, 1947–48; Bill Vukovich, 1953–54; and Al Unser, 1970–71.

Oldest winner Al Unser became the oldest winner when he won the 1987 race at age 47 years 11 months.

Youngest winner Troy Ruttman became the youngest winner when he won the 1952 race at age 22 years 2 months.

Closest finish The closest margin of victory was 0.16 seconds in 1982 when Gordon Johncock edged Rick Mears.

Lap leader Al Unser has led the race for a cumulative 625 laps during his 25 starts, 1965–90.

Highest earnings The record prize fund is $7,009,150, and the individual prize record is $1,219,704, by Rick Mears, both in 1991. Mears also leads the field in career earnings at $4,162,989 from 14 starts, 1978–91.

QUALIFYING

Official time trials are held on the two weekends prior to the race to allow entrants to qualify for the 33 starting positions. A completed trial consists of four consecutive laps around the track with the course cleared of all other traffic. Pole position is determined at the "first day" trials. Qualifiers on each subsequent day are lined up behind the qualifiers of previous days. In 1991 Rick Mears gained pole position with an average speed of 224.113 mph, but Gary Bettenhausen recorded the fastest overall average speed of 224.468 mph on the fol-

INDIANAPOLIS 500 WINNERS (1953–1991)

Year	Driver	Av. Speed (mph)	Year	Driver	Av. Speed (mph)
1953	Bill Vukovich	128.740	1973	Gordon Johncock	159.036
1954	Bill Vukovich	130.840	1974	Johnny Rutherford	158.589
1955	Bob Sweikert	128.209	1975	Bobby Unser	149.213
1956	Pat Flaherty	128.490	1976	Johnny Rutherford	148.725
1957	Sam Hanks	135.601	1977	A. J. Foyt Jr.	161.331
1958	Jim Bryan	133.791	1978	Al Unser	161.363
1959	Rodger Ward	135.857	1979	Rick Mears	158.899
1960	Jim Rathmann	138.767	1980	Johnny Rutherford	142.862
1961	A. J. Foyt Jr.	139.131	1981	Bobby Unser	139.084
1962	Rodger Ward	140.293	1982	Gordon Johncock	162.029
1963	Parnelli Jones	143.137	1983	Tom Sneva	162.117
1964	A. J. Foyt Jr.	147.350	1984	Rick Mears	163.612
1965	Jim Clark*	150.686	1985	Danny Sullivan	152.982
1966	Graham Hill*	144.317	1986	Bobby Rahal	170.722
1967	A. J. Foyt Jr.	151.207	1987	Al Unser	162.175
1968	Bobby Unser	152.882	1988	Rick Mears	144.809
1969	Mario Andretti	156.867	1989	Emerson Fittipaldi*	167.581
1970	Al Unser	155.749	1990	Arie Luyendyk*	185.981
1971	Al Unser	157.735	1991	Rick Mears	176.457
1972	Mark Donohue	162.962			

* Nationality: Jim Clark (Great Britain), Graham Hill (Great Britain), Emerson Fittipaldi (Brazil), Arie Luyendyk (Netherlands).

FOUR 500'S ■ RICK MEARS CELEBRATES HIS 1991 INDY 500 TRIUMPH, WHICH WAS HIS RECORD-EQUALING FOURTH WIN.

lowing day, yet only gained a spot on Row 5 of the starting grid. This was the fourteenth time that this paradox had happened since the introduction of speed time trials in 1915.

Most starts A. J. Foyt Jr. has started a record 34 races (1959–91).

Pole position Rick Mears has gained a record six poles, in 1979, 1982, 1986, 1988–89 and 1991. Mears's victory in 1991 was the fourteenth time the pole-sitter had won the race.

Fastest qualifier The record average speed for four laps qualifying is 225.301 mph by Emerson Fittipaldi (Brazil) in a 1990 Penske-Chevrolet on May 13, 1991. On the same day he set the one-lap record of 225.575 mph.

First woman driver The only woman to compete in the Indianapolis 500 is Janet Guthrie. She passed her rookie test in 1976 and 1977, became the first woman to compete in the race, but was forced to retire after 27 laps. In 1978, she completed the race, finishing in ninth place.

BORN January 16, 1935, Houston, Tex.

INDY CAR RACING CAREER STATISTICS
1958–91

Starts	Wins	Poles	Race Leader	Earnings	Titles
367*	67*	53	6,621 laps	$5,150,230	7*

INDIANAPOLIS 500 CAREER STATISTICS
1958-91

Starts	Wins	Poles	Laps	Miles	Earnings
34*	4†	4	4,714*	11,785*	$2,448,080

RECORD NOTES Foyt is the only driver to have won the Indy 500 (1961, 1964, 1967, 1977), the Daytona 500 (1972), and the Le Mans 24 Hours (1967). Foyt holds the Indy Car season records for most wins: 10* in 1964; most poles: 10 in 1965; and most wins in different seasons: 18, 1960–81.

† indicates tied record; * indicates all-time record.

INDY CAR RACING

The first Indy Car Championship was held in 1909 under the sponsorship of the American Automobile Association (AAA). In 1956 the United States Automobile Club (USAC) took over the running of the Indy series. Since 1979, Championship Auto Racing Teams Inc. (CART) has organized the Indy Championship, which has been called the PPG Indy Car World Series Championship since 1979.

VICTORY LANE

Most championships A.J. Foyt Jr. has won seven Indy Car National Championships: 1960–61, 1963–64, 1967, 1975 and 1979.

Most consecutive championships Ted Horn won three consecutive national titles from 1946–48.

Most wins (career) A.J. Foyt Jr. has won a career record 67 Indy car races, 1957–91. Foyt's first victory came at the DuQuoin 100 in 1960 and his latest at the Pocono 500 in 1981.

Most wins (season) The record for most victories in a season is 10, shared by two drivers: A.J. Foyt Jr. in 1964 and Al Unser in 1970.

Consecutive winning seasons Bobby Unser won at least one race per season for 11 seasons from 1966–76.

Most wins (road course) Mario Andretti has won a record 21 road course races, 1964–91.

Most wins (500-mile races) A. J. Foyt Jr. has won nine 500-mile races: Indianapolis 500 in 1961, 1964, 1967 and 1977; Pocono 500 in 1973, 1975, 1979 and 1981; California 500 in 1975.

TOP SPEED ■ AL UNSER JR. WON THE 1990 MICHIGAN 500 CLOCKING AN AVERAGE SPEED OF 189.727 MPH—THE FASTEST EVER FOR A 500-MILE INDY CAR EVENT.

Closest races The closest margin of victory in an Indy car race was 0.02 seconds on April 10, 1921 when Ralph DePalma edged Roscoe Sarles to win the Beverly Hills 25. The closest finish in a 500-mile event was Mario Andretti's 0.14 second victory in the 1984 Michigan 500. Andretti also pulled off the closest finish in an Indy road race, when he won the Portland 200 by 0.07 seconds on June 15, 1986. The loser in this memorable showdown was his son, Michael . . . well, it was Father's Day!

Highest earnings (season) The single-season record is $2,461,734, set in 1991 by Michael Andretti.

Highest earnings (career) Through the 1991 season, Rick Mears has the highest career earnings for Indy drivers with $10,638,430.

QUALIFYING

Most poles (career) Mario Andretti has earned a record 64 pole positions, 1964–91.

FASTEST INDY CAR RACES

Distance	Race	Driver	Av. Speed (mph)	Year
100 miles	Ontario 100	Wally Dallenbach	179.910	1973
150 miles	Atlanta 150	Rick Mears	182.094	1979
200 miles	Michigan 200	Rick Mears	182.325	1983
250 miles	Michigan 250	Bobby Rahal	181.701	1986
500 miles	Michigan 500	Al Unser Jr.	189.727	1990

Source: CART

Most poles (season) A.J. Foyt Jr. earned 10 poles in 1965.

Most poles (road courses) Mario Andretti has earned 26 poles on road courses.

Most poles (500-mile races) Rick Mears has earned a record 16 poles in 500-mile races.

Fastest qualifiers The fastest qualifying lap ever for an Indy car race was 225.575 mph by Emerson Fittipaldi on May 13, 1990 in qualifying for the Indianapolis 500.

NASCAR (NATIONAL ASSOCIATION FOR STOCK CAR AUTO RACING)

The National Association for Stock Car Auto Racing, Inc., was founded by Bill France Sr. in 1947. The first NASCAR-sanctioned race was held on February 15, 1948 on Daytona's beach course. The first NASCAR championship, the Grand National series, was held in 1949. Since 1970, the championship series has been called the Winston Cup Championship. The Winston Cup is won by the driver who accumulates the most points during the 29-race series.

Most championships Richard Petty has won a record seven NASCAR titles: 1964, 1967, 1971–72, 1974–75 and 1979.

Most consecutive titles Cale Yarborough is the only driver to "threepeat" as NASCAR champion, winning in 1976–78.

Most wins (career) Richard Petty has won 200 NASCAR Winston Cup races out of 1,152 in which he competed, 1958–91.

Most wins (season) Richard Petty won a record 27 races in 1967.

Fastest average speed The fastest average speed in a Winston Cup race is 186.288 mph, set by Bill Elliott at Talladega Superspeedway, Ala. on May 5, 1985.

Highest earnings (season) Dale Earnhardt earned a record $3,083,056 in 1990.

Highest earnings (career) Dale Earnhardt also holds the career earnings mark at $15,179,319, 1975–91.

DAYTONA 500 WINNERS (1959–1991)

Year	Driver	Av. Speed (mph)	Year	Driver	Av. Speed (mph)
1959	Lee Petty	135.521	1976	David Pearson	152.181
1960	Junior Johnson	124.740	1977	Cale Yarborough	153.218
1961	Marvin Panch	149.601	1978	Bobby Allison	159.730
1962	Fireball Roberts	152.529	1979	Richard Petty	143.977
1963	Tiny Lund	151.566	1980	Buddy Baker	177.602
1964	Richard Petty	154.334	1981	Richard Petty	169.651
1965	Fred Lorenzen	141.539	1982	Bobby Allison	153.991
1966	Richard Petty	160.627	1983	Cale Yarborough	155.979
1967	Mario Andretti	149.926	1984	Cale Yarborough	150.994
1968	Cale Yarborough	143.251	1985	Bill Elliott	172.265
1969	LeeRoy Yarborough	157.950	1986	Geoff Bodine	148.124
1970	Pete Hamilton	149.601	1987	Bill Elliott	176.263
1971	Richard Petty	144.462	1988	Davey Allison	137.531
1972	A. J. Foyt Jr.	161.550	1989	Darrell Waltrip	148.466
1973	Richard Petty	157.205	1990	Derrike Cope	165.761
1974	Richard Petty	140.894	1991	Ernie Irvan	148.148
1975	Benny Parsons	153.649			

Daytona 500

The Daytona 500 has been held at the 2½ mile oval Daytona International Speedway in Daytona Beach, Fla. since 1959. The Daytona 500 is the most prestigious event on the NASCAR calendar.

Victory Lane

Most wins Richard Petty has won a record seven times: 1964, 1966, 1971, 1973–74, 1979 and 1981.

Consecutive wins Richard Petty and Cale Yarborough are the only drivers to have repeated as Daytona 500 winners in consecutive years. Petty's double was in 1973–74 and Yarborough's in 1983–84.

Oldest winner Bobby Allison became the oldest winner of the race in 1988 at age 50 years 2 months 11 days.

Youngest winner Richard Petty became the youngest winner in 1964, at age 26 years 4 months 18 days.

Fastest win The record average speed for the race is 177.602 mph, by Buddy Baker in 1980.

Slowest win The slowest average speed is 124.740 mph, by Junior Johnson in 1960.

Highest earnings The individual race earnings record is $233,000, by Ernie Irvan in 1991. The career earnings record is $860,005, by Bill Elliott in 13 races, 1978–91.

Qualifying

Most starts Richard Petty has competed in 31 Daytona 500 races.

Fastest qualifying time The record average speed for qualifying for the race is 210.364 mph, set by Bill Elliott in 1987.

Most poles Cale Yarborough has earned a record four poles at the Daytona 500 in 1968, 1970, 1978 and 1984.

Formula One (Grand Prix)

The World Drivers' Championship was inaugurated in 1950. Currently the championship is contested over 16 races in 16 different countries worldwide. Points are awarded to the first six finishers in each race; the driver with the most points at the end of the season is the champion.

Victory Lane

Most championships Juan-Manuel Fangio (Argentina) has won the drivers' championship five

Stock Tops ■ Dale Earnhardt won his fifth NASCAR title in 1991, and extended his career earnings record to $15,179,319.

times, 1951 and 1954–57. He also holds the record for consecutive titles with four straight, 1954–57.

Oldest champion Juan-Manuel Fangio is the oldest world champion, winning the 1957 title at age 46 years 41 days.

Youngest champion Emerson Fittipaldi (Brazil) became the youngest champion in 1972, at age 25 years 273 days.

Most wins (career) Alain Prost (France) has won 44 Formula One races, the most of any driver.

Most wins (season) Ayrton Senna (Brazil) won a record eight races in 1988. His victories came in Belgium, Great Britain, Canada, Germany, Hungary, Japan, San Marino and Detroit.

Oldest winner The oldest driver to win an official race was Luigi Fagioli (Italy), who was 53 years 22 days old when he won the 1951 French Grand Prix.

Youngest winner The youngest driver to win an official race was Troy Ruttman, who was 22 years 2 months old when he won the 1952 Indianapolis 500, which counted in the World Drivers' Championship that year.

Closest finish The narrowest margin of victory in a Formula One race was when Ayrton Senna held off Nigel Mansell (Great Britain) by 0.014 seconds to win the Spanish Grand Prix on April 13, 1986.

United States Two Americans have won the Formula One title, Phil Hill in 1961 and Mario Andretti in 1978.

Most starts Riccardo Patrese (Italy) has raced in a record 224 Grand Prix from 1977–91.

Most poles Ayrton Senna (Brazil) has earned a record 60 poles in 126 races, 1985–91.

Fastest qualifying time Keke Rosberg (Finland) set the fastest qualifying lap in Formula One history, when he qualified for the British Grand Prix at Silverstone with an average speed of 160.817 mph on July 20, 1985.

DRAG RACING

Drag racing is an acceleration contest between two cars racing from a standing start over a precisely measured, straight-line, quarter-mile course. Competition is based on two-car elimination heats culminating in a final round. The fastest elapsed time wins the race. Elapsed time is measured over the distance of the course; the top speed is a measurement of the last 66 feet of the track, where a special speed trap electronically computes the speed of the dragster. There are several classifications in drag racing, based on the engine size, type of fuel and vehicle weight limitations of the car. The most prominent drag racing organization is the National Hot Rod Association (NHRA), which was founded in 1951. The NHRA recognizes 12 categories of racers, with the three main categories being Top Fuel, Funny Car and Pro Stock.

TOP FUEL

Top Fuel dragsters are 4,000-horsepower machines that are powered by nitromethane. The engines are mounted behind the driver, and parachutes are the primary braking system.

SPEED RECORDS

Quickest elapsed time in an NHRA event The quickest elapsed time recorded by a Top Fuel dragster from a standing start for 440 yards is 4.881 seconds by Gary Ormsby at the NHRA Heartland Nationals at Topeka, Kan. on September 29, 1990.

Fastest top speed in an NHRA event During his record elapsed time run (see above), Gary Ormsby also recorded the fastest top speed of 296.05 mph.

VICTORIES

Most wins (career) Don Garlits has won a record 35 Top Fuel races.

Most wins (season) Five drivers have won six Top Fuel races in a season: Don Garlits, 1985;

NHRA PERFORMANCE RECORDS

NHRA rules require that for a record to be certified a back-up run within one percent of the record time must be completed at the same event.

Quickest Elapsed Time

Class	Time	Driver	Date
Top Fuel	4.897 secs.	Joe Amato	March 24, 1991
Funny Car	5.140 secs.	Jim White	Oct. 11, 1990
Pro Stock	7.180 secs.	Warren Johnson	Sept. 15, 1991

Fastest Speed

Class	Mph	Time	Driver
Top Fuel	294.88	Gary Ormsby	Oct. 8, 1989
Funny Car	291.82	Jim White	Oct. 25, 1991
Pro Stock	193.21	Bob Glidden	July 28, 1991

Source: NHRA

ROCKET MEN ■ JOE AMATO (LEFT) AND JIM WHITE (RIGHT) HOLD NHRA PERFORMANCE RECORDS FOR TOP FUEL AND FUNNY CAR CLASSES RESPECTIVELY.

Darrel Gwynn, 1988; Gary Ormsby, 1989; Joe Amato, 1990; and Kenny Bernstein, 1991.

FUNNY CAR

A Funny Car is a short-wheelbase version of the Top Fuel dragster. Funny Cars mount a fiberglass replica of a production car with the engine located in front of the driver.

SPEED RECORDS

Quickest elapsed time in an NHRA event The quickest elapsed time recorded in the Funny Car class is 5.132 seconds, by Ed McCulloch on October 7, 1989 at the Chief Auto Parts Nationals, Ennis, Tex.

Fastest top speed in an NHRA event Jim White was timed at 291.82 mph at the Winston National Finals at Pomona Raceway, Calif. on October 25, 1991.

VICTORIES

Most wins (career) Don Prudhomme has won a record 35 Funny Car races.

Most wins (season) Two drivers have won seven races in a season: Don Prudhomme in 1976; and Kenny Bernstein in 1985.

PRO STOCK

Pro Stock dragsters look like their oval-racing counterparts, but feature extensive engine modifications. A maximum 500 cubic inch displacement and a minimum vehicle weight of 2,350 pounds are allowed under NHRA rules.

SPEED RECORDS

Quickest elapsed time in an NHRA event The quickest elapsed time in the Pro Stock class is 7.180 seconds, by Warren Johnson on September 15, 1991 at the Sunoco Keystone Nationals, Mohnton, Pa.

Fastest top speed in an NHRA event The fastest top speed in a Pro Stock race is 193.21 mph by Bob Glidden on July 28, 1991 at the Autolite California Nationals, Sonoma, Cal.

VICTORIES

Most wins (career) Bob Glidden has won a record 80 races, the most victories of any driver in NHRA events.

Most wins (season) Darrell Alderman won a record 11 races in 1991.

NHRA WINSTON SERIES CHAMPIONSHIP This series was inaugurated in 1975.

MOST TITLES

Top Fuel Joe Amato has won a record four national titles: 1984, 1988 and 1990–91.

Funny Car Two drivers have won a record four national titles: Don Prudhomme, 1975–78, and Kenny Bernstein, 1985–88.

Pro Stock Bob Glidden has won a record nine national titles in 1975, 1978–80 and 1985–89.

BADMINTON

ORIGINS Badminton is a descendant of the children's game of battledore and shuttlecock. It is believed that a similar game was played in China more than 2,000 years ago. Badminton takes its name from Badminton House in England, where the Duke of Beaufort's family and guests popularized the game in the 19th century. British army officers took the game to India in the 1870s, where the first modern rules were codified in 1876. The world governing body is the International Badminton Federation, formed in 1934.

United States The earliest known reference to badminton in the United States is a description of battledore shuttlecock in the 1864 *American Boy's Book of Sports and Games*. The first badminton club formed in the United States was the Badminton Club of New York, founded in 1878. The game was not organized at the national level until 1935, when the American Badminton Association (ABA) was founded in Boston, Mass. In 1978 the ABA was renamed the United States Badminton Association.

OLYMPIC GAMES Badminton will be included in the Olympic Games for the first time as an official sport at the Barcelona Games in 1992. The game was included as a demonstration sport at the Munich Games in 1972.

WORLD CHAMPIONSHIPS The first championships were staged in Malmo, Sweden in 1977. Since 1983 the event has been held biennially.

Most titles (overall) Park Joo-bong (South Korea) has won a record five world titles: men's doubles in 1985 and 1991; mixed doubles in 1985, 1989 and 1991. Two women have won three titles: Lin Ying (China), ladies' doubles in 1983, 1987 and 1989; Li Lingwei (China), ladies' singles in 1983 and 1989, ladies' doubles in 1985.

Most titles (singles) Yang Yang (China) is the only man to have won two world singles titles, in 1987 and 1989. Two women have won two singles titles: Li Lingwei (China), 1983 and 1989; Han Aiping (China), 1985 and 1987.

UNITED STATES NATIONAL CHAMPIONSHIPS The first competition was held in 1937.

Most titles Judy Hashman (née Devlin) has won a record 31 titles: 12 women's singles, 1954, 1956–63 and 1965–67; 12 women's doubles, 1953–55, 1957–63 and 1966–67 (10 with her sister Susan); and seven mixed doubles, 1956–59, 1961–62 and 1967. David G. Freeman has won a record seven men's singles titles: 1939–42, 1947–48 and 1953.

SHUTTLE SERVICE ■ YANG YANG (CHINA) HAS WON A RECORD TWO MEN'S BADMINTON WORLD SINGLES TITLES.

BASEBALL

ORIGINS In 1907, baseball's national commission appointed a committee to research the history of the game. The report, filed in 1908, concluded that Abner Doubleday had invented the game in 1839 at Cooperstown, N.Y. At the time, the report was viewed with some skepticism because of the friendship between Doubleday and the committee chairman, A. G. Mills; however, in 1939, major league baseball celebrated its centennial and cemented the legend of Doubleday's efforts in American folklore. Sports historians today discount the Doubleday theory, claiming that baseball in North America evolved from such English games as cricket, paddleball and rounders.

Uncontested is that Alexander Cartwright Jr. formulated the rules of the modern game in 1845, and that the first match under these rules was played on June 19, 1846 when the New York Nine defeated the New York Knickerbockers, 23–1, in four innings. On March 17, 1871 the National Association of Professional Base Ball Players was formed, the first professional league in the United

States. Today there are two main professional baseball associations, the National League (organized in 1876) and the American League (organized in 1901, recognized in 1903), which together form the major leagues, along with approximately 20 associations that make up the minor leagues. The champions of the two leagues first played a World Series in 1903 and have played one continuously since 1905. (For further details on World Series history, see below.)

MAJOR LEAGUE RECORDS

Records listed in this section are for the all-time major league record and the equivalent National League (NL) or American League (AL) record. Where an all-time record is dated prior to 1900, the modern record (1900–present) is also listed.

GAMES PLAYED

Career 3,562, by Pete Rose, Cincinnati Reds (NL), 1963–78, 1984–86; Philadelphia Phillies (NL), 1979–83; Montreal Expos (NL), 1984. The most American League games played is 3,308, by Carl Yastrzemski, Boston Red Sox, 1961–83.

Consecutive 2,130, by Lou Gehrig, New York Yankees (AL), June 1, 1925 through April 30, 1939. The National League record is 1,207 consecutive games, by Steve Garvey, Los Angeles Dodgers and San Diego Padres, September 3, 1975 through July 29, 1983.

BATTING RECORDS

BATTING AVERAGE

Career .367, by Ty Cobb, Detroit Tigers (AL), 1905–26; Philadelphia Athletics (AL), 1927–28. Cobb compiled his record from 4,191 hits in 11,429 at-bats. The National League record is .359, by Rogers Hornsby, St. Louis Cardinals, 1915–1926, 1933; New York Giants, 1927; Boston Braves, 1928; Chicago Cubs, 1929–32. Hornsby compiled his record from 2,895 hits in 8,058 at-bats.

Season .438, by Hugh Duffy, Boston (American Association) in 1894. Duffy compiled 236 hits in 539 at-bats. The modern record is .424, by Rogers Hornsby, St. Louis Cardinals (NL), in 1924. Hornsby compiled 227 hits in 536 at-bats. The modern American League record is .422, by Nap Lajoie, Philadelphia Athletics, in 1901. Lajoie compiled 229 hits from 543 at-bats.

HITS

Career 4,256, by Pete Rose, Cincinnati Reds (NL), 1963–78, 1984–86; Philadelphia Phillies (NL), 1979–83; Montreal Expos (NL), 1984. Rose compiled his record hits total from 14,053 at-bats. The American League record is 4,191, by Ty Cobb, Detroit Tigers, 1905–26; Philadelphia Athletics, 1927–28. Cobb compiled his hits total from 11,429 at-bats.

Season 257, by George Sisler, St. Louis Browns (AL), in 1920, from 631 at-bats. The National League record is 254 hits, by two players: Lefty O'Doul, Philadelphia Phillies, in 1929, from 638 at-bats; Bill Terry, New York Giants, in 1930, from 633 at-bats.

Game Nine, by John Burnett, Cleveland Indians (AL), during an 18-inning game on July 10, 1932. The American League record for a nine-inning game is six hits, achieved by many players. The National League record is seven hits, by two players (both in nine-inning games): Wilbert Robinson, Baltimore Orioles (NL), on June 10, 1892; Rennie Stennett, Pittsburgh Pirates (NL), on September 16, 1975.

SINGLES

Career 3,215, by Pete Rose, Cincinnati Reds (NL), 1963–78, 1984–86; Philadelphia Phillies, 1979–83, Montreal Expos, 1984. The American League record is 3,052, by Ty Cobb, Detroit Tigers, 1905–26; Philadelphia Athletics, 1927–28.

Season 206, by Wee Willie Keeler, Baltimore Orioles (NL) in 1898. The modern-day National League record is 198, by Lloyd Waner, Pittsburgh Pirates, in 1927. The American League record is 187, by Wade Boggs, Boston Red Sox, in 1985.

Game Seven, by John Burnett, Cleveland Indians (AL), in an 18-inning game on July 10, 1932. In regulation play the record for both the National and American leagues is six hits by several players.

DOUBLES

Career 793, by Tris Speaker, Boston Red Sox (AL), 1907–1915; Cleveland Indians (AL), 1916–1926; Washington Senators (AL), 1927; Philadelphia Athletics (AL), 1928. The National League record is 746, by Pete Rose, Cincinnati Reds, 1963–78, 1984–86; Philadelphia Phillies, 1979–83; Montreal Expos, 1984.

Season 67, by Earl Webb, Boston Red Sox (AL), in 1931. The National League record is 64, by Joe Medwick, St. Louis Cardinals, in 1936.

Game Four, by many players in both leagues.

TRIPLES

Career 312, by Sam Crawford, Cincinnati Reds (NL), 1899–1902; Detroit Tigers (AL), 1903–17. The American League record is 297, by Ty Cobb, Detroit Tigers, 1905–26; Philadelphia Athletics, 1927–28. The National League record is 252, by Honus Wagner, Louisville Colonels, 1897–99; Pittsburgh Pirates, 1900–17.

Season 36, by Owen Wilson, Pittsburgh Pirates (NL), in 1912. The American League record is 26, by two players: Shoeless Joe Jackson, Cleveland Indians, in 1912; Sam Crawford, Detroit Tigers, in 1914.

Game Four, by two players: George A. Strief, Philadelphia (American Association) on June 25, 1885; William Joyce, New York Giants (NL) on May 18, 1897. The modern-day record for both leagues is three, achieved by several players.

HOME RUNS

Career 755, by Hank Aaron, Milwaukee/Atlanta Braves (NL), 1954–74; Milwaukee Brewers (AL), 1975–76. Aaron hit his record dingers from 12,364 at-bats. The National League record is 733, by Aaron, Milwaukee/Atlanta Braves, 1954–74. The American League record is 708 by Babe Ruth, Boston Red Sox, 1914–19; New York Yankees, 1920–34. Ruth hit his record total from 8,327 at-bats.

Season 61, Roger Maris, New York Yankees (AL), in 1961. The National League record is 56, by Hack Wilson, Chicago Cubs, in 1930.

Game Four, by 11 players: Bobby Lowe, Boston (NL), May 30, 1894; Ed Delahanty, Philadelphia Phillies (NL), July 13, 1896; Lou Gehrig, New York Yankees (AL), June 3, 1932; Chuck Klein, Philadelphia Phillies (NL), July 10, 1936; Pat Seerey, Chicago White Sox (AL), July 18, 1948; Gil Hodges, Brooklyn Dodgers (NL), August 31, 1950; Joe Adcock, Milwaukee Braves (NL), July 31, 1954; Rocky Colavito, Cleveland Indians (AL), June 10, 1959; Willie Mays, San Francisco Giants (NL), April 30, 1961; Mike Schmidt, Philadelphia Phillies (NL), April 17, 1976; and Bob Horner, Atlanta Braves, July 6, 1986. Klein, Schmidt and Seerey matched the record in extra-inning games.

GRAND SLAMS

Career 23, by Lou Gehrig, New York Yankees (AL), 1923–39. The National League record is 18, by Willie McCovey, San Francisco Giants, 1959–73, 1977–80; San Diego Padres, 1974–76.

Season Six, by Don Mattingly, New York Yankees (AL), in 1987. The National League record is five, by Ernie Banks, Chicago Cubs, in 1955.

Game Two, by seven players: Tony Lazzeri, New York Yankees (AL), May 24, 1936; Jim Tabor, Boston Red Sox (AL), July 4, 1939; Rudy York, Boston Red Sox (AL), July 27, 1946; Jim Gentile, Baltimore Orioles (AL), May 9, 1961; Tony Cloninger, Atlanta Braves (NL), July 3, 1966; Jim Northrup, Detroit Tigers (AL), June 24, 1968; and Frank Robinson, Baltimore Orioles (AL), June 26, 1970. Cloninger is the only player from the National League to achieve this feat, and he was a pitcher!

RUNS BATTED IN

Career 2,297, by Hank Aaron, Milwaukee/Atlanta Braves (NL), 1954–74; Milwaukee Brewers (AL), 1975–76. The National League record is 2,202, by Hank Aaron, Milwaukee/Atlanta Braves, 1954–74. The American League record is 2,192, by Babe Ruth, Boston Red Sox, 1914–19; New York Yankees, 1920–34.

Season 190, by Hack Wilson, Chicago Cubs (NL), in 1930. The American League record is 184, by Lou Gehrig, New York Yankees, in 1931.

Game 12, by Jim Bottomley, St. Louis Cardinals (NL), on September 16, 1924. The American League record is 11, by Tony Lazzeri, New York Yankees, on May 24, 1936.

RUNS SCORED

Career 2,245, by Ty Cobb, Detroit Tigers (AL), 1905–26; Philadelphia Athletics (AL), 1927–28. The National League record is 2,165 runs, scored by Pete Rose, Cincinnati Reds, 1963–78, 1984–86; Philadelphia Phillies, 1979–83; Montreal Expos, 1984.

Season 196, by Billy Hamilton, Philadelphia Phillies (NL), in 1894. The modern-day National League record is 158 runs, scored by Chuck Klein, Philadelphia Phillies, in 1930. The American

League record is 177 runs, scored by Babe Ruth, New York Yankees, in 1921.

Game Seven, by Guy Hecker, Louisville (American Association), on August 15, 1886. The record in both the National League and American League is six runs scored, achieved by 12 players, 10 in the National League and two in the American League.

TOTAL BASES

Career 6,856, by Hank Aaron, Milwaukee/Atlanta Braves (NL), 1954–74; Milwaukee Brewers (AL), 1975–76. Aaron's record is comprised of 2,294 singles, 624 doubles, 98 triples and 755 home runs. The National League record is also held by Aaron, at 6,591 total bases, Milwaukee/Atlanta Braves, 1954–74. The American League record is 5,863 total bases, set by Ty Cobb, Detroit Tigers, 1905–26; Philadelphia Athletics, 1927–28. Cobb's total comprised 3,052 singles, 724 doubles, 297 triples and 118 home runs.

Season 457, by Babe Ruth, New York Yankees (AL) in 1921. Ruth's total comprised 85 singles, 44 doubles, 16 triples and 59 home runs. The National League record is 450 total bases, by Rogers Hornsby, St. Louis Cardinals, in 1922. Hornsby collected 148 singles, 46 doubles, 14 triples and 39 home runs.

Game 18, by Joe Adcock, Milwaukee Braves (NL) on July 31, 1954. Adcock hit four home runs and a double. The American League record is 16, by six players: Ty Cobb, Detroit Tigers, May 5, 1925; Lou Gehrig, New York Yankees, June 3, 1932; Jimmy Foxx, Philadelphia Athletics, July 10, 1932; Pat Seerey, Chicago White Sox, July 18, 1948; Rocky Colavito, Cleveland Indians, June 10, 1959; and Fred Lynn, Boston Red Sox, June 18, 1975. Foxx and Seerey matched the record in extra-inning games.

WALKS

Career 2,056, by Babe Ruth, Boston Red Sox (AL), 1914–19; New York Yankees (AL), 1920–34; Boston Braves (NL), 1935. Ruth also holds the American League record at 2,036. The National League record is 1,799 walks, by Joe Morgan, Houston Astros 1963–71, 1980; Cincinnati Reds, 1972–79; San Francisco Giants, 1981–82; Philadelphia Phillies, 1983.

Season 170, by Babe Ruth, New York Yankees (AL) in 1923. The National League record is 148,

by two players: Eddie Stanky, Brooklyn Dodgers, in 1945; Jimmy Wynn, Houston Astros, in 1969.

STRIKEOUTS

Career 2,597, by Reggie Jackson, Kansas City/Oakland Athletics (AL), 1967–75, 1987; Baltimore Orioles (AL), 1976; New York Yankees (AL), 1977–81; California Angels (AL), 1982–86. The National League record is 1,936, by Willie Stargell, Pittsburgh Pirates, 1962–82.

Season 189, by Bobby Bonds, San Francisco Giants (NL), in 1970. The American League record is 186, by Rob Deer, Milwaukee Brewers, in 1987.

HIT BY PITCH

Career 267, by Don Baylor, Baltimore Orioles (AL), 1970–75; Oakland Athletics (AL), 1976, 1988; California Angels (AL), 1977–82; New York Yankees (AL), 1983–85; Boston Red Sox (AL), 1986–87; Minnesota Twins (AL), 1987. The National League record is 243, by Ron Hunt, New York Mets, 1963–66; Los Angeles Dodgers, 1967; San Francisco Giants, 1968–70; Montreal Expos, 1971–74; St. Louis Cardinals, 1974.

Season 50, by Ron Hunt, Montreal Expos (NL) in 1971. The American League record is 35, by Don Baylor, Boston Red Sox, in 1986.

CONSECUTIVE BATTING RECORDS

Hits in a row 12, by two players: Pinky Higgins, Boston Red Sox (AL), over four games, June 19–21, 1938; and Moose Droppo, Detroit Tigers (AL), over three games, July 14–15, 1952. The National League record is 10, by eight players: Ed Delahanty, Philadelphia Phillies, July 13–14, 1897; Jacob Gettman, Washington Senators, September 10–11, 1897; Ed Konetchy, Brooklyn Dodgers, June 28–July 1, 1919; Hazen Cuyler, Pittsburgh Pirates, September 18–21, 1925; Charles Hafey, St. Louis Cardinals, July 6–9, 1929; Joe Medwick, St. Louis Cardinals, July 19–21, 1936; John Hassett, Boston Braves, June 9–14, 1940; and Woodrow Williams, Cincinnati Reds, September 5–6, 1943.

Games batted safely 56, by Joe DiMaggio, New York Yankees (AL), May 15 through July 16, 1941. During the streak, DiMaggio gained 91 hits from 223 at-bats: 56 singles, 16 doubles, 4 triples and 15 home runs. The National League record is 44 games, shared by two players: Wee Willie Keeler, Balti-

GOLDEN STREAK ■ 1991 MARKED THE FIFTIETH ANNIVERSARY OF JOE DIMAGGIO'S 56-GAME HITTING STREAK.

more Orioles, April 22 through June 18, 1897; Pete Rose, Cincinnati Reds, June 14 through July 31, 1978.

Home runs in a row Four, by four players: Bobby Lowe, Boston (NL), May 30, 1894; Lou Gehrig, New York Yankees (AL), June 3, 1932; Rocky Colavito, Cleveland Indians (AL), June 10, 1959; and Mike Schmidt, Philadelphia Phillies (NL), April 17, 1976.

Games hitting home runs Eight, by two players: Dale Long, Pittsburgh Pirates (NL), May 19–28, 1956; Don Mattingly, New York Yankees (AL), July 8–18, 1987.

Walks in a row Seven, by three players: Billy Rogell, Detroit Tigers (AL), August 17–19, 1938; Mel Ott, New York Giants (NL), June 16–18, 1943; Eddie Stanky, New York Giants (NL), August 29–30, 1950.

Games receiving a walk 22, by Roy Cullenbine, Detroit Tigers (AL), July 2 through July 22, 1947. The National League record is 16, by Jack Clark, St. Louis Cardinals, July 18 through August 10, 1987.

PITCHING RECORDS

GAMES PLAYED

Career 1,070, by Hoyt Wilhelm, New York Giants (NL), 1952–56; St. Louis Cardinals (NL), 1957; Cleveland Indians (AL), 1957–58; Baltimore Orioles (AL), 1958–62; Chicago White Sox (AL), 1963–68; California Angels (AL), 1969; Atlanta Braves (NL), 1969–70; Chicago Cubs (NL), 1970; Atlanta Braves (NL), 1971; Los Angeles Dodgers (NL), 1971–72. The National League record is 1,050, by Kent Tekulve, Pittsburgh Pirates, 1974– 85; Philadelphia Phillies, 1985–88; Cincinnati Reds, 1989. The American League record is 807, by Sparky Lyle, Boston Red Sox, 1967–71; New York Yankees, 1972–78; Texas Rangers, 1979–80; Chicago White Sox, 1982.

Season 106, by Mike Marshall, Los Angeles Dodgers (NL), in 1974. Marshall also holds the American League record, at 90 games pitched for the Minnesota Twins in 1979.

VICTORIES

Career 511, by Cy Young, Cleveland Spiders (NL), 1890–98; St. Louis Cardinals (NL), 1899–1900; Boston Red Sox (AL), 1901–08; Cleveland

Indians (AL), 1909–11; Boston Braves (NL), 1911. The American League record is 416, by Walter Johnson, Washington Senators, 1907–27. The National League record is 373, by two players: Christy Mathewson, New York Giants, 1900–16; Cincinnati Reds, 1916; and Grover Alexander, Philadelphia Phillies, 1911–1917, 1930; Chicago Cubs, 1918–1926; St. Louis Cardinals, 1926–29.

Season 60, by "Old Hoss" Radbourn, Providence Grays (NL), in 1884. The modern-day National League record is 37, by Christy Mathewson, New York Giants, in 1908. The American League record is 41, by Jack Chesbro, New York Yankees, in 1904.

LOSSES

Career 313, by Cy Young, Cleveland Spiders (NL), 1890–98; St. Louis Cardinals (NL), 1899–1900; Boston Red Sox (AL), 1901–08; Cleveland Indians (AL), 1909–11; Boston Braves (NL), 1911. The American League record is 279, by Walter Johnson, Washington Senators, 1907–27. The National League record is 267, by Pud Galvin, Buffalo Bisons, 1879–85; Pittsburgh Pirates, 1887–92. The modern-day National League record is 251, by Eppa Rixey, Philadelphia Phillies, 1912–20; Cincinnati Reds, 1921–33.

Season 48, by John Coleman, Philadelphia Phillies (NL), in 1883. The modern-day National League record is 29, by Vic Willis, Boston Braves, in 1905. The American League record is 26, by two pitchers: Jack Townsend, Washington Senators, in 1904; Bob Groom, Washington Senators, in 1909.

EARNED RUN AVERAGE (ERA)

Career (minimum 2,000 innings) 1.82, by Ed Walsh, Chicago White Sox (AL), 1904–1916; Boston Braves (NL), 1917. Walsh also holds the American League record at 1.80. The National League record is 1.93, by Mordecai "Three Finger" Brown, St. Louis Cardinals, 1903; Chicago Cubs, 1904–12, 1916; Cincinnati Reds, 1913.

Season (minimum 200 innings) 1.01, by Dutch Leonard, Boston Red Sox (AL), in 1914. The National League record is 1.04, by Mordecai "Three Finger" Brown, Chicago Cubs, in 1906.

INNINGS PITCHED

Career 7,356, by Cy Young, Cleveland Spiders (NL), 1890–98; St. Louis Cardinals (NL), 1899–1900; Boston Red Sox (AL), 1901–08; Cleveland Indians (AL), 1909–1911; Boston Braves (NL),

1911. The American League record is 5,923, by Walter Johnson, Washington Senators, 1907–27. The National League record is 5,243.2 innings, by Warren Spahn, Boston/Milwaukee Braves, 1942–64; New York Mets, 1965; San Francisco Giants, 1965.

Season 680, by Will White, Cincinnati Reds (NL), in 1879. The modern-day National League record is 434, by Joe McGinnity, New York Giants, in 1903. The American League record is 464, by Ed Walsh, Chicago White Sox, in 1908.

NO-HITTERS

On September 4, 1991, baseball's Committee for Statistical Accuracy, chaired by Commissioner Fay Vincent, defined a no-hit game as "one in which a pitcher or pitchers complete a game of nine innings or more without allowing a hit." All previously considered no-hit games which did not fit into this definition—such as rain-shortened games; eight-inning, complete game no-hitters hurled by losing pitchers; and games in which hits were recorded in the tenth inning or later—would be considered "notable achievements," not no-hitters.

The first officially recognized no-hitter was pitched by Joe Borden for Philadelphia of the National Association v. Chicago on July 28, 1875. Through the 1991 season 234 no-hitters have been pitched. The most no-hitters pitched in one season is seven, on two occasions: 1990 and 1991.

Career Seven, by Nolan Ryan: California Angels v. Kansas City Royals (3–0), on May 15, 1973; California Angels v. Detroit Tigers (6–0), on July 15, 1973; California Angels v. Minnesota Twins (4–0), on September 28, 1974; California Angels v. Baltimore Orioles (1–0), on June 1, 1975; Houston Astros v. Los Angeles Dodgers (5–0), on September 26, 1981; Texas Rangers v. Oakland Athletics (5–0), on June 11, 1990; and Texas Rangers v. Toronto Blue Jays (3–0), on May 1, 1991. Ryan pitched five of his no-hitters in American League games, thus achieving the league record. The National League record is four, by Sandy Koufax, Los Angeles Dodgers: v. New York Mets (5–0), June 30, 1962; v. San Francisco Giants (8–0), May 11, 1963; v. Philadelphia Phillies (3–0), June 4, 1964; and v. Chicago Cubs (1–0), September 9, 1965.

Season Two, by four players: Johnny Vander Meer, Cincinnati Reds (NL), in 1938; Allie Reynolds, New York Yankees (AL), in 1951; Virgil Trucks, Detroit Tigers (AL) in 1952; and Nolan Ryan, California Angels (AL), in 1973.

PERFECT GAMES

In a perfect game, no batter reaches base during a complete game of at least nine innings.

The first officially recognized perfect game was hurled by John Richmond on June 12, 1880 for Worcester v. Cleveland in a National League game. Through the 1991 season there have been 14 perfect games pitched: Richmond (see above); John Ward, Providence v. Buffalo (NL), June 17, 1880; Cy Young, Boston Red Sox v. Philadelphia Athletics (AL), May 5, 1904; Addie Joss, Cleveland Indians v. Chicago White Sox (AL), October 2, 1908; Ernie Shore, Boston Red Sox v. Washington Senators (AL), June 23, 1917; Charlie Robertson, Chicago White Sox v. Detroit Tigers (AL), April 30, 1922; Don Larsen, New York Yankees v. Brooklyn Dodgers (World Series game), October 8, 1956; Jim Bunning, Philadelphia Phillies v. New York Mets (NL), June 21, 1964; Sandy Koufax, Los Angeles Dodgers v. Chicago Cubs (NL), September 9, 1965; Catfish Hunter, Oakland Athletics v. Minnesota Twins (AL), May 8, 1968; Len Barker, Cleveland Indians v. Toronto Blue Jays (AL), May 15, 1981; Mike Witt, California Angels v. Texas Rangers (AL), September 30, 1984; Tom Browning, Cincinnati Reds v. Los Angeles Dodgers (NL), September 16, 1988; and Dennis Martinez, Montreal Expos v. Los Angeles Dodgers (NL), July 28, 1991.

PERFECTÓ ■ ON JULY 28, 1991, DENNIS MARTINEZ PITCHED THE 14TH PERFECT GAME IN BASEBALL HISTORY.

COMPLETE GAMES

Career 750, by Cy Young, Cleveland Spiders (NL), 1890–98; St. Louis Cardinals (NL), 1899–1900; Boston Red Sox (AL), 1901–08; Cleveland Indians (AL), 1909–11; Boston Braves (NL), 1911. The National League record is 557, by Pud Galvin, Buffalo Bisons, 1879–85; Pittsburgh Pirates, 1887–89, 1892; St. Louis Cardinals, 1892. The modern-day record is 438, by Grover Alexander, Philadelphia Phillies, 1911–17, 1930; Chicago Cubs, 1918–26; St. Louis Cardinals, 1926–29. The American League record is 531, by Walter Johnson, Washington Senators, 1907–27.

Season 75, by Will White, Cincinnati Reds (NL) in 1879. The modern-day National League record is 45, by Vic Willis, Boston Braves, in 1902. The American League record is 48, by Jack Chesbro, New York Yankees, in 1904.

SHUTOUTS

Career 110, by Walter Johnson, Washington Senators (AL), 1907–27. The National League record is 90, by Grover Alexander, Philadelphia Phillies, 1911–17, 1930; Chicago Cubs, 1918–26; St. Louis Cardinals, 1926–29.

Season 16, by two pitchers: George Bradley, St. Louis (NL), in 1876; and Grover Alexander, Philadelphia Phillies (NL), in 1916. The American League record is 13, by Jack Coombs, Philadelphia Athletics, in 1910.

STRIKEOUTS

Career 5,511, by Nolan Ryan, New York Mets (NL), 1966–71; California Angels (AL), 1972–79; Houston Astros (NL), 1980–88; Texas Rangers (AL), 1989–91. The National League record is 4,000, by Steve Carlton, St. Louis Cardinals, 1965–71; Philadelphia Phillies, 1972–86; San Francisco Giants, 1986. The American League record is 3,508, by Walter Johnson, Washington Senators, 1907–27.

Season 513, by Matt Kilroy, Baltimore (American Association), in 1886. The American League record is 383, by Nolan Ryan, California Angels, in 1973. The National League record is 441, by "Old Hoss" Radbourn, Providence Grays, in 1884. The modern-day National League record is 382, by Sandy Koufax, Los Angeles Dodgers, in 1965.

Game (extra innings) 21, by Tom Cheney, Washington Senators (AL), on September 12, 1962 in a 16-inning game.

K-MEN ■ NOLAN RYAN (LEFT) HAS STRUCK OUT A CAREER RECORD 5,511 BATTERS. ROGER CLEMENS (RIGHT) HOLDS THE ALL-TIME NINE-INNING STRIKEOUT MARK OF 20, SET ON APRIL 29, 1986.

Game (nine innings) 20, by Roger Clemens, Boston Red Sox (AL), on April 29, 1986. The all-time National League record is 19, by three players: Charlie Sweeney, Providence Grays, June 7, 1884; Steve Carlton, St. Louis Cardinals, September 15, 1969; and Tom Seaver, New York Mets, April 22, 1970.

WALKS

Career 2,686, by Nolan Ryan, New York Mets (NL), 1966–71; California Angels (AL), 1972–79; Houston Astros (NL), 1980–88; Texas Rangers (AL), 1989–91. The American League record is 1,775, by Early Wynn, Washington Senators, 1939–48; Cleveland Indians, 1949–57, 1963; Chicago White Sox, 1958–62. The National League record is 1,717, by Steve Carlton, St. Louis Cardinals, 1965–71; Philadelphia Phillies, 1972–86; San Francisco Giants, 1986.

Season 218, by Amos Rusie, New York Giants (NL), in 1893. The modern-day National League record is 185, by Sam Jones, Chicago Cubs, in 1955. The American League record is 208, by Bob Feller, Cleveland Indians, in 1938.

Game 16, by two players: Bruno Haas, Philadelphia Athletics (AL), on June 23, 1915 in a nine-inning game; Tom Byrne, St. Louis Brown's (AL) on August 22, 1951 in a 13-inning game. The National

League record is 14, by Henry Mathewson, New York Giants, on October 5, 1906 in a nine-inning game.

SAVES

Career 341, by Rollie Fingers, Oakland Athletics (AL), 1968–76; San Diego Padres (NL), 1977–80; Milwaukee Brewers (AL), 1981–85. The National League record is 300, by Bruce Sutter, Chicago Cubs, 1976–80; St. Louis Cardinals, 1981–84; Atlanta Braves, 1985–88. The American League record is 238, by Dan Quisenberry, Kansas City Royals, 1979–88.

Season 57, by Bobby Thigpen, Chicago White Sox (AL), in 1990. The National League record is 47, by Lee Smith, St. Louis Cardinals, in 1991.

CONSECUTIVE PITCHING RECORDS

Games won 24, by Carl Hubbell, New York Giants (NL), 16 in 1936 and eight in 1937. The American League record is 17, by two players: Jack Allen, Cleveland Indians, two in 1936, 15 in 1937; David McNally, Baltimore Orioles, two in 1968, 15 in 1969.

Starting assignments 544, by Steve Carlton, from May 15, 1971 through 1986 while playing for four teams: St. Louis Cardinals (NL), Philadelphia Phillies (NL), San Francisco Giants (NL), and Chicago White Sox (AL). Carlton also holds the National League record at 534 games. The American

STOPPER ■ LEE SMITH RECORDED A NATIONAL LEAGUE RECORD 47 SAVES IN 1991.

League record is 396 games, by Jack Morris, Detroit Tigers, September 30, 1978 through 1990.

Scoreless innings 59, by Orel Hershiser, Los Angeles Dodgers (NL), from sixth inning, August 30 through tenth inning, September 28, 1988. The American League record is 55.2, by Walter Johnson, Washington Senators, from second inning, April 10 through third inning, May 14, 1913.

No-hitters Two, by Johnny Vander Meer, Cincinnati Reds (NL), on June 11 and June 15, 1938. No American League pitcher has thrown consecutive no-hitters.

Shutouts Six, by Don Drysdale, Los Angeles Dodgers (NL), May 14 through June 4, 1968. The American League record is five, by Doc White, Chicago White Sox, September 12 through 30, 1904.

Strikeouts 10, by Tom Seaver, New York Mets (NL) on April 22, 1970. The American League record is eight, by three pitchers: Nolan Ryan, California Angels, who has done it twice: July 9, 1972, and July 15, 1973; Ron Davis, New York Yankees, May 4, 1981; and Roger Clemens, Boston Red Sox, April 29, 1986.

BASERUNNING

STOLEN BASES

Career 994, by Rickey Henderson, Oakland Athletics (AL), 1979–84, 1989–91; New York Yankees (AL), 1985–89. Henderson broke Lou Brock's all-time mark of 938 on May 1, 1991 when he stole

---

RECORD FILE: RICKEY HENDERSON

BORN December 25, 1957, Chicago, Ill.

REGULAR SEASON CAREER STATISTICS
OAKLAND ATHLETICS, 1979-84, 1989-91
NEW YORK YANKEES, 1985–89

Year	AB	R	H	HR	RBI	Avg.	Walks	SB
1979–84	2,916	586	850	51	271	.291	520	493
1985–89	2,608	585	753	87	290	.289	476	378
1990–91	959	224	285	46	118	.297	195	123
Totals	6,483	1,395	1,888	184	679	.291	1,191	994*

AMERICAN LEAGUE CHAMPIONSHIP SERIES CAREER STATISTICS
OAKLAND ATHLETICS, 1981, 1989–90

Year	AB	R	H	HR	RBI	Avg.	Walks	SB
1981	11	0	4	0	1	.364	1	2
1989	15	8	6	2	5	.400	7	8
1990	17	1	5	0	3	.294	1	2
Totals	43	9	15	2	9	.349	9	12*

WORLD SERIES CAREER STATISTICS
OAKLAND ATHLETICS, 1989–90

Year	AB	R	H	HR	RBI	Avg.	Walks	SB
1989	19	4	9	1	3	.474	2	3
1990	15	2	5	1	1	.333	3	3
Totals	34	6	14	2	4	.412	5	6

RECORD NOTES Henderson holds the modern-day single-season stolen base mark of 130 set in 1982. That year Henderson also set the season record for most times caught stealing at 42. Henderson also holds the career record for times caught stealing at 211. Besides base-stealing records, Henderson also holds the major league record for most home runs as a leadoff batter, hitting 50, 1979–91.

* indicates all-time record.

third base off New York Yankees catcher Matt Nokes. The National League record is 938, by Lou Brock, Chicago Cubs, 1961–64; St. Louis Cardinals, 1964–79.

Season 130, by Rickey Henderson, Oakland Athletics (AL), in 1982. The National League record is 118, by Lou Brock, St. Louis Cardinals, in 1974.

Game Seven, by two players: George Gore, Chicago Cubs (NL), on June 25, 1881; Billy Hamilton, Philadelphia Phillies (NL), on August 31, 1894. The modern-day National League record is six, by Otis Nixon, Atlanta Braves, on June 17, 1991. The American League record is six, by Eddie Collins, Philadelphia Athletics, on September 11, 1912.

40/40 Club The only player to steal at least 40 bases and hit at least 40 home runs in one season is Jose Canseco, Oakland Athletics (AL), in 1988, when he stole 40 bases and hit 42 home runs.

FIELDING

HIGHEST FIELDING PERCENTAGE

Career .995, by two players: Wes Parker, Los Angeles Dodgers (NL), 1964–72; and Jim Spencer, California Angels (AL), 1968–73; Texas Rangers (AL), 1973–75; Chicago White Sox (AL), 1976–77; New York Yankees (AL), 1978–81; Oakland Athletics (AL), 1981–82. Parker played 1,108 games at first base and 155 in the outfield. Spencer played 1,221 games at first base and 24 in the outfield.

ASSISTS

Career 8,133, by Bill Dahlen, Chicago Cubs (NL), 1891–98; Brooklyn Dodgers (NL), 1899–1903, 1910–11; New York Giants (NL), 1904–07; Boston Braves (NL), 1908–09. Dahlen played 2,132 games at shortstop, 223 at third base, 19 at second base and 58 in the outfield. The American League record is 8,016, by Luis Aparicio, Chicago White Sox, 1956–62, 1968–70; Baltimore Orioles, 1963–67; Boston Red Sox, 1971–73. Aparicio played 2,581 games at shortstop.

MANAGERS

Most games managed 7,755, by Connie Mack, Pittsburgh Pirates (NL), 1894–96; Philadelphia Athletics (AL), 1901–50. Mack's career record was 3,731 wins, 3,948 losses, 75 ties and one no-decision. Mack also holds the American League record at 7,466 games, Philadelphia Athletics,

1901–50. The National League record is 4,608 games, by John McGraw, Baltimore, 1899; New York Giants, 1902–32.

Most wins 3,731, by Connie Mack, Pittsburgh Pirates (NL), 1894–96; Philadelphia Athletics (AL), 1901–50. Mack also holds the American League record at 3,582, Philadelphia Athletics, 1901–50. The National League record is 2,690 wins by John McGraw, Baltimore Orioles, 1899; New York Giants, 1902–32.

Most losses 3,948, by Connie Mack, Pittsburgh Pirates (NL), 1894-96; Philadelphia Athletics (AL), 1901-50. Mack also holds the American League record at 3,814, Philadelphia Athletics, 1901-50. The National League record is 1,863, by John McGraw, Baltimore Orioles, 1899; New York Giants, 1902-32.

Highest winning percentage .615, by Joe McCarthy, Chicago Cubs (NL), 1926-30; New York Yankees (AL), 1931-46; Boston Red Sox (AL), 1948-50. McCarthy's career record was 2,125 wins, 1,333 losses, 26 ties and three no-decisions.

MISCELLANEOUS

Youngest player The youngest major league player of all time was the Cincinnati Reds (AL) pitcher Joe Nuxhall, who played one game in June 1944, at age 15 years 314 days. He did not play again in the National League until 1952.

Oldest player Satchel Paige pitched for the Kansas City A's (AL) at age 59 years 80 days on September 25, 1965.

Shortest and tallest players The shortest major league player was Eddie Gaedel, a 3 foot 7 inch, 65 pound midget, who pinch-hit for the St. Louis Browns (AL) *v.* the Detroit Tigers (AL) on August 19, 1951. Wearing number ⅛, the batter with the smallest-ever major league strike zone walked on four pitches. Following the game, major league rules were hastily rewritten to prevent any recurrence. The tallest major leaguer of all time is Randy Johnson, a 6 foot 10 inch pitcher, who played in his first game for the Montreal Expos (NL) on September 15, 1988.

Father and son On August 31, 1990, Ken Griffey Sr. and Ken Griffey Jr., of the Seattle Mariners (AL), became the first father and son to play for the same major league team at the same time. In

1989 the Griffeys became the first father/son combination to play in the major leagues at the same time. Griffey Sr. played for the Cincinnati Reds (NL) during that season.

Record attendances The all-time season record for attendance for both leagues is 56,813,760 in 1991 (32,117,558 for the 14-team American League, and 24,696,172 for the 12-team National League). The American League record is 32,117,558, set in 1991; the National League record is 25,324,963, set in 1989. The record for home-team attendance is held by the Toronto Blue Jays (AL) at 4,001,526 in 1991. The National League record is held by the Los Angeles Dodgers at 3,608,881 in 1982.

Shortest game The New York Giants (NL) beat the Philadelphia Phillies (NL), 6–1, in nine innings in 51 minutes on September 28, 1919.

Longest games The Brooklyn Dodgers (NL) and the Boston Braves (NL) played to a 1–1 tie after 26 innings on May 1, 1920. The Chicago White Sox (AL) played the longest ballgame in elapsed time—

8 hours 6 minutes—before beating the Milwaukee Brewers, 7–6, in the 25th inning on May 9, 1984 in Chicago. The game started on a Tuesday night and was tied at 3–3 when the 1 A.M. curfew caused suspension until Wednesday night.

The actual longest game was a minor league game in 1981 that lasted 33 innings. At the end of nine innings the score was tied, 1–1, with the Rochester (N.Y.) Red Wings battling the home team Pawtucket (R.I.) Red Sox. At the end of 21 innings it was tied, 2–2, and at the end of 32 innings the score was still 2–2, when the game was suspended. Two months later, play was resumed, and 18 minutes later, Pawtucket scored one run and won. The winning pitcher was the Red Sox Bob Ojeda.

MOST VALUABLE PLAYER AWARD (MVP)

There have been three different MVP Awards in baseball: the Chalmers Award (1911–14), the League Award (1922–29), and the Baseball Writers' Association of America Award (1931– present).

CHALMERS AWARD (1911–1914)

National League				American League			
Year	Player	Team	Position	Year	Player	Team	Position
1911	Wildfire Schulte	Chicago Cubs	OF	1911	Ty Cobb	Detroit Tigers	OF
1912	Larry Doyle	New York Giants	2B	1912	Tris Speaker	Boston Red Sox	OF
1913	Jake Daubert	Brooklyn Dodgers	1B	1913	Walter Johnson	Washington Senators	P
1914	Johnny Evers	Boston Braves	2B	1914	Eddie Collins	Philadelphia A's	2B

LEAGUE AWARD (1922–1929)

National League				American League			
Year	Player	Team	Position	Year	Player	Team	Position
1922	no selection			1922	George Sisler	St. Louis Browns	1B
1923	no selection			1923	Babe Ruth	New York Yankees	OF
1924	Dazzy Vance	Brooklyn Dodgers	P	1924	Walter Johnson	Washington Senators	P
1925	Rogers Hornsby	St. Louis Cardinals	2B	1925	Roger Peckinpaugh	Washington Senators	SS
1926	Bob O'Farrell	St. Louis Cardinals	C	1926	George Burns	Cleveland Indians	1B
1927	Paul Waner	Pittsburgh Pirates	OF	1927	Lou Gehrig	New York Yankees	1B
1928	Jim Bottomley	St. Louis Cardinals	1B	1928	Mickey Cochrane	Philadelphia A's	C
1929	Rogers Hornsby	Chicago Cubs	2B	1929	no selection		

BASEBALL WRITERS' AWARD (1931–1966)

National League				American League			
Year	Player	Team	Position	Year	Player	Team	Position
1931	Frankie Frisch	St. Louis Cardinals	2B	1931	Lefty Grove	Philadelphia A's	P
1932	Chuck Klein	Philadelphia Phillies	OF	1932	Jimmie Foxx	Philadelphia A's	1B
1933	Carl Hubbell	New York Giants	P	1933	Jimmie Foxx	Philadelphia A's	1B
1934	Dizzy Dean	St. Louis Cardinals	P	1934	Mickey Cochrane	Detroit Tigers	C
1935	Gabby Hartnett	Chicago Cubs	C	1935	Hank Greenberg	Detroit Tigers	1B
1936	Carl Hubbell	New York Giants	P	1936	Lou Gehrig	New York Yankees	1B
1937	Joe Medwick	St. Louis Cardinals	OF	1937	Charlie Gehringer	Detroit Tigers	2B
1938	Ernie Lombardi	Cincinnati Reds	C	1938	Jimmie Foxx	Boston Red Sox	1B
1939	Bucky Walters	Cincinnati Reds	P	1939	Joe DiMaggio	New York Yankees	OF
1940	Frank McCormick	Cincinnati Reds	1B	1940	Hank Greenberg	Detroit Tigers	OF
1941	Dolf Camilli	Brooklyn Dodgers	1B	1941	Joe DiMaggio	New York Yankees	OF
1942	Mort Cooper	St. Louis Cardinals	P	1942	Joe Gordon	New York Yankees	2B
1943	Stan Musial	St. Louis Cardinals	OF	1943	Spud Chandler	New York Yankees	P
1944	Marty Marion	St. Louis Cardinals	SS	1944	Hal Newhouser	Detroit Tigers	P
1945	Phil Cavarretta	Chicago Cubs	1B	1945	Hal Newhouser	Detroit Tigers	P
1946	Stan Musial	St. Louis Cardinals	1B–OF	1946	Ted Williams	Boston Red Sox	OF
1947	Bob Elliott	Boston Braves	3B	1947	Joe DiMaggio	New York Yankees	OF
1948	Stan Musial	St. Louis Cardinals	OF	1948	Lou Boudreau	Cleveland Indians	SS
1949	Jackie Robinson	Brooklyn Dodgers	2B	1949	Ted Williams	Boston Red Sox	OF
1950	Jim Konstanty	Philadelphia Phillies	P	1950	Phil Rizzuto	New York Yankees	SS
1951	Roy Campanella	Brooklyn Dodgers	C	1951	Yogi Berra	New York Yankees	C
1952	Hank Sauer	Chicago Cubs	OF	1952	Bobby Shantz	Philadelphia A's	P
1953	Roy Campanella	Brooklyn Dodgers	C	1953	Al Rosen	Cleveland Indians	3B
1954	Willie Mays	New York Giants	OF	1954	Yogi Berra	New York Yankees	C
1955	Roy Campanella	Brooklyn Dodgers	C	1955	Yogi Berra	New York Yankees	C
1956	Don Newcombe	Brooklyn Dodgers	P	1956	Mickey Mantle	New York Yankees	OF
1957	Hank Aaron	Milwaukee Braves	OF	1957	Mickey Mantle	New York Yankees	OF
1958	Ernie Banks	Chicago Cubs	SS	1958	Jackie Jensen	Boston Red Sox	OF
1959	Ernie Banks	Chicago Cubs	SS	1959	Nellie Fox	Chicago White Sox	2B
1960	Dick Groat	Pittsburgh Pirates	SS	1960	Roger Maris	New York Yankees	OF
1961	Frank Robinson	Cincinnati Reds	OF	1961	Roger Maris	New York Yankees	OF
1962	Maury Wills	Los Angeles Dodgers	SS	1962	Mickey Mantle	New York Yankees	OF
1963	Sandy Koufax	Los Angeles Dodgers	P	1963	Elston Howard	New York Yankees	C
1964	Ken Boyer	St. Louis Cardinals	3B	1964	Brooks Robinson	Baltimore Orioles	3B
1965	Willie Mays	San Francisco Giants	OF	1965	Zoilo Versalles	Minnesota Twins	SS
1966	Roberto Clemente	Pittsburgh Pirates	OF	1966	Frank Robinson	Baltimore Orioles	OF

BASEBALL WRITERS' AWARD (1967–1991)

National League

Year	Player	Team	Position
1967	Orlando Cepeda	St. Louis Cardinals	1B
1968	Bob Gibson	St. Louis Cardinals	P
1969	Willie McCovey	San Francisco Giants	1B
1970	Johnny Bench	Cincinnati Reds	C
1971	Joe Torre	St. Louis Cardinals	3B
1972	Johnny Bench	Cincinnati Reds	C
1973	Pete Rose	Cincinnati Reds	OF
1974	Steve Garvey	Los Angeles Dodgers	1B
1975	Joe Morgan	Cincinnati Reds	2B
1976	Joe Morgan	Cincinnati Reds	2B
1977	George Foster	Cincinnati Reds	OF
1978	Dave Parker	Pittsburgh Pirates	OF
1979	Willie Stargell	Pittsburgh Pirates	1B*
	Keith Hernandez	St. Louis Cardinals	1B*
1980	Mike Schmidt	Philadelphia Phillies	3B
1981	Mike Schmidt	Philadelphia Phillies	3B
1982	Dale Murphy	Atlanta Braves	OF
1983	Dale Murphy	Atlanta Braves	OF
1984	Ryne Sandberg	Chicago Cubs	2B
1985	Willie McGee	St. Louis Cardinals	OF
1986	Mike Schmidt	Philadelphia Phillies	3B
1987	Andre Dawson	Chicago Cubs	OF
1988	Kirk Gibson	Los Angeles Dodgers	OF
1989	Kevin Mitchell	San Francisco Giants	OF
1990	Barry Bonds	Pittsburgh Pirates	OF
1991	Terry Pendleton	Atlanta Braves	3B

American League

Year	Player	Team	Position
1967	Carl Yastrzemski	Boston Red Sox	OF
1968	Denny McLain	Detroit Tigers	P
1969	Harmon Killebrew	Minnesota Twins	3–1B
1970	Boog Powell	Baltimore Orioles	1B
1971	Vida Blue	Oakland A's	P
1972	Dick Allen	Chicago White Sox	1B
1973	Reggie Jackson	Oakland A's	OF
1974	Jeff Burroughs	Texas Rangers	OF
1975	Fred Lynn	Boston Red Sox	OF
1976	Thurman Munson	New York Yankees	C
1977	Rod Carew	Minnesota Twins	1B
1978	Jim Rice	Boston Red Sox	OF-DH
1979	Don Baylor	California Angels	OF-DH
1980	George Brett	Kansas City Royals	3B
1981	Rollie Fingers	Milwaukee Brewers	P
1982	Robin Yount	Milwaukee Brewers	SS
1983	Cal Ripken Jr.	Baltimore Orioles	SS
1984	Willie Hernandez	Detroit Tigers	P
1985	Don Mattingly	New York Yankees	1B
1986	Roger Clemens	Boston Red Sox	P
1987	George Bell	Toronto Blue Jays	OF
1988	Jose Canseco	Oakland A's	OF
1989	Robin Yount	Milwaukee Brewers	OF
1990	Rickey Henderson	Oakland A's	OF
1991	Cal Ripken Jr.	Baltimore Orioles	SS

* Tied vote

Most wins Three, by seven players: Jimmie Foxx, Philadelphia Athletics (AL), 1932–33, 1938; Joe DiMaggio, New York Yankees (AL), 1939, 1941, 1947; Stan Musial, St. Louis Cardinals (NL), 1943, 1946, 1948; Roy Campanella, Brooklyn Dodgers (NL), 1951, 1953, 1955; Yogi Berra, New York Yankees (AL), 1951, 1954–55; Mickey Mantle, New York Yankees (AL), 1956–57, 1962; and Mike Schmidt, Philadelphia Phillies (NL), 1980–81, 1986.

Wins in both leagues The only player to win the award in both leagues is Frank Robinson, Cincinnati Reds (NL), in 1961; Baltimore Orioles (AL), in 1966.

CY YOUNG AWARD (1956–1991)

Inaugurated in 1956, this award is given to the best pitcher in baseball as judged by the Baseball Writers' Association of America. From 1967 on separate awards have been given to the best pitcher in each league.

CY YOUNG AWARD WINNERS (1956–1966)

Year	Pitcher	Team	Year	Pitcher	Team
1956	Don Newcombe	Brooklyn Dodgers (NL)	1962	Don Drysdale	Los Angeles Dodgers (NL)
1957	Warren Spahn	Milwaukee Braves (NL)	1963	Sandy Koufax	Los Angeles Dodgers (NL)
1958	Bob Turley	New York Yankees (AL)	1964	Dean Chance	Los Angeles Angels (AL)
1959	Early Wynn	Chicago White Sox (AL)	1965	Sandy Koufax	Los Angeles Dodgers (NL)
1960	Vernon Law	Pittsburgh Pirates (NL)	1966	Sandy Koufax	Los Angeles Dodgers (NL)
1961	Whitey Ford	New York Yankees (AL)			

CY YOUNG AWARD WINNERS (1967–1991)

National League			American League		
Year	Pitcher	Team	Year	Pitcher	Team
1967	Mike McCormick	San Francisco Giants	1967	Jim Lonborg	Boston Red Sox
1968	Bob Gibson	St. Louis Cardinals	1968	Denny McLain	Detroit Tigers
1969	Tom Seaver	New York Mets	1969*	Mike Cuellar Denny McLain	Baltimore Orioles Detroit Tigers
1970	Bob Gibson	St. Louis Cardinals	1970	Jim Perry	Minnesota Twins
1971	Ferguson Jenkins	Chicago Cubs	1971	Vida Blue	Oakland Athletics
1972	Steve Carlton	Philadelphia Phillies	1972	Gaylord Perry	Cleveland Indians
1973	Tom Seaver	New York Mets	1973	Jim Palmer	Baltimore Orioles
1974	Mike Marshall	Los Angeles Dodgers	1974	Jim "Catfish" Hunter	Oakland Athletics
1975	Tom Seaver	New York Mets	1975	Jim Palmer	Baltimore Orioles
1976	Randy Jones	San Diego Padres	1976	Jim Palmer	Baltimore Orioles
1977	Steve Carlton	Philadelphia Phillies	1977	Sparky Lyle	New York Yankees
1978	Gaylord Perry	San Diego Padres	1978	Ron Guidry	New York Yankees
1979	Bruce Sutter	Chicago Cubs	1979	Mike Flanagan	Baltimore Orioles
1980	Steve Carlton	Philadelphia Phillies	1980	Steve Stone	Baltimore Orioles
1981	Fernando Valenzuela	Los Angeles Dodgers	1981	Rollie Fingers	Milwaukee Brewers
1982	Steve Carlton	Philadelphia Phillies	1982	Pete Vukovich	Milwaukee Brewers
1983	John Denny	Philadelphia Phillies	1983	LaMarr Hoyt	Chicago White Sox
1984	Rick Sutcliffe	Chicago Cubs	1984	Willie Hernandez	Detroit Tigers
1985	Dwight Gooden	New York Mets	1985	Bret Saberhagen	Kansas City Royals
1986	Mike Scott	Houston Astros	1986	Roger Clemens	Boston Red Sox
1987	Steve Bedrosian	Philadelphia Phillies	1987	Roger Clemens	Boston Red Sox
1988	Orel Hershiser	Los Angeles Dodgers	1988	Frank Viola	Minnesota Twins
1989	Mark Davis	San Diego Padres	1989	Bret Saberhagen	Kansas City Royals
1990	Doug Drabek	Pittsburgh Pirates	1990	Bob Welch	Oakland Athletics
1991	Tom Glavine	Atlanta Braves	1991	Roger Clemens	Boston Red Sox

* Tied vote

Most wins Four, by Steve Carlton, Philadelphia Phillies, 1972, 1977, 1980 and 1982. The most wins by an American League pitcher is three, by two players: Jim Palmer, Baltimore Orioles, 1973, 1975–76; Roger Clemens, Boston Red Sox, 1986–87, 1991.

Wins, both leagues The only pitcher to win the Cy Young Award in both leagues is Gaylord Perry: Cleveland Indians (AL), 1972; San Diego Padres (NL), 1978.

Consecutive wins Two, by four pitchers: Sandy Koufax, Los Angeles Dodgers (NL), 1965 and 1966; Denny McLain, Detroit Tigers (AL), 1968 and 1969 (shared with Mike Cuellar); Jim Palmer, Baltimore Orioles (AL), 1975 and 1976; Roger Clemens, Boston Red Sox (AL), 1986 and 1987.

LEAGUE CHAMPIONSHIP SERIES RECORDS (1969–1991)

GAMES PLAYED

Most series played 11, by Reggie Jackson, Oakland Athletics (AL), 1971–75; New York Yankees (AL), 1977–78, 1980–81; California Angels (AL), 1982, 1986.

LEAGUE CHAMPIONSHIP SERIES (1969–1991)

League Championship Series (LCS) playoffs began in 1969 when the American and National Leagues expanded to 12 teams each and created two divisions, East and West. To determine the respective league pennant winners, the division winners played a best-of-five-games series, which was expanded to best-of-seven in 1985.

National League

Year	Winner	Loser	Series
1969	New York Mets (East)	Atlanta Braves (West)	3–0
1970	Cincinnati Reds (West)	Pittsburgh Pirates (East)	3–0
1971	Pittsburgh Pirates (East)	San Francisco Giants (West)	3–1
1972	Cincinnati Reds (West)	Pittsburgh Pirates (East)	3–2
1973	New York Mets (East)	Cincinnati Reds (West)	3–2
1974	Los Angeles Dodgers (West)	Pittsburgh Pirates (East)	3–1
1975	Cincinnati Reds (West)	Pittsburgh Pirates (East)	3–0
1976	Cincinnati Reds (West)	Philadelphia Phillies (East)	3–0
1977	Los Angeles Dodgers (West)	Philadelphia Phillies (East)	3–1
1978	Los Angeles Dodgers (West)	Philadelphia Phillies (East)	3–1
1979	Pittsburgh Pirates (East)	Cincinnati Reds (West)	3–0
1980	Philadelphia Phillies (East)	Houston Astros (West)	3–2
1981	Los Angeles Dodgers (West)	Montreal Expos (East)	3–2
1982	St. Louis Cardinals (East)	Atlanta Braves (West)	3–0
1983	Philadelphia Phillies (East)	Los Angeles Dodgers (West)	3–1
1984	San Diego Padres (West)	Chicago Cubs (East)	3–2
1985	St. Louis Cardinals (East)	Los Angeles Dodgers (West)	4–2
1986	New York Mets (East)	Houston Astros (West)	4–2
1987	St. Louis Cardinals (East)	San Francisco Giants (West)	4–3
1988	Los Angeles Dodgers (West)	New York Mets (East)	4–3
1989	San Francisco Giants (West)	Chicago Cubs (East)	4–1
1990	Cincinnati Reds (West)	Pittsburgh Pirates (East)	4–2
1991	Atlanta Braves (West)	Pittsburgh Pirates (East)	4–3

Most games played 45, by Reggie Jackson, Oakland Athletics (AL), 1971–75; New York Yankees (AL), 1977–78, 1980–81; California Angels (AL), 1982, 1986.

HITTING RECORDS (CAREER)

Batting average (minimum 50 at-bats) .386, by Mickey Rivers, New York Yankees (AL), 1976–78. Rivers collected 22 hits in 57 at-bats in 14 games.

Hits 45, by Pete Rose, Cincinnati Reds (NL), 1970, 1972–73, 1975–76; Philadelphia Phillies (NL), 1980, 1983.

Home runs Nine, by George Brett, Kansas City Royals (AL), 1976–78, 1980, 1984–85.

Runs batted in (RBIs) 21, by Steve Garvey, Los Angeles Dodgers (NL), 1974, 1977–78, 1981; San Diego Padres (NL), 1984.

Runs scored 22, by George Brett, Kansas City Royals (AL), 1976–78, 1980, 1984–85.

Walks 23, by Joe Morgan, Cincinnati Reds (NL), 1972–73, 1975–76, 1979; Houston Astros (NL), 1980; Philadelphia Phillies (NL), 1983.

Stolen bases 12, by Rickey Henderson, Oakland Athletics (AL), 1981, 1989–90.

LEAGUE CHAMPIONSHIP SERIES (1969–1991)

American League

Year	Winner	Loser	Series
1969	Baltimore Orioles (East)	Minnesota Twins (West)	3–0
1970	Baltimore Orioles (East)	Minnesota Twins (West)	3–0
1971	Baltimore Orioles (East)	Oakland A's (West)	3–0
1972	Oakland A's (West)	Detroit Tigers (East)	3–2
1973	Oakland A's (West)	Baltimore Orioles (East)	3–2
1974	Oakland A's (West)	Baltimore Orioles (East)	3–1
1975	Boston Red Sox (East)	Oakland A's (West)	3–0
1976	New York Yankees (East)	Kansas City Royals (West)	3–2
1977	New York Yankees (East)	Kansas City Royals (West)	3–2
1978	New York Yankees (East)	Kansas City Royals (West)	3–1
1979	Baltimore Orioles (East)	California Angels (West)	3–1
1980	Kansas City Royals (West)	New York Yankees (East)	3–0
1981	New York Yankees (East)	Oakland A's (West)	3–0
1982	Milwaukee Brewers (East)	California Angels (West)	3–2
1983	Baltimore Orioles (East)	Chicago White Sox (West)	3–1
1984	Detroit Tigers (East)	Kansas City Royals (West)	3–0
1985	Kansas City Royals (West)	Toronto Blue Jays (East)	4–3
1986	Boston Red Sox (East)	California Angels (West)	4–3
1987	Minnesota Twins (West)	Detroit Tigers (East)	4–1
1988	Oakland A's (West)	Boston Red Sox (East)	4–0
1989	Oakland A's (West)	Toronto Blue Jays (East)	4–1
1990	Oakland A's (West)	Boston Red Sox (East)	4–0
1991	Minnesota Twins (West)	Toronto Blue Jays (East)	4–1

PLAYOFF PERFORMERS ■ GEORGE BRETT (LEFT) HOLDS THE LCS RECORD FOR MOST HOME RUNS (NINE) AND MOST RUNS SCORED (22). YA GOTTA BELIEVE THAT TUG McGRAW (RIGHT) HAS PITCHED IN A RECORD 15 LCS GAMES.

PITCHING RECORDS (CAREER)

Most series pitched Seven, by Bob Welch, Los Angeles Dodgers (NL), 1978, 1981, 1983, 1985; Oakland Athletics (AL), 1988–90.

Most games pitched 15, by Tug McGraw, New York Mets (NL), 1969, 1973; Philadelphia Phillies (NL), 1976–78, 1980.

Wins Five, by Dave Stewart, Oakland Athletics (AL), 1988–90.

Losses Seven, by Jerry Reuss, Pittsburgh Pirates (NL), 1974–75; Los Angeles Dodgers (NL), 1981, 1983, 1985.

Innings pitched 69⅓, by Jim "Catfish" Hunter, Oakland Athletics (AL), 1971–74, New York Yankees (AL), 1976, 1978.

Complete games Five, by Jim Palmer, Baltimore Orioles (AL), 1969–71, 1973–74, 1979.

Strikeouts 46, by two players: Nolan Ryan, New York Mets (NL), 1969; California Angels (AL), 1979; Houston Astros (NL), 1980, 1986; and Jim Palmer, Baltimore Orioles (AL), 1969–71, 1973–74, 1979.

Saves Nine, by Dennis Eckersley, Chicago Cubs (NL), 1984; Oakland Athletics (AL), 1988–90.

Most Valuable Player Award Two, by Steve Garvey, Los Angeles Dodgers (NL), 1978; San Diego Padres (NL), 1984.

WORLD SERIES

ORIGINS Played annually between the champions of the National League and the American League, the World Series was first staged unofficially in 1903, and officially from 1905 on.

WORLD SERIES RECORDS (1903–1991)

TEAM RECORDS

Most wins 22, by the New York Yankees (AL), 1923, 1927–28, 1932, 1936–39, 1941, 1943, 1947, 1949–53, 1956, 1958, 1961–62, 1977–78.

WORLD SERIES (1903–1938)

Year	Winner	Loser	Series
1903	Boston Red Sox (AL)	Pittsburgh Pirates (NL)	5–3
1904	no series		
1905	New York Giants (NL)	Philadelphia A's (AL)	4–1
1906	Chicago White Sox (AL)	Chicago Cubs (NL)	4–2
1907	Chicago Cubs (NL)	Detroit Tigers (AL)	4–0–1 *
1908	Chicago Cubs (NL)	Detroit Tigers (AL)	4–1
1909	Pittsburgh Pirates (NL)	Detroit Tigers (AL)	4–3
1910	Philadelphia A's (AL)	Chicago Cubs (NL)	4–1
1911	Philadelphia A's (AL)	New York Giants (NL)	4–2
1912	Boston Red Sox (AL)	New York Giants (NL)	4–3–1*
1913	Philadelphia A's (AL)	New York Giants (NL)	4–1
1914	Boston Braves (NL)	Philadelphia A's (AL)	4–0
1915	Boston Red Sox (AL)	Philadelphia Phillies (NL)	4–1
1916	Boston Red Sox (AL)	Brooklyn Dodgers (NL)	4–1
1917	Chicago White Sox (AL)	New York Giants (NL)	4–2
1918	Boston Red Sox (AL)	Chicago Cubs (NL)	4–2
1919	Cincinnati Reds (NL)	Chicago White Sox (AL)	5–3
1920	Cleveland Indians (AL)	Brooklyn Dodgers (NL)	5–2
1921	New York Giants (NL)	New York Yankees (AL)	5–3
1922	New York Giants (NL)	New York Yankees (AL)	4–0–1*
1923	New York Yankees (AL)	New York Giants (NL)	4–2
1924	Washington Senators (AL)	New York Giants (NL)	4–3
1925	Pittsburgh Pirates (NL)	Washington Senators (AL)	4–3
1926	St. Louis Cardinals(NL)	New York Yankees (AL)	4–3
1927	New York Yankees (AL)	Pittsburgh Pirates (NL)	4–0
1928	New York Yankees (AL)	St. Louis Cardinals (NL)	4–0
1929	Philadelphia A's (AL)	Chicago Cubs (NL)	4–1
1930	Philadelphia A's (AL)	St. Louis Cardinals (NL)	4–2
1931	St. Louis Cardinals (NL)	Philadelphia A's (AL)	4–3
1932	New York Yankees (AL)	Chicago Cubs (NL)	4–0
1933	New York Giants (NL)	Washington Senators (AL)	4–1
1934	St. Louis Cardinals (NL)	Detroit Tigers (AL)	4–3
1935	Detroit Tigers (AL)	Chicago Cubs (NL)	4–2
1936	New York Yankees (AL)	New York Giants (NL)	4–2
1937	New York Yankees (AL)	New York Giants (NL)	4–1
1938	New York Yankees (AL)	Chicago Cubs (NL)	4–0

* Tied game

WORLD SERIES (1939–1975)

Year	Winner	Loser	Series
1939	New York Yankees (AL)	Cincinnati Reds (NL)	4–0
1940	Cincinnati Reds (NL)	Detroit Tigers (AL)	4–3
1941	New York Yankees (AL)	Brooklyn Dodgers (NL)	4–1
1942	St. Louis Cardinals (NL)	New York Yankees (AL)	4–1
1943	New York Yankees (AL)	St. Louis Cardinals (NL)	4–1
1944	St. Louis Cardinals (NL)	St. Louis Browns (AL)	4–2
1945	Detroit Tigers (AL)	Chicago Cubs (NL)	4–3
1946	St. Louis Cardinals (NL)	Boston Red Sox (AL)	4–3
1947	New York Yankees (AL)	Brooklyn Dodgers (NL)	4–3
1948	Cleveland Indians (AL)	Boston Braves (NL)	4–2
1949	New York Yankees (AL)	Brooklyn Dodgers (NL)	4–1
1950	New York Yankees (AL)	Philadelphia Phillies (NL)	4–0
1951	New York Yankees (AL)	New York Giants (NL)	4–2
1952	New York Yankees (AL)	Brooklyn Dodgers (NL)	4–3
1953	New York Yankees (AL)	Brooklyn Dodgers (NL)	4–2
1954	New York Giants (NL)	Cleveland Indians (AL)	4–0
1955	Brooklyn Dodgers (NL)	New York Yankees (AL)	4–3
1956	New York Yankees (AL)	Brooklyn Dodgers (NL)	4–3
1957	Milwaukee Braves (NL)	New York Yankees (AL)	4–3
1958	New York Yankees (AL)	Milwaukee Braves (NL)	4–3
1959	Los Angeles Dodgers (NL)	Chicago White Sox (AL)	4–2
1960	Pittsburgh Pirates (NL)	New York Yankees (AL)	4–3
1961	New York Yankees (AL)	Cincinnati Reds (NL)	4–1
1962	New York Yankees (AL)	San Francisco Giants (NL)	4–3
1963	Los Angeles Dodgers (NL)	New York Yankees (AL)	4–0
1964	St. Louis Cardinals (NL)	New York Yankees (AL)	4–3
1965	Los Angeles Dodgers (NL)	Minnesota Twins (AL)	4–3
1966	Baltimore Orioles (AL)	Los Angeles Dodgers (NL)	4–0
1967	St. Louis Cardinals (NL)	Boston Red Sox (AL)	4–3
1968	Detroit Tigers (AL)	St. Louis Cardinals (NL)	4–3
1969	New York Mets (NL)	Baltimore Orioles (AL)	4–1
1970	Baltimore Orioles (AL)	Cincinnati Reds (NL)	4–1
1971	Pittsburgh Pirates (NL)	Baltimore Orioles (AL)	4–3
1972	Oakland A's (AL)	Cincinnati Reds (NL)	4–3
1973	Oakland A's (AL)	New York Mets (NL)	4–3
1974	Oakland A's (AL)	Los Angeles Dodgers (NL)	4–1
1975	Cincinnati Reds (NL)	Boston Red Sox (AL)	4–3

WORLD SERIES (1976–1991)

Year	Winner	Loser	Series
1976	Cincinnati Reds (NL)	New York Yankees (AL)	4–0
1977	New York Yankees (AL)	Los Angeles Dodgers (NL)	4–2
1978	New York Yankees (AL)	Los Angeles Dodgers (NL)	4–2
1979	Pittsburgh Pirates(NL)	Baltimore Orioles (AL)	4–3
1980	Philadelphia Phillies (NL)	Kansas City Royals (AL)	4–2
1981	Los Angeles Dodgers (NL)	New York Yankees (AL)	4–2
1982	St. Louis Cardinals (NL)	Milwaukee Brewers (AL)	4–3
1983	Baltimore Orioles (AL)	Philadelphia Phillies (NL)	4–1
1984	Detroit Tigers (AL)	San Diego Padres (NL)	4–1
1985	Kansas City Royals (AL)	St. Louis Cardinals (NL)	4–3
1986	New York Mets (NL)	Boston Red Sox (AL)	4–3
1987	Minnesota Twins (AL)	St. Louis Cardinals (NL)	4–3
1988	Los Angeles Dodgers (NL)	Oakland A's (AL)	4–1
1989	Oakland A's (AL)	San Francisco Giants (NL)	4–0
1990	Cincinnati Reds (NL)	Oakland A's (AL)	4–0
1991	Minnesota Twins (AL)	Atlanta Braves (NL)	4–3

Most appearances 33, by the New York Yankees (AL), 1921–23, 1926–28, 1932, 1936–39, 1941–43, 1947, 1949–53, 1955–58, 1960–64, 1976–78, 1981.

INDIVIDUAL RECORDS

GAMES PLAYED

Most series 14, by Yogi Berra, New York Yankees (AL), 1947, 1949–53, 1955–58, 1960–63.

Most series (pitcher) 11, by Whitey Ford, New York Yankees (AL), 1950, 1953, 1955–58, 1960–64.

Most games 75, by Yogi Berra, New York Yankees (AL), 1947, 1949–53, 1955–58, 1960–63.

Most games (pitcher) 22, by Whitey Ford, New York Yankees (AL), 1950, 1953, 1955–58, 1960–64.

HITTING RECORDS

BATTING AVERAGE

Career (minimum 20 games) .391, by Lou Brock, St. Louis Cardinals (NL), 1964, 1967–68. Brock collected 34 hits in 87 at-bats over 21 games.

Series (minimum four games) .750, by Billy Hatcher, Cincinnati Reds (NL), in 1990. Hatcher collected 9 hits in 12 at-bats in four games.

HITS

Career 71, by Yogi Berra, New York Yankees (AL), 1947– 63. In 259 at-bats, Berra hit 12 home runs, 10 doubles and 49 singles.

Series 13, by three players: Bobby Richardson, New York Yankees (AL), in 1960; Lou Brock, St. Louis Cardinals (NL), in 1968; Marty Barrett, Boston Red Sox (AL), in 1986.

HOME RUNS

Career 18, by Mickey Mantle, New York Yankees (AL), 1951–53, 1955–58, 1960–64. Mantle hit his record 18 homers from 230 at-bats in 65 games.

Series Five, by Reggie Jackson, New York Yankees (AL), in 1977.

Game Three, by two players: Babe Ruth, New York Yankees (AL), who did it twice: on October 6, 1926 v. St. Louis Cardinals, and on October 9, 1928 v. St. Louis Cardinals; and Reggie Jackson, New York Yankees (AL), on October 18, 1977 v. Los Angeles Dodgers.

RUNS BATTED IN (RBIs)

Career 40, by Mickey Mantle, New York Yankees (AL), 1951–53, 1955–58, 1960–64.

RECORD FILE: MICKEY MANTLE

BORN October 20, 1931, Spavinaw, Okla.

REGULAR SEASON CAREER STATISTICS
NEW YORK YANKEES, 1951–68

Years	AB	R	H	HR	RBI	Avg.	SO	Walks
1951–68	8,102	1,677	2,415	536	1,509	.298	1,710	1,734

WORLD SERIES CAREER STATISTICS
NEW YORK YANKEES, 1951–53; 1955–58; 1960–64

Years	AB	R	H	HR	RBI	Avg.	Walks
1951	5	1	1	0	0	.200	2
1952	29	5	10	2	3	.345	3
1953	24	3	5	2	7	.208	3
1955	10	1	2	1	1	.200	0
1956	24	6	6	3	4	.250	6
1957	19	3	5	1	2	.263	3
1958	24	4	6	2	3	.250	7
1960	25	8	10	3	11	.400	8
1961	6	0	1	0	0	.167	0
1962	25	2	3	0	0	.120	4
1963	15	1	2	1	1	.133	1
1964	24	8	8	3	8	.333	6
Totals	230	42*	59	18*	40*	.257	43*

RECORD NOTES Mantle holds several switch-hitting records: most home runs (season), 54 in 1961; most RBIs (season), 130 in 1956; most walks (season), 146 in 1957; most total bases (season), 376 in 1956. Mantle also holds the career World Series record for most total bases at 123.

* indicates all-time record.

Series 12, by Bobby Richardson, New York Yankees (AL), in 1960.

Game Six, by Bobby Richardson, New York Yankees (AL), on October 8, 1960 *v.* Pittsburgh Pirates.

PITCHING RECORDS

WINS

Career Ten, by Whitey Ford, New York Yankees (AL), in 11 series, 1950–64. Ford's career record was 10 wins, 8 losses in 22 games.

Series Three, by 12 pitchers. Only two pitchers have won three games in a five-game series: Christy Matthewson, New York Giants (NL) in 1905; Jack Coombs, Philadelphia Athletics (AL) in 1910.

STRIKEOUTS

Career 94, by Whitey Ford, New York Yankees (AL), in 11 series, 1950–64.

Series 35, by Bob Gibson, St. Louis Cardinals (NL) in 1968, from seven games.

Game 17, by Bob Gibson, St. Louis Cardinals (NL), on October 2, 1968 *v.* Detroit Tigers.

INNINGS PITCHED

Career 146, by Whitey Ford, New York Yankees (AL), in 11 series, 1950, 1953, 1955–58, 1960–64.

Series 44, by Deacon Phillippe, Pittsburgh Pirates (NL), in 1903 in an eight-game series.

Game 14, by Babe Ruth, Boston Red Sox (AL), on October 9, 1916 *v.* Brooklyn Dodgers.

SAVES

Career Six, by Rollie Fingers, Oakland Athletics (AL), 1972–74.

Series Three, by Kent Tekulve, Pittsburgh Pirates (NL), in 1979 in a seven-game series.

PERFECT GAME The only perfect game in World Series history was hurled by Don Larson, New York Yankees (AL), on October 8, 1956 *v.* Brooklyn Dodgers.

MOST VALUABLE PLAYER AWARD The World Series MVP award has been won a record two times by three players: Sandy Koufax, Los Angeles Dodgers (NL), 1963 and 1965; Bob Gibson, St. Louis Cardinals (NL), 1964 and 1967; and Reggie Jackson, Oakland Athletics (AL), 1973, New York Yankees (AL), 1977.

MANAGERS

Most series Ten, by Casey Stengel, New York Yankees (AL), 1949–53, 1955–58, 1960. Stengel's record was seven wins, three losses.

Most wins Seven, by two managers: Joe McCarthy, New York Yankees (AL), 1932, 1936–39, 1941, 1943; and Casey Stengel, New York Yankees (AL), 1949–53, 1956, 1958.

Most losses Six, by John McGraw, New York Giants (NL), 1911–13, 1917, 1923–24.

Wins, both leagues The only manager to lead a team from each league to a World Series title is Sparky Anderson, who skippered the Cincinnati Reds (NL) to championships in 1975–76, and the Detroit Tigers (AL) in 1984.

COLLEGE BASEBALL

ORIGINS Various forms of college baseball have been played throughout the 20th century; however, the NCAA did not organize a championship until 1947 and did not begin to keep statistical records until 1957.

COLLEGE WORLD SERIES The first College World Series was played in 1947 at Kalamazoo, Mich. The University of California at Berkeley defeated Yale University 8–7. Since 1950 the College World Series has been played at Rosenblatt Stadium, Omaha, Neb.

Most championships The most wins is 11, by Southern Cal., in 1948, 1958, 1961, 1963, 1968, 1970–74 and 1978.

COLLEGE WORLD SERIES (1947–1991)

Year	Winner	Loser	Score	Year	Winner	Loser	Score
1947	California	Yale	8–7	1970	Southern Cal.	Florida St.	2–1
1948	Southern Cal.	Yale	9–2	1971	Southern Cal.	Southern Ill.	7–2
1949	Texas	Wake Forest	10–3	1972	Southern Cal.	Arizona St.	1–0
1950	Texas	Washington St.	3–0	1973	Southern Cal.	Arizona St.	4–3
1951	Oklahoma	Tennessee	3–2	1974	Southern Cal.	Miami (Fla.)	7–3
1952	Holy Cross	Missouri	8–4	1975	Texas	South Carolina	5–1
1953	Michigan	Texas	7–5	1976	Arizona	Eastern Mich.	7–1
1954	Missouri	Rollins	4–1	1977	Arizona St.	South Carolina	2–1
1955	Wake Forest	Western Mich.	7–6	1978	Southern Cal.	Arizona St.	10–3
1956	Minnesota	Arizona	12–1	1979	Cal. St. Fullerton	Arkansas	2–1
1957	California	Penn State	1–0	1980	Arizona	Hawaii	5–3
1958	Southern Cal.	Missouri	8–7	1981	Arizona St.	Oklahoma St.	7–4
1959	Oklahoma St.	Arizona	5–3	1982	Miami (Fla.)	Wichita St.	9–3
1960	Minnesota	Southern Cal.	2–1	1983	Texas	Alabama	4–3
1961	Southern Cal.	Oklahoma St.	1–0	1984	Cal. St. Fullerton	Texas	3–1
1962	Michigan	Santa Clara	5–4	1985	Miami (Fla.)	Texas	10–6
1963	Southern Cal.	Arizona	5–2	1986	Arizona	Florida St.	10–2
1964	Minnesota	Missouri	5–1	1987	Stanford	Oklahoma St.	9–5
1965	Arizona St.	Ohio St.	2–1	1988	Stanford	Arizona St.	9–4
1966	Ohio St.	Oklahoma St.	8–2	1989	Wichita St.	Texas	5–3
1967	Arizona St.	Houston	11–2	1990	Georgia	Oklahoma St.	2–1
1968	Southern Cal.	Southern Ill.	4–3	1991	Louisiana St.	Wichita St.	6–3
1969	Arizona St.	Tulsa	10–1				

LITTLE LEAGUE BASEBALL

ORIGINS Little League Baseball was founded in 1939 in Williamsport, Pa., by Carl Stotz and George and Bert Bebble. In 1947, the inaugural Little League World Series was played—Maynard, Pa. defeating Lock Haven, Pa. 16–7. By this time there were 12 leagues throughout Pennsylvania, and Little League had expanded beyond the state borders to Hammonton, N.J. By 1950, there were 307 leagues throughout the United States, and Little League Baseball was quickly establishing itself as an American institution. In 1957 Monterrey, Mexico became the first international team to win the title. In 1989 Carl Yastrzemski became the first Little League graduate to be inducted into the Baseball Hall of Fame.

LITTLE LEAGUE WORLD SERIES

Most championships Taiwan (Chinese Taipei), 15 (1969, 1971–74, 1977–81, 1986–88, 1990–91).

Most championships (U.S.—state) Four, from two states: Pennsylvania (Maynard–1947, Lock Haven–1948, Morrisville–1955, Levittown–1960); Connecticut (Stamford–1951, Norwalk–1952, Windsor Locks–1965, Trumbull–1989).

BASKETBALL

ORIGINS Basketball was devised by the Canadian-born Dr. James Naismith at the Training School of the International YMCA College at Springfield, Mass. in mid-December 1891. The first game played under modified rules was on January 20, 1892. The International Amateur Basketball Federation (FIBA) was founded in 1932; it has now dropped the word Amateur from its title.

NATIONAL BASKETBALL ASSOCIATION (NBA)

ORIGINS The Amateur Athletic Union (AAU) organized the first national tournament in the United States in 1897. The first professional league was the National Basketball League (NBL), founded in 1898, but this league only lasted two seasons. The American Basketball League was formed in 1925, but declined, and the NBL was refounded in 1937. This organization merged with the Basketball Association of America in 1949 to form the National Basketball Association (NBA).

GIVE AND TAKE ■ ON DECEMBER 30, 1990, SCOTT SKILES (BELOW) SET THE NBA SINGLE-GAME ASSISTS MARK OF 30. DURING THE 1985–86 SEASON, ALVIN ROBERTSON (ABOVE) SET THE SINGLE-SEASON STEALS MARK OF 301.

NBA REGULAR SEASON INDIVIDUAL RECORDS (1947–1991)

Games Played

		Player(s)	Team(s)	Date(s)
Season	88	Walt Bellamy	New York Knicks, Detroit Pistons	1968–69
Career	1,560	Kareem Abdul-Jabbar	Milwaukee Bucks, Los Angeles Lakers	1969–89

Points

Game	100	Wilt Chamberlain	Philadelphia Warriors v. New York Knicks	March 2, 1962
Season	4,029	Wilt Chamberlain	Philadelphia Warriors	1961–62
Career	38,387	Kareem Abdul-Jabbar	Milwaukee Bucks, Los Angeles Lakers	1969–89

Field Goals

Game	36	Wilt Chamberlain	Philadelphia Warriors v. New York Knicks	March 2, 1962
Season	1,597	Wilt Chamberlain	Philadelphia Warriors	1961–62
Career	15,837	Kareem Abdul-Jabbar	Milwaukee Bucks, Los Angeles Lakers	1969–89

Free Throws

Game	28	Wilt Chamberlain Adrian Dantley	Philadelphia Warriors v. New York Knicks Utah Jazz v. Houston Rockets	March 2, 1962 January 4, 1984
Season	840	Jerry West	Los Angeles Lakers	1965–66
Career	8,195*	Moses Malone	Buffalo Braves, Houston Rockets, Philadelphia 76ers, Washington Bullets, Atlanta Hawks, Milwaukee Bucks	1976–92

Assists

Game	30	Scott Skiles	Orlando Magic v. Denver Nuggets	December 30, 1990
Season	1,164	John Stockton	Utah Jazz	1990–91
Career	9,921	Magic Johnson	Los Angeles Lakers	1979–91

Rebounds

Game	55	Wilt Chamberlain	Philadelphia Warriors v. Boston Celtics	November 24, 1960
Season	2,149	Wilt Chamberlain	Philadelphia Warriors	1960–61
Career	23,924	Wilt Chamberlain	Philadelphia/San Francisco Warriors, Philadelphia 76ers, Los Angeles Lakers	1959–73

Steals

Game	11	Larry Kenon	San Antonio Spurs v. Kansas City Kings	December 26, 1976
Season	301	Alvin Robertson	San Antonio Spurs	1985–86
Career	2,231*	Maurice Cheeks	Philadelphia 76ers, San Antonio Spurs, New York Knicks, Phoenix Suns	1978–92

* As of January 4, 1992
Source: NBA

REGULAR SEASON TEAM RECORDS (1937–1991)

SCORING

Most points (one team) 186, by the Detroit Pistons, defeating the Denver Nuggets, 186–184, at Denver, on December 13, 1983 after three overtimes.

Most points, regulation (one team) 173, by two teams: Boston Celtics *v.* Minneapolis Lakers (139 points), at Boston, on February 27, 1959; Phoenix Suns *v.* Denver Nuggets (143 points), at Phoenix, on November 10, 1990.

Highest-scoring game (aggregate) 370 points, Detroit Pistons defeated the Denver Nuggets, 186–184, at Denver, on December 13, 1983 after three overtimes.

Highest-scoring game (aggregate), regulation 320 points, Golden State Warriors defeated the Denver Nuggets, 162–158, at Denver, on November 2, 1990.

Lowest-scoring game (aggregate) 37 points, Fort Wayne Pistons defeated the Minneapolis Lakers, 19–18, at Minneapolis, on November 22, 1950.

PASS MASTER ■ MAGIC JOHNSON HOLDS THE NBA ALL-TIME ASSISTS RECORD OF 9,921.

RECORD FILE: KAREEM ABDUL-JABBAR

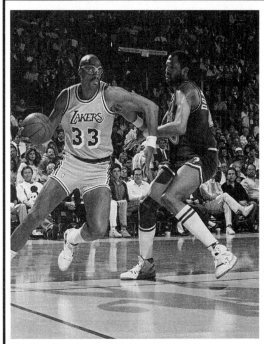

BORN April 17, 1947, New York City, N.Y.

NBA REGULAR SEASON CAREER STATISTICS
MILWAUKEE BUCKS, 1969–74; LOS ANGELES LAKERS, 1975–89

Years	Games	FGA	FGM	Pct.	Reb.	Pts.	Avg.
1969–74	467	10,787	5,902	.579	7,161	14,211	30.4
1975–89	1,093	17,520	9,935	.567	10,279	24,176	22.1
Totals	1,560*	28,307*	15,837*	.559	17,440	38,387*	24.6

NBA PLAYOFFS CAREER STATISTICS
MILWAUKEE BUCKS, 1969–74; LOS ANGELES LAKERS, 1976–89

Years	Games	FGA	FGM	Pct.	Reb.	Pts.	Avg.
1969–74	57	1,398	713	.510	956	1,692	29.7
1976–89	180	3,024	1,643	.543	1,525	4,070	22.6
Totals	237*	4,422*	2,356*	.533	2,481	5,762*	24.3

RECORD NOTES Abdul-Jabbar set numerous NBA regular-season records during his stellar career: most minutes played, 57,446; most seasons played, 20; most blocked shots, 3,189; most personal fouls, 4,657; most defensive rebounds, 9,394; and most seasons scoring over 1,000 points (19), and over 2,000 points (nine). Abdul-Jabbar also holds several playoff records, including most minutes played, 8,851; most blocked shots, 476; and most personal fouls, 797. In addition to his scoring records, Abdul-Jabbar has been named NBA Most Valuable Player a record six times: 1971–72, 1974, 1976–77, 1980.

* indicates all-time record.

Greatest margin of victory 68 points, by the Cleveland Cavaliers, defeating the Miami Heat, 148–80, on December 17, 1991.

WINS AND LOSSES

Most wins (season) 69, by the Los Angeles Lakers in 1971–72.

Most consecutive wins 33, by the Los Angeles Lakers. The Lakers' streak began with a 110–106 victory over the Baltimore Bullets on November 5, 1971 in Los Angeles, and ended on January 9, 1972 when they were beaten 120–104 by the Milwaukee Bucks in Milwaukee.

Most losses (season) 73, by the Philadelphia 76ers in 1972–73.

Most consecutive losses 24, by the Cleveland Cavaliers. The Cavs' undesirable roll started on March 19, 1982 when they lost to the Milwaukee Bucks, 119–97, in Milwaukee, and ended on November 10, 1982 when they defeated the Golden State Warriors 132–120 in overtime on November 10, 1982. During the streak the Cavs lost the last 19 games of the 1981–82 season, and the first five of the 1982–83 season.

CONSECUTIVE RECORDS (INDIVIDUAL, 1937–1991)

Games played 906, by Randy Smith, from February 18, 1972 to March 13, 1983. During his streak, Smith played for the Buffalo Braves, San Diego Clippers (twice), Cleveland Cavaliers, and New York Knicks.

Games scoring 50+ points Seven, by Wilt Chamberlain, Philadelphia Warriors, December 16–29, 1961.

Games scoring 10+ points 787, by Kareem Abdul-Jabbar, Los Angeles Lakers, from December 4, 1977 through December 2, 1987.

Free throws 78, by Calvin Murphy, Houston Rockets, from December 27, 1980 through February 28, 1981.

MOST VALUABLE PLAYER AWARD The Maurice Podoloff Trophy was instituted in 1956 to be awarded to the NBA's most valuable player. From 1956 to 1980 the award was decided by a vote of eligible NBA players; since 1980 the winner has been decided by a vote of eligible writers and broadcasters.

NBA MOST VALUABLE PLAYER AWARD (1956–1991)

Year	Player	Team	Year	Player	Team
1956	Bob Pettit	St. Louis Hawks	1974	Kareem Abdul-Jabbar	Milwaukee Bucks
1957	Bob Cousy	Boston Celtics	1975	Bob McAdoo	Buffalo Braves
1958	Bill Russell	Boston Celtics	1976	Kareem Abdul-Jabbar	Los Angeles Lakers
1959	Bob Pettit	St. Louis Hawks	1977	Kareem Abdul-Jabbar	Los Angeles Lakers
1960	Wilt Chamberlain	Philadelphia Warriors	1978	Bill Walton	Portland Trail Blazers
1961	Bill Russell	Boston Celtics	1979	Moses Malone	Houston Rockets
1962	Bill Russell	Boston Celtics	1980	Kareem Abdul-Jabbar	Los Angeles Lakers
1963	Bill Russell	Boston Celtics	1981	Julius Erving	Philadelphia 76ers
1964	Oscar Robertson	Cincinnati Royals	1982	Moses Malone	Houston Rockets
1965	Bill Russell	Boston Celtics	1983	Moses Malone	Philadelphia 76ers
1966	Wilt Chamberlain	Philadelphia 76ers	1984	Larry Bird	Boston Celtics
1967	Wilt Chamberlain	Philadelphia 76ers	1985	Larry Bird	Boston Celtics
1968	Wilt Chamberlain	Philadelphia 76ers	1986	Larry Bird	Boston Celtics
1969	Wes Unseld	Baltimore Bullets	1987	Magic Johnson	Los Angeles Lakers
1970	Willis Reed	New York Knicks	1988	Michael Jordan	Chicago Bulls
1971	Kareem Abdul-Jabbar	Milwaukee Bucks	1989	Magic Johnson	Los Angeles Lakers
1972	Kareem Abdul-Jabbar	Milwaukee Bucks	1990	Magic Johnson	Los Angeles Lakers
1973	Dave Cowens	Boston Celtics	1991	Michael Jordan	Chicago Bulls

MVP ■ LARRY BIRD IS ONE OF ONLY THREE PLAYERS TO HAVE WON THE MVP AWARD IN THREE CONSECUTIVE YEARS.

Most wins Six, by Kareem Abdul-Jabbar, Milwaukee Bucks, 1971–72, 1974; Los Angeles Lakers, 1976–77, 1980.

Consecutive wins Three, by three players: Bill Russell, Boston Celtics, 1961–63; Wilt Chamberlain, Philadelphia 76ers, 1966–68; Larry Bird, Boston Celtics, 1984–86.

COACHES (REGULAR SEASON, 1947–1991)

Most wins 938, by Red Auerbach, Washington Capitols (115 wins, 1946–49); Tri-Cities Blackhawks (28 wins, 1949–50); Boston Celtics (795 wins, 1950–66).

Highest winning percentage .733, by Pat Riley, Los Angeles Lakers, 1981–90. Riley's record was 533 wins, 194 losses with the Lakers.

Most games 1,719, by Dick Motta, Chicago Bulls, 1968–76; Washington Bullets, 1976–80; Dallas Mavericks, 1980–87; Sacramento Kings, 1989–91. Motta's career totals are 856 wins, 863 losses.

NBA CHAMPIONSHIP

The NBA recognizes the 1946–47 season as its first championship; however, at that time the league was known as the Basketball Association of America (BAA).

Most titles 16, by the Boston Celtics, 1957, 1959–66, 1968–69, 1974, 1976, 1981, 1984, 1986.

Consecutive titles Eight, by the Boston Celtics, 1959–66.

NBA CHAMPIONSHIP FINALS (1947–1968)

Year	Winner	Loser	Series	Year	Winner	Loser	Series
1947	Philadelphia Warriors	Chicago Stags	4–1	1958	St. Louis Hawks	Boston Celtics	4–2
1948	Baltimore Bullets	Philadelphia Warriors	4–2	1959	Boston Celtics	Minneapolis Lakers	4–0
1949	Minneapolis Lakers	Washington Capitols	4–2	1960	Boston Celtics	St. Louis Hawks	4–3
1950	Minneapolis Lakers	Syracuse Nationals	4–2	1961	Boston Celtics	St. Louis Hawks	4–1
1951	Rochester Royals	New York Knicks	4–3	1962	Boston Celtics	Los Angeles Lakers	4–3
1952	Minneapolis Lakers	New York Knicks	4–3	1963	Boston Celtics	Los Angeles Lakers	4–2
1953	Minneapolis Lakers	New York Knicks	4–1	1964	Boston Celtics	San Francisco Warriors	4–1
1954	Minneapolis Lakers	Syracuse Nationals	4–3	1965	Boston Celtics	Los Angeles Lakers	4–1
1955	Syracuse Nationals	Fort Wayne Pistons	4–3	1966	Boston Celtics	Los Angeles Lakers	4–3
1956	Philadelphia Warriors	Fort Wayne Pistons	4–1	1967	Philadelphia 76ers	San Francisco Warriors	4–2
1957	Boston Celtics	St. Louis Hawks	4–3	1968	Boston Celtics	Los Angeles Lakers	4–2

Most titles (coach) Nine, by Red Auerbach, Boston Celtics, 1957, 1959–66.

NBA CHAMPIONSHIP RECORDS (FINALS SERIES) (1947–1991)

INDIVIDUAL RECORDS (GAME)

Most points scored 61, by Elgin Baylor, Los Angeles Lakers *v.* Boston Celtics on April 14, 1962 in Boston.

Most field goals made 22, by two players: Elgin Baylor, Los Angeles Lakers *v.* Boston Celtics on April 14, 1962 in Boston; Rick Barry, San Francisco Warriors *v.* Philadelphia 76ers on April 18, 1967 in San Francisco.

Most free throws made 19, by Bob Pettit, St. Louis Hawks *v.* Boston Celtics on April 9, 1958 in Boston.

Most rebounds 40, by Bill Russell, Boston Celtics, who has performed this feat twice: *v.* St. Louis Hawks on March 29, 1960; *v.* Los Angeles Lakers on April 18, 1962, in an overtime game.

Most assists 21, by Magic Johnson, Los Angeles Lakers *v.* Boston Celtics on June 3, 1984.

Most steals Six, by four players: John Havlicek, Boston Celtics *v.* Milwaukee Bucks, May 3, 1974; Steve Mix, Philadelphia 76ers *v.* Portland Trail Blazers, May 22, 1977; Maurice Cheeks, Philadel-

PARQUET BULLY ■ ON APRIL 20, 1986, MICHAEL JORDAN SCORED A PLAYOFF GAME RECORD 63 POINTS V. THE BOSTON CELTICS IN THE FAMED BOSTON GARDEN.

NBA CHAMPIONSHIP FINALS (1969–1991)

Year	Winner	Loser	Series	Year	Winner	Loser	Series
1969	Boston Celtics	Los Angeles Lakers	4–3	1981	Boston Celtics	Houston Rockets	4–2
1970	New York Knicks	Los Angeles Lakers	4–3	1982	Los Angeles Lakers	Philadelphia 76ers	4–2
1971	Milwaukee Bucks	Baltimore Bullets	4–0	1983	Philadelphia 76ers	Los Angeles Lakers	4–0
1972	Los Angeles Lakers	New York Knicks	4–1	1984	Boston Celtics	Los Angeles Lakers	4–3
1973	New York Knicks	Los Angeles Lakers	4–1	1985	Los Angeles Lakers	Boston Celtics	4–2
1974	Boston Celtics	Milwaukee Bucks	4–3	1986	Boston Celtics	Houston Rockets	4–2
1975	Golden State Warriors	Washington Bullets	4–0	1987	Los Angeles Lakers	Boston Celtics	4–2
1976	Boston Celtics	Phoenix Suns	4–2	1988	Los Angeles Lakers	Detroit Pistons	4–3
1977	Portland Trail Blazers	Philadelphia 76ers	4–2	1989	Detroit Pistons	Los Angeles Lakers	4–0
1978	Washington Bullets	Seattle SuperSonics	4–3	1990	Detroit Pistons	Portland Trail Blazers	4–1
1979	Seattle SuperSonics	Washington Bullets	4–1	1991	Chicago Bulls	Los Angeles Lakers	4–1
1980	Los Angeles Lakers	Philadelphia 76ers	4–2				

NBA INDIVIDUAL PLAYOFF RECORDS (1947–1991)

Points

		Player(s)	Team(s)	Date(s)
Game	63	Michael Jordan	Chicago Bulls v. Boston Celtics	April 20, 1986 (2 OT)
	61	Elgin Baylor	Los Angeles Lakers v. Boston Celtics	April 14, 1962*
Series	284	Elgin Baylor	Los Angeles Lakers v. Boston Celtics	1962
Career	5,762	Kareem Abdul-Jabbar	Milwaukee Bucks, Los Angeles Lakers	1969–89

Field Goals

Game	24	Wilt Chamberlain	Philadelphia Warriors v. Syracuse Nationals	March 14, 1960
		John Havlicek	Boston Celtics v. Atlanta Hawks	April 1, 1973
		Michael Jordan	Chicago Bulls v. Cleveland Cavaliers	May 1, 1988
Series	113	Wilt Chamberlain	San Francisco Warriors v. St. Louis	1964
Career	2,356	Kareem Abdul-Jabbar	Milwaukee Bucks, Los Angeles Lakers	1970–89

Free Throws

Game	30	Bob Cousy	Boston Celtics v. Syracuse Nationals	March 21, 1953 (4 OT)
	23	Michael Jordan	Chiacgo Bulls v. New York Knicks	May 14, 1989*
Series	86	Jerry West	Los Angeles Lakers v. Baltimore Bullets	1965
Career	1,213	Jerry West	Los Angeles Lakers	1960–74

Assists

Game	24	Magic Johnson	Los Angeles Lakers v. Phoenix Suns	May 15, 1984
		John Stockton	Utah Jazz v. Los Angeles Lakers	May 17, 1988
Series	115	John Stockton	Utah Jazz v. Los Angeles Lakers	1988
Career	2,320	Magic Johnson	Los Angeles Lakers	1979–91

Rebounds

Game	41	Wilt Chamberlain	Philadelphia 76ers v. Boston Celtics	April 5, 1967
Series	220	Wilt Chamberlain	Philadelphia 76ers v. Boston Celtics	1965
Career	4,104	Bill Russell	Boston Celtics	1956–69

Steals

Game	8	Rick Barry	Golden State Warriors v. Seattle SuperSonics	April 14, 1975
		Lionel Hollins	Portland Trail Blazers v. Los Angeles Lakers	May 8, 1977
		Maurice Cheeks	Philadelphia 76ers v. New Jersey Nets	April 11, 1979
		Craig Hodges	Milwaukee Bucks v. Philadelphia 76ers	May 9, 1986
		Tim Hardaway	Golden State Warriors v. Los Angeles Lakers	May 8, 1991
Series	28	John Stockton	Utah Jazz v. Los Angeles Lakers	1988
Career	358	Magic Johnson	Los Angeles Lakers	1979–91

* Regulation play
Source: NBA

DEFENSE! ■ ISIAH THOMAS (LEFT) SHARES THE PLAYOFF GAME STEALS MARK OF SIX, AND HAKEEM OLAJUWON (RIGHT) SHARES THE FINALS GAME BLOCKED SHOTS RECORD OF EIGHT.

phia 76ers *v.* Los Angeles Lakers, May 7, 1980; Isiah Thomas, Detroit Pistons *v.* Los Angeles Lakers, June 19, 1988.

Most blocked shots Eight, by two players: Bill Walton, Portland Trail Blazers *v.* Philadelphia 76ers, June 5, 1977; Hakeem Olajuwon, Houston Rockets *v.* Boston Celtics, June 5, 1986.

TEAM RECORDS (GAME)

Most points (one team) 148, by the Boston Celtics *v.* Los Angeles Lakers (114 points) on May 27, 1985.

Highest-scoring game (aggregate) 276 points, Philadelphia 76ers defeated the San Francisco Warriors, 141–135, in overtime, on April 14, 1967.

Highest-scoring game, regulation (aggregate) 263 points, Los Angeles Lakers defeated the Boston Celtics, 141–122, on June 4, 1987.

Greatest margin of victory 35 points, Washington Bullets shot down the Seattle SuperSonics, 117–82, on June 4, 1978.

NCAA COLLEGE BASKETBALL

MEN'S BASKETBALL (NCAA)

The National Collegiate Athletic Association (NCAA) has compiled statistics for its men's basketball competitions since the 1937–38 season. NCAA men's basketball is classified by three divisions: I, II and III.

NCAA CAREER REGULAR SEASON RECORDS (DIVISIONS I, II, III, 1937–1991)

POINTS SCORED

Game 113, by Clarence "Bevo" Francis, Rio Grande (Division II), *v.* Hillsdale on February 2, 1954.

Season 1,381, by Pete Maravich, Louisiana State (Division I). Pistol Pete hit 522 field goals and 337 free throws in 31 games.

Career 4,045, by Travis Grant, Kentucky State (Division II), 1969–72.

BORN: June 22, 1947, Aliquippa, Pa. Died January 5, 1988.

NCAA COLLEGIATE CAREER, LOUISIANA STATE
1967–70

Years	Games	FGA	FGM	Pct.	Reb.	Pts.	Avg.
1967–68	26	1,022	432	.423	195	1,138	43.8
1968–69	26	976	433	.444	169	1,148	44.2
1969–70	31	1,168*	522*	.447	164	1,381*	44.5*
Totals	83	3,166*	1,387*	.438	528	3,667*	44.2*

RECORD NOTES Maravich holds several other NCAA scoring records: most 50-point games in a career, 28; most in a season, 10 in 1970; and most consecutively, three, from February 10–15, 1969. Maravich also holds the record for most free throws made in a game, 30 from 31 attempts *v.* Oregon State on December 22, 1969.

* indicates all-time record.

DEFENSE ANCHOR ■ IN 1986, NAVY'S DAVID ROBERTSON SET GAME AND SEASON NCAA DIVISION I RECORDS FOR BLOCKED SHOTS, 14 AND 207 RESPECTIVELY.

100 POINTS! ■ FRANK SELVY, FURMAN, SCORED AN NCAA DIVISION 1 GAME RECORD 100 POINTS V. NEWBERRY ON FEBRUARY 13, 1954.

NCAA DIVISION I MEN'S INDIVIDUAL REGULAR SEASON RECORDS (1937–1991)

Points

		Player(s)	Team(s)	Date(s)
Game	100	Frank Selvy	Furman v. Newberry	February 13, 1954
	72	Kevin Bradshaw	U.S. International v. Loyola–Marymount	January 5, 1991*
Season	1,381	Pete Maravich	Louisiana State	1970
Career	3,667	Pete Maravich	Lousiana State	1968–70

Field Goals

Game	41	Frank Selvy	Furman v. Newberry	February 13, 1954
Season	522	Pete Maravich	Lousiana State	1970
Career	1,387	Pete Maravich	Lousiana State	1968–70

Free Throws

Game	30	Pete Maravich	Louisiana State v. Oregon State	December 22, 1969
Season	355	Frank Selvy	Furman	1954
Career	905	Dickie Hemric	Wake Forest	1952–55

Assists

Game	22	Tony Fairley	Charleston South v. Armstrong State	February 9, 1987
		Avery Johnson	Southern-B.R. v. Texas Southern	January 25, 1988
		Sherman Douglas	Syracuse v. Providence	January 28, 1989
Season	406	Mark Wade	UNLV	1987
Career	1,038	Chris Corchiani	North Carolina State	1988–91

Rebounds

Game	51	Bill Chambers	William & Mary v. Virginia	February 14, 1953
Season	734	Walt Dukes	Seton Hall	1953
Career	2,243	Tom Gola	La Salle	1952–55

Blocked Shots

Game	14	David Robinson	Navy v. N.C.–Wilmington	January 4, 1986
		Shawn Bradley	BYU v. Eastern Kentucky	December 7, 1990
Season	207	David Robinson	Navy	1986
Career	399	Rodney Blake	St. Joseph's (Pa.)	1985–88

Steals

Game	13	Mookie Blaylock	Oklahoma v. Centenary	December 12, 1987
		Mookie Blaylock	Oklahoma v. Loyola–Marymount	December 17, 1988
Season	150	Mookie Blaylock	Oklahoma	1988
Career	376	Eric Murdock	Providence	1988–91

* Game between two Division I teams
Source: NCAA

FIELD GOALS MADE

Game 41, by Frank Selvy, Furman (Division I), *v.* Newberry on February 13, 1954. Selvy amassed his record total from 66 attempts.

Season 539, by Travis Grant, Kentucky State (Division II) in 1972. Grant's season record was gained from 869 attempts.

Career 1,760, by Travis Grant, Kentucky State (Division II), 1969–72. Grant achieved his career record from 2,759 attempts.

ASSISTS

Game 26, by Robert James, Kean (Division III), *v.* New Jersey Tech on March 11, 1989.

Season 406, by Mark Wade, UNLV (Division I) in 1987. Wade played in 38 games.

Career 1,038, by Chris Corchiani, North Carolina State (Division I), 1988–91. During his record-setting career Corchiani played in 124 games.

REBOUNDS

Game 51, by Bill Chambers, William & Mary (Division I), *v.* Virginia on February 14, 1953.

Season 799, by Elmore Smith, Kentucky State (Division II) in 1971.

Career 2,334, by Jim Smith, Steubenville (Division II), 1955–58. Smith amassed his record total from 112 games.

NCAA TEAM RECORDS (DIVISION I, 1937–1991)

Most points scored (one team) 186, by Loyola Marymount (Cal.) *v.* U.S. International (140 points), on January 5, 1991.

Highest-scoring game (aggregate) 331 points, Loyola Marymount (Cal.) defeating U.S. International, 181–150, on January 31, 1989.

Fewest points scored (team) Six, by two teams: Temple *v.* Tennessee (11 points), on December 15, 1973; Arkansas State *v.* Kentucky (75 points), on January 8, 1945.

Lowest-scoring game (aggregate) 17 points, Tennessee defeating Temple, 11–6, on December 15, 1973.

Widest margin of victory 95 points, Oklahoma defeating Northeastern Illinois, 146–51, on December 2, 1989.

Greatest deficit overcome 28 points, New Mexico State defeating Bradley, 117–109, on January 27, 1977, after trailing 0–28 with 13:49 left in the first half.

Most wins (season) 37, by two teams: Duke in 1986 (37 wins, 3 losses); UNLV in 1987 (37 wins, 2 losses).

Most losses (season) 27, by four teams: Washington State in 1953 (6 wins, 27 losses); Pacific in 1984 (3 wins, 27 losses); U.S. International in 1985 (1 win, 27 losses); George Washington in 1989 (1 win, 27 losses).

CONSECUTIVE RECORDS (INDIVIDUAL, DIVISION I)

Games scoring 10+ points 115, by Lionel Simmons, La Salle, 1987–90.

Games scoring 50+ points Three, by Pete Maravich, Louisiana State, February 10 to February 15, 1969.

Field goals 25, by Ray Voelkel, American, over nine games from November 24 through December 16, 1978.

Field goals (game) 16, by Doug Grayson, Kent *v.* North Carolina on December 6, 1967.

Three-point field goals 15, by Todd Leslie, Northwestern, over four games from December 15 through December 28, 1990.

Three-point field goals (game) 11, by Gary Bossert, Niagara *v.* Sienna, January 7, 1987.

Free throws 64, by Joe Dykstra, Western Illinois, over eight games, December 1, 1981 through January 4, 1982.

Free throws (game) 24, by Arlen Clark, Oklahoma State *v.* Colorado, March 7, 1959.

CONSECUTIVE RECORDS (TEAM, DIVISION I)

Wins (regular season) 76, by UCLA, from January 30, 1971 through January 17, 1974. The streak was ended on January 19, 1974 when the Bruins were defeated by Notre Dame, 71–70.

Wins (regular season and playoffs) 88, by UCLA, from January 30, 1971 through January 17, 1974.

Losses 37, by Citadel, from January 16, 1954 through December 12, 1955.

Winning seasons 46, by Louisville, 1945–90.

COACHES (DIVISION I)

Most wins 875, by Adolph Rupp, Kentucky, 1931–72.

Highest winning percentage .833, by Jerry Tarkanian, Long Beach State, 1969–73; UNLV, 1974–present. Through the 1990–91 season, the shark's career record was 599 wins, 120 losses.

Most games 1,105, by Henry Iba, Northwest Missouri State, 1930–33; Colorado, 1934; Oklahoma State, 1935–70. Iba's career record was 767 wins, 338 losses.

Most years 48, by Phog Allen, Baker, 1906–08; Kansas, 1908–09; Haskell, 1909, Central Missouri State, 1913–19, Kansas, 1920–56.

NCAA CHAMPIONSHIP TOURNAMENT (1939–1991)

The NCAA finals were first contested in 1939 at Northwestern University, Evanston, Ill. The Uni-

NCAA DIVISION I CHAMPIONS (1939–1991)

Year	Winner	Loser	Score	Year	Winner	Loser	Score
1939	Oregon	Ohio State	46–33	1966	UTEP	Kentucky	72–65
1940	Indiana	Kansas	60–42	1967	UCLA	Dayton	79–64
1941	Wisconsin	Washington State	39–34	1968	UCLA	North Carolina	78–55
1942	Stanford	Dartmouth	53–38	1969	UCLA	Purdue	92–72
1943	Wyoming	Georgetown	46–34	1970	UCLA	Jacksonville	80–69
1944	Utah	Dartmouth	42–40	1971	UCLA	Villanova*	68–62
1945	Oklahoma State	NYU	49–45	1972	UCLA	Florida State	81–76
1946	Oklahoma State	North Carolina	43–40	1973	UCLA	Memphis State	87–66
1947	Holy Cross	Oklahoma	58–47	1974	N. Carolina State	Marquette	76–64
1948	Kentucky	Baylor	58–42	1975	UCLA	Kentucky	92–85
1949	Kentucky	Oklahoma A&M	46–36	1976	Indiana	Michigan	86–68
1950	CCNY	Bradley	71–68	1977	Marquette	North Carolina	67–59
1951	Kentucky	Kansas State	68–58	1978	Kentucky	Duke	94–88
1952	Kansas	St. John's	80–63	1979	Michigan State	Indiana State	75–64
1953	Indiana	Kansas	69–68	1980	Louisville	UCLA*	59–54
1954	LaSalle	Bradley	92–76	1981	Indiana	North Carolina	63–50
1955	San Francisco	LaSalle	77–63	1982	North Carolina	Georgetown	63–62
1956	San Francisco	Iowa	83–71	1983	N. Carolina State	Houston	54–52
1957	North Carolina	Kansas	54–53	1984	Georgetown	Houston	84–75
1958	Kentucky	Seattle	84–72	1985	Villanova	Georgetown	66–64
1959	California	West Virginia	71–70	1986	Louisville	Duke	72–69
1960	Ohio State	California	75–55	1987	Indiana	Syracuse	74–73
1961	Cincinnati	Ohio State	70–65	1988	Kansas	Oklahoma	83–79
1962	Cincinnati	Ohio State	71–59	1989	Michigan	Seton Hall	80–79
1963	Loyola (Ill.)	Cincinnati	60–58	1990	UNLV	Duke	103–73
1964	UCLA	Duke	98–83	1991	Duke	Kansas	72–65
1965	UCLA	Michigan	91–80				

* The teams were disqualified by the NCAA for rules violations uncovered following the completion of the tournament.

versity of Oregon, University of Oklahoma, Villanova University and Ohio State University were the first "final four." Oregon defeated Ohio State 46–33 to win the first NCAA title.

Most wins (team) 10, by UCLA, 1964–65, 1967–73, 1975.

Most wins (coach) 10, by John Wooden. Wooden coached UCLA to each of its NCAA titles.

CHAMPIONSHIP GAME RECORDS (INDIVIDUAL, 1939–1991)

Most points 44, by Bill Walton, UCLA *v.* Memphis State in 1973.

Most field goals 21, by Bill Walton, UCLA *v.* Memphis State in 1973.

Most rebounds 21, by Bill Spivey, Kentucky *v.* Kansas State in 1951.

Most assists Nine, by three players: Alvin Franklin, Houston *v.* Georgetown, 1984; Michael Jackson, Georgetown *v.* Villanova, 1985; Bobby Hurley, Duke *v.* Kansas, 1991.

MARCH WIZARDRY ■ **JOHN WOODEN LED UCLA TO AN UNPRECEDENTED 10 NCAA CHAMPIONSHIPS.**

WOMEN'S BASKETBALL

ORIGINS Senda Berenson and Clara Baer are generally credited as the pioneers of women's basketball. In 1892, Berenson, a physical education instructor at Smith College, adapted James Naismith's rules of basketball to create a "divided-court" version, which required the players to remain in their assigned sections of the court, making the game less physically demanding and thus, presumably, more suitable for women. Clara Baer introduced women's basketball to Sophie Newcomb Memorial College in her native New Orleans, La., in 1893. Baer also adapted the style of Naismith's game, and published her own set of rules in 1895; these became known as the Newcomb College rules.

The game spread rapidly in the late 19th century, with the first women's collegiate game being played between California and Stanford on April 4, 1896. Women's basketball was unable to sustain its growth in the 20th century, however, due to controversy over whether it was safe for women to play the game. It wasn't until after World War II that attitudes changed and women's basketball began to organize itself on a national level and bring its rules into line with the men's game.

In 1969, Carol Eckman, coach at West Chester University, Pa., organized the first national invitation tournament. Under the auspices of the Association for Intercollegiate Athletics for Women (AIAW) the national tournament was expanded, and in 1982 the NCAA was invited to take over the tournament.

FINAL FOUR FLOURISH ■ **BILL WALTON HOLDS NCAA TITLE GAME RECORDS FOR MOST POINTS (44) AND MOST FIELD GOALS (21).**

NCAA REGULAR SEASON RECORDS (DIVISIONS I, II, III, 1982–1991)

POINTS SCORED

Game 67, by Jackie Givens, Fort Valley State (Division II), *v.* Knoxville on February 22, 1991. Givens hit 25 field goals, six three-point field goals, and 11 free throws.

Season 1,075, by Jackie Givens, Fort Valley State (Division II), in 1991. Givens' record-setting season consisted of 369 field goals, 120 three-point field goals, and 217 free throws in 28 games.

Career 3,171, by Jeannie Demers, Buena Vista (Division III), 1983–87. Demers' career totals are 1,386 field goals and 399 free throws in 105 games.

FIELD GOALS MADE

Game 28, by Ann Gilbert, Oberlin (Division III), *v.* Allegheny on February 6, 1991.

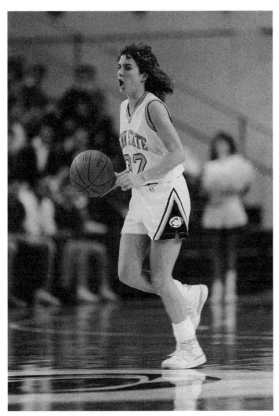

Season 392, by Barbara Kennedy, Clemson (Division I) in 1982. Kennedy set her record total from 760 attempts.

Career 1,386, by Jeannie Demers, Buena Vista (Division III), 1983–87. Demers made her record total from 2,838 attempts.

ASSISTS

Game 23, by Michelle Burden, Kent (Division I), *v.* Ball State on February 6, 1991.

Season 355, by Suzie McConnell, Penn State (Division I), in 1987.

Career 1,307, by Suzie McConnell, Penn State (Division I), 1984–88.

REBOUNDS

Game 40, by Deborah Temple, Delta State (Division I), *v.* Alabama–Birmingham, on February 14, 1983.

Season 635, by Francine Perry, Quinnipac (Division II), in 1982.

Career 1,887, by Wanda Ford, Drake (Division I), 1983–86.

NCAA TEAM RECORDS (DIVISION I)

Most points scored (one team) 149, by Long Beach State *v.* San Jose State (69 points), on February 16, 1987.

Highest-scoring game (aggregate) 243 points, Virginia defeating North Carolina State, 123–120, after three overtimes on January 12, 1991.

Fewest points scored (one team) 12, by Bennett *v.* North Carolina A&T (85 points), on November 21, 1990.

Lowest scoring game (aggregate) 72 points, Virginia defeating San Diego State, 38–34, on December 29, 1981.

Most wins (season) 35, by three teams: Texas, 1982; Louisiana Tech, 1982; Tennessee, 1989.

Most losses (season) 28, by Charleston South in 1991.

COACHES (DIVISION I)

Most wins 577, by Jody Conradt, Texas, 1970–91.

Highest winning percentage .879, by Leon Barmore, Louisiana Tech, 1983–91. Barmore's career record through the 1990–91 season is 261 wins, 36 losses.

NCAA DIVISION I WOMEN'S INDIVIDUAL REGULAR SEASON RECORDS (1982–1991)

Points

		Player(s)	Team(s)	Date(s)
Game	60	Cindy Brown	Long Beach State v. San Jose State	February 16, 1987
Season	974	Cindy Brown	Long Beach State	1987
Career	3,122	Patricia Hoskins	Mississippi Valley	1985–89

Field Goals

Game	27	Lorri Bauman	Drake v. Southwest Missouri State	January 6, 1984
Season	392	Barbara Kennedy	Clemson	1982
Career	1,259	Joyce Walker	Louisiana State	1981–84

Free Throws

Game	22	Lorri Bauman	Drake v. Northern Illinois	November 26, 1982
		Tammy Hinchee	Northern Illinois v. Marquette	February 25, 1989
Season	275	Lorri Bauman	Drake	1982
Career	907	Lorri Bauman	Drake	1981–84

Assists

Game	23	Michelle Burden	Kent v. Ball State	February 6, 1991
Season	355	Suzie McConnell	Penn State	1987
Career	1,307	Suzie McConnel	Penn State	1984–88

Rebounds

Game	40	Deborah Temple	Delta State v. Alabama– Birmingham	February 14, 1983
Season	534	Wanda Ford	Drake	1985
Career	1,887	Wanda Ford	Drake	1983–86

Blocked Shots

Game	13	Stefanie Kasperski	Oregon v. Western Kentucky	December 29, 1987
		Suzanne Johnson	Monmouth v. Delaware	December 13, 1990
Season	151	Michelle Wilson	Texas Southern	1989
Career	428	Genia Miller	Cal. St. Fullerton	1987–91

Steals

Game	13	Tammy Stover	Wright St. v. Maryland–East Shore	January 20, 1988
		Ann Thomas	Tennessee St. v. Monmouth	Novermber 25, 1989
Season	160	Shelly Barton	Florida A&M	1990
Career	429	Neacole Hall	Alabama St.	1987–89

Source: NCAA

NCAA CHAMPIONSHIP TOURNAMENT (1982–1991)

The NCAA instituted a women's basketball championship in 1982.

NCAA CHAMPIONS (1982–1991)

Year	Winner	Loser	Score
1982	Louisiana Tech.	Cheyney	76–62
1983	Southern Cal.	Louisiana Tech.	69–67
1984	Southern Cal.	Tennessee	72–61
1985	Old Dominion	Georgia	70–65
1986	Texas	Southern Cal.	97–81
1987	Tennessee	Louisiana Tech.	67–44
1988	Louisiana Tech.	Auburn	56–54
1989	Tennessee	Auburn	76–60
1990	Stanford	Auburn	88–81
1991	Tennessee	Virginia	70–67*

* Overtime

Most wins (team) Three, by Tennessee, 1987, 1989 and 1991.

Most wins (coach) Three, by Pat Summitt. Summitt coached Tennessee to all three NCAA titles.

CHAMPIONSHIP GAME RECORDS (INDIVIDUAL, 1982–1991)

Most points 28, by two players in the 1991 championship game between Virginia and Tennessee: Dawn Staley (Virginia); Dena Head (Tennessee).

Most field goals 12, by Erica Westbrooks, Louisiana Tech *v.* Auburn, in 1988.

Most rebounds 20, by Tracy Claxton, Old Dominion *v.* Georgia, in 1985.

Most assists 10, by two players: Kamie Ethridge, Texas *v.* Southern Cal, in 1986; Melissa McCray, Tennessee *v.* Auburn, in 1989.

OLYMPIC GAMES The men's basketball competition was introduced at the Berlin Olympics in 1936. In April 1989, the International Olympic Committee voted to allow professional players to compete in the Games.

The women's basketball competition was introduced at the Montreal Olympics in 1976.

OLYMPIC GAMES MEDALISTS (1936–1988)

Men			
Year	Gold	Silver	Bronze
1936	United States	Canada	Mexico
1948	United States	France	Brazil
1952	United States	USSR	Uruguay
1956	United States	USSR	Uruguay
1960	United States	USSR	Brazil
1964	United States	USSR	Brazil
1968	United States	Yugoslavia	USSR
1972	USSR	United States	Cuba
1976	United States	Yugoslavia	USSR
1980	Yugoslavia	Italy	USSR
1984	United States	Spain	Yugoslavia
1988	USSR	Yugoslavia	United States
Women			
1976	USSR	United States	Bulgaria
1980	USSR	Bulgaria	Yugoslavia
1984	United States	South Korea	China
1988	United States	Yugoslavia	USSR

Most gold medals (men) The United States has won nine gold medals in Olympic basketball competition: 1936, 1948, 1952, 1956, 1960, 1964, 1968, 1976 and 1984.

Most gold medals (women) In the women's basketball tournament the gold medal has been won twice by two countries: USSR, 1976 and 1980; United States, 1984 and 1988.

Most gold medals (individual) Three players have played on two United States gold-medal-winning teams: Bob Kurland, 1948 and 1952; Bill Houghland, 1952 and 1956; and Burdette Haldorson, 1956 and 1960.

Most medals (country) The United States has won 14 medals in Olympic competition: nine gold, one silver and one bronze in men's events; two gold and one silver in women's.

Most medals (individual) Two players have won four medals: Sergey Belov (USSR), one gold in 1972, two silver in 1960 and 1964, one bronze in

1968; Gennadiy Volnov (USSR), one gold in 1972, three bronzes in 1968, 1976 and 1980.

WORLD CHAMPIONSHIPS An official men's world championship was first staged in 1950 in Buenos Aires, Argentina, and has been held quadrennially since. A women's world championship was first staged in 1953 and is now also staged as a quadrennial event.

Most titles (men) Two countries have won the men's title three times: USSR, 1967, 1974 and 1982; Yugoslavia, 1970, 1978 and 1990.

Most titles (women) The USSR has won the women's event a record six times: 1959, 1964, 1967, 1971, 1975 and 1983.

United States The United States has won the women's title five times: 1953, 1957, 1979, 1986 and 1990; and the men's title twice: 1954 and 1986.

BIATHLON

The biathlon is a composite test of cross-country skiing and rifle marksmanship. Competitors ski over a prepared course carrying a small-bore rifle; at designated ranges the skiers stop and complete the shooting assignment for the race. Time penalties are assessed for missed shots; the winner of the event is the one with the fastest time.

ORIGINS The sport reflects one of the earliest techniques of human survival; rock carvings in Roedoey, Norway dating to 3000 B.C. seem to depict hunters stalking their prey on skis. Biathlon as a modern sport evolved from military ski patrol maneuvers, which tested the soldier's ability as a fast skier and accurate marksman. In 1958 the *Union Internationale de Pentathlon Moderne et Biathlon* (UIPMB) was formed as the international governing body of biathlon and modern pentathlon. Biathlon was included in the Olympic Games for the first time in 1960.

United States The 1960 Olympic Games at Squaw Valley, Calif. introduced biathlon to this country. National championships were first held in 1965. The current governing body of the sport is the United States Biathlon Association, founded in 1980 and based in Essex Junction, Vt.

OLYMPIC GAMES Biathlon was included in the Winter Games for the first time at Squaw Valley, Calif. in 1960. Women's events are to be included for the first time at the 1992 Games at Albertville, France.

Most gold medals Aleksandr Tikhonov (USSR) has won four gold medals as a member of the Soviet relay team that won the 4 x 7,500 meter races in 1968, 1972, 1976 and 1980. The Soviet Union has won the men's relay on all six occasions that the event has been staged. Magnar Solberg (Norway) and Franz-Peter Rotsch (East Germany) have both won two gold medals in individual events. Solberg won the 20,000 meters in 1968 and 1972; Rotsch won the 10,000 meters and 20,000 meters in 1988.

Most medals Aleksandr Tikhonov has won a record five medals in Olympic competition. In addition to his four gold medals (see above), he won the silver medal in the 20,000 meters in 1968.

Most medals (country) The Soviet Union has won 19 medals: nine gold, five silver and five bronze.

United States No American biathlete has ever won an Olympic medal.

WORLD CHAMPIONSHIPS First held in 1958 for men and in 1984 for women, the world championships are an annual event. In Olympic years, the Games are considered the world championships; therefore, records in this section include results from the Games.

Most titles (overall) Aleksandr Tikhonov (USSR) has won 14 world titles: 10 in the 4 x 7,500 meter relay, 1968–74, 1976–77 and 1980; four individual events, 10,000 meter in 1977 and 20,000 meter in 1969–70 and 1973. In women's events, Kaya Parve (USSR) has won a record six gold medals: four in the 3 x 5,000 meter relay, 1984–86, 1988; two individual titles, the 5,000 meter in 1986 and the 10,000 meter in 1985.

Most titles (individual) Frank Ullrich (East Germany) has won a record six individual titles: 10,000 meter, 1978–81; 20,000 meter, 1982–83.

UNITED STATES NATIONAL CHAMPIONSHIPS In this competition, first held in 1965 in Rosendale, N.Y., men's events have been staged annually. Women's events were included in 1985.

Most titles Lyle Nelson has won seven national championships: five in the 10,000 meter, 1976, 1979, 1981, 1985 and 1987; two in the 20,000 meter, 1977 and 1985. Anna Sonnerup holds the women's record with five titles: two in the 10,000 meter, 1986–87; two in the 15,000 meter, 1989 and 1991; and one in the 7,500 meter in 1989.

BOBSLED AND LUGE

BOBSLED

ORIGINS The earliest known sled is dated c. 6500 B.C. and was found at Heinola, Finland. There are references to sled racing in Norwegian folklore dating from the 15th century. The first tracks built for sled racing were constructed in the mid-18th century in St. Petersburg, Russia. The modern sport of bobsled dates to the late 19th century, when British enthusiasts organized competitions in Switzerland. The first run built for bobsled racing was constructed in St. Moritz, Switzerland in 1902. The *Federation Internationale de Bobsleigh de Tobagganing* (FIBT) was founded in 1923 and is the world governing body of bobsled racing.

United States The United States Bobsled & Skeleton Federation was founded in 1941 and is still the governing body for the sport in this country.

OLYMPIC GAMES A four-man bob competition was included in the first Winter Games in 1924 at Chamonix, France. Bobsled events have been included in every Games except 1960, when the Squaw Valley organizing committee refused to build a bobsled track.

Four-man bob Switzerland has won a record five Olympic titles: 1924, 1936, 1956, 1972 and 1988.

Two-man bob Five countries have won the two-man title twice: United States, 1932 and 1936; Switzerland, 1948 and 1980; West Germany, 1952 and 1972; Italy, 1956 and 1968; East Germany, 1976 and 1984.

Most gold medals Meinhard Nehmer and Bernhard Germeshausen (both East Germany) have both won a record three gold medals. They were both members of the 1976 two-man and four-man winning crews and the 1980 four-man winning crews.

SWISS PRECISION ■ SWITZERLAND HAS DOMINATED OLYMPIC BOBSLED COMPETITION, WINNING 20 MEDALS, INCLUDING A RECORD SEVEN GOLDS.

Most medals Eugenio Monti (Italy) has won six medals: two gold, two silver and two bronze, 1956–68.

Most medals (country) Switzerland has won 20 medals in bobsled competition: seven gold, six silver and seven bronze.

United States The United States has won 14 medals in Olympic competition. Billy Fiske III and Clifford Gray are the only Americans to win two gold medals in bobsled, being members of the four-man bob champion crews in 1928 and 1932.

WORLD CHAMPIONSHIPS A world championship staged independently of the Olympic Games was first held in 1930 for four-man bob, and from 1931 for two-man bob. In Olympic years the Games are considered the world championship; therefore, records in this section include the Games of 1924 and 1928.

Four-man bob Switzerland has won the world title a record 19 times: 1924, 1936, 1939, 1947, 1954–57, 1971–73, 1975, 1982–83 and 1986–90.

Two-man bob Italy has won the world title 14 times: 1954, 1956–63, 1966, 1968–69, 1971 and 1975.

Most titles Eugenio Monti (Italy) has won 11 bobsled world championships: eight in the two-man, 1957–1961, 1963, 1966 and 1968; three in the four-man, 1960–61 and 1968.

UNITED STATES NATIONAL CHAMPIONSHIPS The United States Championship was first held in 1941 and has been held annually since. The United States Bobsled & Skeleton Federation does not have complete files on its championship, making it impossible to calculate records for this section at this time.

LUGE

In luge the rider adopts a supine as opposed to a sitting position.

ORIGINS The first international luge race took place in 1883. Organized by the hotel keepers of Davos, Switzerland to promote their town, the race attracted 21 entrants from seven countries, including the United States. The course was 2½ miles, from St. Wolfgang to Klosters. The FIBT governed luge racing until 1957, when the *Fédération Internationale de Luge* (FIL) was formed.

United States The United States has participated in all Olympic luge events since the sport was sanctioned for the 1964 Games, but there was no organized governing body for the sport in this country until 1979, when the United States Luge Association was formed. The only luge run in the United States accredited for international competition is the refrigerated run used for the Lake Placid Olympics in 1980.

OLYMPIC GAMES One-man skeleton races were included in the 1928 and 1948 Games; however, in skeleton races riders race face down rather than lying on their backs as in luge. Luge was included in the Games for the first time in 1964 in Innsbruck, Austria.

Most gold medals Thomas Kohler, Hans Rinn, Norbert Hahn and Steffi Martin-Walter (all East Germany) have each won two Olympic titles: Kohler won the single-seater in 1964 and the two-seater in 1968; Rinn and Hahn won the two-seater in 1976 and 1980; Martin-Walter won the women's single-seater in 1984 and 1988.

Most medals (country) East Germany has won 29 medals in luge competition: in men's events, nine gold, three silver and five bronze; in women's events, four gold, five silver and three bronze.

United States No American luger has won a medal at the Olympic Games. In the skeleton sled races held in 1928 and 1948, the United States won one gold and two silvers out of six races. Jennison Heaton was the winner of the 1928 single skeleton sled event.

WORLD CHAMPIONSHIPS First held in 1955, the world championships have been staged biennially since 1981. In Olympic years the Games are considered the world championships; therefore, records in this section include results from the Games.

Most titles Thomas Kohler and Hans Rinn (both East Germany) have both won six world titles: Kohler won the single-seater in 1962, 1964 and 1966–67, and the two-seater in 1967–68; Rinn won the single-seater in 1973 and 1977, and the two-seater in 1976–77 and 1980 (two world championships were held in 1980, with Rinn winning each time). Margit Schumann (East Germany) holds the women's mark with five world titles, 1973–77.

UNITED STATES NATIONAL CHAMPIONSHIPS This competition was inaugurated in 1974.

Most titles Frank Masley has won a record six men's championships: 1979, 1981–83 and 1987–88. Bonny Warner has won a record five women's titles: 1983–84, 1987–88 and 1990.

Fastest speed The fastest recorded photo-timed speed is 85.38 mph, by Asle Strand (Norway) at Tandådalens Linbana, Sälen, Sweden on May 1 1982.

BOWLING

ORIGINS The ancient German game of nine-pins (*Heidenwerfen*—"knock down pagans") was exported to the United States in the early 17th century. In 1841, the Connecticut state legislature prohibited the game, and other states followed. Eventually a tenth pin was added to evade the ban. The first body to standardize rules was the American Bowling Congress (ABC), established in New York City on September 9, 1895.

PROFESSIONAL BOWLERS ASSOCIATION (PBA)

The PBA was founded in 1958 by Eddie Elias and is based in Akron, Ohio.

Most titles (career) Earl Anthony of Dublin, Calif. has won a career record 41 PBA titles, 1970–83.

Most titles (season) The record number of titles won in one PBA season is eight, by Mark Roth of North Arlington, N.J., in 1978.

TRIPLE CROWN The United States Open, the PBA National Championship and the Firestone Tournament of Champions comprise the Triple Crown of men's professional bowling. No bowler has won all three titles in the same year, and only three have managed to win all three during a career. The first bowler to accumulate the three legs of the triple crown was Billy Hardwick: National Championship (1963); Firestone Tournament of Champions (1965); U.S. Open (1969). Hardwick's feat was matched by Johnny Petraglia: Firestone (1971); U.S. Open (1977); National (1980); and by Pete Weber: Firestone (1987); U.S. Open (1988 and 1991); National (1989).

U.S. OPEN In this tournament, inaugurated in 1942, the most wins is four, by two bowlers: Don Carter in 1953–54 and 1957–58, and Dick Weber in 1962–63 and 1965–66.

PBA NATIONAL CHAMPIONSHIP In this contest, inaugurated in 1960, the most wins is six, by Earl Anthony in 1973–75 and 1981–83.

PBA TOUR SCORING RECORDS

Games	Score	Bowler	Site	Year
6	1,613	Tom Baker	Denver, Colo.	1981
8	2,165	Billy Hardwick	Japan	1968
12	3,037	Tom Baker	Denver, Colo.	1981
16	4,015	Carmen Salvino	Sterling Heights, Mich.	1980
18	4,515	Earl Anthony	New Orleans, La.	1977
24	5,825	Earl Anthony	Seattle, Wash.	1970

Source: PBA Tour

FIRESTONE TOURNAMENT OF CHAMPIONS In this tournament, inaugurated in 1965, the most wins is three, by Mike Durbin in 1972, 1982 and 1984.

PEFECT GAMES

A total of 141 perfect (300 score) games were bowled in PBA tournaments in 1990, the most ever for one year.

Most perfect games (career) Since 1977, when the PBA began to keep statistics on perfect games, Wayne Webb has bowled 32 in tournament play.

Most perfect games (season) Amleto Monacelli rolled seven perfect games on the 1989 tour.

Highest earnings Marshall Holman has won a career record $1,555,851 in PBA competitions through 1991. Mike Aulby of Indianapolis, Ind. set a single-season earnings mark of $298,237 in 1989.

PIN MONEY ■ MARSHALL HOLMAN HAS WON A PBA CAREER EARNINGS RECORD $1,555,851.

LADIES PROFESSIONAL BOWLERS TOUR (LPBT)

Founded in 1981, the LPBT is based in Rockford, Ill.

Most titles (career) Lisa Wagner has won 26 tournaments in her twelve-year career, 1980–91.

Most titles (season) Patty Costello won a season record seven tournaments in 1976.

PERFECT GAMES

Most bowled (career) Jeanne Maiden has bowled an LPBT-approved record 19 perfect games (300 score) in her career.

Most bowled (season) The record for most perfect games in a season is four, bowled by three bowlers: Betty Morris, 1986; Nikki Gianulias, 1986; and Debbie McMullen in 1991.

Highest earnings Lisa Wagner has won a career record $464,444 in prize money, 1980–91. Robin Romeo won a season record $113,750 in 1989.

AMERICAN BOWLING CONGRESS (ABC)

SCORING RECORDS

Highest individual score (three games) The highest individual score for three games is 899, by Thomas Jordan at Union, N.J. on March 7, 1989.

Highest team score (one game) The all-time ABC-sanctioned two-man single-game record is 600, held jointly by four teams: John Cotta and Steve Larson, May 1, 1981 at Manteca, Calif.; Jeff

Mraz and Dave Roney, November 8, 1987 at Canton, Ohio.; William Gruner and Dave Conway, February 27, 1990 at Oceanside, Calif.; Scott Williams and Willie Hammar, June 7, 1990 at Utica, N.Y.

Highest team score (three games) The highest three-game team score is 3,858, by Budweisers of St. Louis on March 12, 1958.

Highest season average The highest season average attained in sanctioned competition is 245.63, by Doug Vergouven of Harrisonville, Mo. in the 1989–90 season.

Juniors Brentt Arcement, at age 16, bowled a three-game series of 888, the highest ever bowled in a league or tournament sanctioned by the Young American Bowling Alliance, which is the national organization serving junior bowlers (age 21 and under).

Consecutive strikes The record for consecutive strikes in sanctioned match play is 33, by John Pezzin at Toledo, Ohio on March 4, 1976.

PERFECT GAMES

Most bowled (career) The highest number of sanctioned 300 games is 42, by Bob Learn Jr. of Erie, Pa.

Consecutive Two perfect games were rolled back-to-back *twice* by Al Spotts of West Reading, Pa. on March 14, 1982 and again on February 1, 1985.

WOMEN'S INTERNATIONAL BOWLING CONGRESS (WIBC)

SCORING RECORDS

Highest individual score (three games) The highest individual score for three games is 864, by Jeanne Maiden at Sodon, Ohio on November 23, 1986.

Highest team score (one game) Jean Reeder and Janice James bowled the all-time two-woman single-game highest score of 553 in Cleveland, Ohio during the 1982–83 season.

Highest team score (three games) The highest three-game team score is 3,437, by Goebel Beer of Detroit, Mich. during the 1988–89 season.

Highest season average The highest season average attained in sanctioned WIBC-competition is

232.0, by Patty Ann of Appleton, Wis., in the 1983–84 season.

Consecutive strikes Jeanne Maiden bowled a record 40 consecutive strikes during her record-breaking 864 performance on November 23, 1986.

PERFECT GAMES

Most bowled (career) The highest number of WIBC-sanctioned perfect games (300) is 18, by Jeanne Maiden.

Oldest The oldest woman to bowl a perfect game was Helen Duval of Berkeley, Calif., at age 65 in 1982.

Bowled, lowest average Of all the women who have rolled a perfect game, the one with the lowest average was Diane Ponza of Santa Cruz, Calif., who had a 112 average in the 1977–78 season.

PERFECT FORM ■ JEANNE MAIDEN HOLDS BOTH THE LBPT AND WIBC RECORDS FOR THE MOST PERFECT GAMES BOWLED.

BOXING

The nationality of the competitors in this section is U.S. unless stated otherwise.

ORIGINS Boxing with gloves is depicted on a fresco from the Isle of Thera, Greece that has been dated to 1520 B.C. The earliest prize-ring code of rules was formulated in England on August 16, 1743 by the champion pugilist Jack Broughton, who reigned from 1734 to 1750. In 1867, boxing came under the Queensberry Rules, formulated for John Sholto Douglas, 8th Marquess of Queensberry.

United States New York was the first state to legalize boxing, in 1896. Today professional boxing is regulated in each state by athletic or boxing commissions.

Longest fights The longest recorded fight with gloves was between Andy Bowen and Jack Burke at New Orleans, La. on April 6–7, 1893. It lasted 110 rounds, 7 hours 19 minutes (9:15 P.M.–4:34 A.M.) and was declared a no contest (later changed to a draw). The longest bare-knuckle fight was 6 hours 15 minutes between James Kelly and Jack Smith at Fiery Creek, Dalesford, Victoria, Australia on December 3, 1855.

The greatest number of rounds was 276 in 4 hours 30 minutes when Jack Jones beat Patsy Tunney in Cheshire, England in 1825.

Shortest fights The shortest fight on record appears to be one in a Golden Gloves tournament at Minneapolis, Minn. on November 4, 1947, when Mike Collins floored Pat Brownson with the first punch and the contest was stopped, without a count, 4 seconds after the bell. The World Boxing Council reports that the shortest fight in the history of professional boxing occured on June 19, 1991, when Paul Rees (Australia) scored a technical knockout over Charlie Hansen (Australia) in five seconds in a junior-middleweight bout in Brisbane, Australia.

The shortest world title fight was 45 seconds, when Lloyd Honeyghan (Great Britain) beat Gene Hatcher in an IBF welterweight bout at Marbella, Spain on August 30, 1987. Some sources also quote the Al McCoy first-round knockout of George Chip in a middleweight contest on April 7, 1914 as being in 45 seconds.

Most fights without loss Of boxers with complete records, Packey McFarland had 97 fights (five draws) from 1905 to 1915 without a defeat.

Consecutive wins Pedro Carrasco (Spain) won 83 consecutive fights from April 22, 1964 to September 3, 1970.

Most knockouts The greatest number of finishes classified as "knockouts" in a career is 145 (129 in professional bouts), by Archie Moore.

Consecutive knockouts The record for consecutive knockouts is 44, by Lamar Clark from 1958 to January 11, 1960.

HEAVYWEIGHT DIVISION

Long accepted as the first world heavyweight title fight, with gloves and three-minute rounds, was that between John L. Sullivan and James J. "Gentleman Jim" Corbett in New Orleans, La. on September 7, 1892. Corbett won in 21 rounds.

Longest reign Joe Louis was champion for 11 years 252 days, from June 22, 1937, when he knocked out James J. Braddock in the eighth round at Chicago, Ill., until announcing his retirement on March 1, 1949. During his reign, Louis defended his title a record 25 times.

Shortest reign The shortest reign was 64 days for IBF champion Tony Tucker, May 30–August 1, 1987.

Most recaptures Muhammad Ali is the only man to have regained the heavyweight championship twice. Ali first won the title on Februrary 25, 1964, defeating Sonny Liston. He defeated George Foreman on October 30, 1974, having been stripped of the title by the world boxing authorities on April 28, 1967. He won the WBA title from Leon Spinks on September 15, 1978, having previously lost to him on Februrary 15, 1978.

Undefeated Rocky Marciano is the only world champion at any weight to have won every fight of his entire professional career (1947–56); 43 of his 49 fights were by knockouts or stoppages.

Oldest successful challenger Jersey Joe Walcott was 37 years 168 days when he knocked out Ezzard Charles on July 18, 1951 in Pittsburgh, Pa.

Lightest champion Bob Fitzsimmons (Great Britain) weighed 167 pounds when he won the title

"THE GREATEST" ■ MUHAMMAD ALI IS THE ONLY BOXER TO HAVE WON THE HEAVYWEIGHT TITLE THREE TIMES. HERE HE CELEBRATES HIS FIRST TITLE WIN IN 1964.

by knocking out James J. Corbett at Carson City, Nev. on March 17, 1897.

Heaviest champion Primo Carnera (Italy) weighed in at 270 pounds for the defense of his title *v.* Tommy Loughran on March 1, 1934. Carnera won a unanimous point decision.

Quickest knockout The quickest knockout in a heavyweight title fight was 55 seconds, by James J. Jeffries over Jack Finnegan at Detroit, Mich. on April 6, 1900.

WORLD CHAMPIONS (ANY WEIGHT)

Reign (longest) Joe Louis's heavyweight duration record of 11 years 252 days stands for all divisions.

Reign (shortest) Tony Canzoneri was world light welterweight champion for 33 days, May 21 to June 23, 1933, the shortest period for a boxer to have won and lost the world title in the ring.

Most recaptures The only boxer to win a world title five times at one weight is Sugar Ray Robinson, who beat Carmen Basilio in Chicago Stadium, Ill. on March 25, 1958 to regain the world middleweight title for the fourth time.

Greatest weight difference Primo Carnera (Italy) outweighed his opponent, Tommy Loughran, by 86 pounds (270 pounds to 184 pounds) when they fought for the heavyweight title on March 1, 1934 in Miami, Fla. Surprisingly, the bout went the distance, with Carnera winning on points.

Greatest tonnage The greatest tonnage recorded in any fight is 700 pounds, when Claude "Humphrey" McBride, 340 pounds, knocked out Jimmy Black, 360 pounds, in the third round of their bout at Oklahoma City, Okla. on June 1, 1971. The greatest combined weight for a world title fight is 488¾ pounds, when Primo Carnera (Italy), 259½ pounds, fought Paolino Uzcudun (Spain), 229¼ pounds, in Rome, Italy on October 22, 1933.

AMATEUR

OLYMPIC GAMES Boxing contests were included in the ancient games, and were included in the modern Games in 1904.

Most gold medals Two boxers have won three gold medals: Laszlo Papp (Hungary) won the middleweight title in 1948, and the light middleweight in 1952 and 1956; Teofilo Stevenson (Cuba) won the heavyweight division in 1972, 1976 and 1980. The only man to win two titles at the same Games was Oliver L. Kirk, who won both the bantamweight and featherweight titles in 1904. It should be noted that Kirk only had to fight one bout in each class.

Most medals (country) The United States has won 93 medals in boxing: 45 gold, 20 silver and 28 bronze.

WORLD CHAMPIONSHIPS The world championships were first staged in 1974, and are held quadrennially.

Most titles Two boxers have won three world championships: Teofilo Stevenson (Cuba), heavyweight champion in 1974 and 1978 and super-heavyweight champion in 1986, and Adolfo Horta (Cuba), bantamweight champion in 1978, featherweight champion in 1982 and lightweight champion in 1986.

UNITED STATES NATIONAL CHAMPIONSHIPS U.S. amateur championships were first staged in 1888.

Most titles The most titles won is five, by middleweight W. Rodenbach, 1900–04.

CANOEING

ORIGINS The most influential pioneer of canoeing as a sport was John MacGregor, a British attorney, who founded the Canoe Club in Surrey, England in 1866. The sport's world governing body is the International Canoe Federation, founded in 1924.

United States The New York Canoe Club, founded in Staten Island, N.Y., in 1871, is the oldest in the United States. The American Canoe Association was formed on August 3, 1880.

OLYMPIC GAMES Canoeing was first included in the Games as a demonstration sport in 1924. At the 1936 Games, canoeing was included as an official Olympic sport for the first time.

Most gold medals Gert Fredriksson (Sweden) won a record six Olympic gold medals: 1,000 meter Kayak Singles (K1), 1948, 1952 and 1956; 10,000 meter K1, 1948 and 1956; 1,000 meter Kayak Pairs (K2), 1960. In women's competition, two canoeists have won three golds: Ludmila Pinayeva (née Khvedosyuk; USSR), 500 meter K1, 1964 and 1968, 500 meter K2, 1972; and Birgit Schmidt (née Fischer; East Germany), 500 meter K1, 1980, 500 meter K2, 1988, 500 meter K4, 1988.

Most medals (country) The Soviet Union has won 52 medals in canoeing competition: in men's events, 21 golds, 11 silver and seven bronze; in women's events, eight gold, two silver and three bronze.

United States Greg Barton is the only American canoeist to win two gold medals: 1,000 meter K1, 1,000 meter K2 in 1988. Overall the United States has won 11 canoeing medals: in men's events four gold, two silver and three bronze; in women's events, one silver and one bronze.

WORLD CHAMPIONSHIPS In Olympic years, the Games also serve as the world championship.

Most titles Birgit Schmidt (East Germany) has won a record 22 titles, 1978–88. The men's record is 13, by three canoeists: Gert Fredriksson (Sweden), 1948–60; Rudiger Helm (East Germany), 1976–83; and Ivan Patzaichin (Romania), 1968–84.

UNITED STATES NATIONAL CHAMPIONSHIPS

Most titles Marcia Ingram Jones Smoke won 35 national titles from 1962–81. The men's record is 33 by Ernest Riedel from 1930–48.

Fastest speed The Hungarian four-man kayak Olympic champions in 1988 at Seoul, South Korea covered 1,000 meters in 2 minutes 58.54 seconds in a heat. This represents an average speed of 12.53 mph. In this same race, the Norwegian four achieved a 250 meter split of 42.08 seconds between 500 meters and 750 meters for a speed of 13.29 mph.

CROQUET

ORIGINS Its exact beginnings are unknown; however, it is believed that croquet developed from the French game *jeu de mail*. A game resembling croquet was played in Ireland in the 1830s and introduced to England 20 years later. Although croquet was played in the United States for a number of years, a national body was not established until the formation of the United States Croquet Association (USCA) in 1976. The first United States championship was played in 1977.

USCA NATIONAL CHAMPIONSHIPS J. Archie Peck has won the singles title a record four times (1977, 1979–80, 1982). Ted Prentis has won the doubles title four times with three different partners (1978, 1980–81, 1988). The teams of Ted Prentis and Ned Prentis (1980–81) and Dana Dribben and Ray Bell (1985–86) have each won the doubles title twice. The New York Croquet Club has won a record six National Club Championships (1980–83, 1986, 1988).

CROSS-COUNTRY RUNNING

ORIGINS The earliest recorded international cross-country race took place on March 20, 1898 between England and France. The race was staged at Ville d'Avray, near Paris, France over a course 9 miles 18 yards long.

WORLD CHAMPIONSHIPS The first official world championship was staged in 1973. Currently the men's competition is run over a 12 kilometer course, and the women's over a 5 kilometer course.

Most titles (country) Kenya has won the men's event a record six times, 1986–91. In women's competition the Soviet Union has won a record eight times, 1976–77, 1980–82, 1988–90.

Most titles (individual) Grete Waitz (Norway) has won a record five women's titles, 1978–81 and 1983. John Ngugi (Kenya) has won the men's title a record four times, 1986– 89.

United States The United States has never won either of the team events. Craig Virgin has won the men's individual title twice, 1980–81, and Lynn Jennings has won the women's title twice, 1990–91.

UNITED STATES NATIONAL CHAMPIONSHIPS This competition was first staged in 1890 for men, and in 1972 for women.

Most titles Pat Porter has won the men's event a record eight times, 1982–89. Lynn Jennings has won the women's event five times, 1985 and 1987–90.

NCAA CHAMPIONSHIPS The first NCAA cross-country championship was held in 1938, and was open only to men's teams. A women's event was not staged until 1981.

Most titles (team) In men's competition, Michigan State has won the team title a record eight times: 1939, 1948–49, 1952, 1955–56, 1958–59.

Most titles (individuals) Three athletes have won the men's individual title three times: Gerry Lindgren (Washington State), 1966–67 and 1969; Steve Prefontaine (Oregon), 1970–71 and 1973; Henry Rono (Washington State), 1976–77 and 1979.

Most titles (team) In women's competition, Villanova has won the team title three times, 1989–91.

Most titles (individual) Two runners have won the title twice: Betty Springs (North Carolina State), 1981 and 1983; Sonia O'Sullivan (Villanova), 1990 and 1991.

CURLING

ORIGINS The traditional home of curling is Scotland; some historians, however, believe that the sport originated in the Netherlands in the 15th century. There is evidence of a curling club in Kilsyth, Scotland in 1716, but the earliest recorded club is the Muthill Curling Club, Tayside, Scotland, formed in 1739, which produced the first known written rules of the game on November 17, 1739. The Grand (later Royal) Caledonian Curling Club was founded in 1838 and was the international governing body of the sport until 1966,

when the International Curling Federation was formed; this was renamed the World Curling Federation in 1991.

United States and Canada Scottish immigrants introduced curling to North America in the 18th century. The earliest known club was the Royal Montreal Curling club, founded in 1807. The first international game was between Canada and the United States in 1884—the inaugural Gordon International Medal series. In 1832, Orchard Lake Curling Club, Mich., was founded, the first in the United States. The oldest club in continuous existence in the U.S. is the Milwaukee Curling Club, Wis., formed *c.* 1850. Regional curling associations governed the sport in the U.S. until 1947, when the United States Women's Curling Association was formed, followed in 1958 by the Men's Curling Association. In 1986, the United States Curling Association was formed and is the current governing body for the sport. In Canada, the Dominion Curling Association was formed in 1935, renamed the Canadian Curling Association in 1968.

OLYMPIC GAMES Curling has been a demonstration sport at the Olympic Games of 1924, 1932, 1964 and 1988.

WORLD CHAMPIONSHIPS First held in 1959, these championships are held annually. Women's competition was introduced in 1979.

Most titles (men) Canada has dominated this event, winning 20 titles; 1959–64, 1966, 1968–72, 1980, 1982–83, 1985–87 and 1989–90. Ernie Richardson (Canada) has been winning skip a record four times, 1959–60, 1962–63.

Most titles (women) Canada has won six championships, in 1980, 1984–87 and 1989. Djordy Nordby (Norway) has been skip of two winning teams, 1990–91.

UNITED STATES NATIONAL CHAMPIONSHIPS A men's tournament was first held in 1957. A women's event was introduced in 1977.

Men Two curlers have been skips on five championship teams: Bud Somerville (Superior Curling Club, Wis. in 1965, 1968–69, 1974 and 1981), and Bruce Roberts (Hibbing Curling Club, Minn.— 1966–67, 1976–77 and 1984).

Women In this competition, Nancy Langley of Seattle, Wash. has been the skip of a record four championship teams: 1979, 1981, 1983 and 1988.

THE LABATT BRIER (FORMERLY THE MACDONALD BRIER 1927–79) The Brier is the Canadian men's curling championship. The competition was first held at the Granite Club, Toronto in 1927. Sponsored by Macdonald Tobacco Inc., it had been known as the Macdonald Brier; since 1980 Labatt Brewery has sponsored the event.

Most titles The most wins is 22, by Manitoba (1928–32, 1934, 1936, 1938, 1940, 1942, 1947, 1949, 1952–53, 1956, 1965, 1970–72, 1979, 1981 and 1984). Ernie Richardson (Saskatchewan) has been winning skip a record four times (1959–60 and 1962–63).

Perfect game Stu Beagle, of Calgary, Alberta, played a perfect game (48 points) against Nova Scotia in the Canadian Championships (Brier) at Fort William (now Thunder Bay), Ontario on March 8, 1960. Andrew McQuiston skipped the Scotland team to a perfect game *v.* Switzerland at the Uniroyal Junior Men's World Championship at Kitchener, Ontario, Canada in 1980.

Bernice Fekete, of Edmonton, Alberta, Canada, skipped her rink to two consecutive eight-enders on the same ice at the Derrick Club, Edmonton on January 10 and February 6, 1973.

Two eight-enders in one bonspiel were scored at the Parry Sound Curling Club, Ontario, Canada from January 6–8, 1983.

CYCLING

ORIGINS The forerunner of the bicycle, the *celerifere*, was demonstrated in the garden of the Palais Royale, Paris, France in 1791. The velocipede, the first practical pedal-propelled vehicle, was built in March 1861 by Pierre Michaux and his son Ernest and demonstrated in Paris. The first velocipede race occurred on May 31, 1868 at the Parc St. Cloud, Paris, over a distance of 1.24 miles. The first international organization was the International Cyclist Association (ICA), founded in 1892, which launched the first world championships in 1893. The current governing body, the

Union Cycliste Internationale (UCI), was founded in 1900.

OLYMPIC GAMES Cycling was included in the first modern Games held in 1896, and has been part of every Games since, with the exception of 1904. Women's events were first staged in 1984.

Most gold medals Four men have won three gold medals: Paul Masson (France), 1,000 meter time-trial, 1,000 meter sprint, 10,000 meter track in 1896; Francesco Verri (Italy), 1,000 meter time-trial, 1,000 meter sprint, 5,000 meter track in 1906; Robert Charpentier (France), individual road race, team road race, 4,000 meter team pursuit in 1936; Daniel Morelon (France), 1,000 meter sprint in 1968 and 1972, 2,000 meter tandem in 1968.

Most medals Daniel Morelon (France) has won five Olympic medals: three gold (see above); one silver, 1,000 meter sprint in 1972; one bronze, 1,000 meter sprint in 1964.

Most medals (country) France has won 62 Olympic medals: 27 gold, 15 silver and 20 bronze, all gained in men's events.

United States The United States has won 13 medals in Olympic competition: four gold, three silver and six bronze.

WORLD CHAMPIONSHIPS World championships are contested annually. They were first staged for amateurs in 1893 and for professionals in 1895.

Most titles (one event) The most wins in a particular event is 10, by Koichi Nakano (Japan), professional sprint 1977–86. The most wins in a men's amateur event is seven, by two cyclists: Daniel Morelon (France), sprint, 1966–67, 1969–71, 1973, 1975; and Leon Meredith (Great Britain), 100 kilometer motor-paced, 1904–05, 1907–09, 1911 and 1913.

The most women's titles is eight, by Jeannie Longo (France), pursuit 1986 and 1988–89 and road 1985–87 and 1989–90.

United States The most world titles won by a U.S. cyclist is four, in women's 3 kilometer pursuit by Rebecca Twigg, 1982, 1984–85 and 1987. The most successful man has been Greg LeMond, winner of the individual road race in 1983 and 1989.

UNITED STATES NATIONAL CHAMPIONSHIPS National cycling championships have been held annually since 1899. Women's events were first included in 1937.

WORLD CYCLING RECORDS

These marks are recognized by the Union Cycliste Internationale (UCI). UCI recognizes records for both amateur and professional racers; in this listing only the overall record is shown.

Indoor Track Standing Start (Men)

Distance	Time	Cyclist (Country)	Date
1 km	1:02.576	Aleksandr Kirchenko (USSR)	Aug. 2, 1989
4 km	4:28.900	Vyacheslav Ekimov (USSR)	Sept. 20, 1986
5 km	5:39.316	Vyacheslav Ekimov (USSR)	Oct. 26, 1990
10 km	11:31.968	Vyacheslav Ekimov (USSR)	Jan. 7, 1989
20 km	23:14.553	Vyacheslav Ekimov (USSR)	Feb. 3, 1989
100 km	2:10:08.287	Beat Meister (Switzerland)	Sept. 22, 1989

Indoor Track Flying Start

200 m	10.117	Nikolay Kovch (USSR)	Feb. 5, 1988
500 m	26.649	Aleksandr Kirichenko (USSR)	Oct. 29, 1988
1 km	57.260	Aleksandr Kirichenko (USSR)	April 25, 1989

Indoor Track Standing Start (Women)

Distance	Time	Cyclist (Country)	Date
1 km	1:08.247	Erika Salumyae (USSR)	Aug. 19, 1984
3 km	3:43.490	Jeannie Longo (France)	Nov. 14, 1986
5 km	6:22.713	Jeannie Longo (France)	Nov. 2, 1986
10 km	12:54.260	Jeannie Longo (France)	Oct. 29, 1989
20 km	26:51.222	Jeannie Longo (France)	Oct. 29, 1989
100 km	2:24:57.618	Tea Vikstedt-Nyman (Finland)	Oct. 30, 1990

Source: U.S. National Cycling Association

Most titles Leonard Nitz has won 16 titles: five pursuit (1976 and 1980–83); eight team pursuit (1980–84, 1986 and 1988–89); two 1 kilometer time-trial (1982 and 1984); one criterium (1986). Connie Carpenter has won 11 titles in women's events: four road race (1976–77, 1979 and 1981); three pursuit (1976–77 and 1979); two criterium (1982–83); two points (1981–82).

TOUR DE FRANCE

First staged in 1903, the Tour meanders throughout France and sometimes neighboring countries over a four-week period.

Most wins Three riders have each won the event five times: Jacques Anquetil (France), 1957, 1961–64; Eddy Merckx (Belgium), 1969–72, 1974; Bernard Hinault (France), 1978–79, 1981–82, 1985.

Longest race The longest race held was 3,569 miles in 1926.

Closest race The closest race ever was in 1989, when after 2,030 miles over 23 days (July 1–23) Greg LeMond (U.S.), who completed the Tour in 87 hours 38 minutes 35 seconds, beat Laurent Fignon (France) in Paris by only 8 seconds.

Fastest speed The fastest average speed was 24.16 mph by Pedro Delgado (Spain) in 1988.

TOUR DE FRANCE CHAMPIONS (1903–1946)

Year	Winner	Country	Year	Winner	Country
1903	Maurice Garin	France	1925	Ottavio Bottecchia	Italy
1904	Henri Cornet	France	1926	Lucien Buysse	Belgium
1905	Louis Trousselier	France	1927	Nicholas Frantz	Luxembourg
1906	Rene Pottier	France	1928	Nicholas Frantz	Luxembourg
1907	Lucien Petit-Breton	France	1929	Maurice Dewaele	Belgium
1908	Lucien Petit-Breton	France	1930	Andre Leducq	France
1909	Francois Faber	Luxembourg	1931	Antonin Magne	France
1910	Octave Lapize	France	1932	Andre Leducq	France
1911	Gustave Garrigou	France	1933	Georges Speicher	France
1912	Odile Defraye	Belgium	1934	Antonin Magne	France
1913	Philippe Thys	Belgium	1935	Romain Maes	Belgium
1914	Philippe Thys	Belgium	1936	Sylvere Maes	Belgium
1915	not held		1937	Roger Lapebie	France
1916	not held		1938	Gino Bartali	Italy
1917	not held		1939	Sylvere Maes	Belgium
1918	not held		1940	not held	
1919	Firmin Labot	Belgium	1941	not held	
1920	Philippe Thys	Belgium	1942	not held	
1921	Leon Scieur	Belgium	1943	not held	
1922	Firmin Labot	Belgium	1944	not held	
1923	Henri Pelissier	France	1945	not held	
1924	Ottavio Bottecchia	Italy	1946	Jean Lazarides	France

TOUR TRIUMPHS ■ EDDY MERCKX (BELGIUM) (6) HAS WON THE TOUR DE FRANCE FIVE TIMES, A RECORD HE SHARES WITH JACQUES ANQUETIL AND BERNARD HINAULT (BOTH FRANCE).

Longest stage The longest-ever stage was the 486 kilometers from Les Sables d'Olonne to Bayonne in 1919.

Most participants The most participants was 204 starters in 1987.

United States Greg LeMond became the first American winner in 1986; he returned from serious injury to win again in 1989 and 1990.

WOMEN'S TOUR DE FRANCE

The inaugural women's Tour de France was staged in 1984.

Most wins Jeannie Longo (France) has won the event a record four times, 1987–90.

TOUR DE FRANCE CHAMPIONS (1947–1991)

Year	Winner	Country	Year	Winner	Country
1947	Jean Robic	France	1970	Eddy Merckx	Belgium
1948	Gino Bartali	Italy	1971	Eddy Merckx	Belgium
1949	Fausto Coppi	Italy	1972	Eddy Merckx	Belgium
1950	Ferdinand Kubler	Switzerland	1973	Luis Ocana	Spain
1951	Hugo Koblet	Switzerland	1974	Eddy Merckx	Belgium
1952	Fausto Coppi	Italy	1975	Bernard Thevenet	France
1953	Louison Bobet	France	1976	Lucien van Impe	Belgium
1954	Louison Bobet	France	1977	Bernard Thevenet	France
1955	Louison Bobet	France	1978	Bernard Hinault	France
1956	Roger Walkowiak	France	1979	Bernard Hinault	France
1957	Jacques Anquetil	France	1980	Joop Zoetemilk	Netherlands
1958	Charly Gaul	Luxembourg	1981	Bernard Hinault	France
1959	Federico Bahamontes	Spain	1982	Bernard Hinault	France
1960	Gastone Nencini	Italy	1983	Laurent Fignon	France
1961	Jacques Anquetil	France	1984	Laurent Fignon	France
1962	Jacques Anquetil	France	1985	Bernard Hinault	France
1963	Jacques Anquetil	France	1986	Greg LeMond	U.S.
1964	Jacques Anquetil	France	1987	Stephen Roche	Ireland
1965	Felice Gimondi	Italy	1988	Pedro Delgado	Spain
1966	Lucien Aimar	France	1989	Greg LeMond	U.S.
1967	Roger Pingeon	France	1990	Greg LeMond	U.S.
1968	Jan Janssen	Netherlands	1991	Miguel Indurain	Spain
1969	Eddy Merckx	Belgium			

FOCUSED ■ **FRANCE'S JEANNE LONGO HAS DOMI-NATED WOMEN'S CYCLING, WINNING EIGHT WORLD AND FOUR TOUR DE FRANCE TITLES.**

TRANSCONTINENTAL CYCLING RECORDS

UNITED STATES

Fastest time (men) Michael Secrest, Scottsdale, Ariz., set a transcontinental record of seven days 23 hours 16 minutes in June 1990, riding from Huntington Beach, Cal. to Atlantic City, N.J., a distance of 2,916 miles. Secrest's average speed was 15.24 mph.

Fastest time (women) Susan Notorangelo, Harvard, Ill., completed the 2,910 mile 1989 Race Across America course in a record 9 days 9 hours 9 minutes in August 1989.

Fastest average speed (men) Pete Penseyres, Fallbrook, Cal., rode at an average speed of 15.40

SIBERIAN PASSAGE

From June 20 to October 25, 1989, seven adventurers completed what is believed to be the first crossing of the Soviet Union (at that time the world's largest country) by bicycle—a trip which they dubbed the Siberian Passage. The group was comprised of three Americans—Tom Freisem, Torie Scott and Mark Jenkins—and four Russians: Tanya Kirova, Natasha Traviynskay, Fyodor Konyukhov and Pavel Konyukhov. They pedaled 11,330 kilometers (7,035.93 miles), riding west from Nakhodka on the Sea of Japan to Leningrad on the Baltic Sea. The journey was a severe test of both rider and equipment: three complete drive chains (freewheels, bottom brackets, chain rings, chains), three sets of tires, and five to ten tubes per rider were required to complete the trip. So why do it? Says Jenkins: "To see a remote and mysterious country at a human pace, and develop an understanding of the Russian people and their world," and, punctures permitting, "to be the first to traverse the largest country in the world by bicycle."

THE MOST ARDUOUS PART OF THE JOURNEY WAS CROSSING THE 1,270-KILOMETER SWAMP KNOWN LOCALLY AS "THE BALOTA" (THE SLOUGH). WITHOUT ANY IDENTIFIABLE ROADWAYS, THE CYCLISTS WERE FORCED TO PUSH, CARRY OR DRAG THEIR BIKES THROUGH FLOODED BOGLANDS AND MUDDY TROUGHS.

THE SECOND HALF OF "THE PASSAGE" (KRASNOYARSK TO LENINGRAD VIA MOSCOW) WAS COMPLETED UNDER MORE CIVILIZED CONDITIONS, AND ALLOWED THE RIDERS TO EXPERIENCE THE VASTNESS AND FLAVOR OF THE SOVIET UNION—THE PRIMARY MOTIVATION FOR THEIR TRIP.

ACKNOWLEDGMENT ■ THANKS TO MARK JENKINS FOR PROVIDING THE MAP, LOG AND PHOTOGRAPHS USED IN THIS FEATURE. FOR READERS WHO WOULD LIKE TO KNOW MORE ABOUT THIS REMARKABLE JOURNEY, JENKINS HAS WRITTEN HIS OWN ACCOUNT, ENTITLED OFF THE MAP: BICYCLING ACROSS SIBERIA, PUBLISHED BY WILLIAM MORROW.

Stage	Road Conditions	Distance	Dates
Nakhodka–Khabarovsk	pavement	1,001 km	June 20–28
Khabarovsk–Blagoveschensk	pavement	804 km	June 29–July 5
Blagoveschensk–Shimanovsk	dirt	315 km	July 7–9
Shimanovsk–Shilka Camp	swamp	1,270 km	July 10–29
Shilka Camp–Chita	dirt	410 km	July 30–Aug. 2
Chita (rest period)			Aug. 3–6
Chita–Irkutsk	pavement	1,275 km	Aug. 7–15
Irkutsk (rest period)			Aug. 16–18
Irkutsk–Krasnoyarsk	dirt	945 km	Aug. 19–27
Krasnoyarsk (rest period)			Aug. 28–31
Krasnoyarsk–Novosibirsk	dirt	840 km	Sept. 1–6
Novosibirsk (rest period)			Sept. 7–8
Novosibirsk–Omsk	dirt	860 km	Sept. 9–14
Omsk (rest period)			Sept. 15–16
Omsk–Chelyabinsk	pavement	910 km	Sept. 17–23
Chelyabinsk (rest period)			Sept. 24–25
Chelyabinsk–Tol'yatti	pavement	905 km	Sept. 26–Oct. 3
Tol'yatti (rest period)			Oct. 4–5
Tol'yatti–Moscow	pavement	1,090 km	Oct. 6–16
Moscow (rest period)			Oct. 17–19
Moscow–Leningrad	pavement	705 km	Oct. 20–25
Total		**11,330 km**	**June 20–October 25**

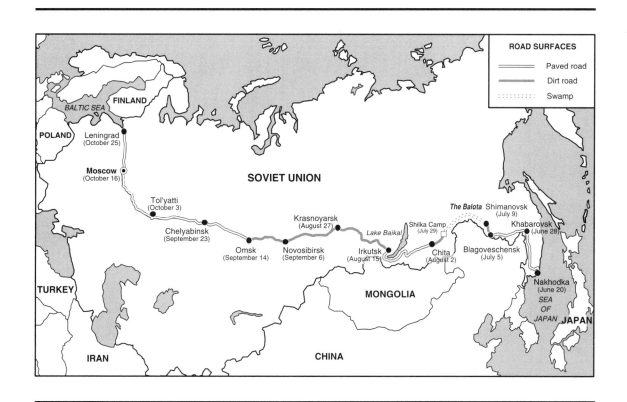

mph in his 1986 Race Across America victory. Penseyres completed the 3,107.3 mile course in 8 days 9 hours 47 minutes, which averages out to 369.55 miles per day.

Fastest average speed (women) In 1989, Susan Notorangelo attained the fastest average speed of 12.92 mph.

CANADA

Fastest time The trans-Canada record is 13 days 9 hours 6 minutes by William Narasnek, from Vancouver, British Columbia to Halifax, Nova Scotia on July 5–18, 1991, a distance of 3,698 miles.

Fastest speed The fastest speed ever achieved on a bicycle is 152.284 mph, by John Howard (U.S.) behind a windshield at Bonneville Salt Flats, Utah on July 20, 1985. It should be noted that considerable help was provided by the slipstreaming effect of the lead vehicle.

DARTS

ORIGINS Darts, or dartes (heavily weighted 10-inch throwing arrows) were first used in Ireland in the 16th century, as a weapon for self-defense. The Pilgrims played darts for recreation aboard the *Mayflower* in 1620. The modern game dates to 1896, when Brian Gamlin of Bury, England devised the present board numbering system. The first recorded score of 180, the maximum with three darts, was by John Reader at the Highbury Tavern, Sussex, England in 1902.

WORLD CHAMPIONSHIP This competition was instituted in 1978.

Most titles Eric Bristow of England has won the title a record five times (1980–81, 84–86).

SCORING RECORDS

Fewest darts Scores of 201 in four darts, 301 in six darts, 401 in seven darts and 501 in nine darts have been achieved on various occasions.

501 Roy Blowes (Canada) was the first person to achieve a 501 in nine darts, "double-on, double-off," at the Widgeons Pub, Calgary, Canada on March 9, 1987. His scores were: Bull, treble 20, treble 17, five treble 20s and a double 20 to finish.

1,001 The lowest number of darts thrown for a score of 1,001 is 19, by Cliff Inglis (England) (160, 180, 140, 180, 121, 180, 40) at the Bromfield Men's Club, Devon, England on November 11, 1975, and by Jocky Wilson (Scotland) (140, 140, 180, 180, 180, 131, Bull) at The London Pride, Bletchley, England on March 23, 1989.

2,001 A score of 2,001 in 52 darts was achieved by Alan Evans (Wales) at Ferndale, Wales on September 3, 1976.

3,001 A score of 3,001 in 73 darts was thrown by Tony Benson (England) at the Plough Inn, Gorton, England on July 12, 1986. Linda Batten (England) set a women's 3,001 record of 117 darts at the Old Wheatsheaf, Enfield, England on April 2, 1986.

100,001 A score of 100,001 was achieved in 3,732 darts by Alan Downie of Stornoway, Scotland on November 21, 1986.

DIVING

ORIGINS Diving traces its roots to the gymnastics movement that developed in Germany and Sweden in the 17th century. During the summer, gymnasts would train at the beach, and acrobatic techniques would be performed over water as a safety measure. From this activity the sport of diving developed. The world governing body for diving is the *Fédération Internationale de Natation Amateur* (FINA), founded in 1980. FINA is also the governing body for swimming and water polo.

United States Ernst Bransten and Mike Peppe are considered the two main pioneers of diving in the United States. Bransten, a Swede, came to the United States following World War I. He introduced Swedish training methods and diving techniques, which revolutionized the sport in this country. Peppe's highly successful program at Ohio State University, 1931–68, produced several Olympic medalists and helped promote the sport here.

OLYMPIC GAMES Men's diving events were introduced at the 1904 Games, and women's events in 1912.

Most gold medals Two divers have won four gold medals: Pat McCormick (U.S.), who won both the women's springboard and the highboard events in 1952 and 1956; and Greg Louganis (U.S.), who performed the highboard/springboard double in 1984 and 1988.

RECORD FILE: GREG LOUGANIS

BORN January 29, 1960, San Diego, Calif.

UNITED STATES NATIONAL CHAMPIONSHIPS TITLES
1978–88

1-meter Titles	3-meter Titles	Platform	Total
17*	17*	13*	47*

WORLD CHAMPIONSHIP TITLES
1978–86

3-meter Titles	Platform	Total
2*	3*	5*

OLYMPIC GAMES TITLES
1976–88

3-meter Titles	Platform	Total
2*	2	4*

RECORD NOTES Louganis holds the record for the highest marks scored in diving competition for both 3-meter springboard and platform: springboard, 755.49 points at the 1983 U.S. International; platform, 717.41 points at the 1986 Mission Bay Challenge. At the 1984 Olympic Games, Louganis set the record score for both springboard and platform, with scores of 754.41 points and 710.91 points respectively.

*indicates all-time record.

Most medals Two divers have won five medals: Klaus Dibiasi (Italy), three golds, highboard in 1968, 1972 and 1976, and two silver, highboard in 1964 and springboard in 1968; and Greg Louganis, four golds (see above) and one silver, highboard in 1976.

Most medals (country) The United States has dominated the diving events, winning 122 medals out of a possible 224 awarded. In men's events the tally is 26 gold, 19 silver and 19 bronze; in women's, 19 gold, 20 silver and 19 bronze.

WORLD CHAMPIONSHIPS Diving events were included in the first world aquatic championships staged in 1973.

Most titles Greg Louganis (U.S.) has won a record five world titles—highboard in 1978 and the highboard/springboard double in 1982 and 1986. Philip Boggs (U.S.) is the only diver to win three gold medals at one event, springboard, in 1973, 1975 and 1978.

UNITED STATES NATIONAL CHAMPIONSHIPS The Amateur Athletic Union (AAU) organized the first national diving championships in 1909. Since 1981, United States Diving has been the governing body of the sport in this country, and thus responsible for the national championships.

Most titles Greg Louganis has won a record 47 national titles: 17, one-meter springboard; 17, three-meter springboard; 13, platform. In women's competition, Cynthia Potter has won a record 28 titles.

HIGH DIVING

The most famous head-first "high dives" are those performed from *La Quebrada* (The Break in the Rocks) at Acapulco, Mexico. The divers leap from a height of 87½ feet above the water. The base rocks jut out 21 feet, necessitating a takeoff leap of 27 feet to clear them. The water at the "landing" area is only 12 feet deep.

Highest dive The world record high dive is 176 feet 10 inches, by Oliver Favre (Switzerland) at Villers-le-Lac, France on August 30, 1987. The women's record is 120 feet 9 inches, by Lucy Wardle (U.S.) at Ocean Park, Hong Kong on April 6, 1985.

EQUESTRIAN SPORTS

ORIGINS Evidence of horseback riding dates from a Persian engraving dated *c.* 3000 B.C. The three separate equestrian competitions recognized at the Olympic level are show jumping, dressage and the three-day event. The earliest known show jumping competition was in Ireland, when the Royal Dublin Society held its first "Horse Show" on April 15, 1864. Dressage competition derived from the exercises taught at 16th century Italian and French horsemanship academies, while the three-day event developed from cavalry endurance rides. The world governing body for all three disciplines is the *Fédération Equestre Internationale* (FEI), founded in Brussels, Belgium in 1921.

OLYMPIC GAMES In the ancient games, chariot races featured horses, and later riding contests were included. Show jumping was included in the 1900 Games; the three-day event and dressage disciplines were not added until 1912. In 1956 the equestrian events were held in Stockholm, Sweden, separate from the main Games in Melbourne, Australia, because of the strict Australian quarantine laws.

Most medals (all events) Germany has dominated the equestrian events, winning 57 medals overall: 24 gold, 15 silver and 18 bronze. The United States has won 32 medals: eight gold, 15 silver and nine bronze.

SHOW JUMPING

OLYMPIC GAMES

Most gold medals (rider) Hans-Gunther Winkler (West Germany) has won five titles, 1956, 1960, 1964 and 1972 in the team competition, and the individual championship in 1956. The only rider to win two individual titles is Pierre Jonqueres d'Oriola (France), in 1952 and 1964.

Most gold medals (horse) The most successful horse is Halla, ridden by Hans-Gunther Winkler during his individual and team wins in 1956, and during the team win in 1960.

Most medals Hans-Gunther Winkler has won a record seven medals: five gold (see above), one silver and one bronze in the team competition in 1976 and 1968.

Most medals (country) Germany has won a record 17 medals in show jumping: nine gold, three silver and five bronze.

United States Two American riders have won the individual event: Bill Steinkraus in 1968, and Joe Fargis in 1984. The United States won the team event in 1984. Overall, the United States has won eleven medals: three gold, six silver, and two bronze.

WORLD CHAMPIONSHIPS The men's world championship was inaugurated in 1953. In 1965, 1970 and 1974 separate women's championships were held. An integrated championship was first held in 1978 and is now held every four years.

Most titles Two riders share the record for most men's championships with two victories: Hans-Gunther Winkler (West Germany), 1954–55, and Raimondo d'Inzeo (Italy), 1956 and 1960. The women's title was won twice by Janou Tissot (née Lefebvre) of France, in 1970 and 1974. No rider has won the integrated competition more than once.

JUMPING RECORDS The official *Fédération Equestre Internationale* records are:

High jump 8 feet 1¼ inches, by Huasó, ridden by Captain Alberto Larraguibel Morales (Chile) at Viña del Mar, Santiago, Chile on February 5, 1949.

FAULTLESS ■ BILL STEINKRAUS RODE SNOW-BOUND TO THE 1968 OLYMPIC INDIVIDUAL TITLE, THE FIRST AMERICAN RIDER TO WIN THE GOLD MEDAL.

Long jump over water 27 feet 6¾ inches, by Something, ridden by André Ferreira (South Africa) at Johannesburg, South Africa on April 25, 1975.

THREE-DAY EVENT

OLYMPIC GAMES

Most gold medals Charles Pahud de Mortanges (Netherlands) has won four gold medals—the individual title in 1928 and 1932, and the team event in 1924 and 1928. Mark Todd (New Zealand) is the only other rider to have won the individual title twice, in 1984 and 1988.

Most medals (rider) Charles Pahud de Mortanges has won five medals: four gold (see above) and one silver in the 1932 team event.

Most medals (horse) Marcroix was ridden by Charles Pahud de Mortanges in four of his five medal rounds, including three gold, 1928–32.

Most medals (country) The United States has won 17 medals: five gold, eight silver, four bronze.

UNITED STATES The most medals won for the U.S. is six, by J. Michael Plumb: team gold, 1976 and 1984, and four silver medals, team 1964, 1968 and 1972, and individual 1976. Tad Coffin is the only U.S. rider to have won both team and individual gold medals, in 1976.

WORLD CHAMPIONSHIP First held in 1966, the event is held quadrenially and is open to both men and women.

Most titles (rider) Bruce Davidson (U.S.) is the only rider to have won two world titles, on Irish Cap in 1974, and on Might Tango in 1978.

Most titles (country) Great Britain has won the team title a record three times, 1970, 1982 and 1986. The United States won the team event in 1974.

DRESSAGE

OLYMPIC GAMES

Most gold medals (rider) Reiner Klimke (West Germany) has won six gold medals: one individual in 1984, and five team in 1964, 1968, 1976, 1984 and 1988. Henri St. Cyr (Sweden) is the only rider to have won two individual titles, in 1952 and 1956.

Most gold medals (horse) Ahlerich was ridden by Reiner Klimke in three of his gold medal rounds, individual in 1984, and team in 1984 and 1988.

Most medals Reiner Klimke won eight medals: six gold (see above), and two bronze in the individual event in 1968 and 1976.

Most medals (country) Germany has won 24 medals in dressage competition: 12 gold, six silver and six bronze.

United States The United States has never won a gold medal in dressage. In the team event the United States has won one silver, 1948, and two bronze, in 1932 and 1976. Hiram Tuttle is the only rider to have won an individual medal, earning the bronze in 1932.

WORLD CHAMPIONSHIPS This competition was instituted in 1966.

Most titles (country) West Germany has won a record six times: 1966, 1974, 1978, 1982, 1986 and 1990.

Most titles (rider) Reiner Klimke (West Germany) is the only rider to have won two individual titles, on Mehmed in 1974 and on Ahlerich in 1982.

FENCING

ORIGINS Evidence of swordsmanship can be traced back to Egypt as early as *c.* 1360 B.C., where it was demonstrated during religious ceremonies. Fencing, "fighting with sticks," gained popularity as a sport in Europe in the 16th century.

The modern foil, a light court sword, was introduced in France in the mid-17th century; in the late 19th century, the fencing "arsenal" was expanded to include the épée, a heavier dueling weapon, and the sabre, a light cutting sword.

The *Fédération Internationale d'Escrime* (FIE), the world governing body, was founded in Paris, France in 1913. The first European championships were held in 1921 and were expanded into world championships in 1935.

United States In the United States, the Amateur Fencers League of America (AFLA) was founded on April 22, 1891 in New York City. This group assumed supervision of the sport in the U.S., staging the first national championship in 1892. In

June 1981, the AFLA changed its name to the United States Fencing Association (USFA).

OLYMPIC GAMES Fencing was included in the first Olympic Games of the modern era at Athens in 1896, and is one of only six sports to be featured in every Olympiad.

Most gold medals Aladar Gerevich (Hungary) has won a record seven gold medals, all in sabre: individual, 1948; team, 1932, 1936, 1948, 1952, 1956 and 1960. In individual events, two fencers have won three titles: Ramon Fonst (Cuba), épée, 1900 and 1904, and foil, 1904; Nedo Nadi (Italy), foil, 1912 and 1920, and sabre, 1920. The most golds won by a woman is four, by Yelena Novikova (née Belova; USSR), all in foil: individual, 1968; team, 1968, 1972 and 1976.

Most medals Edoardo Mangiarotti (Italy) has won a record 13 medals in fencing: six gold, five silver and two bronze in foil and épée events from 1936 to 1960.

Oldest and youngest champions Aladar Gerevich was a member of the sabre team champions in 1960 at age 50 years 178 days. Ramon Fonst is the youngest champion, winning the épée title in 1900, aged 16 years 289 days.

Most medals (country) France has won 92 medals in fencing competition: 32 gold, 31 silver and 24 bronze in men's events; two gold, one silver and two bronze in women's events.

United States Albertson Van Zo Post is the only American to have won an Olympic title. He won the single sticks competition and teamed with two Cubans to win the team foil title in 1904. In overall competition the United States has won 19 medals (both Cuba and the United States are credited with a gold medal for the 1904 team foil): two gold, six silver and 11 bronze—all in men's events.

WORLD CHAMPIONSHIPS The first world championships were staged in Paris, France in 1937. Foil, épée and sabre events were held for men and just foil for women. In 1989, a women's épée event was added. The tournament is staged annually.

Most titles The greatest number of individual world titles won is five, by Aleksandr Romankov (USSR), at foil, 1974, 1977, 1979, 1982 and 1983. Five women foilists have won three world titles: Hélène Mayer (Germany), 1929, 1931 and 1937; Ilona Schacherer-Elek (Hungary), 1934–35, 1951;

Ellen Müller-Preis (Austria), 1947, 1949–50; Cornelia Hanisch (West Germany), 1979, 1981 and 1985; and Anja Fichtel (West Germany), 1986, 1988 and 1990.

UNITED STATES NATIONAL CHAMPIONSHIPS

Most titles The most U.S. titles won at one weapon is 12 at sabre, by Peter Westbrook, in 1974, 1975, 1979–86, 1988 and 1989. The women's record is 10 at foil, by Janice Romary in 1950–51, 1956–57, 1960–61, 1964–66 and 1968.

The most individual foil championships won is seven, by Michael Marx in 1977, 1979, 1982, 1985–87 and 1990. L. G. Nunes won the most épée championships, with six—1917, 1922, 1924, 1926, 1928 and 1932. Vincent Bradford won a record number of women's épée championships with four in 1982–84 and 1986.

NCAA CHAMPIONSHIP DIVISION I (MEN) This competition was inaugurated in 1941.

Most titles (team) New York University has won the most titles: 12 (1947, 1954, 1957, 1960–61, 1966–67, 1970–71, 1973–74, and 1976).

Most consecutive titles The longest consecutive title streak is four wins by Wayne State (Mich.), 1982–85.

Most titles (fencer) Michael Lofton, New York University, has won the most titles in a career, with four victories in the sabre, 1984–87. Abraham Balk, New York University, is the only man to win two individual titles in one year, 1947 (foil and épée).

NCAA CHAMPIONSHIP DIVISION I (WOMEN) This competition was inaugurated in 1982.

Most titles (team) Wayne State (Mich.) has won the most titles: three (1982, 1988–89).

Most titles (fencer) Caitlin Bilodeaux (Columbia-Barnard) and Molly Sullivan (Notre Dame) have both won the individual title twice: Bilodeaux in 1985 and 1987, Sullivan in 1986 and 1988.

NCAA CHAMPIONSHIP DIVISION I (COMBINED EVENT) In 1990, the NCAA team competition was combined for the first time.

Most wins (team) Penn State has won both the 1990 and 1991 titles.

Duel Champions ■ Molly Sullivan (left) and Caitlin Bilodeaux (right) share the record for most women's NCAA fencing titles with two each.

FIELD HOCKEY

ORIGINS Hitting a ball with a stick is a game that dates back to the origins of the human race. Bas-reliefs and frescoes discovered in Egypt and Greece depict hockey-like games. A drawing of a "bully" on the walls of a tomb at Beni Hassan in the Nile Valley has been dated to *c.* 2050 B.C. The birthplace of modern hockey is Great Britain, where the first definitive code of rules was established in 1886. The *Fédération Internationale de Hockey* (FIH), the world governing body, was founded on January 7, 1924.

United States The sport was introduced to this country in 1921 by a British teacher, Constance M. K. Applebee. The Field Hockey Association of America (FHAA) was founded in 1928 by Henry Greer. The first game was staged between the Germantown Cricket Club and the Westchester Field Hockey Club, also in 1928.

OLYMPIC GAMES Field hockey was added to the Olympic Games in 1908 and became a permanent feature in 1928; a women's tournament was added in 1980.

Most gold medals (team) In the men's competition, India has won eight gold medals: 1928, 1932, 1936, 1948, 1952, 1956, 1964 and 1980. In the women's competition, no team has won the event more than once.

Most gold medals (individual) Seven Indian players were members of three winning teams: Richard Allen, 1928–36; Dhyan Chand, 1928–36; Randhir Singh, 1948–56; Balbir Singh, 1948–56; Leslie Claudius, 1948–56; Ranganandhan Francis, 1948–56; and Udham Singh, 1952, 1956 and 1964.

Most medals (country) India has won 11 medals, all in the men's tournament: eight gold (see above), one silver in 1960, and two bronze in 1968 and 1972.

United States The United States has never won either the men's or women's events; the best result has been a bronze in 1932 (men), and in 1984 (women).

SCORING RECORDS

Highest score The highest score in an international game was India's 24–1 defeat of the United States at Los Angeles, Calif., in the 1932 Olympic Games. In women's competition, England hammered France 23–0 at Merton, England on February 3, 1923.

Most goals Paul Litjens (Netherlands) holds the record for most goals by one player in international play. He scored 267 goals in 177 games.

Fastest goal The fastest goal scored in an international game was netted only seven seconds after the bully by John French for England *v.* West Germany at Nottingham, England on April 25, 1971.

NCAA DIVISION I (WOMEN) The women's championship was inaugurated in 1981.

Most titles Old Dominion has won the most championships with five titles: 1982–84, 1988 and 1991.

FIGURE SKATING

ORIGINS The earliest reference to ice skating is in Scandinavian literature dating to the 2nd century A.D. Jackson Haines, a New Yorker, is regarded as the pioneer of the modern concept of figure skating, a composite of skating and dancing. Although not initially favored in the United States, Haines moved to Europe in the mid-1860s, where his "International Style of Figure Skating" was warmly received and promoted. The first artificial rink was opened in London, England on January 7, 1876. The world governing body is the International Skating Union (ISU), founded in 1892. The sport functioned informally in the United States until 1921, when the United States Figure Skating Association (USFSA) was formed to oversee skating in this country—a role it still performs.

OLYMPIC GAMES Figure skating was first included in the 1908 Summer Games in London, and has been featured in every Games since 1920. Uniquely, both men's and women's events have been included in the Games from the first introduction of the sport.

Most gold medals Three skaters have won three gold medals: Gillis Grafstrom (Sweden) in 1920, 1924 and 1928; Sonja Henie (Norway) in 1928, 1932 and 1936; Irina Rodnina (USSR), with two different partners, in the pairs in 1972, 1976 and 1980.

Most medals Gillis Gafstrom has won four medals: three gold (see above) and one silver in 1932.

Most medals (country) The United States has won a record 34 medals: 10 gold, 10 silver and 14 bronze. The Soviet Union has won the most gold medals with 11.

United States Dick Button is the only American skater to win two gold medals, in 1948 and 1952. American skaters have won the men's title six times and the women's four. No American team has won either the pairs or dance titles.

WORLD CHAMPIONSHIPS This competition was first staged in 1896.

Most titles (individual) The greatest number of men's individual world figure skating titles is 10, by Ulrich Salchow (Sweden), in 1901–05 and 1907–11. The women's record (instituted 1906) is also 10 individual titles, by Sonja Henie (Norway) between 1927 and 1936.

Most titles (pairs) Irina Rodnina (USSR) has won 10 pairs titles (instituted 1908), four with Aleksey Ulanov, 1969–72, and six with her husband, Aleksandr Zaitsev, 1973–78.

Most titles (ice dance) The most ice dance titles (instituted 1952) won is six, by Lyudmila Pakhomova and her husband, Aleksandr Gorshkov (USSR), 1970–74 and 1976.

United States Dick Button won five world titles, 1948–52. Five women's world titles were won by Carol Heise, 1956–60.

UNITED STATES NATIONAL CHAMPIONSHIPS The U.S. championships were first held in 1914.

Most titles The most titles won by an individual is nine, by Maribel Y. Vinson, 1928–33 and 1935–37. She also won six pairs titles, and her aggregate of 15 titles is equaled by Therese Blanchard (née Weld), who won six individual and nine pairs titles between 1914 and 1927. The men's individual record is seven, by Roger Turner, 1928–34, and by Dick Button, 1946–52.

HIGHEST MARKS The highest tally of maximum six marks awarded in an international championship was 29, to Jayne Torvill and Christopher Dean (Great Britain) in the World Ice Dance Championships at Ottawa, Canada on March 22–24, 1984. This comprised seven in the compulsory dances, a perfect set of nine for presentation in the set pattern dance, and 13 in the free dance, including another perfect set from all nine judges for artistic presentation. They previously gained a perfect set of nine sixes for artistic presentation in the free dance at the 1983 World Championships in Helsinki, Finland and at the 1984 Winter Olympic Games in Sarajevo, Yugoslavia. In their career, Torvill and Dean received a record total of 136 sixes.

The highest tally by a soloist is seven, by Donald Jackson (Canada) in the World Men's Championship at Prague, Czechoslovakia in 1962; and by Midori Ito (Japan) in the World Ladies' Championships at Paris, France in 1989.

FOOTBALL

ORIGINS On November 6, 1869, Princeton and Rutgers staged what is generally regarded as the first intercollegiate football game at New Brunswick, N.J. In October 1873 the Intercollegiate Football Association was formed (Columbia, Princeton, Rutgers and Yale), with the purpose of standardizing rules. At this point football was a modified version of soccer. The first significant move toward today's style of play came when Harvard accepted an invitation to play McGill University (Montreal, Canada) in a series of three challenge matches, the first being in May 1874, under modified rugby rules. Walter Camp is credited with organizing the basic format of the current game. Between 1880 and 1906, Camp sponsored the concepts of scrimmage lines, 11-man teams, reduction in field size, "downs" and "yards to gain" and a new scoring system.

NATIONAL FOOTBALL LEAGUE (NFL)

ORIGINS William (Pudge) Heffelfinger became the first professional player on November 12, 1892, when he was paid $500 by the Allegheny Athletic Association (AAA) to play for them against the Pittsburgh Athletic Club (PAC). In 1893, PAC signed one of its players, believed to have been Grant Dibert, to the first known professional contract. The first game to be played with admitted professionals participating was played at Latrobe, Pa., on August 31, 1895, with Latrobe YMCA defeating the Jeanette Athletic Club 12–0. Professional leagues existed in Pennsylvania and Ohio at the turn of the 20th century; however, the major breakthrough for

RECORD FILE: WALTER PAYTON

BORN: July 25, 1954, Columbia, Miss.

NFL REGULAR SEASON STATISTICS
CHICAGO BEARS, 1975–87

Games	Att.	Rushing Yards	Avg	TD
190	3,838*	16,726*	4.4	110

Receptions	Receiving Yards	Avg.	TD
492	4,538	9.2	15

Yardage	Total Offense TD	Points
21,803*	125	750

RECORD NOTES Payton set several NFL records during his stellar career: most yards rushing in a game, 275; most games gaining 100 yards rushing in a career, 77; most seasons gaining 1,000 yards rushing, 10.

* indicates all-time career record.

professional football was the formation of the American Professional Football Association (APFA), founded in Canton, Ohio on September 17, 1920. Reorganized a number of times, the APFA was renamed the National Football League (NFL) on June 24, 1922. Since 1922, several rival leagues have challenged the NFL, the most significant being the All-America Football Conference (AAFL) and the American Football League (AFL). The AAFL began play in 1946 but after four seasons merged with the NFL for the 1950 season. The AFL challenge was stronger and more acrimonious. Formed in 1959, it had its inaugural season in 1960. The AFL–NFL "war" was halted on June 4, 1966, when an agreement to merge the leagues was announced. The leagues finally merged for the 1970 season, but an AFL–NFL championship game, the Super Bowl, was first played in January 1967.

REGULAR SEASON RECORDS (1922–1991)

ENDURANCE

Most games played (career) George Blanda played in a record 340 games in a record 26 seasons in the NFL, for the Chicago Bears (1949, 1950–58), the Baltimore Colts (1950), the Houston Oilers (1960–66), and the Oakland Raiders (1967–75).

Most consecutive games played Jim Marshall played 282 consecutive games from 1960–79 for two teams: the Cleveland Browns, 1960, and the Minnesota Vikings, 1961–79.

LONGEST PLAYS

Run from scrimmage Tony Dorsett, Dallas Cowboys, ran through the Minnesota Vikings defense for a 99-yard touchdown on January 3, 1983.

Pass completion The longest pass completion, all for touchdowns, is 99 yards, performed by six quarterbacks: Frank Filchock (to Andy Farkas), Washington Redskins v. Pittsburgh Steelers, October 15, 1939; George Izo (to Bobby Mitchell), Washington Redskins v. Cleveland Browns, September 15, 1963; Karl Sweetan (to Pat Studstill), Detroit Lions v. Baltimore Colts, October 16, 1966; Sonny Jurgensen (to Gerry Allen), Washington Redskins v. Chicago Bears, September 15, 1968; Jim Plunkett (to Cliff Branch), Los Angeles Raiders v. Washington Redskins, October 2, 1983; Ron

Jaworski (to Mike Quick), Philadelphia Eagles v. Atlanta Falcons, November 10, 1985.

Field goal The longest was 63 yards, by Tom Dempsey, New Orleans Saints v. Detroit Lions, on November 8, 1970.

Punt Steve O'Neal, New York Jets, boomed a 98-yard punt on September 21, 1969 v. Denver Broncos.

Interception return Vencie Glenn, San Diego Chargers, intercepted a Denver Broncos' pass and returned it 103 yards for a touchdown on November 29, 1987.

Kickoff return Three players share the record for a kickoff return at 106 yards: Al Carmichael, Green Bay Packers v. Chicago Bears, October 7, 1956; Noland Smith, Kansas City Chiefs v. Denver Broncos, December 17, 1967; and Roy Green, St. Louis Cardinals v. Dallas Cowboys, October 21, 1979. All three players scored touchdowns.

Missed field goal return Al Nelson, Philadelphia Eagles, returned a Dallas Cowboys' missed field goal 101 yards for a touchdown on September 26, 1971.

Punt return Four players share the record for the longest punt return at 98 yards: Gil LeFebvre, Cincinnati Reds v. Brooklyn Dodgers, December 3, 1933; Charlie West, Minnesota Vikings v. Washington Redskins, November 3, 1968; Dennis Morgan, Dallas Cowboys v. St. Louis Cardinals, October 13, 1974; Terance Mathis, New York Jets

PACKER POINTS ■ IN 1960, THE PACKERS' PAUL HORNUNG SCORED AN NFL SEASON RECORD 176 POINTS.

NATIONAL FOOTBALL LEAGUE RECORDS (1920–1991)

Points Scored

		Player(s)	Team(s)	Date(s)
Game	40	Ernie Nevers	Chicago Cardinals v. Chicago Bears	Nov. 18, 1929
Season	176	Paul Hornung	Green Bay Packers	1960
Career	2,002	George Blanda	Chicago Bears, Baltimore Colts, Houston Oilers, Oakland Raiders	1949–75

Touchdowns Scored

Game	6	Ernie Nevers	Chicago Cardinals v. Chicago Bears	Nov. 28, 1929
		Dub Jones	Cleveland Browns v. Chicago Bears	Nov. 25, 1951
		Gale Sayers	Chicago Bears v. San Francisco 49ers	Dec. 12, 1965
Season	24	John Riggins	Washington Redskins	1983
Career	126	Jim Brown	Cleveland Browns	1957–65

Passing

Yards Gained

Game	554	Norm Van Brocklin	Los Angeles Rams v. New York Yankees	Sept. 28, 1951
Season	5,084	Dan Marino	Miami Dolphins	1984
Career	47,003	Fran Tarkenton	Minnesota Vikings, New York Giants	1961–78

Completions

Game	42	Richard Todd	New York Jets v. San Francisco 49ers	Sept. 21, 1980
Season	404	Warren Moon	Houston Oilers	1991
Career	3,686	Fran Tarkenton	Minnesota Vikings, New York Giants	1961–78

Attempts

Game	68	George Blanda	Houston Oilers v. Buffalo Bills	Nov. 1, 1964
Season	655	Warren Moon	Houston Oilers	1991
Career	6,467	Fran Tarkenton	Minnesota Vikings, New York Giants	1961–78

Touchdowns Thrown

Game	7	Sid Luckman	Chicago Bears v. New York Giants	Nov. 14, 1943
		Adrian Burk	Philadelphia Eagles v. Washington Redskins	Oct. 17, 1954
		George Blanda	Houston Oilers v. New York Titans	Nov. 19, 1961
		Y. A. Tittle	New York Giants v. Washington Redskins	Oct. 28, 1962
		Joe Kapp	Minnesota Vikings v. Baltimore Colts	Sept. 28, 1969
Season	48	Dan Marino	Miami Dolphins	1984
Career	342	Fran Tarkenton	Minnesota Vikings, New York Giants	1961–78

NATIONAL FOOTBALL LEAGUE RECORDS (1920–1991)

Passing (cont.)

Average Yards Gained

		Player(s)	Team(s)	Date(s)
Game (min. 20 attempts)	18.58	Sammy Baugh	Washington	Oct. 31, 1948
Season (qualifiers)	11.17	Tommy O'Connell	Cleveland Browns (110–1,229)	1957
Career (min. 1,500 attempts)	8.63	Otto Graham	Cleveland Browns (1,565–13,499)	1950–55

Pass Receiving

Receptions

Game	18	Tom Fears	Los Angeles Rams v. Green Bay Packers	Dec. 3, 1950
Season	106	Art Monk	Washington Redskins	1984
Career	819	Steve Largent	Seattle Seahawks	1976–89

Yards Gained

Game	336	Willie Anderson	Los Angeles Rams v. New Orleans Saints	Nov. 26, 1989*
Season	1,746	Charley Hennigan	Houston Oilers	1961
Career	13,089	Steve Largent	Seattle Seahawks	1976–89

Touchdown Receptions

Game	5	Bob Shaw	Chicago Cardinals v. Baltimore Colts	Oct. 2, 1950
		Kellen Winslow	San Diego Chargers v. Oakland Raiders	Nov. 22, 1981
		Jerry Rice	San Francisco 49ers v. Atlanta Falcons	Oct. 14, 1990
Season	22	Jerry Rice	San Francisco 49ers	1987
Career	100	Steve Largent	Seattle Seahawks	1976–89

Average Yards Gained

Game (min. 3 catches)	60.67	Bill Groman	Houston Oilers v. Denver Broncos (3–182)	Nov. 20, 1960
		Homer Jones	New York Giants v. Washington Redskins	Dec. 12, 1965
Season (min. 24 catches)	32.58	Don Currivan	Boston Yanks (24–782)	1947
Career (min. 200 catches)	22.26	Homer Jones	New York Giants, Cleveland Browns (224–4,986)	1964–70

---

* Overtime

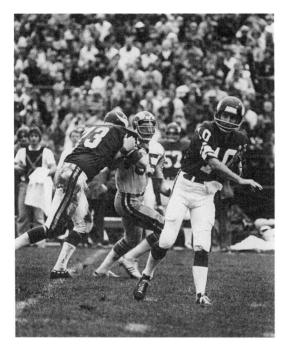

PASS AND CATCH ■ FRAN TARKENTON (LEFT) HOLDS NFL CAREER PASSING RECORDS FOR ATTEMPTS, COMPLETIONS, YARDS GAINED AND TOUCHDOWNS. STEVE LARGENT (RIGHT) HOLDS NFL CAREER RECEPTION RECORDS FOR TOUCHDOWNS, RECEPTIONS, AND YARDS GAINED.

SEVEN DOWN ■ CHIEFS' LINEBACKER DERRICK THOMAS GAINED AN NFL GAME RECORD SEVEN SACKS ON NOVEMBER 11, 1990.

v. Dallas Cowboys, November 4, 1990. All four players scored touchdowns.

Fumble return Jack Tatum, Oakland Raiders, returned a Green Bay Packers fumble 104 yards for a touchdown on September 24, 1972.

CONSECUTIVE RECORDS

Scoring (games) 181, Jim Breech, Oakland Raiders, 1979; Cincinnati Bengals, 1980–91.

Scoring touchdowns (games) 18, Lenny Moore, Baltimore Colts, 1963–65.

Points after touchdown (PATs), consecutive kicked 234, Tommy Davis, San Francisco 49ers, 1959–65.

Field goals, consecutive kicked 24, Kevin Butler, Chicago Bears, 1988–89.

Field goals (games) 31, Fred Cox, Minnesota Vikings, 1968–70.

100+ yards rushing (games) 11, Marcus Allen, Los Angeles Raiders, 1985–86.

NATIONAL FOOTBALL LEAGUE RECORDS (1920–1991)

Rushing

Yards Gained

		Player(s)	Team(s)	Date(s)
Game	275	Walter Payton	Chicago Bears v. Minnesota Vikings	Nov. 20, 1977
Season	2,105	Eric Dickerson	Los Angeles Rams	1984
Career	16,726	Walter Payton	Chicago Bears	1975–87

Attempts

Game	45	Jamie Morris	Washington Redskins v. Cincinnati Bengals	Dec. 17, 1988
Season	407	James Wilder	Tampa Bay Buccaneers	1984
Career	3,838	Walter Payton	Chicago Bears	1975–87

Touchdowns Scored

Game	6	Ernie Nevers	Chicago Cardinals v. Chicago Bears	Nov. 28, 1929
Season	24	John Riggins	Washington Redskins	1983
Career	110	Walter Payton	Chicago Bears	1975–87

Average Yards Gained

Game (min. 10 attempts)	17.09	Marion Mottley	Cleveland Browns v. Pittsburgh Steelers (11–188)	Oct. 29, 1950
Season (qualifiers)	9.94	Beattie Feathers	Chicago Bears (101–1,004)	1934
Career (min. 700 attempts)	5.22	Jim Brown	Cleveland Browns (2,359–12,312)	1957–65

Interceptions

Game	4	16 players have achieved this feat.		
Season	14	Dick "Night Train" Lane	Los Angeles Rams	1952
Career	81	Paul Krause	Washington Redskins, Minnesota Vikings	1964–79

Interceptions Returned for Touchdowns

Game	2	15 players have achieved this feat.		
Season	4	Ken Houston Jim Kearney	Houston Oilers Kansas City Chiefs	1971 1972
Career	9	Ken Houston	Houston Oilers, Washington Redskins	1967–80

NATIONAL FOOTBALL LEAGUE RECORDS (1920–1991)

Sacks
(compiled since 1982)

		Player(s)	Team(s)	Date(s)
Game	7	Derrick Thomas	Kansas City v. Seattle Seahawks	Nov. 11, 1990
Season	22	Mark Gastineau	New York Jets	1984
Career	121.5	Lawrence Taylor	New York Giants	1982–91

Kicking

Field Goals

Game	7	Jim Bakken	St. Louis Cardinals v. Pittsburgh Steelers	Sept. 24, 1967
		Rich Karlis	Minnesota Vikings v. Los Angeles Rams	Nov. 5, 1989 (OT)
Season	35	Ali Haji-Sheikh	New York Giants	1983
Career	373	Jan Stenerud	Kansas City Chiefs, Green Bay Packers, Minnesota Vikings	1967–85

Highest Percentage

Game	100.00	This has been achieved by many kickers. The most field goals kicked with no misses is 7, by Rich Karlis, Minnesota Vikings v. Los Angeles Rams on Nov. 5, 1989 in an overtime game.		
Season	100.00	Tony Zendejas	Los Angeles Rams (17–17)	1991
Career	79.33	Nick Lowery	New England Patriots, Kansas City Chiefs	1978, 1980–91

Field Goals 50 or More Yards

Game	2	This record has been achieved 25 times; Nick Lowery, Kansas City Chiefs, is the only kicker to have done it 3 times.		
Season	6	Dean Biasucci	Indianapolis Colts	1988
Career	18	Nick Lowery	New England Patriots, Kansas City Chiefs	1978, 1980–91

Points After Touchdown (PATs)

Game	9	Pat Harder	Chicago Cardinals v. New York Giants	Oct. 17, 1948
		Bob Waterfield	Los Angeles Rams v. Baltimore Colts	Oct. 22, 1950
		Charlie Gogolak	Washington Redskins v. New York Giants	Nov. 27, 1966
Season	66	Uwe von Schamann	Miami Dolphins	1984
Career	943	George Blanda	Chicago Bears, Baltimore Colts, Houston Oilers, Oakland Raiders	1949–75

NATIONAL FOOTBALL LEAGUE RECORDS (1920–1991)

Punting

Punts

		Player(s)	Team(s)	Date(s)
Game	15	John Teltschik	Philadelphia Eagles v. New York Giants	Dec. 6, 1987
Season	114	Bob Parsons	Chicago Bears	1981
Career	1,154	Dave Jennings	New York Giants, New York Jets	1974–87

Average Yards Gained

		Player(s)	Team(s)	Date(s)
Game (min. 4 punts)	61.75	Bob Cifers	Detroit Lions v. Chicago Bears (4–247)	Nov. 24, 1946
Season (qualifiers)	51.40	Sammy Baugh	Washington Redskins (35–1,799)	1940
Career (min. 300 punts)	45.10	Sammy Baugh	Washington Redskins (338–15,245)	1937–52

Special Teams

Punt Returns for Touchdowns

Game	2	Jack Christiansen	Detroit Lions v. Los Angeles Rams	Oct. 14, 1951
		Jack Christiansen	Detroit Lions v. Green Bay Packers	Nov. 22, 1951
		Dick Christy	New York Titans v. Denver Broncos	Sept. 24, 1961
		Rick Upchurch	Denver Broncos v. Cleveland Browns	Sept. 26, 1976
		LeRoy Irvin	Los Angeles Rams v. Atlanta Falcons	Oct. 11, 1981
		Vai Sikahema	St. Louis Cardinals v. Tampa Bay Buccaneers	Dec. 21, 1986
Season	4	Jack Christiansen	Detroit Lions	1951
		Rick Upchurch	Denver Broncos	1976
Career	8	Jack Christiansen	Detroit Lions	1951–58
		Rick Upchurch	Denver Broncos	1975–83

Kickoff Returns for Touchdowns

Game	2	Timmy Brown	Philadelphia Eagles v. Dallas Cowboys	Nov. 6, 1966
		Travis Williams	Green Bay Packers v. Cleveland Browns	Nov. 12, 1967
		Ron Brown	Los Angeles Rams v. Green Bay Packers	Nov. 24, 1985
Season	4	Travis Williams	Green Bay Packers	1967
		Cecil Turner	Chicago Bears	1970
Career	6	Ollie Matson	Chicago Cardinals, Los Angeles Rams, Detroit Lions, Philadelphia Eagles	1952–64
		Gale Sayers	Chicago Bears	1965–71
		Travis Williams	Green Bay Packers, Los Angeles Rams	1967–71

Source: NFL

200+ yards rushing (games) 2, by two players: O.J. Simpson, Buffalo Bills, 1973, 1976; Earl Campbell, Houston Oilers, 1980.

Touchdown passes (games) 47, Johnny Unitas, Baltimore Colts, 1956–60.

Touchdown rushes (games) 13, by two players: John Riggins, Washington Redskins, 1982–83; George Rogers, Washington Redskins, 1985–86.

Touchdown receptions (games) 13, Jerry Rice, San Francisco 49ers, 1986–87.

Passes completed (consecutive) 22, Joe Montana, San Francisco 49ers *v*. Cleveland Browns, November 29, 1987 (5); *v*. Green Bay Packers, December 6, 1987 (17).

300+ yards passing (games) 5, Joe Montana, San Francisco 49ers, 1982.

Four or more touchdown passes (games) 4, Dan Marino, Miami Dolphins, 1984.

Pass receptions (games) 177, Steve Largent, Seattle Seahawks, 1977–89.

LEAGUE LEADERS, MOST SEASONS

Scoring 5, Don Hutson, Green Bay Packers, 1940–44; Gino Cappelletti, Boston Patriots, 1961, 1963–66.

Touchdowns 8, Don Hutson, Green Bay Packers, 1935–38, 1941–44.

Rushing 8, Jim Brown, Cleveland Browns, 1957–61, 1963–65.

Passing 6, Sammy Baugh, Washington Redskins, 1937, 1940, 1943, 1945, 1947, 1949.

Receiving 8, Don Hutson, Green Bay Packers, 1936–37, 1939, 1941–45.

Field goals 5, Lou Groza, Cleveland Browns, 1950, 1952–54, 1957.

TEAM RECORDS (REGULAR SEASON)

WINS AND LOSSES

Most consecutive games won The Chicago Bears won 17 straight regular-season games, covering the 1933–34 seasons.

Most consecutive games unbeaten The Canton Bulldogs played 25 regular-season games without a defeat, covering the 1921–23 seasons. The Bulldogs won 22 games and tied three.

Most games won in a season Two teams have compiled 15-win seasons: the San Francisco 49ers in 1984, and the Chicago Bears in 1985.

Most consecutive games lost This most undesirable of records is held by the Tampa Bay Buccaneers, who lost 26 straight games from 1976–77.

Most games lost in a season Four teams hold the dubious honor of having lost 15 games in one season: the New Orleans Saints in 1980, the Dallas Cowboys in 1989, the New England Patriots in 1990 and the Indianapolis Colts in 1991.

SCORING

Most points scored, game The Washington Redskins scored 72 points *v*. the New York Giants on November 27, 1966 to set the single-game NFL regular season record for most points scored by one team.

Highest aggregate score On November 27, 1966, the Washington Redskins defeated the New York Giants 72–41 in Washington D.C. The Redskins' total was an NFL record for most points (see above).

Largest deficit overcome On December 7, 1980, the San Francisco 49ers, playing at home, trailed the New Orleans Saints 35–7 at halftime. In the second half, the 49ers, led by Joe Montana, scored 31 unanswered points to win the game 38–35 in overtime. The 49ers had overcome a deficit of 28 points—the largest in NFL history.

TRADES

Largest in NFL history Based on the number of players and/or draft choices involved, the largest trade in NFL history is 15, which has happened twice. On March 26, 1953 the Baltimore Colts and the Cleveland Browns exchanged 15 players; and on January 28, 1971, the Washington Redskins and the Los Angeles Rams completed the transfer of seven players and eight draft choices.

COACHES

Most seasons 40, George Halas, Decatur/Chicago Staleys/Chicago Bears: 1920–29, 1933–42, 1946–55, 1958–67.

Most wins (including playoffs) 325, George Halas, Decatur/Chicago Staleys/Chicago Bears: 1920–29, 1933–42, 1946–55, 1958–67.

NFL CHAMPIONSHIP

The first NFL championship was awarded in 1920 to the Akron Pros, as the team with the best record. From 1920 to 1931, the championship was based

NFL CHAMPIONS (1920–1957)

Season	Winner	Loser	Score
1920	Akron Pros	—	—
1921	Chicago Staleys	—	—
1922	Canton Bulldogs	—	—
1923	Canton Bulldogs	—	—
1924	Cleveland Bulldogs	—	—
1925	Chicago Cardinals	—	—
1926	Frankford Yellowjackets	—	—
1927	New York Giants	—	—
1928	Providence Steam Roller	—	—
1929	Green Bay Packers	—	—
1930	Green Bay Packers	—	—
1931	Green Bay Packers	—	—
1932	Chicago Bears	Portsmouth Spartans	9–0
1933	Chicago Bears	New York Giants	23–21
1934	New York Giants	Chicago Bears	30–13
1935	Detroit Lions	New York Giants	26–7
1936	Green Bay Packers	Boston Redskins	21–6
1937	Washington Redskins	Chicago Bears	28–21
1938	New York Giants	Green Bay Packers	23–17
1939	Green Bay Packers	New York Giants	27–0
1940	Chicago Bears	Washington Redskins	73–0
1941	Chicago Bears	New York Giants	37–9
1942	Washington Redskins	Chicago Bears	14–6
1943	Chicago Bears	Washington Redskins	41–21
1944	Green Bay Packers	New York Giants	14–7
1945	Cleveland Rams	Washington Redskins	15–14
1946	Chicago Bears	New York Giants	24–14
1947	Chicago Cardinals	Philadelphia Eagles	28–21
1948	Philadelphia Eagles	Chicago Cardinals	7–0
1949	Philadelphia Eagles	Los Angeles Rams	14–0
1950	Cleveland Browns	Los Angeles Rams	30–28
1951	Los Angeles Rams	Cleveland Browns	24–17
1952	Detroit Lions	Cleveland Browns	17–7
1953	Detroit Lions	Cleveland Browns	17–16
1954	Cleveland Browns	Detroit Lions	56–10
1955	Cleveland Browns	Los Angeles Rams	38–14
1956	New York Giants	Chicago Bears	47–7
1957	Detroit Lions	Cleveland Browns	59–14

NFL CHAMPIONS (1958–1965)

Season	Winner	Loser	Score
1958	Baltimore Colts	New York Giants	23–17
1959	Baltimore Colts	New York Giants	31–16
1960	Philadelphia Eagles	Green Bay Packers	17–13
1961	Green Bay Packers	New York Giants	37–0
1962	Green Bay Packers	New York Giants	16–7
1963	Chicago Bears	New York Giants	14–10
1964	Cleveland Browns	Baltimore Colts	27–0
1965	Green Bay Packers	Cleveland Browns	23–12

SUPER BOWL RESULTS (1967–1992)

Bowl	Date	Winner	Loser	Score	Site
I	Jan. 15, 1967	Green Bay Packers	Kansas City Chiefs	35–10	Los Angeles, Calif.
II	Jan. 14, 1968	Green Bay Packers	Oakland Raiders	33–14	Miami, Fla.
III	Jan. 12, 1969	New York Jets	Baltimore Colts	16–7	Miami, Fla.
IV	Jan. 11, 1970	Kansas City Chiefs	Minnesota Vikings	23–7	New Orleans, La.
V	Jan. 17, 1971	Baltimore Colts	Dallas Cowboys	16–13	Miami, Fla.
VI	Jan. 16, 1972	Dallas Cowboys	Miami Dolphins	24–3	New Orleans, La.
VII	Jan. 14, 1973	Miami Dolphins	Washington Redskins	14–7	Los Angeles, Calif.
VIII	Jan. 13, 1974	Miami Dolphins	Minnesota Vikings	24–7	Houston, Tex.
IX	Jan. 12, 1975	Pittsburgh Steelers	Minnesota Vikings	16–6	New Orleans, La.
X	Jan. 18, 1976	Pittsburgh Steelers	Dallas Cowboys	21–17	Miami, Fla.
XI	Jan. 9, 1977	Oakland Raiders	Minnesota Vikings	32–14	Pasadena, Calif.
XII	Jan. 15, 1978	Dallas Cowboys	Denver Broncos	27–10	New Orleans, La.
XIII	Jan. 21, 1979	Pittsburgh Steelers	Dallas Cowboys	35–31	Miami, Fla.
XIV	Jan. 20, 1980	Pittsburgh Steelers	Los Angeles Rams	31–19	Pasadena, Calif.
XV	Jan. 25, 1981	Oakland Raiders	Philadelphia Eagles	27–10	New Orleans, La.
XVI	Jan. 24, 1982	San Francisco 49ers	Cincinnati Bengals	26–21	Pontiac, Mich.
XVII	Jan. 30, 1983	Washington Redskins	Miami Dolphins	27–17	Pasadena, Calif.
XVIII	Jan. 22, 1984	Los Angeles Raiders	Washington Redskins	38–9	Tampa, Fla.
XIX	Jan. 20, 1985	San Francisco 49ers	Miami Dolphins	38–16	Stanford. Calif.
XX	Jan. 26, 1986	Chicago Bears	New England Patriots	46–10	New Orleans, La.
XXI	Jan. 25, 1987	New York Giants	Denver Broncos	39–20	Pasadena, Calif.
XXII	Jan. 31, 1988	Washington Redskins	Denver Broncos	42–10	San Diego, Calif.
XXIII	Jan. 22, 1989	San Francisco 49ers	Cincinnati Bengals	20–16	Miami, Fla.
XXIV	Jan. 28, 1990	San Francisco 49ers	Denver Broncos	55–10	New Orleans, La.
XXV	Jan. 27, 1991	New York Giants	Buffalo Bills	20–19	Tampa, Fla.
XXVI	Jan. 25, 1992	Washington Redskins	Buffalo Bills	37–24	Minneapolis, Minn.

on regular-season records. The first championship game was played in 1932.

In 1966, the National Football League (NFL) and the American Football League (AFL) agreed to merge their competing leagues to form an expanded NFL. Regular-season play would not begin until 1970, but the two leagues agreed to stage an annual AFL–NFL world championship game beginning in January 1967. The proposed championship game was dubbed the Super Bowl, and in 1969 the NFL officially recognized the title.

Most NFL titles The Green Bay Packers have won 11 NFL championships: 1929–31, 1936, 1939, 1944, 1961–62, 1965, and Super Bowls I and II (1966 and 1967 seasons).

THE SUPER BOWL (1967–1992)

Super Bowl I was played on January 15, 1967, with the Green Bay Packers (NFL) defeating the Kansas City Chiefs (AFL), 35–10.

Most wins Two teams have won the Super Bowl four times: the Pittsburgh Steelers, Super Bowls IX, X, XIII and XIV; and the San Francisco 49ers, XVI, XIX, XXIII and XXIV.

Consecutive wins Four teams have won Super Bowls in successive years: the Green Bay Packers, I and II; the Miami Dolphins, VII and VIII; the Pittsburgh Steelers (twice), IX and X, and XIII and XIV; and the San Francisco 49ers, XXIII and XXIV.

Most appearances Two teams have played in five Super Bowls: the Dallas Cowboys, V, VI, X, XII and XIII; the Miami Dolphins, VI, VII, VIII, XVII and XIX. Both teams won two and lost three games.

SCORING RECORDS

Most points scored The San Francisco 49ers scored 55 points *v.* the Denver Broncos in Super Bowl XXIV.

Highest aggregate score The highest aggregate score is 66 points when the Pittsburgh Steelers beat the Dallas Cowboys 35–31 in Super Bowl XIII.

Greatest margin of victory The greatest margin of victory is 45 points, set by the San Francisco

RECORD FILE: JOE MONTANA

BORN: June 11, 1956, Monongahela, Pa.

NFL REGULAR SEASON CAREER STATISTICS
SAN FRANCISCO 49ERS, 1979–90

			Passing				
Games	Att.	Comp.	Pct.	Yards	Avg.	TDs	Int.
166	4,579	2,914	63.6*	34,998	7.64	242	123

NFL PLAYOFF CAREER STATISTICS
SAN FRANCISCO 49ERS, 1981, 1983–90

			Passing				
Games	Att.	Comp.	Pct.	Yards	Avg.	TDs	Int.
19	593*	375*	63.2	4,758*	8.02	39*	17

SUPER BOWL CAREER STATISTICS
SAN FRANCISCO 49ERS, XVI, XIX, XXIII, XXIV

			Passing				
Games	Att.	Comp.	Pct.	Yards	Avg.	TDs	Int.
4	122*	83*	68.0*	1,142*	9.36	11*	0*

RECORD NOTES Montana holds NFL regular-season records for most consecutive completed passes, 22; most consecutive 300 yards or more games passing, five; and the highest career quarterback rating, 93.4. Montana has played in four Super Bowls and holds game records for most yards gained passing, 357; most touchdowns thrown, five. Montana has won the Super Bowl MVP award a record three times.

* indicates all-time record

SUPER BOWL RECORDS (1967–1992)

Points Scored

		Player(s)	Team(s)	Super Bowl
Game	18	Roger Craig	San Francisco 49ers	XIX
		Jerry Rice	San Francisco 49ers	XXIV
Career	24	Franco Harris	Pittsburgh Steelers	IX, X, XIII, XIV
		Roger Craig	San Francisco 49ers	XIX, XXIII, XXIV
		Jerry Rice	San Francisco 49ers	XXIII, XXIV

Touchdowns Scored

Game	3	Roger Craig	San Francisco 49ers	XIX
		Jerry Rice	San Francisco 49ers	XXIV
Career	4	Franco Harris	Pittsburgh Steelers	IX, X, XIII, XIV
		Roger Craig	San Francisco 49ers	XIX, XXIII, XXIV
		Jerry Rice	San Francisco 49ers	XXIII, XXIV

Passing

Yards Gained

Game	357	Joe Montana	San Francisco 49ers	XXIII
Career	1,142	Joe Montana	San Francisco 49ers	XVI, XIX, XXIII, XXIV

Completions

Game	29	Dan Marino	Miami Dolphins	XIX
Career	83	Joe Montana	San Francisco 49ers	XVI, XIX, XXIII, XXIV

Touchdowns Thrown

Game	5	Joe Montana	San Francisco 49ers	XXIV
Career	11	Joe Montana	San Francisco 49ers	XVI, XIX, XXIII, XXIV

Highest Completion Percentage

Game (min. 20 attempts)	88.0	Phil Simms	New York Giants (22–25)	XXI
Career (min. 40 attempts)	68.0	Joe Montana	San Francisco 49ers (83–122)	XVI, XIX, XXIII, XXIV

SUPER BOWL RECORDS (1967–1992)

Pass Receiving

		Player(s)	Team(s)	Super Bowl

Receptions

		Player(s)	Team(s)	Super Bowl
Game	11	Dan Ross	Cincinnati Bengals	XVI
		Jerry Rice	San Francisco 49ers	XXIII
Career	20	Roger Craig	San Francisco 49ers	XIX, XXIII, XXIV

Yards Gained

Game	215	Jerry Rice	San Francisco 49ers	XXIII
Career	364	Lynn Swann	Pittsburgh Steelers	IX, X, XIII, XIV

Touchdown Receptions

Game	3	Jerry Rice	San Francisco 49ers	XXIV
Career	4	Jerry Rice	San Francisco 49ers	XXIII, XXIV

Rushing

Yards Gained

Game	204	Timmy Smith	Washington Redskins	XXII
Career	354	Franco Harris	Pittsburgh Steelers	IX, X, XIII, XIV

Touchdowns Scored

Game	2	This feat has been achieved by 8 players		
Career	4	Franco Harris	Pittsburgh Steelers	IX, X, XIII, XIV

Interceptions

Game	3	Rod Martin	Oakland Raiders	XV
Career	3	Chuck Howley	Dallas Cowboys	V, VI
		Rod Martin	Oakland/Los Angeles Raiders	XV, XVIII

Field Goals Kicked

Game	4	Don Chandler	Green Bay Packers	II
		Ray Wersching	San Francisco 49ers	XVI
Career	5	Ray Wersching	San Francisco 49ers	XVI, XIX

Longest Plays

Run from Scrimmage	74 yards	Marcus Allen	Los Angeles Raiders	XVIII
Pass Completion	80 yards	Jim Plunkett	(to Kenny King) Oakland Raiders	XV
		Doug Williams	(to Ricky Sanders) Washington Redskins	XXII
Field Goal	48 yards	Jan Stenerud	Kansas City Chiefs	IV
		Rich Karlis	Denver Broncos	XXI
Punt	63 yards	Lee Johnson	Cincinnati Bengals	XXIII

Source: NFL

49ers when they defeated the Denver Broncos 55–10 in Super Bowl XXIV.

Most MVP awards Joe Montana, quarterback of the San Francisco 49ers, has been voted the Super Bowl MVP on a record three occasions, XVI, XIX, XXIV.

COACHES

Most wins Chuck Noll led the Pittsburgh Steelers to four Super Bowl titles, IX, X, XIII and XIV.

Most appearances Don Shula has been the head coach of six Super Bowl teams: the Baltimore Colts, III; the Miami Dolphins, VI, VII, VIII, XVII and XIX. He won two games and lost four.

COLLEGE FOOTBALL (NCAA)

ORIGINS At the turn of the 20th century, football's popularity was rising rapidly; however, with the increased participation came a rise in serious injuries and even some deaths. Many institutions, alarmed at the violent nature of the game, called for controls to be established.

In December 1905, 13 universities, led by Chancellor Henry M. MacCracken of New York University, outlined a plan to establish an organization to standardize playing rules. On December 28, the Intercollegiate Athletic Association of the United States (IAAUS) was founded in New York City with 62 charter members. The IAAUS was officially constituted on March 31, 1906, and was renamed the National Collegiate Athletic Association (NCAA) in 1910.

The NCAA first began to keep statistics for football in 1937, and the records in this section date from that time. In 1973, the NCAA introduced a classification system creating Divisions I, II, and III to identify levels of college play. In 1978, Division I was subdivided into I-A and I-AA.

INDIVIDUAL RECORDS (1937–1991)

NCAA OVERALL CAREER RECORDS (DIVISIONS I-A, I-AA, II AND III)

POINTS SCORED

Game Three players have scored 48 points in an NCAA game: Junior Wolf, Panhandle State (Div. II), set the mark on November 8, 1958 v. St. Mary's (Kans.); Paul Zaeske, North Park (Div. II), tied the record on October 12, 1968 v. North Central; How-

SUPER DAY ■ IN SUPER BOWL XXI, PHIL SIMMS (ABOVE) COMPLETED A PHENOMENAL 22 OUT OF 25 PASSES. THE FOLLOWING YEAR TIMMY SMITH (BELOW) GAINED 204 YARDS RUSHING, TO SET THE SUPER BOWL RECORD.

ard Griffith, Illinois (Div I-A), created a triumvirate on September 22, 1990.

Season The most points scored in a season is 234, by Barry Sanders, Oklahoma State (Div. I-A) in 1988, all from touchdowns, 37 rushing and two receptions.

Career The career record for most points scored is 474, by Joe Dudek, Plymouth State (Div. III), 1982–85. Dudek scored 79 touchdowns, 76 rushing and three receptions.

RUSHING (YARDS GAINED)

Game Tony Sands, Kansas (Div. I-A) rushed for an NCAA single-game record 396 yards *v.* Missouri on November 23, 1991.

Season The most yards gained in a season is 2,628, by Barry Sanders, Oklahoma State (Div. I-A), in 1988. Sanders played in 11 games and carried the ball 344 times for an average gain of 7.64 yards per carry.

Career The career record for most yards gained is 6,320, by Johnny Bailey, Texas A&I (Div. II), 1986–89. Bailey carried the ball 885 times for an average gain of 7.14 yards per carry.

PASSING (YARDS GAINED)

Game David Klingler, Houston (Div. I-A) threw for an NCAA single-game record 716 yards *v.* Arizona State on December 2, 1990.

Season The single-season NCAA mark is held by Ty Detmer, BYU, who threw for 5,188 yards in 1990.

Career The career passing record is 15,031 yards, set by Ty Detmer, BYU (Div. I-A).

RECEIVING (YARDS GAINED)

Game The most yards gained from pass receptions in a single game is 370, by Barry Wagner, Alabama A&M (Div. II), *v.* Clark Atlanta on November 4, 1989.

Season The single-season NCAA record is 1,812 yards, by Barry Wagner, Alabama A&M (Div. II). Wagner caught 106 passes for an average gain of 17.1 yards.

Career The all-time NCAA mark is held by Jerry Rice, Mississippi Valley (Div. I-AA), 1981–84. He gained 4,693 yards on 301 catches (also an NCAA career record), for an average gain of 15.6 yards.

TOUCHDOWN LEADER ■ 1988 HEISMAN TROPHY WINNER BARRY SANDERS SET DIVISION I-A SEASON RECORDS FOR TOUCHDOWNS SCORED, OVERALL AND IN RUSHING.

READY TO PASS ■ MATT VOGLER HOLDS THE NCAA DIVISION I-A RECORD FOR MOST PASSING ATTEMPTS IN A GAME, 79.

NCAA DIVISION I–A RECORDS

Points Scored

		Player(s)	Team(s)	Date(s)
Game	48	Howard Griffith	Illinois v. Southern Illinois (8 TDs)	Sept. 22, 1990
Season	234	Barry Sanders	Oklahoma State (39 TDs)	1988
Career	394	Anthony Thompson	Indiana (65 TDs, 4 PATs)	1986–89

Touchdowns Scored

Game	8	Howard Griffith	Illinois v. Southern Illinois (all rushing)	Sept. 22, 1990
Season	39	Barry Sanders	Oklahoma State	1988
Career	65	Anthony Thompson	Indiana (64 rushing, 1 reception)	1986–89

2-Point Conversions

Game	6	Jim Pilot	New Mexico State v. Hardin-Simmons	Nov. 25, 1961
Season	6	Pat McCarthy	Holy Cross	1960
		Jim Pilot	New Mexico State	1961
		Howard Twilley	Tulsa	1964
Career	13	Pat McCarthy	Holy Cross	1960–62

Passing

Touchdowns Thrown

Game	11	David Klingler	Houston v. Eastern Washington	Nov. 17, 1990
Season	54	David Klingler	Houston	1990
Career	121	Ty Detmer	BYU	1988–91

Yards Gained

Game	716	David Klingler	Houston v. Arizona State	Dec. 1, 1990
Season	5,188	Ty Detmer	BYU	1990
Career	15,031	Ty Detmer	BYU	1988–91

Completions

Game	48	David Klingler	Houston v. SMU	Oct. 20, 1990
Season	374	David Klingler	Houston	1990
Career	958	Ty Detmer	BYU	1988–91

Attempts

Game	79	Matt Vogler	TCU v. Houston	Nov. 3, 1990
Season	643	David Klingler	Houston	1990
Career	1,530	Ty Detmer	BYU	1988–91

NCAA DIVISION I–A RECORDS

Passing

Average Yards Gained per Attempt

		Player(s)	Team(s)	Date(s)
Game (min. 40 attempts)	13.93	Marc Wilson	BYU v. Utah (41 for 571 yards)	Nov. 5, 1977
Season (min 400 attempts)	11.07	Ty Detmer	BYU (412 for 4,560 yards)	1989
Career (min 1000 attempts)	9.82	Ty Detmer	BYU (1,530 for 15,031 yards)	1988–91

Pass Receiving

Touchdown Receptions

Game	6	Tim Delaney	San Diego State v. New Mexico State	Nov. 15, 1969
Season	22	Emmanuel Hazard	Houston	1989
Career	38	Clarkston Hines	Duke	1986–89

Receptions

Game	22	Jay Miller	BYU v. New Mexico	Nov. 3, 1973
Season	142	Emmanuel Hazard	Houston	1989
Career	263	Terance Mathis	New Mexico	1985–87

Yards Gained

Game	349	Chuck Hughes	UTEP v. North Texas	Sept. 18, 1965
Season	1,779	Howard Tilley	Tulsa	1965
Career	4,254	Terance Mathis	New Mexico	1985–87, 1989

Average Yards Gained per Reception

Game (min. 5 catches)	52.6	Alex Wright	Auburn v. Pacific (5 for 263 yards)	Sept. 9, 1989
Season (min. 50 catches)	24.4	Henry Ellard	Fresno State (62 for 1,510 yards)	1982
Career (min. 100 catches)	22.0	Herman Moore	Virginia (114 for 2,504 yards)	1988–90

NCAA DIVISION I–A RECORDS

Rushing

Yards Gained

		Player(s)	Team(s)	Date(s)
Game	396	Tony Sands	Kansas v. Missouri	Nov. 23, 1991
Season	2,628	Barry Sanders	Oklahoma State	1988
Career	6,082	Tony Dorsett	Pittsburgh	1973–76

Attempts

		Player(s)	Team(s)	Date(s)
Game	58	Tony Sands	Kansas v. Missouri	Nov. 23, 1991
Season	403	Marcus Allen	Southern Cal.	1981
Career	1,215	Steve Bartalo	Colorado State	1983–86

Average Yards Gained per Attempt

		Player(s)	Team(s)	Date(s)
Game (min. 15 rushes)	21.40	Tony Jeffery	TCU v. Tulane (16 for 343 yards)	Sept. 13, 1986
Season (min. 250 rushes)	7.81	Mike Rozier	Nebraska (275 for 2,148 yards)	1983
Career (min. 600 rushes)	7.61	Mike Rozier	Nebraska (668 for 4,780 yards)	1981–83

Touchdowns Scored

		Player(s)	Team(s)	Date(s)
Game	8	Howard Griffith	Illinois v. Southern Illinois	Sept. 22, 1990
Season	37	Barry Sanders	Oklahoma State	1988
Career	64	Anthony Thompson	Indiana	1986–89

Total Offense (Rushing plus Passing)

Yards Gained

		Player(s)	Team(s)	Date(s)
Game	732	David Klingler	Houston v. Arizona State (716 passing, 16 rushing)	Dec. 2, 1990
Season	5,221	David Klingler	Houston (81 rushing, 5,140 passing)	1990
Career	14,665	Ty Detmer	BYU (–366 rushing, 15,031 passing)	1988–91

Interceptions

		Player(s)	Team(s)	Date(s)
Game	5	Lee Cook	Oklahoma State v. Detroit	Nov. 28, 1942
		Walt Pastuszak	Brown v. Rhode Island	Oct. 8, 1949
		Byron Beaver	Houston v. Baylor	Sept. 22, 1962
		Dan Rebsch	Miami (Ohio) v. Western Michigan	Nov. 4, 1972
Season	14	Al Worley	Washington	1968
Career	29	Al Brosky	Illinois	1950–52

NCAA DIVISION I–A RECORDS

Kicking

Field Goals Kicked

		Player(s)	Team(s)	Date(s)
Game	7	Mike Prindle	Western Michigan v. Marshall	Sept. 29, 1984
		Dale Klein	Nebraska v. Missouri	Oct. 19, 1985
Season	29	John Lee	UCLA	1984
Career	80	Jeff Jaeger	Washington	1983–86

Points Scored

Game	24	Mike Prindle	Western Michigan v. Marshall (7 FGs, 3 PATSs)	Sept. 29, 1984
Season	131	Roman Anderson	Houston (22 FGs, 65 PATs)	1989
Career	423	Roman Anderson	Houston (70 FGs, 213 PATs)	1988–91

Points After Touchdown (PATs)

Game	13	Terry Leiweke	Houston v. Tulsa	Nov. 23, 1968
Season	67	Cary Blanchard	Oklahoma State	1988
Career	213	Roman Anderson	Houston	1988–91

Punting

Most Punts

Game	36	Charlie Calhoun	Texas Tech v. Centenary	Nov. 11, 1939
Season	101	Jim Bailey	Virginia Military	1969
Career	320	Cameron Young	TCU	1976–79

Average Yards Gained

Game (min. 5 punts)	60.4	Lee Johnson	BYU v. Wyoming (5 for 302 yds)	Oct. 8, 1983
Season (min. 50 punts)	48.2	Ricky Anderson	Vanderbilt (58 for 2,793)	1984
Career (min. 200 punts)	44.7	Ray Guy	Southern Mississippi (200 for 8,934)	1970–72

Yards Gained

Game	1,318	Charlie Calhoun	Texas Tech v. Centenary	Nov. 11, 1939
Season	4,138	Johnny Pingel	Michigan State	1938
Career	12,947	Cameron Young	TCU	1976–79

Source: NCAA

IT'S GOOD! ■ THE NCAA DIVISION I-A RECORD FOR MOST FIELD GOALS (7) AND MOST POINTS KICKING (24) IN A GAME ARE HELD BY MIKE PRINDLE, SET ON SEPTEMBER 29, 1984.

SUUU-EEE !!! ■ RAZORBACK BILL BURNETT SCORED TOUCHDOWNS IN 23 CONSECUTIVE GAMES TO SET THE NCAA DIVISION I-A RECORD. DURING HIS STREAK, BURNETT SCORED 47 TOUCHDOWNS.

FIELD GOALS (MOST MADE)

Game Goran Lingmerth, Northern Arizona (Div. I-AA) booted 8 out of 8 field goals *v.* Idaho on October 25, 1986. The distances were 39, 18, 20, 33, 46, 27, 22 and 35 yards each.

Season The most kicks made in a season is 29, by John Lee, UCLA (Div. I-A) from 33 attempts in 1984.

Career The NCAA all-time career record is 80, by Jeff Jaeger, Washington (Div. I-A) from 99 attempts, 1983–86.

LONGEST PLAYS (DIVISION I-A)

Run from scrimmage 99 yards, by four players: Gale Sayers (Kansas *v.* Nebraska), 1963; Max Anderson (Arizona State *v.* Wyoming), 1967; Ralph Thompson (West Texas State *v.* Wichita State), 1970; Kelsey Finch (Tennessee *v.* Florida), 1977.

Pass completion 99 yards, on eight occasions, performed by seven players (Terry Peel and Robert Ford did it twice): Fred Owens (to Jack Ford), Portland *v.* St. Mary's, Calif., 1947; Bo Burris (to Warren McVea), Houston *v.* Washington State, 1966; Colin Clapton (to Eddie Jenkins), Holy Cross *v.* Boston U, 1970; Terry Peel (to Robert Ford), Houston *v.* Syracuse, 1970; Terry Peel (to Robert Ford), Houston *v.* San Diego State, 1972; Cris Collingsworth (to Derrick Gaffney), Florida *v.* Rice, 1977; Scott Ankrom (to James Maness), TCU *v.* Rice, 1984; Gino Torretta (to Horace Copeland), Miami *v.* Arkansas, 1991.

Field goal 67 yards, by three players: Russell Erxleben (Texas *v.* Rice), 1977; Steve Little (Arkansas *v.* Texas), 1977; Joe Williams (Wichita State *v.* Southern Illinois), 1978.

Punt 99 yards, by Pat Brady, Nevada-Reno *v.* Loyola, Calif. in 1950.

CONSECUTIVE RECORDS

REGULAR SEASON (INDIVIDUAL—DIVISION I-A)

Scoring touchdowns (games) 23, by Bill Burnett, Arkansas. Burnett amassed 47 touchdowns during his 23-game streak, which ran from October 5, 1968–October 31, 1970.

Touchdown passes (games) 35, Ty Detmer, BYU, September 7, 1989–November 23, 1991.

Touchdown passes (consecutive) 6, by Brooks Dawson, UTEP *v.* New Mexico, October 28, 1967. Dawson completed his first 6 passes for touch-

"The sons of Notre Dame" played their first game on November 23, 1887, losing to Michigan 8–0. From this inauspicious kickoff developed the tradition that is Notre Dame football—the most successful team in college sports. The Fighting Irish can boast the most national championships, eight; the highest winning percentage, .759 (702–209–40); and the most Heisman Trophy winners, seven. However, Notre Dame football goes beyond statistics. It is a mystique, one whose characters and characteristics have become ingrained in American culture: the slogan "Win one for the Gipper," the Four Horsemen, coaches Knute Rockne and Frank Leahy, "Notre Dame Victory March" and "Touchdown Jesus" are recognizable to many who have never watched college football. November 9, 1991 marked the 100th consecutive sellout in Notre Dame stadium. No doubt the rabid Irish fans will continue to cheer their "loyal sons . . . onward to victory."

COACHING LEGENDS ■ **KNUTE ROCKNE (LEFT) AND FRANK LEAHY (ABOVE) RANK FIRST AND SECOND ON THE NCAA ALL-TIME WINNING PERCENTAGE LIST. ROCKNE, CREDITED WITH INVENTING THE FORWARD PASS, COACHED NOTRE DAME FROM 1918 TO 1930, WITH A CAREER RECORD 105 WINS, 12 LOSSES AND 5 TIES, FOR AN .881 WINNING PERCENTAGE. LEAHY COACHED THE IRISH FROM 1941–43 AND FROM 1946–53, WITH A RECORD OF 87–11–9. INCLUDING HIS STINT AT BOSTON COLLEGE, 1939–40, LEAHY'S CAREER RECORD WAS 107–13–9, FOR A WINNING PERCENTAGE OF .864.**

HEISMAN MEN ■ **SEVEN NOTRE DAME PLAYERS HAVE WON THE HEISMAN TROPHY, THE MOST FROM ONE TEAM. FROM LEFT TO RIGHT THEY ARE: JOHN LUJACK, 1947; ANGELO BERTELLI, 1943; LEON HART, 1949; TIM BROWN, 1987; PAUL HORNUNG, 1956; JOHN HUARTE, 1964; JOHN LATTNER, 1953.**

GOLDEN DOME ■ THE FAMED NOTRE DAME GOLD HELMETS ARE MODELED ON THE GOLDEN DOME ATOP THE ADMINISTRATION BUILDING (FAR LEFT). **THE FOUR HORSEMEN** ■ AN INTEGRAL PART OF THE NOTRE DAME MYTH, FROM LEFT TO RIGHT, DON MILLER, ELMER LAYDEN, JIM CROWLEY AND HARRY STUHLDREHER, WERE IMMORTALIZED BY GRANTLAND RICE'S PROSE FOLLOWING THEIR PERFORMANCE IN NOTRE DAME'S DEFEAT OF ARMY 13–7 ON OCTOBER 18, 1924.

CAREER LEADERS ■ JOE THEISMANN, 1968–70 (LEFT) HOLDS NOTRE DAME CAREER RECORDS FOR MOST TOUCHDOWNS THROWN, 31, AND HIGHEST COMPLETION PERCENTAGE, .570 (290–509); ALLEN PINKETT, 1982–85 (CENTER) IS THE CAREER LEADER FOR MOST YARDS RUSHING, 4,131; MOST POINTS SCORED, 320; AND MOST TOUCHDOWNS SCORED, 53; STEVE BEUERLEIN, 1983–86 (RIGHT) SET ALL-TIME PASSING MARKS FOR MOST ATTEMPTS, 850; MOST COMPLETIONS, 473; AND MOST YARDAGE, 6,527.

ALL-AMERICANS ■ NOTRE DAME BOASTS 28 CONSENSUS ALL-AMERICAN SELECTIONS, THE MOST OF ANY TEAM. THEY RANGE FROM THE FIRST, GEORGE GIPP IN 1920 (LEFT), TO RUNNING BACK VAGAS FERGUSON IN 1979 (CENTER), TO FLANKER RAGHIB "ROCKET" ISMAIL IN 1990 (RIGHT).

downs, which must rank as the greatest start to a game ever!

Passes completed 22, shared by two players: Steve Young, BYU *v*. Utah State, October 30, 1982, *v*. Wyoming, November 6, 1982; Chuck Long, Iowa *v*. Indiana, October 27, 1984.

100 yards+ rushing (games) 31, by Archie Griffin, Ohio State, September 15, 1973–November 22, 1975.

200 yards+ rushing (games) 5, shared by two players: Marcus Allen, Southern Calif., 1981; Barry Sanders, Oklahoma State, 1988.

Touchdown receptions (games) 10, by Mike Chronister, BYU, 1976–77.

Pass receptions (caught for touchdowns) 6, by Carlos Carson, Louisiana State, 1977. Carlson scored touchdowns on his last five receptions *v*. Rice on September 24, 1977, and from his first reception *v*. Florida on October 1, 1977. Amazingly, these were the first six receptions of his collegiate career!

Pass receptions (games) 44, by Gary Williams, Ohio State, 1979–82.

Field goals (consecutive) 30, by Chuck Nelson, Washington, 1981–82. Nelson converted his last five kicks of the season *v*. Southern Cal on November 14, 1981, and then booted the first 25 of the 1982 season, missing an attempt *v*. Washington State on November 20, 1982.

Field goals (games) 19, shared by two players: Larry Roach, Oklahoma State (1983–84); Gary Gussman, Miami (Ohio) (1986–87).

TEAM RECORDS (DIVISION I-A)

Most wins Michigan has won 722 games out of 993 played, 1879–1991.

Highest winning percentage The highest winning percentage in college football history is .759 percent by Notre Dame. The Fighting Irish have won 702, lost 209 and tied 40 out of 951 games played, 1887–1991.

NCAA DIVISION I-A NATIONAL CHAMPIONS (1936–1963)

In 1936 the Associated Press introduced the AP poll, a ranking of college teams by a vote of sportswriters and broadcasters. In 1950 the United Press, now UPI, introduced a coaches' poll. The AP and UPI polls are still used as the basis for declaring the national college football champion. AP and UPI have chosen different champions on nine occasions: 1954, 1957, 1965, 1970, 1973, 1974, 1978, 1990, and 1991.

Year	Team	Record	Year	Team	Record
1936	Minnesota	7–1–0	1951	Tennessee	10–0–0
1937	Pittsburgh	9–0–1	1952	Michigan State	9–0–0
1938	TCU	11–0–0	1953	Maryland	10–1–0
1939	Texas A&M	11–0–0	1954	Ohio State (AP)	10–0–0
1940	Minnesota	8–0–0		UCLA (UPI)	9–0–0
1941	Minnesota	8–0–0	1955	Oklahoma	11–0–0
1942	Ohio State	9–1–0	1956	Oklahoma	10–0–0
1943	Notre Dame	9–1–0	1957	Auburn (AP)	10–0–0
1944	Army	9–0–0		Ohio State (UPI)	9–1–0
1945	Army	9–0–0	1958	LSU	11–0–0
1946	Notre Dame	8–0–1	1959	Syracuse	11–0–0
1947	Notre Dame	9–0–0	1960	Minnesota	8–2–0
1948	Michigan	9–0–0	1961	Alabama	11–0–0
1949	Notre Dame	10–0–0	1962	Southern Cal.	11–0–0
1950	Oklahoma	10–0–0	1963	Texas	11–0–0

Longest winning streak The longest winning streak in Division I-A football, including bowl games, is 47 games by Oklahoma from 1953–57. Oklahoma's streak was stopped on November 16, 1957, when Notre Dame defeated them 7–0 in Norman.

Longest undefeated streak Including bowl games, Washington played 63 games, 1907–17, without losing a game. California ended the streak with a 27–0 victory on November 3, 1917. Washington's record during the streak was 59 wins and 4 ties.

Longest losing streak The most consecutive losses in Division I-A football is 34 games, by Northwestern. This undesirable streak started on September 22, 1979 and was finally snapped three years later on September 25, 1982 when Northern Illinois succumbed to the Wildcats 31–6.

Most points scored Wyoming crushed Northern Colorado 103–0 on November 5, 1949 to set the Division I-A mark for most points scored by one team in a single game. The Cowboys scored 15 touchdowns and converted 13 PATs.

Highest-scoring game The most points scored in a Division I-A game is 124, when Oklahoma defeated Colorado 82–42 on October 4, 1980.

Highest-scoring tie game BYU and San Diego State played a 52–52 tie on November 16, 1991.

Most wins (1936–91) Eight, by Notre Dame (1943, 1946–47, 1949, 1966, 1973, 1977, 1988).

BOWL GAMES

The oldest college bowl game is the Rose Bowl. It was first played on January 1, 1902 at Tournament Park, Pasadena, Calif., where Michigan defeated Stanford 49–0. The other three bowl games that make up the "big four" are the Orange Bowl, initiated in 1935; the Sugar Bowl, 1935; and the Cotton Bowl, 1937.

ROSE BOWL In the first game, played on January 1, 1902, Michigan blanked Stanford 49–0.

Most wins Southern Cal. has won the Rose Bowl 19 times: 1923, 1930, 1932–33, 1939–40, 1944–45, 1953, 1963, 1968, 1970, 1973, 1975, 1977, 1979–80, 1985, 1990.

NCAA DIVISION I-A NATIONAL CHAMPIONS (1964–1991)

Year	Team	Record	Year	Team	Record
1964	Alabama	10–1–0	1978	Alabama (AP)	11–1–0
1965	Alabama (AP)	9–1–1		Southern Cal. (UPI)	12–1–0
	Michigan State (UPI)	10–1–0	1979	Alabama	11–0–0
1966	Notre Dame	9–0–1	1980	Georgia	12–0–0
1967	Southern Cal.	10–1–0	1981	Clemson	12–0–0
1968	Ohio State	10–0–0	1982	Penn State	11–1–0
1969	Texas	11–0–0	1983	Miami, Fla.	11–1–0
1970	Nebraska (AP)	11–0–1	1984	BYU	13–0–0
	Texas (UPI)	10–1–0	1985	Oklahoma	11–1–0
1971	Nebraska	12–0–0	1986	Penn State	12–0–0
1972	Southern Cal.	12–0–0	1987	Miami, Fla.	12–0–0
1973	Notre Dame (AP)	11–0–0	1988	Notre Dame	12–0–0
	Alabama (UPI)	11–1–0	1989	Miami, Fla.	10–1–0
1974	Oklahoma (AP)	11–0–0	1990	Colorado (AP)	11–1–1
	Southern Cal. (UPI)	10–1–0		Georgia Tech (UPI)	11–0–1
1975	Oklahoma	11–1–0	1991	Miami, Fla. (AP)	12–0–0
1976	Pittsburgh	12–0–0		Washington (UPI)	12–0–0
1977	Notre Dame	11–1–0			

Most appearances Southern Cal. has played in the Rose Bowl 27 times, with a record of 19 wins and 8 losses.

ORANGE BOWL In the first game, played on January 1, 1935, Bucknell shut out Miami (Fla.) 26–0.

Most wins Oklahoma has won the Orange Bowl 11 times: 1954, 1956, 1958–59, 1968, 1976, 1979–81, 1986–87.

Most appearances Oklahoma has played in the Orange Bowl 16 times, with a record of 11 wins and 5 losses.

SUGAR BOWL In the first game, played on January 1, 1935, Tulane defeated Temple 20–14.

Most wins Alabama has won the Sugar Bowl seven times: 1962, 1964, 1967, 1975, 1978–80.

Most appearances Alabama has played in the Sugar Bowl 11 times, with a record of 7 wins and 4 losses.

COTTON BOWL In the first game, played on January 1, 1937, Texas Christian defeated Marquette 16–6.

Most wins Texas has won the Cotton Bowl nine times: 1943, 1946, 1953, 1962, 1964, 1969–70, 1973, 1982.

Most appearances Texas has played in the Cotton Bowl 18 times, with a record of 9 wins, 8 losses and 1 tie.

BOWL GAME RECORDS Alabama, Georgia and Notre Dame are the only three teams to have won each of the "big four" bowl games.

Most wins Alabama has won a record 24 bowl games: Sugar Bowl, seven times, 1962, 1964, 1967, 1975, 1978–80; Rose Bowl, four times, 1926, 1931, 1935, 1946; Orange Bowl, four times, 1943, 1953, 1963, 1966; Sun Bowl (now John Hancock Bowl), three times, 1983, 1986, 1988; Cotton Bowl, twice, 1942, 1981; Liberty Bowl, twice, 1976, 1982; Aloha Bowl, once, 1985; Blockbuster Bowl, once, 1991.

Consecutive seasons UCLA won a bowl game for seven consecutive seasons: Rose Bowl, 1983–84; Fiesta Bowl, 1985; Rose Bowl, 1986; Freedom Bowl, 1986; Aloha Bowl, 1987; Cotton Bowl, 1989.

Bowl game appearances Alabama has played in 44 bowl games.

HEISMAN TROPHY

Awarded annually since 1935 by the Downtown Athletic Club of New York to the top college football player as determined by a poll of journalists, it was originally called the D.A.C. Trophy, but the

HEISMAN TROPHY WINNERS (1935–1962)

Year	Player	Team	Year	Player	Team
1935	Jay Berwanger	Chicago	1949	Leon Hart	Notre Dame
1936	Larry Kelley	Yale	1950	Vic Janowicz	Ohio State
1937	Clint Frank	Yale	1951	Dick Kazmaier	Princeton
1938	Davey O'Brien	TCU	1952	Billy Vessels	Oklahoma
1939	Nile Kinnick	Iowa	1953	Johnny Lattner	Notre Dame
1940	Tom Harmon	Michigan	1954	Alan Ameche	Wisconsin
1941	Bruce Smith	Minnesota	1955	Howard Cassady	Ohio State
1942	Frank Sinkwich	Georgia	1956	Paul Hornung	Notre Dame
1943	Angelo Bertelli	Notre Dame	1957	John David Crow	Texas A&M
1944	Les Horvath	Ohio State	1958	Pete Dawkins	Army
1945	Doc Blanchard	Army	1959	Billy Cannon	LSU
1946	Glenn Davis	Army	1960	Joe Bellino	Navy
1947	Johnny Lujack	Notre Dame	1961	Ernie Davis	Syracuse
1948	Doak Walker	SMU	1962	Terry Baker	Oregon State

HEISMAN DOUBLE ■ ARCHIE GRIFFIN IS THE ONLY PLAYER TO HAVE WON THE HEISMAN TROPHY TWICE, IN 1974 AND 1975.

COACHES

Wins (Division I-A) In Division I-A competition, Paul "Bear" Bryant has won more games than any other coach, with 323 victories over 38 years. Bryant coached four teams: Maryland, 1945 (6–2–1); Kentucky, 1956–53 (60–23–5); Texas A&M, 1954–57 (25–14–2); and Alabama, 1958–82 (232–46–9). His completed record was 323 wins–85 losses–17 ties, with a .780 winning percentage.

Wins (all divisions) In overall NCAA competition, Eddie Robinson, Grambling (Division I-AA) holds the mark for most victories with 366.

Highest winning percentage (Division I-A) The highest winning percentage in Division I-A competition is .881, held by Knute Rockne of Notre Dame. Rockne coached the Irish from 1918 to 1930, with a record of 105 wins–12 losses–5 tied.

Highest winning percentage (all divisions) In overall NCAA competition, Mark Duffner compiled a .917 record (60 wins–5 losses–one tie), in six seasons with Holy Cross (Div. I-AA), 1987–91. At the end of the 1991 season Duffner resigned his post at Holy Cross to take the position of head coach of Maryland (Division I-A).

name was changed in 1936. Its full title is the John W. Heisman Memorial Trophy and it is named after the first athletic director of the Downtown Athletic Club. The only double winner has been Archie Griffin of Ohio State, 1974–75. Notre Dame, with seven, has had more Heisman Trophy winners than any other school.

HEISMAN TROPHY WINNERS (1963–1991)

Year	Player	Team	Year	Player	Team
1963	Roger Staubach	Navy	1978	Billy Sims	Oklahoma
1964	John Huarte	Notre Dame	1979	Charles White	Southern Cal.
1965	Mike Garrett	Southern Cal.	1980	George Rogers	South Carolina
1966	Steve Spurrier	Florida	1981	Marcus Allen	Southern Cal.
1967	Gary Beban	UCLA	1982	Herschel Walker	Georgia
1968	O. J. Simpson	Southern Cal.	1983	Mike Rozier	Nebraska
1969	Steve Owens	Oklahoma	1984	Doug Flutie	Boston College
1970	Jim Plunkett	Stanford	1985	Bo Jackson	Auburn
1971	Pat Sullivan	Auburn	1986	Vinny Testaverde	Miami, Fla.
1972	Johnny Rodgers	Nebraska	1987	Tim Brown	Notre Dame
1973	John Cappelletti	Penn State	1988	Barry Sanders	Oklahoma State
1974	Archie Griffin	Ohio State	1989	Andre Ware	Houston
1975	Archie Griffin	Ohio State	1990	Ty Detmer	BYU
1976	Tony Dorsett	Pittsburgh	1991	Desmond Howard	Michigan
1977	Earl Campbell	Texas			

ATTENDANCES

Single game It has been estimated that crowds of 120,000 were present for two Notre Dame games played at Soldier Field, Chicago, Ill.: *v*. Southern Cal. (November 26, 1927); *v*. Navy (October 13, 1928). Official attendance records have been kept by the NCAA since 1948. The highest official crowd for a regular season NCAA game was 106,255 Wolverine fans at Michigan Football Stadium, Ann Arbor Mich., on October 23, 1983 for the Michigan *v*. Ohio State game. As Michigan lost 18–15, a record may have been set for the greatest number of depressed people at a football game!

Bowl game The record attendance for a bowl game is 106,869 people at the 1973 Rose Bowl, where Southern Cal. defeated Ohio State 42–17.

Season average The highest average attendance for home games is 105,588 for the six games played by Michigan in 1985.

CANADIAN FOOTBALL LEAGUE (CFL)

ORIGINS The earliest recorded football game in Canada was an intramural contest between students of the University of Toronto on November 9, 1861. As with football in the U.S., the development of the game in Canada dates from a contest between two universities—McGill and Harvard, played in May 1874.

Canadian football differs in many ways from its counterpart in the U.S. The major distinctions are the number of players (CFL–12, NFL–11); size of field (CFL–110 yards x 65 yards, NFL–100 yards x 53 yards); number of downs (CFL–3, NFL–4); and a completely different system for scoring and penalties.

The current CFL is comprised of eight teams in two divisions, the Western and Eastern. The divisional playoff champions meet in the Grey Cup to decide the CFL champion.

SURE HANDS ■ EDMONTON'S BRIAN KELLY HOLDS CFL CAREER RECEPTION RECORDS FOR TOUCHDOWNS CAUGHT (97) AND RECEPTION YARDS GAINED (11,169).

CANADIAN FOOTBALL LEAGUE (CFL) RECORDS

Games Played

		Player(s)	Team(s)	Date(s)
Most	288	Ron Lancaster	Ottawa/Saskatchewan Roughriders	1960–78
Consecutive	253	Dave Cutler	Edmonton Eskimos	1969–84

Points Scored

Game	36	Bob McNamara	Winnipeg Blue Bombers *v.* B.C. Lions	Oct. 13, 1956
Season	236	Lance Chomyc	Toronto Argonauts	1991
Career	2,522	Lui Passaglia	B.C. Lions	1976–91

Touchdowns Scored

Game	6	Eddie James	Winnipegs *v.* Winnipeg St. Johns	Sept. 28, 1932
		Bob McNamara	Winnipeg Blue Bombers *v.* B.C. Lions	Oct. 13, 1956
Season	20	Pat Abbruzzi	Montreal Alouettes	1956
		Darrell K. Smith	Toronto Argonauts	1990
		Blake Marshall	Edmonton Eskimos	1991
		Jon Volpe	B.C. Lions	1991
Career	137	George Reed	Saskatchewan Roughriders	1963–75

Passing

Yards Gained

Game	586	Sam Etcheverry	Montreal Alouettes *v.* Hamilton Tiger-Cats	Oct. 16, 1954
Season	6,619	Doug Flutie	B. C. Lions	1991
Career	50,535	Ron Lancaster	Ottawa Roughriders/Saskatchewan Roughriders	1960–78

Touchdowns Thrown

Game	8	Joe Zuger	Hamilton Tiger-Cats	Oct. 15, 1962
Season	40	Peter Liske	Calgary Stampeders	1967
Career	333	Ron Lancaster	Ottawa/Saskatchewan Roughriders	1960–78

Completions

Game	41	Dieter Brock	Winnipeg Blue Bombers *v.* Ottawa Roughriders	Oct. 3, 1981
Season	466	Doug Flutie	B. C. Lions	1991
Career	3,384	Ron Lancaster	Ottawa Roughriders/Saskatchewan Roughriders	1960–78

CANADIAN FOOTBALL LEAGUE (CFL) RECORDS

Pass Receiving

Receptions

		Player(s)	Team(s)	Date(s)
Game	16	Terry Greer	Toronto Argonauts v. Ottawa Roughriders	Aug. 19, 1983
Season	118	Allen Pitts	Calgary Stampeders	1991
Career	706	Rocky DiPietro	Hamilton Tiger-Cats	1978–91

Yards Gained

Game	338	Hal Patterson	Montreal Alouettes v. Hamilton Tiger-Cats	Sept. 29, 1956
Season	2,003	Terry Greer	Toronto Argonauts	1983
Career	11,169	Brian Kelly	Edmonton Eskimos	1979–87

Touchdown Receptions

Game	5	Ernie Pitts	Winnipeg Blue Bombers v. Saskatchewan Roughriders	Aug. 29, 1959
Season	20	Darrell K. Smith	Toronto Argonauts	1990
Career	97	Brian Kelly	Edmonton Eskimos	1979–87

Rushing

Yards Gained

Game	287	Ron Stewart	Ottawa Roughriders v. Montreal Alouettes	Oct. 10, 1960
Season	1,896	Willie Burden	Calgary Stampeders	1975
Career	16,116	George Reed	Saskatchewan Roughriders	1963–75

Touchdowns Scored

Game	5	Earl Lunsford	Calgary Stampeders v. Edmonton Eskimos	Sept. 3, 1962
Season	18	Gerry James	Winnipeg Blue Bombers	1957
		Jim Germany	Edmonton Eskimos	1981
Career	134	George Reed	Saskatchewan Roughriders	1963–75

Longest Plays (Yards)

Rushing	109	George Dixon	Montreal Alouettes	Sept. 2, 1963
		Willie Fleming	B.C. Lions	Oct. 17, 1964
Pass Completion	109	Sam Etcheverry to Hal Patterson	Hamilton Tiger-Cats	Sept. 22, 1956
		Jerry Keeling to Terry Evanshen	Calgary Stampeders	Sept. 27, 1966
Field Goal	60	Dave Ridgway	Saskatchewan Roughriders	Sept. 6, 1987
Punt	108	Zenon Andrusyshyn	Edmonton Eskimos	Oct. 23, 1977

Source: CFL

CFL Team Records

Longest winning streak The Calgary Stampeders won 22 consecutive games between August 25, 1948 and October 22, 1949 to set the CFL mark.

Longest winless streak The Hamilton Tiger-Cats hold the dubious distinction of being the CFL's most futile team, amassing a 20-game winless streak (0–19–1), from September 28, 1948 to September 2, 1950.

Highest-scoring game The Toronto Argonauts defeated the B.C. Lions 68–43 on September 1, 1990 to set a CFL combined score record of 111 points.

Highest score by one team The Montreal Alouettes rolled over the Hamilton Tiger-Cats 82–14 on October 20, 1956 to set the CFL highest-score mark.

The Grey Cup

In 1909, Lord Earl Grey, the governor general of Canada, donated a trophy that was to be awarded to the Canadian Rugby Football champion. The competition for the Grey Cup evolved during the first half of the 20th century from an open competition for amateurs, college teams and hybrid rugby teams to the championship of the professional Canadian Football League that was formed in 1958.

Most wins 12, Toronto Argonauts: 1914, 1921, 1933, 1937–38, 1945–47, 1950, 1952, 1983, 1991.

Most consecutive wins Five, Edmonton Eskimos: 1978–83.

Arena Football League

Origins Invented by Jim Foster, arena football had its debut season in 1987. Arena football is a scaled-down version of the outdoor game adapted to indoor arenas. The playing field measures 150 feet long (plus two 24-foot end-zones) by 85 feet wide; the goalposts are 9 feet wide and the crossbar is 15 feet high. The teams are limited to eight players, and four offensive players must be lined up on the line of scrimmage. The game is played over four 15-minute quarters. The scoring system allows six points for a touchdown, one point for a conversion, two points for a "drop kick" conversion, two points for a succcessful run or pass conversion, three points for a field goal, four points for a "drop kick" field goal and two points for a safety. On March 27, 1990, Foster was granted a final issuance on his patent for the Arena Football Game system. It is believed that Arena Football is the only league in sports history to play a patented game.

Most wins Three, Detroit Drive, 1988–90.

ARENA FOOTBALL LEAGUE CHAMPIONS (1987–1991)

Year	Winner	Loser	Score
1987	Denver Dynamite	Pittsburgh Gladiators	45–16
1988	Detroit Drive	Chicago Bruisers	24–13
1989	Detroit Drive	Pittsburgh Gladiators	39–26
1990	Detroit Drive	Dallas Texans	51–27
1991	Tampa Bay Storm	Detroit Drive	48–42

GREY CUP RESULTS (1909–1917)

Year	Winner	Loser	Score
1909	University of Toronto	Toronto Parkdale	26–6
1910	University of Toronto	Hamilton Tigers	16–7
1911	University of Toronto	Toronto Argonauts	14–7
1912	Hamilton Alerts	Toronto Argonauts	11–4
1913	Hamilton Tigers	Toronto Parkdale	44–2
1914	Toronto Argonauts	University of Toronto	14–2
1915	Hamilton Tigers	Toronto Rowing	13–7
1916	not held		
1917	not held		

GREY CUP RESULTS (1918–1954)

Year	Winner	Loser	Score
1918	not held		
1919	not held		
1920	University of Toronto	Toronto Argonauts	16–3
1921	Toronto Argonauts	Edmonton Eskimos	23–0
1922	Queen's University	Edmonton Elks	13–1
1923	Queen's University	Regina Roughriders	54–0
1924	Queen's University	Toronto Balmy Beach	11–3
1925	Ottawa Senators	Winnipeg Tammany Tigers	24–1
1926	Ottawa Senators	University of Toronto	10–7
1927	Toronto Balmy Beach	Hamilton Tigers	9–6
1928	Hamilton Tigers	Regina Roughriders	30–0
1929	Hamilton Tigers	Regina Roughriders	14–3
1930	Toronto Balmy Beach	Regina Roughriders	11–6
1931	Montral AAA Winged Wheelers	Regina Roughriders	22–0
1932	Hamilton Tigers	Regina Roughriders	25–6
1933	Toronto Argonauts	Sarnia Imperials	4–3
1934	Sarnia Imperials	Regina Roughriders	20–12
1935	Winnipeg	Hamilton Tigers	18–12
1936	Sarnia Imperials	Ottawa Rough Riders	26–20
1937	Toronto Argonauts	Winnipeg Blue Bombers	4–3
1938	Toronto Argonauts	Winnipeg Blue Bombers	30–7
1939	Winnipeg Blue Bombers	Ottawa Rough Riders	8–7
1940	Ottawa Rough Riders	Toronto Balmy Beach	8–2
1941	Winnipeg Blue Bombers	Ottawa Rough Riders	18–16
1942	Toronto Hurricanes	Winnipeg Bombers	8–5
1943	Hamilton Flying Wildcats	Winnipeg Bombers	23–14
1944	St. Hyacinthe-Donnacona Navy	Hamilton Wildcats	7–6
1945	Toronto Argonauts	Winnipeg Blue Bombers	35–0
1946	Toronto Argonauts	Winnipeg Blue Bombers	28–6
1947	Toronto Argonauts	Winnipeg Blue Bombers	10–9
1948	Calgary Stampeders	Ottawa Rough Riders	12–7
1949	Montreal Alouettes	Calgary Stampeders	28–15
1950	Toronto Argonauts	Winnipeg Blue Bombers	13–0
1951	Ottawa Rough Riders	Saskatchewan Roughriders	21–14
1952	Toronto Argonauts	Edmonton Eskimos	21–11
1953	Hamilton Tiger-Cats	Winnipeg Blue Bombers	12–6
1954	Edmonton Eskimos	Montreal Alouettes	26–25

GREY CUP RESULTS (1955–1991)

Year	Winner	Loser	Score
1955	Edmonton Eskimos	Montreal Alouettes	34–19
1956	Edmonton Eskimos	Montreal Alouettes	50–27
1957	Hamilton Tiger-Cats	Winnipeg Blue Bombers	32–7
1958	Winnipeg Blue Bombers	Hamilton Tiger-Cats	35–28
1959	Winnipeg Blue Bombers	Hamilton Tiger-Cats	21–7
1960	Ottawa Senators	Edmonton Eskimos	16–6
1961	Winnipeg Blue Bombers	Hamilton Tiger-Cats	21–14
1962	Winnipeg Blue Bombers	Hamilton Tiger-Cats	28–27
1963	Hamilton Tiger-Cats	B.C. Lions	21–10
1964	B.C. Lions	Hamilton Tiger-Cats	34–24
1965	Hamilton Tiger-Cats	Winnipeg Blue Bombers	22–16
1966	Saskatchewan Roughriders	Ottawa Senators	29–14
1967	Hamilton Tiger-Cats	Saskatchewan Roughriders	24–1
1968	Ottawa Senators	Calgary Stampeders	24–21
1969	Ottawa Senators	Saskatchewan Roughriders	29–11
1970	Montreal Alouettes	Calgary Stampeders	23–10
1971	Calgary Stampeders	Toronto Argonauts	14–11
1972	Hamilton Tiger-Cats	Saskatchewan Roughriders	13–10
1973	Ottawa Senators	Edmonton Eskimos	22–18
1974	Montreal Alouettes	Edmonton Eskimos	20–7
1975	Edmonton Eskimos	Montreal Alouettes	9–8
1976	Ottawa Senators	Saskatchewan Roughriders	23–20
1977	Montreal Alouettes	Edmonton Eskimos	41–6
1978	Edmonton Eskimos	Montreal Alouettes	20–13
1979	Edmonton Eskimos	Montreal Alouettes	17–9
1980	Edmonton Eskimos	Hamilton Tiger-Cats	48–10
1981	Edmonton Eskimos	Ottawa Senators	26–23
1982	Edmonton Eskimos	Toronto Argonauts	32–16
1983	Toronto Argonauts	B.C. Lions	18–17
1984	Winnipeg Blue Bombers	Hamilton Tiger-Cats	47–17
1985	B.C. Lions	Hamilton Tiger-Cats	37–24
1986	Hamilton Tiger-Cats	Edmonton Eskimos	39–15
1987	Edmonton Eskimos	Toronto Argonauts	38–36
1988	Winnipeg Blue Bombers	B.C. Lions	22–21
1989	Saskatchewan Roughriders	Hamilton Tiger-Cats	43–40
1990	Winnipeg Blue Bombers	Edmonton Eskimos	50–11
1991	Toronto Argonauts	Calgary Stampeders	36–21

GREY CUP GAME RECORDS

Points Scored

		Player(s)	Team(s)	Date(s)
Game	23	Don Sweet	Montreal Alouettes v. Edmonton Eskimos	Nov. 27, 1977
Career	72	Dave Cutler	Edmonton Eskimos	1973–75, 1977–80, 1982

Touchdowns Scored

Game	3	Ross Craig	Hamilton Tigers v. Toronto Parkdale	Nov. 29, 1913
		Red Storey	Toronto Argonauts v. Hamilton Tiger-Cats	Dec. 10, 1938
		Jackie Parker	Edmonton Eskimos v. Montreal Alouettes	Nov. 24, 1956
		Tommy Scott	Edmonton Eskimos v. Hamilton Tiger-Cats	Nov. 23, 1980
Career	5	Hal Patterson	Montreal Alouettes/Hamilton Tiger-Cats	1955–56, 1963
		Brian Kelly	Edmonton Eskimos	1980, 1982, 1986–87

Converts

Game	7	Pep Leadlay	Queens v. Regina Roughriders	Dec. 1, 1923
Career	17	Don Sutherin	Hamilton Tiger-Cats/Ottawa Roughriders/Toronto Argonauts	1961–65, 1968–69

Field Goals

Game	6	Don Sweet	Montreal Alouettes v. Edmonton Eskimos	Nov. 27, 1977
		Paul Osbaldiston	Hamilton Tiger-Cats v. Edmonton Eskimos	Nov. 30, 1986
Career	18	Dave Cutler	Edmonton Eskimos	1973–75, 1977–80, 1982

Source: CFL

FRISBEE (FLYING DISC THROWING)

ORIGINS The design of a carved plastic flying disc was patented in the United States by Fred Morrison in 1948. In 1957 Wham-O Inc. of San Gabriel, Calif. bought Morrison's patent and trademarked the name *FRISBEE* in 1958. In 1968 Wham-O helped form the International FRISBEE Associa-

FREQUENT FLINGERS ■ AMY BEKKEN (LEFT) AND SAM FERRINS (RIGHT) DEMONSTRATE THEIR WORLD RECORD FRISBEE TECHNIQUE.

FLYING DISC RECORDS

Men's Records

Distance Thrown

Distance	Name	Country	Date
623 feet 7 inches	Sam Ferrins	U.S.	July 2, 1988

Throw, Run, Catch

303 feet 11 inches	Hiroshi Oshima	Japan	July 20, 1988

Time Aloft

Time	Name	Country	Date
16.72 sec	Don Cain	U.S.	May 26, 1984

Women's Records

Distance Thrown

Distance	Name	Country	Date
426 feet 9½ inches	Amy Bekkan	U.S.	June 25, 1990

Throw, Run, Catch

196 feet 11 inches	Judy Horowitz	U.S.	June 29, 1985

Time Aloft

Time	Name	Country	Date
11.81 sec	Amy Bekkan	U.S.	Aug. 1, 1991

Source: World Flying Disc Association

tion (IFA) as a vehicle for organizing the *FRISBEE* craze that had swept across the United States. The IFA folded in 1982 and it wasn't until 1986 that the World Flying Disc Federation was formed to organize and standardize rules for the sport.

GOLF

The nationality of the competitors in this section is U.S. unless stated otherwise.

ORIGINS The Chinese Nationalist Golf Association claims that golf (*ch'ui wan*—"the ball-hitting game") was played in China in the 3rd or 2nd century B.C. There is evidence that a game resembling golf was played in the Low Countries (present-day Belgium, Holland and northern France) in the Middle Ages. Scotland, however, is generally regarded as the home of the modern game. The oldest club of which there is written evidence is the Honourable Company of Edinburgh Golfers, Scotland, founded in 1744. The Royal & Ancient Club of St. Andrews (R&A), has been in existence since 1754. The R&A is credited with formulating the rules of golf upon which the modern game is based.

United States There are claims that golf was played in this country as early as the 18th century in North Carolina and Virginia. The oldest recognized club in North America is the Royal Montreal Golf Club, Canada, formed on November 4, 1873. Two clubs claim to be the first established in the U.S.: the Foxberg Golf Club, Clarion County, Pa. (1887), and St. Andrews Golf Club of Yonkers, N.Y. (1888). The United States Golf Association

(USGA) was founded in 1894 as the governing body of golf in the United States.

PROFESSIONAL GOLF (MEN)

GRAND SLAM CHAMPIONSHIPS (THE MAJORS)

GRAND SLAM In 1930, Bobby Jones won the U.S. and British Open Championships and the U.S. and British Amateur Championships. This feat was christened the "Grand Slam." In 1960, the professional Grand Slam (the Masters, U.S. Open, British Open, and Professional Golfers Association [PGA] Championships) gained recognition when Arnold Palmer won the first two legs, the Masters and the U.S. Open. However, he did not complete the set of titles, and the Grand Slam has still not been attained. Ben Hogan came the closest in 1951, when he won the first three legs, but didn't return to the U.S. from Great Britain in time for the PGA Championship.

Most grand slam titles Jack Nicklaus has won the most majors, with 18 professional titles (6 Masters, 4 U.S. Opens, 3 British Opens, 5 PGA Championships).

THE MASTERS See the feature on pages 112–113.

THE UNITED STATES OPEN Inaugurated in 1895, this event is held on a different course each year.

U.S. OPEN CHAMPIONS (1895–1991)

Year	Champion	Year	Champion	Year	Champion	Year	Champion
1895	Horace Rawlins	1919	Walter Hagen	1943	not held	1967	Jack Nicklaus
1896	James Foulis	1920	Edward Ray*	1944	not held	1968	Lee Trevino
1897	Joe Lloyd	1921	Jim Barnes	1945	not held	1969	Orville Moody
1898	Fred Herd	1922	Gene Sarazen	1946	Lloyd Mangrum	1970	Tony Jacklin*
1899	Willie Smith	1923	Bobby Jones	1947	Lew Worsham	1971	Lee Trevino
1900	Harry Vardon*	1924	Cyril Walker	1948	Ben Hogan	1972	Jack Nicklaus
1901	Willie Anderson	1925	Willie MacFarlane	1949	Cary Middlecoff	1973	Johnny Miller
1902	Laurie Auchterlonie	1926	Bobby Jones	1950	Ben Hogan	1974	Hale Irwin
1903	Willie Anderson	1927	Tommy Armour	1951	Ben Hogan	1975	Lou Graham
1904	Willie Anderson	1928	Johnny Farrell	1952	Julius Boros	1976	Jerry Pate
1905	Willie Anderson	1929	Bobby Jones	1953	Ben Hogan	1977	Hubert Green
1906	Alex Smith	1930	Bobby Jones	1954	Ed Furgol	1978	Andy North
1907	Alex Ross	1931	Billy Burke	1955	Jack Fleck	1979	Hale Irwin
1908	Fred McLeod	1932	Gene Sarazen	1956	Cary Middlecoff	1980	Jack Nicklaus
1909	George Sargent	1933	Johnny Goodman	1957	Dick Mayer	1981	David Graham‡
1910	Alex Smith	1934	Olin Dutra	1958	Tommy Bolt	1982	Tom Watson
1911	John McDermott	1935	Sam Parks Jr.	1959	Billy Casper	1983	Larry Nelson
1912	John McDermott	1936	Tony Manero	1960	Arnold Palmer	1984	Fuzzy Zoeller
1913	Francis Ouimet	1937	Ralph Guldahl	1961	Gene Littler	1985	Andy North
1914	Walter Hagen	1938	Ralph Guldahl	1962	Jack Nicklaus	1986	Raymond Floyd
1915	Jerome Travers	1939	Byron Nelson	1963	Julius Boros	1987	Scott Simpson
1916	Charles Evans Jr.	1940	Lawson Little	1964	Ken Venturi	1988	Curtis Strange
1917	not held	1941	Craig Wood	1965	Gary Player†	1989	Curtis Strange
1918	not held	1942	not held	1966	Billy Casper	1990	Hale Irwin
						1991	Payne Stewart

* Great Britain, † South Africa, ‡ Australia

The Open was expanded from a three-day, 36-hole Saturday finish to four days of 18 holes of play in 1965.

Most wins Four players have won the title four times: Willie Anderson (1901, 1903–05); Bobby Jones (1923, 1926, 1929–30); Ben Hogan (1948, 1950–51, 1953); Jack Nicklaus (1962, 1967, 1972, 1980).

Most consecutive wins Three, by Willie Anderson (1903–05).

Lowest 18-hole total (any round) 63, by three players: Johnny Miller at Oakmont Country Club, Pa., on June 17, 1973; Jack Nicklaus and Tom Weiskopf, both at Baltusrol Country Club, Springfield, N.J., on June 12, 1980.

Lowest 72-hole total 272 (63, 71, 70, 68), by Jack Nicklaus at Baltusrol Country Club, Springfield, N.J., in 1980.

Oldest champion 45 years 15 days, Hale Irwin (1990).

Youngest champion 19 years 317 days, John J. McDermott (1911).

THE BRITISH OPEN In ths event, inaugurated in 1860, the first dozen tournaments were staged at Prestwick, Scotland. Since 1873, the locations have varied, but all venues are coastal links courses.

Most wins Harry Vardon won a record six titles, in 1896, 1898–99, 1903, 1911, 1914.

Most consecutive wins 4, Tom Morris Jr. (1868–70, 1872; the event was not held in 1871).

Lowest 18-hole total (any round) 63, by five players: Mark Hayes at Turnberry, Scotland, on July 7, 1977; Isao Aoki (Japan) at Muirfield, Scotland, on July 19, 1980; Greg Norman (Australia) at

BRITISH OPEN CHAMPIONS (1860–1922)

Year	Champion	Country	Year	Champion	Country	Year	Champion	Country
1860	Willie Park Sr.	Great Britain	1881	Robert Ferguson	Great Britain	1902	Sandy Herd	Great Britain
1861	Tom Morris Sr.	Great Britain	1882	Robert Ferguson	Great Britain	1903	Harry Vardon	Great Britain
1862	Tom Morris Sr.	Great Britain	1883	Willie Fernie	Great Britain	1904	Jack White	Great Britain
1863	Willie Park Sr.	Great Britain	1884	Jack Simpson	Great Britain	1905	James Braid	Great Britain
1864	Tom Morris Sr.	Great Britain	1885	Bob Martin	Great Britain	1906	James Braid	Great Britain
1865	Andrew Strath	Great Britain	1886	David Brown	Great Britain	1907	Arnaud Massy	France
1866	Willie Park Sr.	Great Britain	1887	Willie Park Jr.	Great Britain	1908	James Braid	Great Britain
1867	Tom Morris Sr.	Great Britain	1888	Jack Burns	Great Britain	1909	John H. Taylor	Great Britain
1868	Tom Morris Jr.	Great Britain	1889	Willie Park Jr.	Great Britain	1910	James Braid	Great Britain
1869	Tom Morris Jr.	Great Britain	1890	John Ball	Great Britain	1911	Harry Vardon	Great Britain
1870	Tom Morris Jr.	Great Britain	1891	Hugh Kirkaldy	Great Britain	1912	Edward Ray	Great Britain
1871	not held		1892	Harold H. Hilton	Great Britain	1913	John H. Taylor	Great Britain
1872	Tom Morris Jr.	Great Britain	1893	William Auchterlonie	Great Britain	1914	Harry Vardon	Great Britain
1873	Tom Kidd	Great Britain	1894	John H. Taylor	Great Britain	1915	not held	
1874	Mungo Park	Great Britain	1895	John H. Taylor	Great Britain	1916	not held	
1875	Willie Park Sr.	Great Britain	1896	Harry Vardon	Great Britain	1917	not held	
1876	Bob Martin	Great Britain	1897	Harold H. Hilton	Great Britain	1918	not held	
1877	Jamie Anderson	Great Britain	1898	Harry Vardon	Great Britain	1919	not held	
1878	Jamie Anderson	Great Britain	1899	Harry Vardon	Great Britain	1920	George Duncan	Great Britain
1879	Jamie Anderson	Great Britain	1900	John H. Taylor	Great Britain	1921	Jock Hutchinson	U.S.
1880	Robert Ferguson	Great Britain	1901	James Braid	Great Britain	1922	Walter Hagen	U.S.

BRITISH OPEN CHAMPIONS (1860–1991)

Year	Champion	Country	Year	Champion	Country	Year	Champion	Country
1923	Arthur Havers	Great Britain	1946	Sam Snead	U.S.	1969	Tony Jacklin	Great Britain
1924	Walter Hagen	U.S.	1947	Fred Daly	Great Britain	1970	Jack Nicklaus	U.S.
1925	Jim Barnes	U.S.	1948	Henry Cotton	Great Britain	1971	Lee Trevino	U.S.
1926	Bobby Jones	U.S.	1949	Bobby Locke	South Africa	1972	Lee Trevino	U.S.
1927	Bobby Jones	U.S.	1950	Bobby Locke	South Africa	1973	Tom Weiskopf	U.S.
1928	Walter Hagen	U.S.	1951	Max Faulkner	Great Britain	1974	Gary Player	South Africa
1929	Walter Hagen	U.S.	1952	Bobby Locke	South Africa	1975	Tom Watson	U.S.
1930	Bobby Jones	U.S.	1953	Ben Hogan	U.S.	1976	Johnny Miller	U.S.
1931	Tommy Armour	U.S.	1954	Peter Thomson	Australia	1977	Tom Watson	U.S.
1932	Gene Sarazen	U.S.	1955	Peter Thomson	Australia	1978	Jack Nicklaus	U.S.
1933	Densmore Shute	U.S.	1956	Peter Thomson	Australia	1979	Seve Ballesteros	Spain
1934	Henry Cotton	Great Britain	1957	Bobby Locke	South Africa	1980	Tom Watson	U.S.
1935	Alfred Perry	Great Britain	1958	Peter Thomson	Australia	1981	Bill Rogers	U.S.
1936	Alfred Padgham	Great Britain	1959	Gary Player	South Africa	1982	Tom Watson	U.S.
1937	Henry Cotton	Great Britain	1960	Kel Nagle	Australia	1983	Tom Watson	U.S.
1938	Reg Whitcombe	Great Britain	1961	Arnold Palmer	U.S.	1984	Seve Ballesteros	Spain
1939	Dick Burton	Great Britain	1962	Arnold Palmer	U.S.	1985	Sandy Lyle	Great Britain
1940	not held		1963	Bob Charles	New Zealand	1986	Greg Norman	Australia
1941	not held		1964	Tony Lema	U.S.	1987	Nick Faldo	Great Britain
1942	not held		1965	Peter Thomson	Australia	1988	Seve Ballesteros	Spain
1943	not held		1966	Jack Nicklaus	U.S.	1989	Mark Calcavecchia	U.S.
1944	not held		1967	Roberto de Vicenzo	Argentina	1990	Nick Faldo	Great Britain
1945	not held		1968	Gary Player	South Africa	1991	Ian Baker-Finch	Australia

Turnberry, Scotland, on July 18, 1986; Paul Broadhurst (Great Britain) at St. Andrews, Scotland, on July 21, 1990; Jodie Mudd at Royal Birkdale, England, on July 21, 1991.

Lowest 72-hole total 268 (68, 70, 65, 65) by Tom Watson at Turnberry, Scotland in 1977.

Oldest champion 46 years 99 days, Tom Morris Sr. (Great Britain) (1867).

Youngest champion 17 years 249 days, Tom Morris Jr. (Great Britain) (1868).

THE PROFESSIONAL GOLFERS ASSOCIATION (PGA) CHAMPIONSHIP Inaugurated in 1916, the tournament was a match-play event, but switched to a 72-hole stroke-play event in 1958.

Most wins Two players have won the title five times: Walter Hagen (1921, 1924–27); and Jack Nicklaus (1963, 1971, 1973, 1975, 1980).

Most consecutive wins Four, by Walter Hagen (1924–27).

Lowest 18-hole total (any round) 63, by two players: Bruce Crampton (Australia) at Firestone Country Club, Akron, Ohio, in 1975; Ray Floyd at Southern Hills, Tulsa, Okla., in 1982.

Lowest 72-hole total 271 (64, 71, 69, 67), by Bobby Nichols at Columbus Country Club, Ohio in 1964.

Oldest champion 48 years 140 days, Julius Boros (1968).

Youngest champion 20 years 173 days, Gene Sarazen (1922).

Professional Golfers Association (PGA) Tour Records

Most wins (season) Byron Nelson won a record 18 tournaments in 1945.

Most wins (career) Sam Snead won 81 official PGA tour events from 1936–65.

Most consecutive wins 11, Byron Nelson, 1945.

Most wins (same event) Sam Snead won the Greater Greensboro Open eight times to set the individual tournament win mark. His victories came in 1938, 1946, 1949–50, 1955–56, 1960, 1965.

Most consecutive wins (same event) Four, by Walter Hagen, the PGA Championship, 1924–27.

Oldest winner 52 years 10 months, Sam Snead, 1965 Greater Greensboro Open.

Youngest winner 19 years 10 months, Johnny McDermott, 1911 U.S. Open.

Widest winning margin 16 strokes, by Bobby Locke (South Africa), 1948 Chicago Victory National Championship.

PGA CHAMPIONS (1916–1991)

Year	Champion	Year	Champion	Year	Champion
1916	Jim Barnes	1941	Vic Chezzi	1966	Al Geiberger
1917	not held	1942	Sam Snead	1967	Don January
1918	not held	1943	not held	1968	Julius Boros
1919	Jim Barnes	1944	Bob Hamilton	1969	Raymond Floyd
1920	Jock Hutchinson	1945	Byron Nelson	1970	Dave Stockton
1921	Walter Hagen	1946	Ben Hogan	1971	Jack Nicklaus
1922	Gene Sarazen	1947	Jim Ferrier	1972	Gary Player †
1923	Gene Sarazen	1948	Ben Hogan	1973	Jack Nicklaus
1924	Walter Hagen	1949	Sam Snead	1974	Lee Trevino
1925	Walter Hagen	1950	Chandler Harper	1975	Jack Nicklaus
1926	Walter Hagen	1951	Sam Snead	1976	Dave Stockton
1927	Walter Hagen	1952	Jim Turnesa	1977	Lanny Wadkins
1928	Leo Diegel	1953	Walter Burkemo	1978	John Mahaffey
1929	Leo Diegel	1954	Chick Harbert	1979	David Graham‡
1930	Tommy Armour	1955	Doug Ford	1980	Jack Nicklaus
1931	Tom Creavy	1956	Jack Burke Jr.	1981	Larry Nelson
1932	Olin Dutra	1957	Lionel Hebert	1982	Raymond Floyd
1933	Gene Sarazen	1958	Dow Finsterwald	1983	Hal Sutton
1934	Paul Runyan	1959	Bob Rosburg	1984	Lee Trevino
1935	Johnny Revolta	1960	Jay Herbert	1985	Hubert Green
1936	Densmore Shute	1961	Jerry Barber	1986	Bob Tway
1937	Densmore Shute	1962	Gary Player †	1987	Larry Nelson
1938	Paul Runyan	1963	Jack Nicklaus	1988	Jeff Sluman
1939	Henry Picard	1964	Bobby Nichols	1989	Payne Stewart
1940	Byron Nelson	1965	Dave Marr	1990	Wayne Grady‡
				1991	John Daly

† South Africa, ‡ Australia

Inaugurated in 1934, the Masters is the only one of golf's four grand slam events that is always played on the same course, the Augusta National Golf Club, Augusta, Georgia. Noted for its fast greens and beautiful landscaping, Augusta National was designed by Bobby Jones and Dr. Alister MacKenzie, with construction beginning in 1931. Set on 365 acres, the course currently measures 6,905 yards in length at par 72.

MASTERS CHAMPIONS 1934-1991

Year	Champion	Year	Champion
1934	Horton Smith	1965	Jack Nicklaus
1935	Gene Sarazen	1966	Jack Nicklaus
1936	Horton Smith	1967	Gay Brewer
1937	Byron Nelson	1968	Bob Goalby
1938	Henry Picard	1969	George Archer
1939	Ralph Guldahl	1970	Billy Casper
1940	Jimmy Demaret	1971	Charles Coody
1941	Craig Wood	1972	Jack Nicklaus
1942	Byron Nelson	1973	Tommy Aaron
1943	not held	1974	Gary Player (South Africa)
1944	not held		
1945	not held	1975	Jack Nicklaus
1946	Herman Keiser	1976	Raymond Floyd
1947	Jimmy Demaret	1977	Tom Watson
1948	Claude Harmon	1978	Gary Player (South Africa)
1949	Sam Snead		
1950	Jimmy Demaret	1979	Fuzzy Zoeller
1951	Ben Hogan	1980	Seve Ballesteros (Spain)
1952	Sam Snead		
1953	Ben Hogan	1981	Tom Watson
1954	Sam Snead	1982	Craig Stadler
1955	Cary Middlecoff	1983	Seve Ballesteros (Spain)
1956	Jack Burke Jr.	1984	Ben Crenshaw
1957	Doug Ford	1985	Bernhard Langer (Germany)
1958	Arnold Palmer		
1959	Art Wall Jr.	1986	Jack Nicklaus
1960	Arnold Palmer	1987	Larry Mize
1961	Gary Player (South Africa)	1988	Sandy Lyle (Great Britain)
		1989	Nick Faldo (Great Britain)
1962	Arnold Palmer	1990	Nick Faldo (Great Britain)
1963	Jack Nicklaus	1991	Ian Woosnam (Great Britain)
1964	Arnold Palmer		

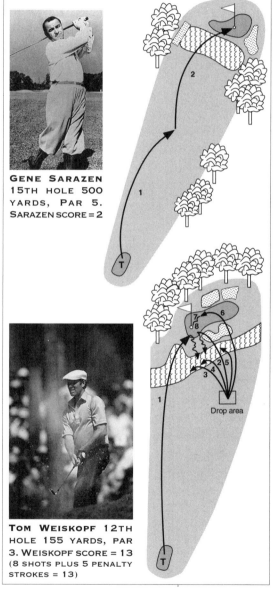

GENE SARAZEN 15TH HOLE 500 YARDS, PAR 5. SARAZEN SCORE = 2

TOM WEISKOPF 12TH HOLE 155 YARDS, PAR 3. WEISKOPF SCORE = 13 (8 SHOTS PLUS 5 PENALTY STROKES = 13)

DOUBLE EAGLE ■ TRAILING BY THREE SHOTS IN THE FINAL ROUND OF THE 1935 EVENT, GENE SARAZEN (UPPER RIGHT) HOLED A 220-YARD FOUR-WOOD AT THE PAR-5 15TH HOLE FOR A DOUBLE EAGLE TWO TO TIE THE LEAD. SARAZEN WON THE TOURNAMENT IN A PLAYOFF. HIS FOUR-WOOD BECAME THE MOST FAMOUS SHOT IN GOLF LORE, AND ESTABLISHED THE MASTERS AS A SPORTS INSTITUTION.

"DECA-BOGEY" ■ THE WORST SCORE IN MASTERS HISTORY, A TEN-OVER-PAR 13, WAS RECORDED BY TOM WEISKOPF (LOWER RIGHT) AT THE 12TH HOLE DURING THE FIRST ROUND OF THE 1980 TOURNAMENT. INCLUDING HIS TEE SHOT, WEISKOPF LOST FIVE BALLS IN RAE'S CREEK, FINALLY FINDING LAND WITH HIS SIXTH, WHERE HE TWO-PUTTED FOR HIS HISTORIC 13.

HIGHEST AND LOWEST SCORES (18 HOLES)

The lowest score is 63, by Nick Price, Zimbabwe, during the third round of the 1986 tournament.
The highest score is 95, by Charles Kunkle, an amateur, during the fourth round of the 1956 tournament.

WORST AND BEST SCORES (AT EACH HOLE)

The worst scores on each hole during the Masters, if done by one player, would have resulted in a round of 162, 90 over par. The best scores would have posted a 35, 37 under par.

Front Nine

Holes	1	2	3	4	5	6	7	8	9	Out
Yards	400	555	360	205	435	180	360	535	435	3,465
Par	4	5	4	3	4	3	4	5	4	36
Price	5	4	4	3	3	2	4	4	4	33
Kunkle	7	6	5	5	6	4	5	6	5	49
Worst	7	10	8	7	8	7	8	12	8	75
Best	2	3	2	2	2	1	2	2	2	18

Back Nine

Holes	10	11	12	13	14	15	16	17	18	In	Out	Total
Yards	485	455	155	465	405	500	170	400	405	3,440	3,465	6,905
Par	4	4	3	5	4	5	3	4	4	36	36	72
Price	3	3	2	4	4	4	2	4	4	30	33	63
Kunkle	5	4	5	6	5	8	4	4	5	46	49	95
Worst	8	9	13	13	7	11	11	7	8	87	75	162
Best	2	2	1	3	2	2	1	2	2	17	18	35

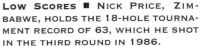

LOW SCORES ■ NICK PRICE, ZIMBABWE, HOLDS THE 18-HOLE TOURNAMENT RECORD OF 63, WHICH HE SHOT IN THE THIRD ROUND IN 1986.

MASTERS RECORDS

1st Round	64	Lloyd Mangrum	1940
		Mike Donald	1990
2nd Round	64	Miller Barber	1979
3rd Round	63	Nick Price (Zimbabwe)	1986
4th Round	64	Maurice Bembridge (Great Britain)	1974
		Hale Irwin	1975
		Gary Player (South Africa)	1978
		Greg Norman (Australia)	1988
Front Nine	30	Johnny Miller, 3rd round	1975
		Greg Norman, 4th round	1988
Back Nine	30	Jimmy Demaret, 1st round	1940
		Gene Littler, 3rd round	1966
		Ben Hogan, 3rd round	1967
		Nick Price, 3rd round	1986
		Miller Barber, 4th round	1970
		Maurice Bembridge, 4th round	1974
		Gary Player, 4th round	1978
		Jack Nicklaus, 4th round	1986
36 Holes	131	Johnny Miller (3rd and 4th rounds)	1975
		Ray Floyd (1st and 2nd rounds)	1976
54 Holes	201	Ray Floyd (1st, 2nd and 3rd rounds)	1976
72 Holes	271	Jack Nicklaus (67–71–64–69)	1965
		Ray Floyd (65–66–70–70)	1976
Most Wins	6	Jack Nicklaus (1963, 1965–66, 1972, 1975, 1986)	
Consecutive Wins	2	Jack Nicklaus	1965–66
		Nick Faldo (Great Britain)	1989–90
Oldest Champion	46 years 81 days	Jack Nicklaus	1986
Youngest Champion	23 years 2 days	Severiano Ballesteros (Spain)	1980

SOURCE ■ BILL INGLISH, MASTERS STATISTICIAN

MOST WINS ■ JACK NICKLAUS HAS WON A RECORD SIX GREEN JACKETS. HE IS SEEN HERE LEAVING THE 18TH GREEN IN 1986, FOLLOWING A BACK NINE CHARGE THAT CATAPULTED HIM TO HIS SIXTH WIN.

LOWEST SCORES

Nine holes 27, by two players: Mike Souchak at the Brackenridge Park Golf Course, San Antonio, Texas, on the back nine of the first round of the 1955 Texas Open; Andy North at the En-Joie Golf Club, Endicott, N.Y., on the back nine of the first round of the 1975 B.C. Open.

18 holes 59, by two players: Al Geiberger at the Colonial Country Club, Memphis, Tenn., during the second round of the 1977 Danny Thomas Memphis Classic; Chip Beck at the Sunrise Golf Club, Las Vegas, Nev., during the third round of the 1991 Las Vegas Invitational.

36 holes 125, by two players: Ron Streck at the Oak Hills Country Club, San Antonio, Texas, during the third and fourth rounds of the 1978 Texas Open; Blaine McCallister at the Oakwood Country Club, Coal Valley, Ill., during the second and third rounds of the 1988 Hardee's Golf Classic.

54 holes 189, by Chandler Harper at the Brackenridge Park Golf Course, San Antonio, Texas, during the last three rounds of the 1954 Texas Open.

72 holes 257, by Mike Souchak at the Brackenridge Park Golf Course, San Antonio, Texas, at the 1955 Texas Open.

Most shots under par 31, by two players: Andrew Magee and D.A. Weibring at the 90-hole 1991 Las Vegas Invitational. Magee won the tournament in a playoff. The most shots under par in a 72-hole tournament is 27, shared by two players: Mike Souchak, at the 1955 Texas Open; and Ben Hogan, at the 1945 Portland Invitational.

HIGHEST EARNINGS

Season Tom Kite, $1,359,278 in 1989.

Career Tom Kite, $6,655,474, 1971–91.

Most times leading money winner Eight, Jack Nicklaus, 1964–65, 1967, 1971–73, 1975–76.

SENIOR PGA TOUR

The Senior PGA tour was established in 1982. Players 50 years and older are eligible to compete on the tour. Tournaments vary between 54- and 72-hole stroke-play.

Most wins 24, by Miller Barber (1981–90).

Most wins (season) Nine, by Peter Thomson, 1985.

Most consecutive wins Three, by two players: Bob Charles and Chi Chi Rodriguez, both in 1987.

HIGHEST EARNINGS

Season $1,190,518, Lee Trevino in 1990.

Career $3,168,642, Bob Charles (New Zealand), 1986–91.

THE PGA EUROPEAN TOUR

Most wins (season) Seven, by two players: Norman von Nida (Australia), 1947; and Flory van Donck (Belgium), 1953.

Most wins (career) 49, by Severiano Ballesteros (Spain), 1976–91.

59 . . . AGAIN ■ CHIP BECK TIED THE PGA TOUR 18-HOLE LOW SCORE RECORD DURING THE THIRD ROUND OF THE 1991 LAS VEGAS INVITATIONAL.

HIGHEST EARNINGS

Season £574,166, by Ian Woosnam (Great Britain) in 1990.

Career £2,889,973, by Severiano Ballesteros (Spain), 1974–91.

Most times leading money winner Six, Severiano Ballesteros, 1976–78, 1986, 1988, 1991.

RYDER CUP A biennial match-play competition between professional representative teams of the United States and Europe (Great Britain and Ireland prior to 1979), this event was launched in 1927. The U.S. leads the series 22–5, with two ties.

Most individual wins Arnold Palmer has won the most matches in Ryder Cup competition with 22 victories out of 32 played.

Most selections Christy O'Connor Sr. (Great Britain and Ireland) has played in the most contests, with 10 selections 1955–73.

PROFESSIONAL GOLF (WOMEN)

GRAND SLAM CHAMPIONSHIPS

GRAND SLAM A Grand Slam in ladies' professional golf has been recognized since 1955. From 1955–66, the United States Open, Ladies Professional Golf Association (LPGA) Championship, Western Open and Titleholders Championship served as the "majors." From 1967–82 the Grand Slam events changed, as first the Western Open (1967) and then the Titleholders Championship (1972) were discontinued. Since 1983, the U.S. Open, LPGA Championship, du Maurier Classic and Nabisco Dinah Shore have comprised the Grand Slam events.

Most grand slam titles Patty Berg has won the most majors, with 15 titles (1 U.S. Open, 7 Titleholders, 7 Western Open).

THE UNITED STATES OPEN In this competition, inaugurated in 1946, the first event was played as a match-play tournament; however, since 1947, the 72-hole stroke-play format has been used.

U.S. OPEN CHAMPIONS (1946–1991)

Year	Champion	Year	Champion	Year	Champion
1946	Patty Berg	1961	Mickey Wright	1976	JoAnne Carner
1947	Betty Jameson	1962	Murle Lindstrom	1977	Hollis Stacy
1948	Babe Zaharias	1963	Mary Mills	1978	Hollis Stacy
1949	Louise Suggs	1964	Mickey Wright	1979	Jerilyn Britz
1950	Babe Zaharias	1965	Carol Mann	1980	Amy Alcott
1951	Betsy Rawls	1966	Sandra Spuzich	1981	Pat Bradley
1952	Louise Suggs	1967	Catherine Lacoste‡	1982	Janet Alex
1953	Betsy Rawls	1968	Susie Berning	1983	Jan Stephenson
1954	Babe Zaharias	1969	Donna Caponi	1984	Hollis Stacy
1955	Fay Crocker	1970	Donna Caponi	1985	Kathy Baker
1956	Kathy Cornelius	1971	JoAnne Carner	1986	Jane Geddes
1957	Betsy Rawls	1972	Susie Berning	1987	Laura Davies*
1958	Mickey Wright	1973	Susie Berning	1988	Liselotte Neumann †
1959	Mickey Wright	1974	Sandra Haynie	1989	Betsy King
1960	Betsy Rawls	1975	Sandra Palmer	1990	Betsy King
				1991	Meg Mallon

* Great Britain, † Sweden, ‡ France

Most wins Two players have won the title four times: Betsy Rawls (1951, 1953, 1957, 1960); Mickey Wright (1958–59, 1961, 1964).

Most consecutive wins Two, by five players: Mickey Wright (1958–59); Donna Caponi (1969–70); Susie Berning (1972–73); Hollis Stacy (1977–78); Betsy King (1989–90).

Lowest 18-hole total 65, by three players: Sally Little at Country Club of Indianapolis, Ind., in 1978; Judy Dickinson at Baltusrol Golf Club, Springfield, N.J., in 1985; Ayako Okamoto (Japan) at Indian Wood Golf and Country Club, Lake Orion, Mich., in 1989.

Lowest 72-hole total 277, by Liselotte Neumann (Sweden) at Baltimore Country Club, Md., in 1988.

Oldest champion 40 years 11 months, Fay Croker (1955).

Youngest champion 22 years 5 days, Catherine Lacoste (France; 1967).

LPGA CHAMPIONSHIP This event was inaugurated in 1955; since 1987, it has been officially called the Mazda LPGA Championship.

Most wins Mickey Wright has won the LPGA a record four times: 1958, 1960–61, 1963.

Most consecutive wins Two, by two players: Mickey Wright (1960–61); Patty Sheehan (1983–84).

DINAH-MITE ■ AMY ALCOTT'S 1991 NABISCO DINAH SHORE VICTORY MARKED HER RECORD-SETTING THIRD WIN IN THE TOURNAMENT.

LPGA CHAMPIONS (1955–1991)

Year	Champion	Year	Champion	Year	Champion
1955	Beverly Hanson	1967	Kathy Whitworth	1979	Donna Caponi
1956	Marlene Hagge	1968	Sandra Post	1980	Sally Little
1957	Louise Suggs	1969	Betsy Rawls	1981	Donna Caponi
1958	Mickey Wright	1970	Shirley Englehorn	1982	Jan Stephenson
1959	Betsy Rawls	1971	Kathy Whitworth	1983	Patty Sheehan
1960	Mickey Wright	1972	Kathy Ahem	1984	Patty Sheehan
1961	Mickey Wright	1973	Mary Mills	1985	Nancy Lopez
1962	Judy Kimball	1974	Sandra Haynie	1986	Pat Bradley
1963	Mickey Wright	1975	Kathy Whitworth	1987	Jane Geddes
1964	Mary Mills	1976	Betty Burfeindt	1988	Sherri Turner
1965	Sandra Haynie	1977	Chako Higuchi	1989	Nancy Lopez
1966	Gloria Ehret	1978	Nancy Lopez	1990	Beth Daniel
				1991	Meg Mallon

Lowest 18-hole total 64, by Patty Sheehan at the Jack Nicklaus Sports Center, Kings Island, Ohio, in 1984.

Lowest 72-hole total 272, by Patty Sheehan at the Jack Nicklaus Sports Center, Kings Island, Ohio in 1984.

NABISCO DINAH SHORE Inaugurated in 1972, this event was formerly called the Colgate-Dinah Shore (1972–82). The event was designated a "major" in 1983. Mission Hills Country Club, Rancho Mirage, Calif. is the permanent site.

NABISCO DINAH SHORE CHAMPIONS (1972–1991)

Year	Champion	Year	Champion
1972	Jane Blalock	1982	Sally Little
1973	Mickey Wright	1983	Amy Alcott
1974	Jo Ann Prentice	1984	Juli Inkster
1975	Sandra Palmer	1985	Alice Miller
1976	Judy Rankin	1986	Pat Bradley
1977	Kathy Whitworth	1987	Betsy King
1978	Sandra Post	1988	Amy Alcott
1979	Sandra Post	1989	Juli Inkster
1980	Donna Caponi	1990	Betsy King
1981	Nancy Lopez	1991	Amy Alcott

Most wins Amy Alcott has won the title three times: 1983, 1988 and 1991.

Most consecutive wins Two, by Sandra Post (1978–79).

Lowest 18-hole total 64, by two players: Nancy Lopez in 1981; Sally Little in 1982.

Lowest 72-hole total 273, by Amy Alcott in 1991.

DU MAURIER CLASSIC Inaugurated in 1973, this event was formerly known as La Canadienne (1973) and the Peter Jackson Classic (1974–82). Granted "major" status in 1979, the tournament is held annually at different sites in Canada.

Most wins Pat Bradley has won this event a record three times, 1980, 1985–86.

Most consecutive wins Two, by Pat Bradley (1985–86).

Lowest 18-hole total 64, by two players: JoAnne Carner at St. George's Country Club, Toronto, Canada in 1978; Jane Geddes at Beaconsfield Country Club, Montreal, Canada in 1985.

Lowest 72-hole total 276, by three players. Pat Bradley and Ayako Okamato (Japan) tied in regulation play in 1986 at the Board of Trade Country Club, Toronto. Bradley defeated Okamoto for the title in a sudden-death playoff. Cathy Johnston matched Bradley and Okamoto in 1990 at Westmont Golf and Country Club, Kitchener, Ontario.

LADIES PROFESSIONAL GOLF ASSOCIATION (LPGA) TOUR

ORIGINS In 1944, three women golfers, Hope Seignious, Betty Hicks and Ellen Griffin, launched the Women's Professional Golf Association (WPGA). By 1947 the WPGA was unable to sustain the tour at the level that was hoped, and it seemed certain that women's professional golf would fade away. However, Wilson Sporting Goods stepped in, overhauled the tour and called it the Ladies Professional Golf Association. In 1950, the LPGA received its official charter.

DU MAURIER CLASSIC CHAMPIONS (1973–1991)

Year	Champion	Year	Champion	Year	Champion
1973	Jocelyne Bourassa	1979	Amy Alcott	1985	Pat Bradley
1974	Carole Jo Skala	1980	Pat Bradley	1986	Pat Bradley
1975	JoAnne Carner	1981	Jan Stephenson	1987	Jody Rosenthal
1976	Donna Caponi	1982	Sandra Haynie	1988	Sally Little
1977	Judy Rankin	1983	Hollis Stacy	1989	Tammie Green
1978	JoAnne Carner	1984	Juli Inkster	1990	Cathy Johnston
				1991	Nancy Scranton

Most wins (career) 88, by Kathy Whitworth, 1962–85.

Most wins (season) 13, by Mickey Wright, in 1963.

Most consecutive wins (scheduled events) Four, by two players: Mickey Wright, on two occasions, 1962, 1963; Kathy Whitworth, 1969.

Most consecutive wins (in events participated in) Five, by Nancy Lopez between May and June 1978.

Most wins (same event) Seven, by Patty Berg, who won two tournaments, the Titleholders Championship and the Western Open, both now defunct, on seven occasions during her illustrious career. She won the Titleholders in 1937–39, 1948, 1953, 1955, 1957; and the Western in 1941, 1943, 1948, 1951, 1955, 1957–58.

Oldest winner 46 years 5 months 9 days, JoAnne Carner at the 1985 Safeco Classic.

Youngest winner 18 years 14 days Marlene Hagge at the 1952 Sarasota Open.

Widest margin of victory 14 strokes, by two players: Louise Suggs in the 1949 U.S. Open; Cindy Mackey in the 1986 Mastercard International.

MOMMA TIME ■ "BIG MOMMA" JOANNE CARNER HOLDS THE LPGA RECORD FOR THE OLDEST PLAYER TO WIN A TOUR EVENT.

RECORD FILE: PAT BRADLEY

BORN March 24, 1951, Westford, Mass.

LPGA TOUR CAREER STATISTICS
1974–91

Year	Events	Wins	Low 18 Holes	Earnings
1974–91	485	30	63	$4,109,165*

RECORD NOTES Bradley has won six majors, including a record three du Maurier Classic wins, 1980, 1985–86. Bradley was the first player to earn $2 million (1986), $3 million (1990), and $4 million (1991) in LPGA Tour prize money. Bradley shares the LPGA Tour nine-hole lowest score record, 28; and holds the 54-hole low score, 197.

*indicates all-time record.

HIGHEST EARNINGS

Season $863,578, by Beth Daniel in 1990.

Career $4,109,165 by Pat Bradley, 1974–91.

Most times leading money winner Eight, Kathy Whitworth, 1965–68, 1970–73.

LOWEST SCORES

Nine holes 28, by four players: Mary Beth Zimmerman at the Rail Golf Club, Springfield, Ill., during the 1984 Rail Charity Golf Classic; Pat Bradley at the Green Gables Country Club, Denver, Colo., during the 1984 Columbia Savings Classic; Muffin Spencer-Devlin at the Knollwood Country Club, Elmsford, N.Y., during the 1985 MasterCard International Pro-Am; Peggy Kirsch at the Squaw-Creek Country Club, Vienna, Ohio during the 1991 Phar-Mar in Youngstown.

18 holes 62, by three players: Mickey Wright at Hogan Park Golf Club, Midland, Texas, in the first round of the 1964 Tall City Open; Vicki Fergon at Alamaden Golf & Country Club, San Jose, Calif., in the second round of the 1984 San Jose Classic; and Laura Davies (Great Britain) at the Rail Golf Club, Springfield, Ill., during the 1991 Rail Charity Golf Classic.

36 holes 129, by Judy Dickinson at Pasadena Yacht & Country Club, St. Petersburg, Fla., during the 1985 S&H Golf Classic.

54 holes 197, by Pat Bradley at the Rail Golf Club, Springfield, Ill., in the 1991 Rail Charity Golf Classic.

72 holes 268, by Nancy Lopez at the Willow Creek Golf Club, High Point, N.C. in the 1985 Henredon Classic.

AMATEUR GOLF (MEN)

UNITED STATES AMATEUR CHAMPIONSHIP Inaugurated in 1895, the initial format was match-play competition. In 1965, the format was changed to stroke-play; however, since 1972, the event has been played under the original match-play format.

Most wins Five, by Bobby Jones, 1924–25, 1927–28, 1930.

Lowest score (stroke-play) 279, Lanny Wadkins, 1970.

Biggest winning margin (match-play: final) 12 & 11, Charles Macdonald, 1895.

WALKER CUP A biennial match-play competition between amateur representative teams of the U.S. and Great Britain and Ireland. It was instituted in 1921, but has been known as the Walker Cup since 1922. The U.S. leads the series 29–3, with one tie.

Most wins (individual) Jay Sigel has won a record 16 matches of 30 played.

Most selections Joseph Carr (Great Britain and Ireland) has played in a record 10 contests, 1947–67.

NCAA CHAMPIONSHIP The men's championship was initiated in 1897 as a match-play championship. In 1967 the format was switched to stroke-play.

Most titles (team) Yale has won the most team championships with 21 victories (1897–98, 1902, 1905–13, 1915, 1924–26, 1931–33, 1936, 1943).

Most titles (individual) The only golfer to win three individual titles is Ben Crenshaw (Texas), 1971–73.

TRIPLE TITLEHOLDER ■ BEN CRENSHAW IS THE ONLY PLAYER TO HAVE WON THE NCAA INDIVIDUAL TITLE THREE TIMES, 1971–73.

AMATEUR GOLF (WOMEN)

UNITED STATES AMATEUR CHAMPIONSHIP This competition was first held in 1895.

Most wins Six, Glenna C. Vare (née Collett), 1922, 1925, 1928–30, 1935.

CURTIS CUP A biennial match-play competition between women's amateur representative teams of the U.S. and Great Britain and Ireland. The U.S. leads the series, first held in 1932, 20–4, with two ties.

NCAA CHAMPIONSHIP This competition was first held in 1982.

Most team titles Two, by three colleges: Florida, 1985–86; Tulsa, 1982, 1988; San Jose State, 1987, 1989.

Most individual titles No golfer has won the title more than once.

GYMNASTICS

ORIGINS The ancient Greeks and Romans were exponents of gymnastics, as shown by demonstration programs in the ancient Olympic Games (776 B.C. to A.D. 393). Modern training techniques were developed in Germany toward the end of the 18th century. Johann Friedrich Simon was the first teacher of the modern methods, at Basedow's School, Dessau, Germany in 1776. Friedrich Jahn, who founded the Turnverein in Berlin, Germany in 1811, is regarded as the most influential of the gymnastics pioneers. The International Gymnastics Federation (IGF) was formed in 1891.

United States Gymnastics was introduced to the United States in the 19th century. With the advent of the modern Olympic Games, interest in the sport grew in this country, and in 1920 the United States entered its first gymnastics team in the Games. The sport was governed by the Amateur Athletic Union (AAU) and then by the National Collegiate Athletic Association (NCAA) until 1963, when the United States Gymnastics Federation (USGF) was formed. The USGF is still the governing body for the sport, and has its headquarters in Indianapolis, Ind.

OLYMPIC GAMES Gymnastics was included in the first modern Olympic Games in 1896; however, women's competition was not included until 1928.

Most gold medals Larissa Latynina (USSR) has won nine gold medals: six individual—all-around title, 1956 and 1960; floor exercise, 1956, 1960 and 1964; vault, 1956; and three team titles—1956, 1960 and 1964. In men's competition, Sawao Kato (Japan) has won eight gold medals: five individual—all-around title, 1968 and 1972; floor exercise, 1968; and parallel bars, 1972 and 1976; and three team titles—1968, 1972 and 1976.

Vera Caslavska (Czechoslovakia) has won a record seven individual gold medals: all-around title, 1964 and 1968; uneven bars, 1968; beam, 1964; floor exercise, 1968; and vault, 1964 and 1968. In men's competition Boris Shakhlin and Nikolai Andrianov (both USSR) have each won six individual titles. Shakhlin won the all-around title, 1960; parallel bars, 1960; pommel horse, 1956, 1960; horizontal bar, 1964; vault, 1960. Andrianov won the all-around title, 1976; floor exercise, 1972, 1976; pommel horse, 1976; and vault, 1976 and 1980.

Most medals Larissa Latynina (USSR) has won 18 medals, the most of any athlete in any sport. She has won nine gold (see above); five silver—all-around title, 1964; uneven bars, 1956 and 1960; beam, 1960; vault, 1964; and four bronze—uneven bars, 1964; beam, 1964; vault, 1964; and the portable apparatus team event (now discontinued) in 1956. Nikolai Andrianov holds the men's record at 15, which is the most by any male athlete in any sport. He won seven gold (see above); five silver—team event, 1972 and 1976; all-around title, 1980; floor exercise, 1980; parallel bars, 1976; and three bronze—pommel horse, 1976; horizontal bar, 1980; and vault, 1972.

Most medals (country) The USSR has dominated the gymnastics competition, winning 186 medals: in men's competition, 40 gold, 38 silver, 18 bronze; in women's competition, 34 gold, 29 silver, 27 bronze.

United States Anton Heida and George Eyser won six medals at the 1904 Games. Heida won five gold and a silver; Eyser, who, remarkably, had a wooden leg, won three gold, two silver and a bronze. In women's competition, Mary Lou Retton won five medals in 1984: gold in the all-around event, two silver and two bronze. Overall, U.S. athletes have won 64 medals: in men's competition, 21 gold, 15 silver and 19 bronze; in women's competition, one gold, three silver and five bronze.

Highest score Nadia Comaneci (Romania) was the first to achieve a perfect score (10.00) in the Olympics, and achieved seven in all at Montreal, Canada in July 1976. The first man to achieve a perfect score in Olympic competition was Aleksandr Dityatin (USSR) in the vault at the 1980 games.

WORLD CHAMPIONSHIPS First held in Antwerp, Belgium in 1903, the championships were discontinued in 1913. Reintroduced in 1922, the event was held quadrenially until 1979, when the format became biennial. Until 1979 the Olympic Games served as the world championships, and results from Olympic competition are included in world championship statistics.

Most titles Larissa Latynina (USSR) won 17 world titles: five team and 12 individual, 1956–64. In men's competition, Boris Shakhlin (USSR) has won 13 titles: three team and 10 individual, 1954–64.

United States The most successful American gymnast has been Kurt Thomas, who has won three gold medals: floor exercise, 1978; floor exercise and horizontal bar, 1979. The only American to win an all-around title is Kim Zmeskal, who won the 1991 women's title.

UNITED STATES NATIONAL CHAMPIONSHIPS

Most titles Alfred A. Jochim won a record seven men's all-around U.S. titles, 1925–30 and 1933, and a total of 34 at all exercises between 1923 and 1934. The women's record is six all-around, 1945–46 and 1949–52, and 39 at all exercises, including 11 in succession at balance beam, 1941–51, by Clara Marie Schroth Lomady.

NCAA CHAMPIONSHIPS (MEN) The men's competition was first held in 1932.

Most team titles The most team championships won is nine, by two colleges: Illinois, 1939–42, 1950, 1955–56, 1958, 1989; Penn State, 1948, 1953–54, 1957, 1959–61, 1965, 1976.

INDIVIDUAL RECORDS, 1932–91

Most titles (one year) Four, by two gymnasts: Jean Cronstedt, Penn State, won the all-around

title, parallel bar, horizontal bar and floor exercise in 1954; Robert Lynn, Southern Cal., won the all-around title, parallel bar, horizontal bar and floor exercise in 1962.

Most titles (career) Seven, by two gymnasts: Joe Giallombardo, Illinois, won the tumbling, 1938–40, all-around title, 1938–40; and floor exercise, 1938; Jim Hartung, Nebraska, won the all-around title, 1980–81; rings, 1980–82; and parallel bar, 1981–82.

NCAA CHAMPIONSHIPS (WOMEN) The women's competition was first held in 1982.

Most team titles The most team championships won is six, by Utah, 1982–86, 1990.

INDIVIDUAL RECORDS, 1982-91

Most titles (one year) Three, by two gymnasts: Kelly Garrison-Steves, Oklahoma, won the all-

ALL-AROUND CHAMPION ■ KIM ZMESKAL WON THE 1991 WOMEN'S ALL-AROUND WORLD CHAMPIONSHIP, BECOMING THE FIRST U.S. GYMNAST TO WIN AN OVERALL TITLE.

around title, balance beam and uneven bars in 1988; Hope Spivey, Georgia, won the all-around title, floor exercise and vault in 1991.

Most titles (career) Four, by three gymnasts: Kelly Garrison-Steves, Oklahoma, won the all-around title, 1987–88; balance beam, 1988; uneven bars, 1988; Kim Hamilton, UCLA, won the floor exercise, 1987–89, and vault, 1989; Penney Hauschild, Alabama, won the all-around title, 1985–86; uneven bars, 1985; and floor exercise, 1986.

MODERN RHYTHMIC GYMNASTICS

Modern rhythmic gymnastics involves complex body movements combined with handling of apparatus such as ropes, hoops, balls, clubs and ribbons. The performance must include required elements, and the choreography must cover the entire floor area and include elements such as jumps, pivots and leaps.

ORIGINS In 1962 the International Gymnastics Federation (IGF) officially recognized rhythmic gymnastics as a distinct sport. The first world championships were held in 1963 and the sport was included in the Olympic Games in 1984.

OLYMPIC GAMES No gymnast has won more than one medal in Olympic competition. Marina Lobach (USSR) won the 1988 Olympic title with perfect scores of 60.00 points in each of her events.

WORLD CHAMPIONSHIPS

Most titles (individual) Maria Gigova (Bulgaria) has won three individual world championships in 1969, 1971 and 1973 (tied).

Most titles (country) Bulgaria has won eight team championships: 1969, 1971, 1973, 1981, 1983, 1985, 1987 and 1989 (tie).

HANG GLIDING

ORIGINS In the 11th century the monk Eilmer is reported to have flown from the 60-foot tower of Malmesbury Abbey, Wiltshire, England. The earliest modern pioneer was Otto Lilienthal (Germany), with about 2,500 flights in gliders of his own construction between 1891 and 1896. In the 1950s, Professor Francis Rogallo of the National Space Agency developed a flexible "wing" from his space capsule reentry research.

WORLD RECORDS The *Fédération Aéronautique Internationale* recognizes world records for flexible-wing, rigid-wing, and multiplace flexible-wing.

FLEXIBLE WING—SINGLE PLACE DISTANCE RECORDS (MEN)

Straight line Larry Tudor (U.S.) piloted a Wills Wing HPAT 158 for a straight-line distance of 303.36 miles, from Hobbs, N. Mex. to Elkhart, Kans., on July 3, 1990.

Single turnpoint Christian Durif (France) piloted a La Mouette Compact 15 a single-turnpoint record 158.94 miles over Owens Valley, Calif. on July 3, 1990.

Triangular course James Lee Jr. (U.S.) piloted a Willis Wing HPAT 158 for a triangular course record 121.82 miles over Garcia, Colo. on July 4, 1991.

Out and return The out and return goal distance record is 192.818 miles, set by two pilots on the same day, July 26, 1988, over Lone Pine, Calif.: Larry Tudor, Wills Wing HPAT 158; Geoffrey Loyns (Great Britain), Enterprise Wings.

Altitude gain Larry Tudor set a height gain record of 14,250.69 feet flying a G2-155 over Horseshoe Meadows, Calif. on August 4, 1985.

FLEXIBLE WING—SINGLE PLACE DISTANCE RECORDS (WOMEN)

Straight line Kari Castle (U.S.) piloted a Wills Wing AT 145 a straight-line distance of 208.63 miles over Lone Pine, Calif. on July 22, 1991.

Single turnpoint Kari Castle piloted a Pacific Airwave Magic Kiss a single-turnpoint distance of 181.47 miles over Hobbs, N.Mex. on July 1, 1990.

Triangular course Judy Leden (Great Britain) flew a triangular course record 70.173 miles over Austria on June 22, 1991.

Out and return The out and return goal distance record is 81.99 miles, set by Tover Buas-Hansen (Norway), piloting an International Axis over Owens Valley, Calif. on July 6, 1989.

Altitude gain Tover Buas-Hansen set an altitude gain record of 11,998.62 feet, piloting an International Axis over Bishop Airport, Calif. on July 6, 1989.

RIGID WING—SINGLE PLACE DISTANCE RECORDS (MEN)

Straight line The straight-line distance record is 139.07 miles, set by William Reynolds (U.S), piloting a Wills Wing over Lone Pine, Calif. on June 27, 1988.

Out and return The out and return goal distance is 47.46 miles, set by Randy Bergum (U.S.), piloting an Easy Riser over Big Pine, Calif. on July 12, 1988.

Altitude gain Rainer Scholl (South Africa) set an altitude gain record of 12,532.80 feet on May 8, 1985.

FLEXIBLE WING—MULTIPLACE DISTANCE RECORDS (MEN)

Straight line The straight line distance record is 100.60 miles, set by Larry Tudor and Eri Fujita, flying a Comet II-185 on July 12, 1985.

Out and return The out and return goal distance record is 81.99 miles, set by Kevin and Tom Klinefelter (U.S.) on July 6, 1989.

Altitude gain Tom and Kevin Klinefelter set an altitude record of 10,997.30 feet on July 6, 1989 over Bishop Airport, Calif. flying a Moyes Delta Glider.

HARNESS RACING

Harness racing involves two styles of racing: trotting and pacing. The distinction between trotters and pacers is in the gait of the horses. The trotting gait requires the simultaneous use of the diagonally opposite legs, while pacers thrust out their fore and hind legs simultaneously on one side.

ORIGINS Trotting races are known to have been held in Valkenburg, the Netherlands in 1554. There is also evidence of trotting races in England in the late 16th century.

United States Harness racing became popular in the United States in the mid-19th century. The National Trotting Association was founded, originally as the National Association for the Promotion of the Interests of the Trotting Turf, in 1870, and is still the governing body for the sport in the United States.

TROTTING

HORSES' RECORDS

VICTORIES

Career Goldsmith Maid won an all-time record 350 races (including dashes and heats) from 1864 through 1877.

Season Make Believe won a record 53 races in 1949.

HIGHEST EARNINGS

Career The greatest career earnings for any harness horse is $4,408,857, by Ourasi (France), 1986–89. The all-time record for trotters racing in North America is $3,907,452, by Mack Lobell, 1986–90.

Season The single-season earnings record for a trotter is $1,610,608, by Prakas in 1985.

Race The richest race in the trotting calendar is the Hambletonian. The richest Hambletonian was the 1990 event, with a total purse of $1,346,000. Harmonious won a record first-place purse of $673,000.

INDIVIDUAL RACES

THE TRIPLE CROWN The Triple Crown for trotters consists of three races: Hambletonian, Kentucky Futurity and Yonkers Trot. Six trotters have won the triple crown.

TRIPLE CROWN WINNERS—TROTTERS

Year	Horse	Driver
1955	Scott Frost	Joe O'Brien
1963	Speedy Scot	Ralph Baldwin
1964	Ayres	John Simpson Sr.
1968	Nevele Pride	Stanley Dancer
1969	Lindy's Pride	Howard Beissinger
1972	Super Bowl	Stanley Dancer

HAMBLETONIAN The most famous race in North American harness racing, the Hambletonian, was first run in 1926. The Hambletonian has been run at six venues: New York State Fairgrounds, Syracuse, N.Y. (1926 and 1928); The Red Mile, Lexington, Ky. (1927 and 1929); Good Time Park, Goshen, N.Y. (1930–42, 1944–56); Empire City,

Yonkers, N.Y. (1943); Du Quoin State Fair, Du Quoin, Ill. (1957–80); and The Meadowlands, N.J. (1981–present). The Hambletonian is open to three-year-olds and is run over one mile.

Fastest time The fastest time is 1 minute 53⅗ seconds, by Mack Lobell, driven by John Campbell, in 1987.

Most wins (driver) Three drivers have won the Hambletonian four times: Ben White, 1933, 1936, 1942 and 1943; Stanley Dancer, 1968, 1972, 1975 and 1983; William Haughton, 1974, 1976–77 and 1980.

KENTUCKY FUTURITY First held in 1893, the Kentucky Futurity is a one-mile race for three-year-olds, raced at The Red Mile, Lexington, Ky.

Fastest time Two trotters hold the race record of 1 minute 54 ⅖ seconds: Peace Corps, driven by John Campbell, in 1989; and Star Mystic, driven by Jan Johnson, in 1990.

Most wins (driver) Ben White has driven the winning trotter seven times: 1916, 1922, 1924–25, 1933, 1936–37.

YONKERS TROT First run in 1955, when it was known as "The Yonkers." This race has been known since 1975 as the Yonkers Trot. Run over one mile for three-year-olds, the race is currently staged at Yonkers Raceway, N.Y.

Fastest time The fastest time is 1 minute 57⅘ seconds, by Mack Lobell, driven by John Campbell, in 1987.

Most wins (driver) Stanley Dancer has driven the winning trotter six times: 1959, 1965, 1968, 1971–72 and 1975.

PACERS

HORSES' RECORDS

VICTORIES

Career Single G won 262 races (including dashes and heats), 1918–26.

Career (modern record) Symbol Allen won 241 races from 1943 through 1958.

Season Victory Hy won a record 65 races in 1950.

Consecutive wins Carty Nagle won 41 consecutive races from 1937 through 1938.

FAST PACE ■ PRECIOUS BUNNY SET THE SINGLE-SEASON PACER EARNINGS RECORD OF $2,217,222 IN 1991.

HIGHEST EARNINGS

Career The all-time earnings record for a pacer is $3,225,653, by Nihilator, 1984–85.

Season The single-season record for a pacer is $2,217,222 by Precious Bunny in 1991.

Race The richest race in harness racing history was the 1984 Woodrow Wilson, which carried a total purse of $2,161,000. The winner, Nihilator, earned a record $1,080,500.

INDIVIDUAL RACES

Triple Crown The Triple Crown for pacers consists of three races: Cane Pace, Little Brown Jug and Messenger Stakes. Seven horses have won the Triple Crown.

TRIPLE CROWN WINNERS—PACERS

Year	Horse	Driver
1959	Adios Butler	Clint Hodgins
1965	Bret Hanover	Frank Ervin
1966	Romeo Hanover	Jerry Silverman
1968	Rum Customer	William Haughton
1970	Most Happy Fella	Stanley Dancer
1980	Niatross	Clint Galbraith
1983	Ralph Hanover	Ron Waples

CANE PACE First run in 1955, this race was originally known as the Cane Futurity. Since 1975, it has been called the Cane Pace. Run over one mile, the race is open to three-year-olds, and is run at Yonkers Raceway, N.Y.

Fastest time The fastest time is 1 minute 53⅗ seconds, by Silky Stallone, driven by Jack Moiseyev, in 1991.

Most wins (driver) Stanley Dancer has driven the winning pacer four times: 1964, 1970–71 and 1976.

LITTLE BROWN JUG First run in 1946, the Jug is raced annually at Delaware County Fair, Delaware, Ohio. The race is for three-year-olds and is run over one mile.

Fastest time The fastest time is 1 minute 52⅕ seconds, by Nihilator, driven by Bill O'Donnell, in 1985.

Most wins (driver) William Haughton has driven five winning pacers, in 1955, 1964, 1968–69 and 1974.

MESSENGER STAKES First run in 1956 at Roosevelt Raceway, this race has been staged at various locations during its history. The race is run over one mile and is open to three-year-olds only.

Fastest time The fastest time is 1 minute 51⅕ seconds, by Die Laughing, driven by Richard Silverman, in 1991.

Most wins (drivers) William Haughton has driven the winning pacer seven times, in 1956, 1967–68, 1972 and 1974–76.

DRIVERS' RECORDS

Most wins (career) Herve Filion (Canada) has won 13,318 harness races as of January 4, 1992.

Most wins (season) Herve Filion won a record 814 races in 1989.

Most wins (day) Mike Lachance won 12 races at Yonkers Raceway, N.Y. on June 23, 1987.

HIGHEST EARNINGS

Career John Campbell has won a career record $100,860,819 in prize money, 1972–91.

Season John Campbell won a season record $11,620,878 in 1990, when he won 543 races.

HOCKEY

ORIGINS There is pictorial evidence that a hockey-like game (*kalv*) was played on ice in the early 16th century in the Netherlands. The game was probably first played in North America on December 25, 1855 at Kingston, Ontario, Canada, but Halifax also lays claim to priority. The International Ice Hockey Federation was founded in 1908.

NATIONAL HOCKEY LEAGUE (NHL) (1917–1991)

ORIGINS The National Hockey League (NHL) was founded on November 22, 1917 in Montreal, Canada. The formation of the NHL was precipitated by the collapse of the National Hockey Association of Canada (NHA). Four teams formed the original league: the Montreal Canadiens, Montreal Wanderers, Ottawa Senators and Quebec Bulldogs. The Toronto Arenas were admitted as a fifth team, but the Bulldogs were unable to operate, and the league began as a four-team competition. The first NHL game was played on December 19, 1917. The NHL is now comprised of 22 teams, seven from Canada and 15 from the United States, divided into two divisions within two conferences: Adams and Patrick Divisions in the Wales Conference; Norris and Smythe Division in the Campbell Conference. At the end of the regular season, 16 teams compete in the Stanley Cup playoffs to decide the NHL Championship. (For further details of the Stanley Cup, see below.)

TEAM RECORDS (1917–1991)

Most wins (season) The Montreal Canadiens won 60 games during the 1976–77 season. In 80 games, "the Habs" won 60, lost 8 and tied 12.

Highest winning percentage (season) The 1929–30 Boston Bruins set an NHL record .875 winning percentage. The Bruins' record was 38 wins, 5 losses and 1 tie.

Most points (season) The Montreal Canadiens accumulated 132 points during their record-setting campaign of 1976–77, when they won a record 60 games.

Most losses (season) The Washington Capitals hold the unenviable record of having lost the most games in one season. During the 1974–75 season,

NATIONAL HOCKEY LEAGUE RECORDS (1917–1991)

Goals

		Player(s)	Team(s)	Date(s)
Period	4	Busher Jackson	Toronto Maple Leafs *v.* St. Louis Eagles	November 20, 1934
		Max Bentley	Chicago Blackhawks *v.* New York Rangers	January 28, 1943
		Clint Smith	Chicago Blackhawks *v.* Montreal Canadiens	March 4, 1945
		Red Berenson	St. Louis Blues *v.* Philadelphia Flyers	November 7, 1968
		Wayne Gretzky	Edmonton Oilers *v.* St. Louis Blues	February 18, 1981
		Grant Mulvey	Chicago Blackhawks *v.* St. Louis Blues	February 3, 1982
		Bryan Trottier	New York Islanders *v.* Philadelphia Flyers	February 13, 1982
		Al Secord	Chicago Blackhawks *v.* Toronto Maple Leafs	January 7, 1987
		Joe Nieuwendyk	Calgary Flames *v.* Winnipeg Jets	January 11, 1989
Game	7	Joe Malone	Quebec Bulldogs *v.*Toronto St. Patricks	January 31, 1920
Season	92	Wayne Gretzky	Edmonton Oilers	1981–82
Career	801	Gordie Howe	Detroit Red Wings, Hartford Whalers;	1946–71, 1979–80

Assists

		Player(s)	Team(s)	Date(s)
Period	5	Dale Hawerchuk	Winnipeg Jets *v.* Los Angeles Kings	March 6, 1984
Game	7	Billy Taylor	Detroit Red Wings *v.* Chicago Blackhawks	March 16, 1947
		Wayne Gretzky	Edmonton Oilers *v.* Washington Capitals	February 15, 1980
		Wayne Gretzky	Edmonton Oilers *v.* Chicago Blackhawks	December 11, 1985
		Wayne Gretzky	Edmonton Oilers *v.* Quebec Nordiques	February 14, 1986
Season	163	Wayne Gretzky	Edmonton Oilers	1985–86
Career	1,462	Wayne Gretzky	Edmonton Oilers, Los Angeles Kings	1979–91*

Points

		Player(s)	Team(s)	Date(s)
Period	6	Bryan Trottier	New York Islanders *v.* New York Rangers	December 23, 1978
Game	10	Darryl Sittler	Toronto Maple Leafs *v.* Boston Bruins	February 7, 1976
Season	215	Wayne Gretzky	Edmonton Oilers	1985–86
Career	2,197	Wayne Gretzky	Edmonton Oilers; Los Angeles Kings	1979–91*

Goaltenders
Shutouts

Season	22	George Hainsworth	Montreal Canadiens	1928–29
Career	103	Terry Sawchuk	Detroit Red Wings, Boston Bruins, Toronto Maple Leafs, Los Angeles Kings, New York Rangers	1949–70

Wins

Season	47	Bernie Parent	Philadelphia Flyers	1973–74
Career	435	Terry Sawchuk	Detroit Red Wings, Boston Bruins, Toronto Maple Leafs, Los Angeles Kings, New York Rangers	1949–70

* As of January 5, 1992
Source: NHL

GOAL KING ■ GORDIE HOWE SCORED AN NHL CA-REER RECORD 801 GOALS IN A RECORD 1,767 GAMES OVER 26 SEASONS.

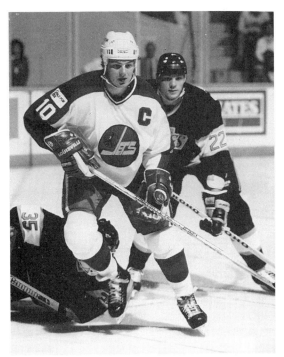

PERIOD PIECE ■ DALE HAWERCHUK WAS CRED-ITED WITH FIVE ASSISTS IN A SINGLE PERIOD ON MARCH 6, 1984 TO SET THE NHL MARK.

the first for the franchise, the Capitals lost 67 of 80 games played.

Most goals (game) The NHL record for goals in one game is 21, which has occurred on two occasions. The mark was set on January 10, 1920, when the Montreal Canadiens defeated the Toronto St. Patricks, 14–7, at Montreal. This record was matched on December 11, 1985, when the Edmonton Oilers beat the Chicago Blackhawks, 12–9, at Chicago.

Most goals (game—one team) The Montreal Canadiens pounded the Quebec Bulldogs 16–3 on March 3, 1920 to set the single-game scoring record. To make matters worse for Quebec, it was on home ice!

Most goals (season) The Edmonton Oilers scored 446 goals in 80 games during the 1983–84 season.

Most assists (season) The Edmonton Oilers recorded 737 assists during the 1985–86 season.

Most points (season) The Edmonton Oilers amassed 1,182 points (446 goals, 736 assists) during the 1983–84 season.

Most power play goals scored (season) The Pittsburgh Penguins scored 120 power-play goals during the 1988–89 season.

Most shorthand goals scored (season) The Edmonton Oilers scored 36 shorthand goals during the 1983–84 season.

Most penalty minutes in one game At the Boston Garden on February 26, 1981, the Boston Bruins and the Minnesota North Stars received a combined 406 penalty minutes, a record for one game. The Bruins received 20 minors, 13 majors, three 10-minute misconducts and six game misconducts for a total of 195 penalty minutes; the North Stars received 18 minors, 13 majors, four 10-minute misconducts and seven game misconducts for a total of 211 penalty minutes. It is also reported that a hockey game broke out between the fights, which the Bruins won 5–1.

Longest winning streak The New York Islanders won 15 consecutive games from January 21–February 20, 1982.

Longest undefeated streak The longest undefeated streak in one season is 35 games by the Philadelphia Flyers. The Flyers won 25 games and tied 10 from October 14, 1979–January 6, 1980.

Longest losing streak The Washington Capitals lost 17 consecutive games from February 18–March 26, 1975.

Longest winless streak The Winnipeg Jets set the mark for the longest winless streak at 30 games. From October 19 to December 20, 1980, the Jets lost 23 games and tied seven.

Longest game The longest game was played between the Detroit Red Wings and the Montreal Maroons at the Forum Montreal and lasted 2 hours 56 minutes 30 seconds. The Red Wings won when Mud Bruneteau scored the only goal of the game in the sixth period of overtime at 2:25 A.M. on March 25, 1936.

INDIVIDUAL RECORDS (1917–1991)

Most games played Gordie Howe played 1,767 games over a record 26 seasons for the Detroit Red Wings (1946–71) and Hartford Whalers (1979–80). The most games played by a goaltender is 971, by Terry Sawchuk, who played 21 seasons for five teams: Detroit Red Wings, Boston Bruins, Toronto Maple Leafs, Los Angeles Kings and New York Rangers (1949–70).

Most consecutive games played Doug Jarvis played 964 consecutive games from October 8, 1975 to October 10, 1987. During the streak, Jarvis played for three teams: the Montreal Canadiens, Washington Capitals and Hartford Whalers.

Fastest goal The fastest goal from the start of a game is 5 seconds by Doug Smail (Winnipeg Jets) *v*. St. Louis Blues at Winnipeg on December 20, 1981, and by Bryan Trottier (New York Islanders) *v*. Boston Bruins at Boston on March 22, 1984. The fastest goal from the start of any period was after 4 seconds by Claude Provost (Montreal Canadiens) *v*. Boston Bruins in the second period at Montreal on November 9, 1957, and by Denis Savard (Chicago Blackhawks) *v*. Hartford Whalers in the third period at Chicago on January 12, 1986.

Most hat tricks The most hat tricks (three or more goals in a game) in a career is 48, by Wayne Gretzky for the Edmonton Oilers and Los Angeles Kings in 12 seasons (1979–91). "The Great One" has recorded 35 three-goal games, nine four-goal games and four five-goal games. Gretzky also holds the record for most hat tricks in a season, 10, in both the 1981–82 and 1983–84 seasons for the Edmonton Oilers.

Longest consecutive goal-scoring streak The most consecutive games scoring at least one goal

RECORD FILE: WAYNE GRETZKY

BORN January 26, 1961, Brantford, Ontario, Canada

NHL REGULAR SEASON CAREER RECORDS
EDMONTON OILERS, 1979–88; LOS ANGELES KINGS, 1988–91

Years	Games	Goals	Assists	Points
1979–88	696	583	1,086	1,669
1988–91	229	135	338	473
1991–92†	25	17	38	55
Totals	950	735	1,462*	2,197*

NHL PLAYOFFS CAREER RECORDS
EDMONTON OILERS, 1979–88; LOS ANGELES KINGS, 1988–91

Years	Games	Goals	Assists	Points
1979–88	120	81	161	252
1988–91	30	12	35	47
Totals	150	93*	206*	299*

RECORD NOTES Gretzky's record-breaking accomplishments have rewritten the NHL record book. He holds career and season records for almost all offensive categories, among them most hat tricks in a career, 48; most 100-point seasons, 12; most 60-goal seasons, five*; most goals, assists and points in a season, 92, 163 and 215 respectively; and longest consecutive point-scoring streak, 51 games. Gretzky has been named NHL MVP a record nine times.

*indicates all-time record.   † as of January 5, 1992.

 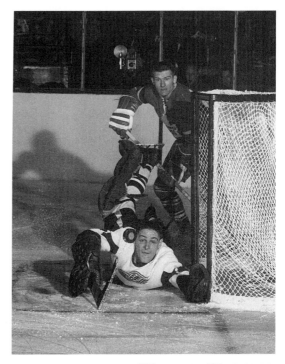

CLEAN SHEETS ■ ALEX CONNELL (LEFT) THWARTED OPPONENTS FOR A RECORD 461 MINUTES 29 SECONDS. TERRY SAWCHUK (RIGHT) HOLDS SEVERAL NHL GOALTENDING RECORDS, INCLUDING MOST CAREER SHUTOUTS, 103.

in a game is 16, by Harry (Punch) Broadbent (Ottawa Senators) in the 1921–22 season. Broadbent scored 25 goals during the streak.

Longest consecutive assist-scoring streak The record for most consecutive games recording at least one assist is 23 games, by Wayne Gretzky (Los Angeles Kings) in 1990–91. Gretzky was credited with 48 assists during the streak.

Most consecutive 50-or-more-goal seasons Mike Bossy (New York Islanders) scored at least 50 goals in nine consecutive seasons from 1977–78 through 1985–86.

Longest consecutive point-scoring streak The most consecutive games scoring at least one point is 51, by Wayne Gretzky (Edmonton Oilers) between October 5, 1983 and January 27, 1984. During the streak, Gretzky scored 61 goals, 92 assists for 153 points.

Longest shutout sequence by a goaltender Alex Connell (Ottawa Senators) played 461 minutes, 29 seconds without conceding a goal in the 1927–28 season.

Longest undefeated streak by a goaltender Gerry Cheevers (Boston Bruins) went 32 games (24 wins, 8 ties) undefeated during the 1971–72 season.

Defensemen On October 17, 1991, Paul Coffey (Edmonton Oilers, 1980–87; Pittsburgh Penguins, 1987–91) broke the career record for assists and points by a defenseman in the NHL, when he recorded two assists in the game v. the New York Islanders, increasing his totals to 744 assists and 1,053 points. On November 8, 1991, Coffey surpassed the record for most goals by a defenseman when he scored his 311th goal v. the Winnipeg Jets. As of January 5, 1992, Coffey's career marks were 315 goals, 776 assists and 1,091 points. Coffey also holds the single-season record for goals scored by a defenseman, 48, which he scored in 1985–86 when he played for the Edmonton Oilers. Bobby Orr (Boston Bruins) holds the single-season marks for assists (102) and points (139), both of which were set in 1970–71.

HART TROPHY Awarded annually since the 1923–24 season by the Professional Hockey Writers Association to the Most Valuable Player of the NHL.

Most wins Wayne Gretzky has won the award a record nine times, 1980–87 and 1989.

HART MEMORIAL TROPHY WINNERS (1924–1991)

Year	Player	Team	Year	Player	Team
1924	Frank Nighbor	Ottawa Senators	1958	Gordie Howe	Detroit Red Wings
1925	Billy Burch	Hamilton Tigers	1959	Andy Bathgate	New York Rangers
1926	Nels Stewart	Montreal Maroons	1960	Gordie Howe	Detroit Red Wings
1927	Herb Gardiner	Montreal Canadiens	1961	Bernie Geoffrion	Montreal Canadiens
1928	Howie Morenz	Montreal Canadiens	1962	Jacques Plante	Montreal Canadiens
1929	Roy Worters	New York Americans	1963	Gordie Howe	Detroit Red Wings
1930	Nels Stewart	Montreal Maroons	1964	Jean Beliveau	Montreal Canadiens
1931	Howie Morenz	Montreal Canadiens	1965	Bobby Hull	Chicago Blackhawks
1932	Howie Morenz	Montreal Canadiens	1966	Bobby Hull	Chicago Blackhawks
1933	Eddie Shore	Boston Bruins	1967	Stan Mikita	Chicago Blackhawks
1934	Aurel Joliat	Montreal Canadiens	1968	Stan Mikita	Chicago Blackhawks
1935	Eddie Shore	Boston Bruins	1969	Phil Esposito	Boston Bruins
1936	Eddie Shore	Boston Bruins	1970	Bobby Orr	Boston Bruins
1937	Babe Siebert	Montreal Canadiens	1971	Bobby Orr	Boston Bruins
1938	Eddie Shore	Boston Bruins	1972	Bobby Orr	Boston Bruins
1939	Toe Blake	Montreal Canadiens	1973	Bobby Clarke	Philadelphia Flyers
1940	Ebbie Goodfellow	Detroit Red Wings	1974	Phil Esposito	Boston Bruins
1941	Bill Cowley	Boston Bruins	1975	Bobby Clarke	Philadelphia Flyers
1942	Tom Anderson	Brooklyn Americans	1976	Bobby Clarke	Philadelphia Flyers
1943	Bill Cowley	Boston Bruins	1977	Guy Lafleur	Montreal Canadiens
1944	Babe Pratt	Toronto Maple Leafs	1978	Guy Lafleur	Montreal Canadiens
1945	Elmer Lach	Montreal Canadiens	1979	Bryan Trottier	New York Islanders
1946	Max Bentley	Chicago Blackhawks	1980	Wayne Gretzky	Edmonton Oilers
1947	Maurice Richard	Montreal Canadiens	1981	Wayne Gretzky	Edmonton Oilers
1948	Buddy O'Connor	New York Rangers	1982	Wayne Gretzky	Edmonton Oilers
1949	Sid Abel	Detroit Red Wings	1983	Wayne Gretzky	Edmonton Oilers
1950	Charlie Rayner	New York Rangers	1984	Wayne Gretzky	Edmonton Oilers
1951	Milt Schmidt	Boston Bruins	1985	Wayne Gretzky	Edmonton Oilers
1952	Gordie Howe	Detroit Red Wings	1986	Wayne Gretzky	Edmonton Oilers
1953	Gordie Howe	Detroit Red Wings	1987	Wayne Gretzky	Edmonton Oilers
1954	Al Rollins	Chicago Blackhawks	1988	Mario Lemieux	Pittsburgh Penguins
1955	Ted Kennedy	Toronto Maple Leafs	1989	Wayne Gretzky	Los Angeles Kings
1956	Jean Beliveau	Montreal Canadiens	1990	Mark Messier	Edmonton Oilers
1957	Gordie Howe	Detroit Red Wings	1991	Brett Hull	St. Louis Blues

BENCHMARK ■ DICK IRVIN COACHED A RECORD 1,437 NHL GAMES, 1930–56.

COACHES

Most wins As of January 5, 1992, Scotty Bowman has coached his teams to 762 victories (110 wins, St. Louis Blues 1967–71; 419 wins, Montreal Canadiens, 1971–79; 210 wins, Buffalo Sa-

bres, 1979–87; 23 wins, Pittsburgh Penguins, 1991–92).

Most games coached Dick Irvin has coached a record 1,437 games with three teams: Chicago Blackhawks, 1930–31, 1955–56; Toronto Maple Leafs, 1931–40; Montreal Canadiens, 1940–55. Irvin's career record was 690 wins, 521 losses, 226 ties.

STANLEY CUP

The Stanley Cup is currently the oldest competition in North American professional sports. The cup was donated to the Canadian Amateur Hockey Association (AHA) by Sir Frederick Arthur Stanley, Lord Stanley of Preston in 1893. The inaugural championship was presented to the AHA champion, but since 1894 there has always been a playoff. The playoff format underwent several changes until 1926 when the National Hockey League (NHL) playoffs became the permanent forum to decide the Stanley Cup champion.

STANLEY CUP CHAMPIONS (1893–1904)

Year	Champion	Loser	Series
1893	Montreal A.A.A.	(no challenger)	——
1894	Montreal A.A.A.	Ottawa Generals	3–1*
1895	Montreal Victorias	(no challenger)	——
1896	Winnipeg Victorias (February)	Montreal Victorias	2–0*
	Montreal Victorias (December)	Winnipeg Victorias	6–5*
1897	Montreal Victorias	Ottawa Capitals	15–2*
1898	Montreal Victorias	(no challenger)	——
1899	Montreal Victorias (February)	Winnipeg Victorias	2–0
1899	Montreal Shamrocks (March)	Queen's University	6–2*
1900	Montreal Shamrocks	Halifax Crescents	**
		Winnipeg Victorias	
1901	Winnipeg Victorias	Montreal Shamrocks	2–0
1902	Montreal A.A.A.	Winnipeg Victorias	2–1
1903	Ottawa Silver Seven	Rat Portage Thistles	**
		Montreal Victorias	
1904	Ottawa Silver Seven	Brandon Wheat Kings	**
		Montreal Wanderers	
		Toronto Marlboros	
		Winnipeg Rowing Club	

STANLEY CUP CHAMPIONS (1905–1932)

Year	Champion	Loser	Series
1905	Ottawa Silver Seven	Rat Portage Thistles	**
		Dawson City Nuggets	
1906	Montreal Wanderers	New Glasgow Clubs	
		Ottawa Silver Seven	**
1907	Kenora Thistles (January)	Montreal Wanderers	2–0
	Montreal Wanderers (March)	Kenora Thistles	1–1†
1908	Montreal Wanderers	Edmonton Eskimos	**
		Toronto Maple Leafs	
		Winnipeg Maple Leafs	
		Ottawa Victorias	
1909	Ottawa Senators	(no challenger)	
1910	Ottawas Senators (January)	Galt	**
		Edmonton Eskimos	
	Montreal Wanderers (March)	Berlin (Kitchener)	7–3*
1911			
1912	Quebec Bulldogs	Moncton Victorias	2–0
1913	Quebec Bulldogs	Sydney Miners	2–0
1914	Toronto Blueshirts	Victoria Cougars	**
		Montreal Canadiens	
1915	Vancouver Millionaires	Ottawa Senators	3–0
1916	Montreal Canadiens	Portland Rosebuds	3–2
1917	Seattle Metropolitans	Montreal Canadiens	3–1
1918	Toronto Arenas	Vancouver Millionaires	3–2
1919	no decision		‡
1920	Ottawa Senators	Seattle Metropolitans	3–2
1921	Ottawa Senators	Vancouver Millionaires	3–2
1922	Toronto St. Patricks	Vancouver Millionaires	3–2
1923	Ottawa Senators	Vancouver Maroons	**
		Edmonton Eskimos	
1924	Montreal Canadiens	Vancouver Maroons	**
		Calgary Tigers	
1925	Victoria Cougars	Montreal Canadiens	3–1
1926	Montreal Maroons	Victoria Cougars	3–1
1927	Ottawa Senators	Boston Bruins	2–0
1928	New York Rangers	Montreal Maroons	3–2
1929	Boston Bruins	New York Rangers	2–0
1930	Montreal Canadiens	Boston Bruins	2–0
1931	Montreal Canadiens	Chicago Blackhawks	3–2
1932	Toronto Maple Leafs	New York Rangers	3–0

STANLEY CUP CHAMPIONS (1933–1969)

Year	Champion	Loser	Series
1933	New York Rangers	Toronto Maple Leafs	3–1
1934	Chicago Blackhawks	Detroit Red Wings	3–1
1935	Montreal Maroons	Toronto Maple Leafs	3–0
1936	Detroit Red Wings	Toronto Maple Leafs	3–1
1937	Detroit Red Wings	New York Rangers	3–2
1938	Chicago Blackhawks	Toronto Maple Leafs	3–1
1939	Boston Bruins	Toronto Maple Leafs	4–1
1940	New York Rangers	Toronto Maple Leafs	4–2
1941	Boston Bruins	Detroit Red Wings	4–0
1942	Toronto Maple Leafs	Detroit Red Wings	4–3
1943	Detroit Red Wings	Boston Bruins	4–0
1944	Montreal Canadiens	Chicago Blackhawks	4–0
1945	Toronto Maple Leafs	Detroit Red Wings	4–3
1946	Montreal Canadiens	Boston Bruins	4–1
1947	Toronto Maple Leafs	Montreal Canadiens	4–2
1948	Toronto Maple Leafs	Detroit Red Wings	4–0
1949	Toronto Maple Leafs	Detroit Red Wings	4–0
1950	Detroit Red Wings	New York Rangers	4–3
1951	Toronto Maple Leafs	Montreal Canadiens	4–1
1952	Detroit Red Wings	Montreal Canadiens	4–0
1953	Montreal Canadiens	Boston Bruins	4–1
1954	Detroit Red Wings	Montreal Canadiens	4–3
1955	Detroit Red Wings	Montreal Canadiens	4–3
1956	Montreal Canadiens	Detroit Red Wings	4–1
1957	Montreal Canadiens	Boston Bruins	4–1
1958	Montreal Canadiens	Boston Bruins	4–2
1959	Montreal Canadiens	Toronto Maple Leafs	4–1
1960	Montreal Canadiens	Toronto Maple Leafs	4–0
1961	Chicago Blackhawks	Detroit Red Wings	4–2
1962	Toronto Maple Leafs	Chicago Blackhawks	4–2
1963	Toronto Maple Leafs	Detroit Red Wings	4–1
1964	Toronto Maple Leafs	Detroit Red Wings	4–3
1965	Montreal Canadiens	Chicago Blackhawks	4–3
1966	Montreal Canadiens	Detroit Red Wings	4–2
1967	Toronto Maple Leafs	Montreal Canadiens	4–2
1968	Montreal Canadiens	St. Louis Blues	4–0
1969	Montreal Canadiens	St. Louis Blues	4–0

STANLEY CUP CHAMPIONS (1970–1991)

Year	Champion	Loser	Series
1970	Boston Bruins	St. Louis Blues	4–0
1971	Montreal Canadiens	Chicago Blackhawks	4–3
1972	Boston Bruins	New York Rangers	4–2
1973	Montreal Canadiens	Chicago Blackhawks	4–2
1974	Philadelphia Flyers	Boston Bruins	4–2
1975	Philadelphia Flyers	Buffalo Sabres	4–2
1977	Montreal Canadiens	Boston Bruins	4–0
1978	Montreal Canadiens	Boston Bruins	4–2
1979	Montreal Canadiens	New York Rangers	4–1
1980	New York Islanders	Philadelphia Flyers	4–2
1981	New York Islanders	Minnesota North Stars	4–1
1982	New York Islanders	Vancouver Canucks	4–0
1983	New York Islanders	Edmonton Oilers	4–0
1984	Edmonton Oilers	New York Islanders	4–1
1985	Edmonton Oilers	Philadelphia Flyers	4–1
1986	Montreal Canadiens	Calgary Flames	4–1
1987	Edmonton Oilers	Philadelphia Flyers	4–3
1988	Edmonton Oilers	Boston Bruins	4–0
1989	Calgary Flames	Montreal Canadiens	4–2
1990	Edmonton Oilers	Boston Bruins	4–1
1991	Pittsburgh Penguins	Minnesota North Stars	4–2

* Final score of single challenge game.

** Multiple challenger series.

† Series decided on total goals scored.

‡ The 1919 final between the Montreal Canadiens and the Seattle Metropolitans was canceled because of an influenza epidemic.

Most championships The Montreal Canadiens have won the Stanley Cup a record 23 times: 1916, 1924, 1930–31, 1944, 1946, 1953, 1956–60, 1965–66, 1968–69, 1971, 1973, 1976–79, 1986.

Most consecutive wins The Montreal Canadiens won the Stanley Cup for five consecutive years, 1956–60.

Most games played Larry Robinson has played in 225 Stanley Cup playoff games for the Montreal Canadiens (1973–89, 203 games) and the Los Angeles Kings (1990–91, 22 games).

GOAL SCORING RECORDS

Fastest goal The fastest goal from the start of any playoff game was scored by Don Kozak (Los An-

STANLEY STAMINA ■ **LARRY ROBINSON HAS PLAYED IN A RECORD 225 STANLEY CUP GAMES.**

geles Kings) past Gerry Cheevers (Boston Bruins) with 6 seconds elapsed. The Kings went on to win 7–4; the game was played on April 17, 1977. Kozak's goal shares the mark for fastest goal from the start of any period with one scored by Pelle Eklund (Philadelphia Flyers). Eklund scored in the second period of a game against the Pittsburgh Penguins in Pittsburgh on April 25, 1989; his effort was in vain, however, as the Penguins won 10–7.

SHORTHANDED GOALS SCORED

Period The most shorthanded goals scored in a single period is two, shared by three players. Bryan Trottier was the first player to perform this feat on April 8, 1990 for the New York Islanders *v.* the Los Angeles Kings. His goals came in the second period of an 8–1 Islanders victory. Bobby Lalonde (Boston Bruins) matched Trottier on April 11, 1981. His double came in the third period of a Bruins 6–3 loss to the Minnesota North Stars. Jari Kurri (Edmonton Oilers) joined this club on April 24, 1983. His goals came in the third period of an Oilers 8–4 win over the Chicago Blackhawks.

Series The record for most shorthanded goals in a playoff series is three, shared by two players: Bill Barber (Philadelphia Flyers) in a Flyers 4–1 series victory over the Minnesota North Stars in 1980; and Wayne Presley (Chicago Blackhawks) in a series *v.* Detroit Red Wings in 1989.

Season The record for shorthanded goals in one season is three, shared by five players: Derek Sanderson (Boston Bruins) in 1969; Bill Barber (Philadelphia Flyers) in 1980; Lorne Henning (New York Islanders) in 1980; Wayne Gretzky (Edmonton Oilers) in 1983; and Wayne Presley (Chicago Blackhawks) in 1989.

Career Mark Messier (Edmonton Oilers) holds the mark for career playoff goals at 11 in 148 games (1979–91).

DEFENSEMEN RECORDS

GOAL SCORING

Game The most goals scored by a defenseman in a playoff game is three, by five players: Bobby Orr, Boston Bruins *v.* Montreal Canadiens, April 11, 1971; Dick Redmond, Chicago Blackhawks *v.* St. Louis Blues, April 4, 1973; Denis Potvin, New York Islanders *v.* Edmonton Oilers, April 17, 1981; Paul Reinhart, Calgary Flames, who performed the feat twice, *v.* Edmonton Oilers, April 14, 1983; *v.* Van-

COFFEY CUP ■ PAUL COFFEY HOLDS DEFENSE-MAN PLAYOFF MARKS FOR MOST POINTS IN A GAME (SIX) AND IN A SEASON (37).

couver Canucks, April 8, 1984; and Doug Halward, Vancouver Canucks *v.* Calgary Flames, April 7, 1984.

Season Paul Coffey (Edmonton Oilers) scored 12 goals in 18 games during the 1985 playoffs.

Career Denis Potvin (New York Islanders) 1973–88, has scored a playoff record 56 goals.

POINT SCORING

Game Paul Coffey earned a record six points on one goal and five assists, for the Edmonton Oilers *v.* Chicago Blackhawks on May 14, 1985.

Season Paul Coffey also holds the record for most points by a defenseman in a season, with 37 in 1985 for the Edmonton Oilers. Coffey's total comprised 12 goals and 25 assists in 18 games.

Career Denis Potvin (New York Islanders) 1973–88, has scored a playoff record 164 points. Potvin scored 56 goals and 108 assists in 185 games.

STANLEY CUP INDIVIDUAL RECORDS (1917–1991)

Records in this section are listed only from the formation of the National Hockey League in 1917.

Goals Scored

		Player(s)	Team(s)	Date(s)
Period	4	Tim Kerr	Philadelphia Flyers v. New York Rangers	April 13, 1985
		Mario Lemieux	Pittsburgh Penguins v. New York Rangers	April 25, 1989
Game	5	Newsy Lalonde	Montreal Canadiens v. Ottawa Senators	March 1, 1919
		Maurice Richard	Montreal Canadiens v. Toronto Maple Leafs	March 23, 1944
		Darryl Sittler	Toronto Maple Leafs v. Philadelphia Flyers	April 22, 1976
		Reggie Leach	Philadelphia Flyers v. Boston Bruins	May 6, 1976
		Mario Lemieux	Pittsburgh Penguins v. Philadelphia Flyers	April 25, 1989
Series (any round)	12	Jari Kurri	Edmonton Oilers v. Chicago Blackhawks	1985
Series (final)	9	Babe Dye	Toronto St. Patricks v. Vancouver Millionaires	1922
Season	19	Reggie Leach	Philadelphia Flyers	1976
		Jari Kurri	Edmonton Oilers	1985
Career	93	Wayne Gretzky	Edmonton Oilers, Los Angeles Kings	1979–91

Power-Play Goals Scored

Period	3	Tim Kerr	Philadelphia Flyers v. New York Rangers	April 13, 1985
Series	6	Chris Kontos	Los Angeles Kings v. Edmonton Oilers	1989
Season	9	Mike Bossy	New York Islanders	1981
		Cam Neely	Boston Bruins	1991
Career	35	Mike Bossy	New York Islanders	1977–87

Points Scored

Period	4	Maurice Richard	Montreal Canadiens v. Toronto Maple Leafs	March 29, 1945
		Dickie Moore	Montreal Canadiens v. Boston Bruins	March 25, 1954
		Barry Pederson	Boston Bruins v. Buffalo Sabres	April 8, 1982
		Peter McNab	Boston Bruins v. Buffalo Sabres	April 11, 1982
		Tim Kerr	Philadelphia Flyers v. New York Rangers	April 13, 1985
		Ken Linseman	Boston Bruins v. Montreal Canadiens	April 14, 1985
		Wayne Gretzky	Edmonton Oilers v. Los Angeles Kings	April 12, 1987
		Glenn Anderson	Edmonton Oilers v. Winnipeg Jets	April 6, 1988
		Mario Lemieux	Pittsburgh Penguins v. Philadelphia Flyers	April 25, 1989
		Dave Gagner	Minnesota North Stars v. Chicago Blackhawks	April 8, 1991
Game	8	Patrik Sundstrom	New Jersey Devils v. Washington Capitals	April 22, 1988
		Mario Lemieux	Pittsburgh Penguins v. Philadelphia Flyers	April 25, 1989
Series (any round)	19	Rick Middleton	Boston Bruins v. Buffalo Sabres	1983
Series (final)	13	Wayne Gretzky	Edmonton Oilers v. Boston Bruins	1988
Season	47	Wayne Gretzky	Edmonton Oilers	1985
Career	299	Wayne Gretzky	Edmonton Oilers, Los Angeles Kings	1979–91

STANLEY CUP INDIVIDUAL RECORDS (1917–1991)

Assists

		Player(s)	Team(s)	Date(s)
Period	3	This feat has been achieved 54 times.		
Game	6	Mikko Leinonen	New York Rangers v. Philadelphia Flyers	April 8, 1982
		Wayne Gretzky	Edmonton Oilers v. Los Angeles Kings	April 9, 1987
Series (any round)	14	Rick Middleton	Boston Bruins v. Buffalo Sabres	1983
		Wayne Gretzky	Edmonton Oilers v. Chicago Blackhawks	1985
Series (final)	10	Wayne Gretzky	Edmonton Oilers v. Boston Bruins	1988
Season	31	Wayne Gretzky	Edmonton Oilers	1988
Career	206	Wayne Gretzky	Edmonton Oilers, Los Angeles Kings	1979–91

Goaltenders

Shutouts

Season	4	Clint Benedict	Montreal Maroons	1926
		Clint Benedict	Montreal Maroons	1928
		Dave Kerr	New York Rangers	1937
		Frank McCool	Toronto Maple Leafs	1945
		Terry Sawchuk	Detroit Tigers	1952
		Bernie Parent	Philadelphia Flyers	1975
		Ken Dyrden	Montreal Canadiens	1977
Career	15	Clint Benedict	Ottawa Senators, Montreal Maroons	1917–30

Minutes Played

Season	1,540	Ron Hextall	Philadelphia Flyers	1987
Career	7,645	Billy Smith	New York Islanders	1971–89

Wins

Season	16	Grant Fuhr	Edmonton Oilers	1988
		Mike Vernon	Calgary Flames	1989
		Bill Ranford	Edmonton Oilers	1990
Career	88	Billy Smith	New York Islanders	1975–88

Penalty Minutes

Game	42	Dave Schultz	Philadelphia Flyers v. Toronto Maple Leafs	April 22, 1976
Career	548	Dale Hunter	Quebec Nordiques, Washington Capitals	1980–91

Source: NHL

CONSECUTIVE RECORDS

Point-scoring streak Bryan Trottier (New York Islanders) scored a point in 27 consecutive playoff games over three seasons (1980–82), scoring 16 goals and 26 assists for 42 points.

Goal-scoring streak Reggie Leach (Philadelphia Flyers) scored at least one goal in nine consecutive playoff games in 1976. The streak started on April 17 *v.* the Toronto Maple Leafs, and ended on May 9 when he was shut out by the Montreal Canadiens. Overall, Leach scored 14 goals during his record-setting run.

Consecutive wins by a goaltender Gerry Cheevers (Boston Bruins) set a playoff record 10 straight victories, anchoring the Bruins to a Stanley Cup title in 1970.

Longest shutout sequence In the 1936 semifinal contest between the Detroit Red Wings and the Montreal Maroons, Norm Smith, the Red Wings goaltender, shut out the Maroons for 248 minutes, 32 seconds. The Maroons failed to score in the first two games (the second game lasted 116 minutes, 30 seconds, the longest overtime game in playoff history), and finally breached Smith's defenses at 12:02 of the first period in game three. After such a stellar performance, it is no surprise that the Red Wings swept the series 3–0.

COACHES

Most championships Toe Blake coached the Montreal Canadiens to eight Stanley Cups, 1956–60, 1965–66, 1968.

Most playoff wins Through the 1990–91 season the record for playoff wins is 114 games by two coaches: Scotty Bowman, St. Louis Blues, 1967–71 (26 wins), Montreal Canadiens, 1971–79 (70 wins), Buffalo Sabres, 1979–87 (18 wins); Al Arbour, St. Louis Blues, 1971–73 (four wins), New York Islanders, 1973–86, 1988–91 (110 wins).

Most games Dick Irvin holds the mark for most games coached, at 190 with three teams: Chicago Blackhawks, 1930–31, 1955–56; Toronto Maple Leafs, 1931–40; Montreal Canadiens, 1940–55.

OLYMPIC GAMES

Hockey was included in the 1920 Summer Olympics in Antwerp, Belgium, and has been an integral part of the Winter Olympics since its introduction in 1924.

Most gold medals (country) The USSR has won seven Olympic titles, in 1956, 1964, 1968, 1972, 1976, 1984 and 1988.

Most medals (country) Canada has won a record 10 medals in Olympic competition: six gold, two silver and two bronze.

Most gold medals (player) Five Soviet players have each been on three gold-medal-winning teams: Vitaliy Davydov, Anatoliy Firssov, Viktor Kuzkin, Aleksandr Ragulin in 1964, 1968 and 1972; and Vladislav Tretyak in 1972, 1976 and 1984.

Most medals (player) Vladislav Tretyak has won four medals: three gold (see above), and one silver in 1980.

United States The United States has won the gold medal twice, in 1960 and 1980. Overall the United States has won nine medals: two golds, six silver and one bronze.

WORLD CHAMPIONSHIPS (MEN) The world championships were first held in 1920 in conjunction with the Olympic Games. Since 1930, the world championships have been held annually. Through the 1964 Olympics, the Games were considered the world championships, and records for those Games are included in this section. Since 1977, the championships have been open to professionals.

Most titles The USSR has won the world championship 22 times: 1954, 1956, 1963–71, 1973–75, 1978–79, 1981–83, 1986, 1989–90.

Most consecutive titles The USSR won nine consecutive championships from 1963–71.

WORLD CHAMPIONSHIPS (WOMEN) The inaugural tournament was held in 1990. Canada won the inaugural event, defeating the United States 5–2 in the final, staged in Ottawa, Canada on March 24, 1990.

NCAA CHAMPIONSHIPS A men's Division I hockey championship was first staged in 1948, and has been held annually since.

Most wins Michigan has won the title seven times: 1948, 1951–53, 1955–56 and 1964.

HORSE RACING

ORIGINS Horsemanship was an important part of the Hittite culture of Anatolia, Turkey, dating from

1400 B.C. The 33rd ancient Olympic Games of 648 B.C. in Greece featured horse racing. Horse races can be traced in England from the 3rd century. The first sweepstakes race was originated by the 12th Earl of Derby at his estate in Epsom in 1780. The Epsom Derby is still run today and is the classic race of the English flat racing season.

United States Horses were introduced to the North American continent from Spain by Cortéz in 1519. In colonial America, horse racing was common. Colonel Richard Nicholls, commander of English forces in New York, is believed to have staged the first organized race at Salisbury Plain, Long Island, N.Y. in 1665. The first Jockey Club to be founded was at Charleston, S.C. in 1734. Thoroughbred racing was first staged at Saratoga Springs, N.Y. in 1863.

RACING RECORDS (UNITED STATES)

HORSES

CAREER RECORDS

Most wins The most wins in a racing career is 89, by Kingston, from 138 starts, 1886–94.

Most wins (graded stakes races) John Henry won 25 graded stakes races, including 16 Grade I races, 1978–84.

HIGHEST EARNINGS

Career The career record for earnings is $6,679,242, by Alysheba, 1986–88. Alysheba's career record was 11 wins, eight seconds and two thirds from 26 races.

Season The single-season earnings record is $4,578,454, by Sunday Silence, in 1989, from nine starts (seven wins and two seconds).

Single race The richest race in the United States is the Breeders' Cup Classic, which carries a purse of $3 million, with first place prize money of $1,560,000 to the winner.

JOCKEYS

CAREER RECORDS

Most wins Bill Shoemaker rode a record 8,833 winners from 40,350 mounts. "The Shoe" made his debut aboard Waxahachie on March 19, 1949, and raced for the last time on Patchy Groundfog on February 3, 1990. His first victory came on April

SPORTING KINGS ■ BILL SHOEMAKER (8) WON A CAREER RECORD 8,833 RACES. HE IS SEEN HERE ABOARD JOHN HENRY, WHO WON A CAREER RECORD 25 GRADED STAKES RACES.

20, 1949 aboard Shafter V, his last on January 20, 1990 aboard Beau Genius at Gulfstream Park, Fla.

SEASON RECORDS

Most wins Kent Desormeaux rode a season record 598 winners, from 2,312 mounts, in 1989.

Most wins (stakes races) Pat Day rode a season record 60 stakes race winners in 1991.

DAILY RECORDS

Most wins (single day) The most winners ridden in one day is nine, by Chris Antley on October 31, 1987. Antley rode four winners in the afternoon at Aqueduct, N.Y. and five in the evening at The Meadowlands, N.J.

Most wins (one card) The most winners ridden on one card is eight, achieved by four jockeys: Hubert Jones, from 13 rides, at Caliente, Calif., on June 11, 1944; Dave Gall, from 10 rides, at Cahokia Downs, East St. Louis, Ill., on October 18, 1978; Robert Williams, from 10 rides, at Lincoln, Neb., on September 29, 1984; and Pat Day, from nine rides, at Arlington, Ill., on September 13, 1989.

Consecutive wins The longest consecutive winning streak by a jockey is nine races, by Albert Adams, at Marlboro Racetrack, Md., over three days, September 10–12, 1930. He won the last two races on September 10, all six races on September 11, and the first race on September 12.

HIGHEST EARNINGS

Career Angel Cordero has won a career record $164,409,204 from 1962 through December 31, 1991.

Season The greatest prize money earned in a single season is $14,877,298, by Jose Santos in 1988.

JOCKEYS (WOMEN)

Most wins Julie Krone has won a record 2,272 races from 1980 through 1991.

Highest earnings Julie Krone has won a record $38,269,864 from 1980 through 1991.

THE TRIPLE CROWN The races that make up the Triple Crown are the Kentucky Derby, Preakness Stakes and the Belmont Stakes. The Triple Crown is for three-year-olds only and has been achieved by 11 horses.

TRIPLE CROWN WINNERS

Year	Horse	Jockey	Trainer	Owner
1919	Sir Barton	Johnny Loftus	H. Guy Bedwell	J. K. L. Ross
1930	Gallant Fox	Earle Sanders	J. E. Fitzsimmons	Belair Stud
1935	Omaha	Willie Saunders	J. E. Fitzsimmons	Belair Stud
1937	War Admiral	Chas. Kurtsinger	George Conway	Samuel Riddle
1941	Whirlaway	Eddie Arcaro	Ben A. Jones	Calumet Farm
1943	Count Fleet	Johnny Longden	Don Cameron	Mrs. J. D. Hertz
1946	Assault	Warren Mehrtens	Max Hirsch	King Ranch
1948	Citation	Eddie Arcaro	Ben A. Jones	Calumet Farm
1973	Secretariat	Ron Turcpotte	Luciren Laurin	Meadow Stable
1977	Seattle Slew	Jean Cruguet	Billy Turner	Karen Taylor
1978	Affirmed	Steve Cauthen	Laz Barrera	Harbor View Farm

Jim Fitzsimmons and Ben Jones are the only trainers to have trained two Triple Crown winners. Eddie Arcaro is the only jockey to have ridden two Triple Crown winners.

TRIPLE DOUBLE ■ JOCKEY EDDIE ARCARO AND TRAINER BEN JONES TEAMED UP TO WIN TWO TRIPLE CROWNS: WITH WHIRLAWAY (RIGHT) IN 1941, AND CITATION (LEFT) IN 1948.

KENTUCKY DERBY This event is held on the first Saturday in May at Churchill Downs, Louisville, Ky. The first race was run in 1875 over 1½ miles; the distance was shortened to 1¼ miles in 1896 and is still run at that length.

Most Wins

Jockey Five, by two jockeys: Eddie Arcaro (1938, 1941, 1945, 1948, 1952); Bill Hartack (1957, 1960, 1962, 1964, 1969).

Trainer Six, by Ben Jones (1938, 1941, 1944, 1948–49, 1952).

Owner Eight, by Calumet Farm (1941, 1944, 1948–49, 1952, 1957–58, 1968).

Fastest time 1 minute 59⅖ seconds, by Secretariat, 1973.

Largest field 23 horses in 1974.

KENTUCKY DERBY WINNERS (1875–1991)

Year	Horse	Year	Horse	Year	Horse	Year	Horse
1875	Aristides	1904	Elwood	1933	Brokers Tip	1962	Decidedly
1876	Vagrant	1905	Agile	1934	Cavalcade	1963	Chateaugay
1877	Baden-Baden	1906	Sir Huon	1935	Omaha	1964	Northern Dancer
1878	Day Star	1907	Pink Star	1936	Bold Venture	1965	Lucky Debonair
1879	Lord Murphy	1908	Stone Street	1937	War Admiral	1966	Kauai King
1880	Fonso	1909	Wintergreen	1938	Lawrin	1967	Proud Clarion
1881	Hindoo	1910	Donau	1939	Johnstown	1968	Forward Pass
1882	Apollo	1911	Meridian	1940	Gallahadion	1969	Majestic Prince
1883	Leonatus	1912	Worth	1941	Whirlaway	1970	Dust Commander
1884	Buchanan	1913	Donerail	1942	Shut Out	1971	Canonero II
1885	Joe Cotton	1914	Old Rosebud	1943	Count Fleet	1972	Riva Ridge
1886	Ben Ali	1915	Regret	1944	Pensive	1973	Secretariat
1887	Montrose	1916	George Smith	1945	Hoop Jr.	1974	Cannonade
1888	MacBeth II	1917	Omar Khayyam	1946	Assault	1975	Foolish Pleasure
1889	Spokane	1918	Exterminator	1947	Jet Pilot	1976	Bold Forbes
1890	Riley	1919	Sir Barton	1948	Citation	1977	Seattle Slew
1891	Kingman	1920	Paul Jones	1949	Ponder	1978	Affirmed
1892	Azra	1921	Behave Yourself	1950	Middleground	1979	Spectacular Bid
1893	Lookout	1922	Morvich	1951	Count Turf	1980	Genuine Risk
1894	Chant	1923	Zev	1952	Hill Gail	1981	Pleasant Colony
1895	Halma	1924	Black Gold	1953	Dark Star	1982	Gato Del Sol
1896	Ben Brush	1925	Flying Ebony	1954	Determine	1983	Sunny's Halo
1897	Typhoon II	1926	Bubbling Over	1955	Swaps	1984	Swale
1898	Plaudit	1927	Whiskery	1956	Needles	1985	Spend A Buck
1899	Manuel	1928	Reigh Count	1957	Iron Liege	1986	Ferdinand
1900	Lt. Gibson	1929	Clyde Van Dusen	1958	Tim Tam	1987	Alysheba
1901	His Eminence	1930	Gallant Fox	1959	Tomy Lee	1988	Winning Colors
1902	Alan-a-Dale	1931	Twenty Grand	1960	Venetian Way	1989	Sunday Silence
1903	Judge Himes	1932	Burgoo King	1961	Carry Back	1990	Unbridled
						1991	Strike the Gold

PREAKNESS STAKES Inaugurated in 1873, this event is held annually at Pimlico Race Course, Baltimore, Md. Originally run at 1½ miles, the distance was changed several times before being settled at the current length of 1³⁄₁₆ miles in 1925.

Most Wins

Jockey Six, by Eddie Arcaro (1941, 1948, 1950–51, 1955, 1957).

Trainer Seven, by Robert Wyndham Walden (1875, 1878–82, 1888).

Owner Five, by George Lorillard (1878–82).

Fastest time 1 minute 53⅕ seconds, by Tank's Prospect, 1985.

Largest field 18 horses in 1928.

PREAKNESS STAKES WINNERS (1873–1991)

Year	Horse	Year	Horse	Year	Horse	Year	Horse
1873	Survivor	1903	Flocarline	1933	Head Play	1963	Candy Spots
1874	Culpepper	1904	Bryn Mawr	1934	High Quest	1964	Northern Dancer
1875	Tom Ochiltree	1905	Cairngorm	1935	Omaha	1965	Tom Rolfe
1876	Shirley	1906	Whimsical	1936	Bold Venture	1966	Kauai King
1877	Cloverbrook	1907	Don Enrique	1937	War Admiral	1967	Damascus
1878	Duke of Magenta	1908	Royal Tourist	1938	Dauber	1968	Forward Pass
1879	Harold	1909	Effendi	1939	Challedon	1969	Majestic Prince
1880	Grenada	1910	Layminister	1940	Bimelech	1970	Personality
1881	Saunterer	1911	Watervale	1941	Whirlaway	1971	Canonero II
1882	Vanguard	1912	Colonel Holloway	1942	Alsab	1972	Bee Bee Bee
1883	Jacobus	1913	Buskin	1943	Count Fleet	1973	Secretariat
1884	Knight of Ellerslie	1914	Holiday	1944	Pensive	1974	Little Current
1885	Tecumseh	1915	Rhine Maiden	1945	Polynesian	1975	Master Derby
1886	The Bard	1916	Damrosch	1946	Assault	1976	Elocutionist
1887	Dunboyne	1917	Kalitan	1947	Faultless	1977	Seattle Slew
1888	Refund	1918	Jack Hare Jr.	1948	Citation	1978	Affirmed
1889	Buddhist	1919	Sir Barton	1949	Capot	1979	Spectacular Bid
1890	Montague	1920	Man o'War	1950	Hill Prince	1980	Codex
1891	not held	1921	Broomspun	1951	Bold	1981	Pleasant Colony
1892	not held	1922	Pillory	1952	Blue Man	1982	Aloma's Ruler
1893	not held	1923	Vigil	1953	Native Dancer	1983	Deputed Testamony
1894	Assignee	1924	Nellie Morse	1954	Hasty Road	1984	Gate Dancer
1895	Belmar	1925	Coventry	1955	Nashua	1985	Tank's Prospect
1896	Margrave	1926	Display	1956	Fabius	1986	Snow Chief
1897	Paul Kauvar	1927	Bostonian	1957	Bold Ruler	1987	Alysheba
1898	Sly Fox	1928	Victorian	1958	Tim Tam	1988	Risen Star
1899	Half Time	1929	Dr. Freeland	1959	Royal Orbit	1989	Sunday Silence
1900	Hindus	1930	Gallant Fox	1960	Bally Ache	1990	Summer Squall
1901	The Parader	1931	Mate	1961	Carry Back	1991	Hansel
1902	Old England	1932	Burgoo King	1962	Greek Money		

BELMONT STAKES This race is the third leg of the Triple Crown, first run in 1867 at Jerome Park, N.Y. Since 1905 the race has been staged at Belmont Park, N.Y. Originally run over 1 mile 5 furlongs, the current distance of 1½ miles has been set since 1926.

Most Wins

Jockey Six, by two jockeys: Jim McLaughlin (1882–84, 1886–88); Eddie Arcaro (1941–42, 1945, 1948, 1952, 1955).

Trainer Eight, by James Rowe Sr. (1883–84, 1901, 1904, 1907–08, 1910, 1913).

BELMONT STAKES WINNERS (1867–1991)

Year	Horse	Year	Horse	Year	Horse	Year	Horse
1867	Ruthless	1898	Bowling Brook	1929	Blue Larkspur	1960	Celtic Ash
1868	General Duke	1899	Jean Bereaud	1930	Gallant Fox	1961	Sherluck
1869	Fenian	1900	Ildrim	1931	Twenty Grand	1962	Jaipur
1870	Kingfisher	1901	Commando	1932	Faireno	1963	Chateaugay
1871	Harry Bassett	1902	Masterman	1933	Hurryoff	1964	Quadrangle
1872	Joe Daniels	1903	Africander	1934	Peace Chance	1965	Hail to All
1873	Springbok	1904	Delhi	1935	Omaha	1966	Amberoid
1874	Saxon	1905	Tanya	1936	Granville	1967	Damascus
1875	Calvin	1906	Burgomaster	1937	War Admiral	1968	Stage Door Johnny
1876	Algerine	1907	Peter Pan	1938	Pasteurized	1969	Arts and Letters
1877	Cloverbrook	1908	Colin	1939	Johnstown	1970	High Echelon
1878	Duke of Magenta	1909	Joe Madden	1940	Bimelech	1971	Pass Catcher
1879	Spendthrift	1910	Sweep	1941	Whirlaway	1972	Riva Ridge
1880	Grenada	1911	not held	1942	Shut Out	1973	Secretariat
1881	Saunterer	1912	not held	1943	Count Fleet	1974	Little Current
1882	Forester	1913	Prince Eugene	1944	Bounding Home	1975	Avatar
1883	George Kinney	1914	Luke McLuke	1945	Pavot	1976	Bold Forbes
1884	Panique	1915	The Finn	1946	Assault	1977	Seattle Slew
1885	Tyrant	1916	Friar Rock	1947	Phalanx	1978	Affirmed
1886	Inspector B	1917	Hourless	1948	Citation	1979	Coastal
1887	Hanover	1918	Johren	1949	Capot	1980	Temperence Hill
1888	Sir Dixon	1919	Sir Barton	1950	Middleground	1981	Summing
1889	Eric	1920	Man o' War	1951	Counterpoint	1982	Conquistador Cielo
1890	Burlington	1921	Grey Lag	1952	One Count	1983	Caveat
1891	Foxford	1922	Pillory	1953	Native Dancer	1984	Swale
1892	Patron	1923	Zev	1954	High Gun	1985	Creme Fraiche
1893	Comanche	1924	Mad Play	1955	Nashua	1986	Danzig Connection
1894	Henry of Navarre	1925	American Flag	1956	Needles	1987	Bet Twice
1895	Belmar	1926	Crusader	1957	Gallant Man	1988	Risen Star
1896	Hastings	1927	Chance Shot	1958	Cavan	1989	Easy Goer
1897	Scottish Chieftain	1928	Vito	1959	Sword Dancer	1990	Go and Go
						1991	Hansel

Owner Five, by three owners: Dwyer Brothers (1883–84, 1886–88); James R. Keene (1901, 1904, 1907–08, 1910); and William Woodward Sr. (Belair Stud) (1930, 1932, 1935–36, 1939).

Fastest time 2 minutes 24 seconds, by Secretariat, 1973.

Largest field 15 horses, in 1983.

BREEDERS' CUP CHAMPIONSHIP

The Breeders' Cup Championship has been staged annually since 1984. It was devised by John R. Gaines, a leading thoroughbred owner and breeder, to provide a season-ending championship for each division of thoroughbred racing. The Breeders' Cup Championship consists of seven races: Juvenile, Juvenile Fillies, Sprint, Mile, Distaff, Turf and the Classic, with a record purse of $10 million.

CHAMPIONSHIP RECORDS

HORSES

Most wins The only horse to win two Breeders' Cup races is Bayakoa, which won the Distaff in 1989 and 1990.

Highest earnings Alysheba has won a record $2,133,000 in Breeders' Cup races, from three starts, 1986–88.

JOCKEYS

Most wins Two riders have ridden six winners in the Breeders' Cup Championship: Laffit Pincay Jr., Juvenile (1985, 1986, 1988), Classic (1986), Distaff (1989, 1990); Pat Day, Classic (1984, 1990), Distaff (1986, 1991), Juvenile Fillies (1987), Turf (1987).

Highest earnings Pat Day has won a record $8,235,000 in Breeders' Cup racing, 1984–91.

BREEDERS' CUP CLASSIC This race, the principle event of the Breeders' Cup Championship, is run over 1 ¼ miles. The Classic offers a single-race record $3 million purse, with $1,560,000 to the winner.

Most wins (horse) The Classic has been won by a different horse on each occasion.

Most wins (jockey) Two jockeys have won the Classic twice: Pat Day, 1984 and 1990; Chris McCarron, 1988 and 1989.

INTERNATIONAL RACES

VRC Melbourne Cup This contest, Australia's most prestigious classic race, has been staged annually since 1861. The race is run over one mile at the Flemington Racetrack, Victoria.

Fastest time The fastest time is 3 minutes 16.3 seconds by Kingston Rule, ridden by Darren Beadman in 1990.

Most wins (jockeys) Two jockeys have won the race four times: Bobby Lewis, 1902, 1915, 1919 and 1927; Harry White, 1974–75 and 1978–79.

Derby England's most prestigious classic race has been staged annually since 1780. The race is contested over 1 mile 4 furlongs at Epsom Downs, Surrey.

Fastest time The fastest time is 2 minutes 33.8 seconds, by Mahmoud, ridden by Charlie Smirke, in 1936. Kahyasi, ridden by Ray Cochrane, won the 1988 Derby in an electronically timed 2 minutes 33.84 seconds.

Most wins (jockey) Lester Piggott has won the Derby a record nine times: 1954, 1957, 1960, 1968, 1970, 1972, 1976–77 and 1983.

Grand National England's most famous steeplechase race, and most beloved sporting event, has been staged annually since 1839. The race is contested over a 4½ mile course of 30 fences at Aintree, Liverpool.

Fastest time The fastest time is 8 minutes 47.8 seconds, by Mr. Frisk, ridden by Marcus Armytage, in 1990.

Most wins (jockey) George Stevens has won the National five times: 1856, 1863–64 and 1869–70.

Prix de l'Arc de Triomphe France's most prestigious classic race, and Europe's richest thoroughbred race, has been staged annually since 1920. The race is contested over 1 mile 864 yards at Longchamps, Paris.

Fastest time The fastest time is 2 minutes 26.3 seconds, by Trempolino, ridden by Pat Eddery, in 1987.

Most wins (jockey) Four jockeys have won the Arc four times: Jacques Doyasbere, 1942, 1944, 1950–51; Freddy Head, 1966, 1972, 1976, 1979; Yves Saint-Martin, 1970, 1974, 1982, 1984; Pat Eddery, 1980, 1985–87.

Irish Derby Ireland's most prestigious classic race has been staged annually since 1866. The race is contested over 1½ miles at The Curragh, County Kildare.

Fastest time The fastest time is 2 minutes 28.8 seconds, by Tambourine II, ridden by Roger Poincelet, in 1962.

Most wins (jockey) Morny Wing has won the Irish Derby a record six times: 1921, 1923, 1930, 1938, 1942 and 1946.

HORSESHOE PITCHING

The object of the game of horseshoes is to toss a horseshoe over an iron stake so that it "comes to rest encircling the stake." The playing area, the horseshoe court, requires two stakes to be securely grounded 40 feet apart within a six-foot-square pitcher's box. Each contestant pitches two shoes in succession from the pitcher's box to the stake at the opposite end of the court. The pitching distance is 40 feet for men, and 30 feet for women. The winner is determined by a point system based on the shoe that is pitched closest to the stake. The pitcher with the most points wins the contest.

ORIGINS Historians claim that a variation of horseshoe pitching was first played by Roman soldiers to relieve the monotony of guard duty. Horseshoes was introduced to North America by the first settlers, and every town had its own horseshoe courts and competitions. The game was a popular pastime for soldiers during the Revolutionary War, and the famed British officer the Duke of Wellington wrote in his memoirs that "The War was won by pitchers of horse hardware!" The modern sport of horseshoes dates to the formation of the National Horseshoe Pitcher's Association (NHPA) in 1914.

WORLD CHAMPIONSHIPS First staged in 1909, the tournament was staged intermittently until 1946; since then it has been an annual event.

Most titles (men) Ted Allen (U.S.) has won 10 world titles: 1933-35, 1940, 1946, 1953, 1955-57 and 1959.

Most titles (women) Vicki Winston (née Chappelle) has won a record 10 women's titles: 1956, 1958–59, 1961, 1963, 1966-67, 1969, 1975 and 1981.

JUDO

ORIGINS Judo is a modern combat sport that developed from an amalgam of several old Japanese martial arts, the most popular of which was jujitsu (jiujitsu), which is thought to be of Chinese origin. Judo has developed greatly since 1882, when it was first devised by Dr. Jigoro Kano. The International Judo Federation was founded in 1951.

Highest grades The efficiency grades in judo are divided into pupil (*kyu*) and master (*dan*) grades. The highest awarded is the extremely rare red belt *judan* (10th dan), given to only 13 men so far. The Judo protocol provides for an 11th dan (*juichidan*) who also would wear a red belt, a 12th dan (*junidan*) who would wear a white belt twice as wide as an ordinary belt, and the highest of all, *shihan* (doctor), but these have never been bestowed, save for the 12th dan, to the founder of the sport, Dr. Jigoro Kano.

OLYMPIC GAMES Judo was first included in the Games in 1964 in Tokyo, Japan, and has been included in every Games since 1972. Women's events were included as a demonstration sport in the 1988 Games in Seoul, and will be recognized as official events at the Barcelona Games in 1992.

Most gold medals Three men have won two gold medals: Willem Ruska (Netherlands), open class and over 93 kilograms class, in 1972; Hiroshi Saito (Japan), over 95 kilograms class, in 1984 and 1988; and Peter Seisenbacher (Austria), up to 86 kilograms class, in 1984 and 1988.

Most medals (individual) Angelo Parisi has won a record four Olympic medals, while representing two countries. In 1972 Parisi won a bronze medal in the open class, representing Great Britain. In 1980 Parisi represented France and won a gold, over 95 kilograms class, and a silver, open class; and won a second silver in the open class in 1984.

Most medals (country) The Soviet Union has won 23 medals in judo competition: five gold, five silver and 13 bronze. Japan has won a record 14 gold medals.

United States No American athlete has won a gold medal in judo. Overall the United States has won six medals in Olympic competition: two silver and four bronze.

WORLD CHAMPIONSHIPS The first men's world championships were held in Tokyo, Japan in 1956. The event has been staged biennially since 1965. A world championship for women was first staged in New York City in 1980.

Most titles (men) Two men have won four world titles: Yasuhiro Yamashita (Japan), open class, 1981; over 95 kilograms class, 1979, 1981, 1983; and Shozo Fujii (Japan), under 80 kilograms class, 1971, 1973, 1975; under 78 kilograms class, 1979.

Most titles (women) Ingrid Berghmans (Belgium) has won a record six world titles: open class, 1980, 1982, 1984 and 1986; under 72 kilograms class, 1984 and 1989.

KARATE

ORIGINS Karate is a martial art developed in Japan. Karate (empty hand) techniques evolved from the Chinese art of shoalin boxing, known as kempo, which was popularized in Okinawa in the 16th century as a means of self-defense, and became known as Tang Hand. Tang Hand was introduced to Japan by Funakoshi Gichin in the 1920s, and the name karate was coined in the 1930s. Gichin's style of karate, known as shotokan, is one of five major styles adapted for competition, the others being wado-ryu, gojuryu, shito-ryu and kyokushinkai. Each style places different emphasis on the elements of technique, speed and power. Karate's popularity grew in the West in the late 1950s.

WORLD CHAMPIONSHIPS The first men's world championships were staged in Tokyo, Japan in 1970; a women's competition was first staged in 1980. Both tournaments are now staged biennially. The competition consists of two types: kumite, in which combatants fight each other, and kata events, in which contestants perform routines.

KUMITE CHAMPIONSHIPS (MEN)

Most titles (team) Great Britain has won six kumite world team titles, in 1975, 1982, 1984, 1986, 1988 and 1990.

Most titles (individual) Three men have won two individual world titles: Pat McKay (Great Britain) in the under 80 kilograms class, 1982, 1984; Emmanuel Pinda (France), in the open class, 1984, and the over 80 kilograms class, 1988; Theirry Masci (France), in the under 70 kilograms class, 1986 and 1988.

KATA CHAMPIONSHIPS (MEN)

Most titles (team) Japan has won two kata world team titles, in 1986 and 1988.

Most titles (individual) Tsuguo Sakumoto (Japan) has won three world titles, in 1984, 1986, 1988.

KUMITE CHAMPIONSHIPS (WOMEN)

Most titles (individual) Guus van Mourik (Netherlands) has won four world titles in the over 60 kilograms class, in 1982, 1984, 1986 and 1988.

KATA CHAMPIONSHIPS (WOMEN)

Most titles (individual) Mie Nakayama (Japan) has won three world titles, in 1982, 1984 and 1986.

LACROSSE

LACROSSE (MEN)

ORIGINS The sport is of Native American origin, derived from the intertribal game of *baggataway*, which has been recorded as being played by Iroquois tribes as early as 1492. French settlers in North America coined the name "La Crosse", (the French word for a crozier or staff). The National Lacrosse Association was formed in Canada in 1867. The United States Amateur Lacrosse Association was founded in 1879. The International Federation of Amateur Lacrosse (IFAL) was founded in 1928.

OLYMPIC GAMES Lacrosse was included in the Olympic program as an official sport in 1904 and 1908. It was also included as a demonstration sport in the Games of 1928, 1932 and 1948.

Most gold medals (country) Canada has won both of the official Olympic tournaments, in 1904 and 1908.

United States The American team won the silver medal at the 1904 Games.

WORLD CHAMPIONSHIPS The men's world championships were first staged in Toronto, Canada in 1967.

Most titles The United States has won five world titles, in 1967, 1974, 1982, 1986 and 1990.

NCAA CHAMPIONSHIPS (DIVISION I) The men's NCAA championship was first staged in 1971.

Most titles Johns Hopkins has won seven lacrosse titles, in 1974, 1978–80, 1984–85 and 1987.

LACROSSE (WOMEN)

ORIGINS Women were first reported to have played lacrosse in 1886. The women's game evolved separately from the men's, developing different rules; thus two distinct games were created:

the women's game features 12-a-side and six-a-side games, while men's games field 10-a-side teams.

WORLD CHAMPIONSHIPS A women's world championship was first held in 1969. Since 1982 the world championships have been known as the World Cup.

Most titles The United States has won three world titles, in 1974, 1982 and 1989.

NCAA CHAMPIONSHIPS (DIVISION I) The NCAA first staged a women's national championship in 1982.

Most titles Two teams have won two titles: Temple, 1984 and 1988; and Penn State, 1987 and 1989.

MODERN PENTATHLON

ORIGINS The modern pentathalon is comprised of five activities: fencing, horseback riding, pistol shooting, swimming and cross-country running. The sport derives from military training in the 19th century, which was based on a messenger's being able to travel across country on horseback, fighting his way through with sword and pistol, and being prepared to swim across rivers and complete his journey on foot. Each event is scored on points, determined either against other contestants or against scoring tables. There is no standard course; therefore, point totals are not comparable. *L'Union Internationale de Pentathlon Moderne* (UIPM) was formed in 1948 and expanded to include the administration of the biathlon in 1957. (For further information on the biathlon, see pages 50–51.)

United States The United States Modern Pentathlon and Biathlon Association was established in 1971, but this body was split to create the U.S. Modern Pentathlon Association in 1978.

OLYMPIC GAMES Modern pentathlon was first included in the 1912 Games held in Stockholm, Sweden, and has been part of every Olympic program since.

Most gold medals (overall) Andras Balczo (Hungary) has won three gold medals in Olympic competition: team event, 1960 and 1968; individual title, 1972.

Most gold medals (individual event) Lars Hall (Sweden) is the only athlete to win two individual Olympic titles, in 1952 and 1956.

Most gold medals (team event) Two countries have won the team event four times: Hungary, 1952, 1960, 1968 and 1988; USSR, 1956, 1964, 1972 and 1980.

Most medals (individual) Pavel Lednev (USSR) has won a record seven medals in Olympic competition: two gold—team event, 1972 and 1980; two silver—team event, 1968; individual event, 1976; and three bronze—individual event, 1968, 1972 and 1980.

Most medals (country) Sweden has won 21 medals in Olympic competition: nine gold, seven silver and five bronze.

United States No American team or athlete has won a gold medal in Olympic competition. Overall the United States has won eight medals: five silver and three bronze. The only individual medal in this tally was gained by Robert Beck, who won the bronze medal in 1960.

WORLD CHAMPIONSHIPS An official men's world championship was first staged in 1949, and has been held annually since. In Olympic years the Games are considered the world championships, and results from those events are included in world championship statistics. A women's world championship was inaugurated in 1981.

MEN'S CHAMPIONSHIP

Most titles (overall) Andras Balczo (Hungary) has won a record 13 world titles, including a record six individual titles: seven team, 1960, 1963, 1965–68 and 1970; six individual, 1963, 1965–67, 1969 and 1972.

Most titles (team event) The USSR has won 17 world championships: 1956–59, 1961–62, 1964, 1969, 1971–74, 1980, 1982–83, 1985 and 1991.

United States The United States won its only team world title in 1979, when Bob Nieman became the first American athlete, and so far the only man, to win an individual world championship.

WOMEN'S CHAMPIONSHIP

Most titles (individual event) Irina Kiselyeva (USSR) is the only woman to win the individual title twice, in 1986 and 1987.

Most titles (team event) Poland has won five world titles: 1985, 1988–91.

United States The best result for the U.S. in the team event is second place, which has been achieved twice, in 1981 and 1989. Lori Norwood won the individual championship in 1989.

UNITED STATES NATIONAL CHAMPIONSHIPS The men's championship was inaugurated in 1955, and the women's in 1977.

Most titles (men) Mike Burley has won four men's titles, in 1977, 1979, 1981 and 1985.

Most titles (women) Kim Arata (née Dunlop) has won nine titles, in 1979–80, 1984–89 and 1991.

MOTORCYCLE RACING

ORIGINS The first recorded motorcycle race took place in France on September 20, 1896, when eight riders took part in a 139-mile race from Paris to Nantes and back. The winner was M. Chevalier on a Michelin-Dion tricycle; he covered the course in 4 hours 10 minutes 37 seconds. The first race for two-wheeled motorcycles was held on a one-mile oval track at Sheen House, Richmond, England on November 29, 1897. The *Fédération Internationale Motorcycliste* (FIM) was founded in 1904 and is the world governing body.

WORLD CHAMPIONSHIPS The FIM instituted world championships in 1949 for 125, 250, 350 and 500cc classes. In 1962, a 50cc class was introduced, which was upgraded to 80cc in 1983. In 1982, the 350cc class was discontinued.

Most Championships

Overall 15, by Giacomo Agostini (Italy): 7—350cc (1968–74); 8—500cc (1966–72, 1975).

50cc 6, by Angel Nieto (Spain), 1969–70, 1972, 1975–77.

80cc 3, by Jorge Martinez (Spain), 1986–88.

125cc 7, by Angel Nieto (Spain), 1971–72, 1979, 1981–84.

250cc 4, by Phil Read (Great Britain), 1964–65, 1968, 1971.

350cc 7, by Giacomo Agostini (Italy), 1968–74.

500cc 8, by Giacomo Agostini (Italy), 1966–72, 1975.

Multiple titles The only rider to win more then one world chmpionship in one year is Freddie Spencer (U.S.), who won the 250cc and 500cc titles in 1985.

United States The most world titles won by an American rider is four, by Eddie Lawson at 500cc in 1984, 1986, 1988–89.

Most Grand Prix Wins

Overall 122, by Giacomo Agostini (Italy): 54—350cc; 68—500cc.

50cc 27, by Angel Nieto (Spain).

80cc 21, by Jorge Martinez (Spain).

125cc 62, by Angel Nieto (Spain).

250cc 33, by Anton Mang (West Germany).

350cc 54, by Giacomo Agostini (Italy).

500cc 68, by Giacomo Agostini (Italy).

Most successful machines Japanese Yamaha machines won 41 world championships between 1964 and 1991.

Fastest circuits The highest average lap speed attained on any closed circuit is 160.288 mph, by Yvon du Hamel (Canada) on a modified 903cc four-cylinder Kawasaki Z1 at the 31-degree banked 2.5 mile Daytona International Speedway, Fla. in March 1973. His lap time was 56.149 seconds.

The fastest road circuit was the Francorchamps circuit near Spa, Belgium, then 8.74 miles long. It was lapped in 3 minutes 50.3 seconds (average speed 137.150 mph) by Barry Sheene (Great Britain) on a 495cc four-cylinder Suzuki during the Belgian Grand Prix on July 3, 1977. On that occasion he set a record time for this 10-lap (87.74-mile) race of 38 minutes 58.5 seconds (average speed 135.068 mph).

Longest race The longest race was the Liège 24-hour run on the old Francorchamps circuit. The greatest distance ever covered is 2,761.9 miles (average speed 115.08 mph) by Jean-Claude Chemarin and Christian Leon, both of France, on a 941cc four-cylinder Honda on August 14–15, 1976.

Longest circuit The 37.73-mile "Mountain" circuit on the Isle of Man, over which the principal Tourist Trophy races have been run since 1911 (with minor amendments in 1920), has 264 curves and corners and is the longest used for any motorcycle race.

OLYMPIC GAMES

Records in this section include results from the Intercalated Games staged in 1906.

ORIGINS The exact date of the first Olympic Games is uncertain. The earliest date for which there is documented evidence is July 776 B.C. By order of Theodosius I, emperor of Rome, the Games were prohibited in A.D. 394. The revival of the Olympic Games is credited to Pierre de Fredi, Baron de Coubertin, a French aristocrat, who was commissioned by his government to form a universal sports association in 1889. Coubertin presented his proposals for a modern Games on November 25, 1892 in Paris; this led to the formation of the International Olympic Committee (IOC) in 1894 and thence to the staging of the first modern Olympic Games, which were opened in Athens, Greece on April 6, 1896. In 1906, the IOC organized the Intercalated Games in Athens, to celebrate the 10th anniversary of the revival of the

GRAND OPENING ■ THE RAISING OF THE OLYMPIC FLAG, AND THE LIGHTING OF THE OLYMPIC FLAME, HIGHLIGHT THE GAMES' OPENING CEREMONY, AND SERVE AS TWO ENDURING SYMBOLS OF DE COUBERTIN'S IDEAL.

GOLDEN GYMNAST ■ LARISSA LATYNINA (USSR) (CENTER) IS THE MOST SUCCESSFUL COMPETITOR IN OLYMPIC HISTORY, WINNING 18 MEDALS, INCLUDING A RECORD NINE GOLDS.

Games. In 1924, the first Winter Olympics were held in Chamonix, France.

OLYMPIC GAMES MEDAL RECORDS

INDIVIDUAL RECORDS

Most gold medals Ray Ewry (U.S.) has won 10 gold medals in Olympic competition: standing high jump, 1900, 1904, 1906 and 1908; standing long jump, 1900, 1904, 1906 and 1908; standing triple jump, 1900 and 1904. The most gold medals won by a woman is nine, by gymnast Larissa Latynina (USSR): all-around, 1956 and 1960; vault, 1956; floor exercise, 1956, 1960 and 1964; team title, 1956, 1960 and 1964.

Most medals Gymnast Larissa Latynina (USSR) has won 18 medals (nine gold, five silver and four bronze), 1956–64. The most medals won by a man is 15 (seven gold, five silver and three bronze), by gymnast Nikolai Andrianov (USSR), 1972–80.

Most gold medals at one Olympics Swimmer Mark Spitz (U.S.) won a record seven gold medals at Munich in 1972. His victories came in the 100-meter freestyle, 200-meter freestyle, 100-meter butterfly, 200-meter butterfly, and three relay events. The most gold medals won at one Games by a woman athlete is six, by swimmer Kristin Otto (East Germany), who won six gold medals at the 1988 Games. Her victories came in the 50-meter freestyle, 100-meter freestyle, 100-meter backstroke, 100-meter butterfly, and two relay events. The most individual events won at one Games is five, by speed skater Eric Heiden (U.S.) in 1980. Heiden won the 500 meters, 1,000 meters, 1,500 meters, 5,000 meters, and 10,000 meters.

Most medals at one Olympics Gymnast Aleksandr Dityatin (USSR) won eight medals (three gold, four silver and one bronze) at Moscow, USSR in 1980. The most medals won by a woman athlete is seven (two gold and five silver), by gymnast Maria Gorokhovskaya (USSR) in 1952.

Most consecutive gold medals (same event) Al Oerter (U.S.) is the only athlete to win the same event, the discus, at four consecutive Games, 1956–68. Yachtsman Paul Elvstrom (Denmark) won four successive golds at monotype events, 1948–60, but there was a class change: Firefly in 1948; Finn class, 1952–60. Including the Intercalated Games of 1906, Ray Ewry (U.S.) won four consecutive gold medals in two events: standing high jump, 1900–1908; standing long jump, 1900–1908.

Oldest gold medalist Oscar Swahn (Sweden) was aged 64 years 258 days when he won an Olympic gold medal in 1912 as a member of the team that won the running deer shooting single-shot title. The oldest woman to win a gold medal was Queenie Newall (Great Britain), who won the 1908 national round archery event at age 53 years 275 days.

Youngest gold medalist The youngest-ever winner was an unnamed French boy who coxed the Netherlands pair to victory in the 1900 rowing event. He was believed to be 7–10 years old. The youngest-ever woman champion was Marjorie Gestring (U.S.), who at age 13 years 268 days won the 1936 women's springboard diving event.

Most Games Three Olympians have competed in eight Games: show jumper Raimondo d'Inzeo (Italy), 1948–76; yachtsman Paul Elvstrom (Denmark), 1948–60, 1968–72, 1984–88; yachtsman Durwood Knowles (Great Britain/Bahamas), 1948–72, 1988. The most appearances by a woman is seven, by fencer Kerstin Palm (Sweden), 1964–88.

Summer/Winter Games gold medalist The only person to have won gold medals in both Summer and Winter Olympiads is Edward Eagan (U.S.), who won the 1920 light-heavyweight boxing title and was a member of the 1932 winning four-man bobsled team.

Summer/Winter Games medalist (same year) The only athlete to have won medals at both the Winter and Summer Games held in the same year is Christa Rothenburger-Luding (East Germany). At the 1988 Winter Games in Calgary, Canada, Rothenburger-Luding won two speed skating medals: gold medal, 1,000 meters, and silver medal, 500 meters; and at the Seoul Games that summer she won a silver medal in the women's sprint cycling event.

UNITED STATES RECORDS

Most gold medals The records for most gold medals overall and at one Games are both held by American athletes (see above). The most gold medals won by an American woman is four, by Patricia McCormick (née Keller), both in highboard and springboard diving, 1952 and 1956.

Most medals (gold, silver, bronze) The most medals won by an American Olympian is 11, by two athletes: Carl Osburn, shooting—five gold, four silver and two bronze (1912–24); Mark Spitz, swimming—nine gold, one silver and one bronze (1968–72). The most medals won by an American woman is eight, by Shirley Babashoff, swimming—two gold and six silver (1972–76).

Oldest gold medalist The oldest U.S. Olympic champion was Galen Spencer, who won a gold medal in the Team Round archery event in 1904, at age 64 years 2 days.

Youngest gold medalist The youngest gold medalist was Jackie Fields, who won the 1924 featherweight boxing title at age 16 years 162 days.

Oldest medalist The oldest U.S. medalist was Samuel Duvall, who was a member of the 1904 silver-medal-winning team in the team round archery event, at age 68 years 194 days.

Youngest medalist The youngest American medal winner, and the youngest-ever participant, was Dorothy Poynton, who won a silver medal in springboard diving at the 1928 Games at age 13 years 23 days. The youngest men's medalist was Donald Douglas Jr., who won a silver medal at six-meter yachting in 1932, at age 15 years 40 days.

SUMMER GAMES CHRONOLOGY (1896–1996)

1896 ATHENS, GREECE

The first Olympic Games of the modern era were staged in Athens, Greece from April 6–15, 1896. Thirteen countries participated in the inaugural Games: Australia, Austria, Bulgaria, Chile, Denmark, France, Germany, Great Britain, Greece, Hungary, Sweden, Switzerland and the United States. These nations competed in seven sports: cycling, fencing, shooting, swimming, tennis, track and field, and weightlifting. Rowing and yachting events had been scheduled for the Games, but severe storms forced the organizers to abandon them.

General records The first event of the Olympics was the 100-meter heats. The first heat was won by Francis Lane (U.S.). The first gold medal of the modern era was won by James Connolly (U.S.), who won the triple jump, which was known at that time as the "hop, step and jump."

Most gold medals The United States won 11 gold medals in 1896.

Most medals Greece won 47 medals in 1896: ten gold, 19 silver and 18 bronze.

United States U.S. athletes won 19 medals in 1896: 11 gold, seven silver and one bronze.

1900 PARIS, FRANCE

The second Summer Games were staged in Paris, France from May 20–October 28, 1900. Twenty-two countries entered teams for the second Games, which for the first time included events for women. The Games were held in conjunction with the Paris Universal Exposition; this proved to be a mistake, since the events were relegated to a series of sideshows to attract crowds to the fair. Facilities were poor, and many of the athletes were unaware that they were competing in the Olympic Games.

It wasn't until 1912 that the International Olympic Committee (IOC) finally tabulated all the results.

General records The first female Olympic champion was Charlotte Cooper (Great Britain), who won the the ladies' singles tennis title. Alvin Kraenzlein (U.S.) won four gold medals in individual track and field events, a feat that is yet to be matched. The youngest Olympic champion was crowned at these games—an unnamed French boy, believed to be seven to ten years old, who coxed the winning Dutch crew in the coxed pairs rowing events.

Most gold medals France won 27 gold medals in 1900.

Most medals France won 99 medals in 1900: 27 gold, 39 silver and 33 bronze.

United States U.S. athletes won 49 medals in 1900: 19 gold, 15 silver and 15 bronze.

1904 ST. LOUIS, MO.

The third Olympic Games were staged in St. Louis, Mo. from July 1–November 23, 1904. The Games were held in conjunction with the Louisiana Purchase Exposition, and the Games again became a sideshow to attract crowds to the fair. St. Louis' geographic location made it difficult and expensive for European nations to send teams, and only 13 countries participated. The Games in fact were little more than an American sports festival, with "international guest athletes" competing in the occasional event.

General records At 64 years 2 days, Galen Spencer became the oldest American athlete to win an Olympic title, when his team won the team round archery event. In the same competition, Samuel Duvall became the oldest American athlete to win a medal, when his team won the silver medal; he was 68 years 194 days old.

Most gold medals The United States won 81 out of a possible 100 gold medals in 1904.

Most medals The United States won 244 medals in 1904: 81 gold, 85 silver and 78 bronze.

1906 ATHENS, GREECE

The reputation of the Games had been damaged by the lack of public support and the minimal international participation at the Paris and St. Louis Games. To revive interest, the IOC agreed to a proposal, forwarded by Greece, to hold a series of sports festivals quadrennially, between the staging of the Olympics, with Athens as the permanent location. The first, and only, Intercalated (or Interim) Games were held in Athens, Greece, from April 22–May 2, 1906. Twenty countries participated in the Intercalated Games, which were viewed by large crowds. The Games were held with the approval of the IOC, but were not numbered in the official sequence of the Games. Medals awarded at these Games are included by most historians in tabulating Olympics records.

Most gold medals France won 15 gold medals in 1906.

Most medals France won 40 medals in 1906: 15 gold, nine silver and 16 bronze.

United States U.S. athletes won 23 medals at the 1906 Games: 12 gold, six silver and five bronze.

1908 LONDON, ENGLAND

The fourth Summer Games were staged in London, England from April 27–October 31, 1908, with 22 countries participating. For the first time, applications for entry to the events by individual athletes were not accepted; only countries could apply to compete in the Games from 1908 onwards. The facilities for the events were a marked improvement, but British officiating was regarded as biased, causing many disputes and blighting an otherwise successful Games.

General records Ray Ewry (U.S.) completed his remarkable Olympic career by winning two gold medals, to increase his haul to an unsurpassed record 10 gold medals.

Most gold medals Great Britain won 56 gold medals in 1908.

Most medals Great Britain won 145 medals in 1908: 56 gold, 50 silver and 39 bronze.

United States U.S. athletes won 47 medals in 1908: 23 gold, 12 silver and 12 bronze.

1912 STOCKHOLM, SWEDEN

The fifth Summer Games were staged in Stockholm, Sweden from May 5–July 22, 1912, with 28 countries participating. The Stockholm Games are widely regarded as the prototype for the Games as we now know them, being well organized and featuring independent officiating, multinational participation, and high standards of competition. Although a tremendous success, the 1912 Games are the source of one of the greatest controversies in Olympic history: Jim Thorpe (U.S.) had been the outstanding performer of the Games, winning the pentathlon and decathlon, leading the King of Sweden to dub him "the world's greatest athlete." However, Thorpe was later declared a professional for having played minor league baseball, and his gold medals were revoked. This decision was disputed until 1982, when Thorpe was reinstated and his medals presented to his family.

General records At age 64 years 258 days, Oscar Swahn (Sweden) became the oldest gold medal winner in the history of the Games, as a member of the Swedish team that won the running deer shooting single-shot team event.

Most gold medals The United States won 25 gold medals, including Thorpe's two golds, in 1912.

Most medals Sweden won 64 medals in 1912: 24 gold, 24 silver and 16 bronze.

United States U.S. athletes won 62 medals in 1912: 25 gold, 19 silver and 18 bronze.

1916

The sixth Summer Games were scheduled to be staged in Berlin, Germany in 1916, but the Games were canceled because of World War I, which lasted from 1914 to 1918.

1920 ANTWERP, BELGIUM

The seventh Summer Games were staged in Antwerp, Belgium, April 20–September 12, 1920, with 29 countries participating. Three permanent fixtures of Olympic pageantry were introduced in Antwerp: the Olympic motto, *"Citius, Altius, Fortius"* (Faster, Higher, Stronger), was adopted; the Olympic flag was unveiled; and the Olympic oath was introduced, being taken for the first time by Victor Boin (Belgium).

General records At age 72 years 280 days, Oscar Swahn (Sweden) became the oldest medalist in Olympic history, as a member of the Swedish team that won the silver medal in the running deer shooting double-shot team event.

Most gold medals The United States won 41 gold medals in 1920.

Most medals The United States won 96 medals in 1920: 41 golds, 27 silver and 28 bronze.

1924 PARIS, FRANCE

The eighth Summer Games were staged in Paris, France from May 4–July 27, 1924, with 44 countries participating. The 1924 Games were the site of one the most remarkable performances in Olympic history: Paavo Nurmi (Finland), on his way to a record five gold medals (see below), won the 1,500 meters and the 5,000 meters within the space of two hours.

General records Paavo Nurmi (Finland) won five gold medals, a record for track and field titles at one Games. Carl Osburn (U.S.) won a silver medal at the 1924 Games, increasing his career medal total to 11, a record for a U.S. athlete, later matched by swimmer Mark Spitz in 1972. Jackie Fields became the youngest American male athlete to win a gold medal, when he won the feather-weight boxing title at age 16 years 162 days.

Most gold medals The United States won 45 gold medals in 1924.

Most medals The United States won 99 medals in 1924: 45 gold, 27 silver and 27 bronze.

1928 AMSTERDAM, NETHERLANDS

The ninth Summer Games were held in Amsterdam, Netherlands from May 17–August 12, 1928, with 46 countries participating. The Olympic flame was introduced for the first time at Amsterdam, with the flame burning for the duration of the Games. Another significant first was the introduction of track and field events for women, although there were only five events: 100 meters, 800 meters, high jump, discus, and 4 x 100 meter relay.

General records Dorothy Poynton became the youngest American medalist, when she won the silver medal in springboard diving at age 13 years 23 days.

Most gold medals The United States won 22 gold medals in 1928.

Most medals The United States won 56 medals in 1928: 22 gold, 18 silver and 16 bronze.

1932 LOS ANGELES, CALIF.

The 10th Summer Games were held in Los Angeles, Calif. from July 30–August 14, 1932, with 37 countries participating. The Los Angeles Games saw the introduction of the current medal ceremony, complete with three-tiered podium, flags, and anthems.

General records Babe Didriksen (U.S.) won the javelin and 800 meters, and came in second in the high jump, thus becoming the only track and field athlete to win medals in running, throwing, and jumping events. In field hockey, India defeated the U.S., 24–1, a result which still stands as the most goals ever scored in an international field hockey game.

Most gold medals The United States won 41 gold medals in 1932.

Most medals The United States won 103 medals in 1932: 41 gold, 32 silver and 30 bronze.

1936 BERLIN, GERMANY

The 11th Summer Games were held in Berlin, Germany from August 1–16, 1936, with 49 countries participating. The Nazi propaganda cloud hung menacingly over these Games, with Adolf Hitler using the Games as a vehicle to demonstrate his ideology of racial superiority. From this cauldron of racism emerged Jesse Owens, the black American track champion, who won four gold medals in track events. Owens's outstanding performance transcended sports, and marked these Games as the most famous in history. On a lighter note, the Berlin Games saw the introduction of the Olympic Torch relay from Olympia, Greece to the host city.

General records Marjorie Gestring (U.S.) became the youngest woman in Olympic history to win a gold medal, when she won the springboard diving event at age 13 years 267 days.

Most gold medals Germany won 33 gold medals in 1936.

NAZIS' NEMESIS ■ JESSE OWENS OVERCAME NAZI PROPAGANDA, AS WELL AS HIS OPPONENTS, TO WIN FOUR GOLD MEDALS AT THE 1936 GAMES.

Most medals Germany won 89 medals in 1936: 33 gold, 26 silver and 30 bronze.

United States U.S. athletes won 56 medals in 1936: 24 gold, 20 silver and 12 bronze.

1940

The 12th Summer Games were scheduled to be staged in Tokyo, Japan, but were transferred to Helsinki, Finland following the outbreak of war between China and Japan in 1938. With the outbreak of World War II, 1939–45, the Games were canceled.

1944

The 13th Summer Games were awarded to London, England in the summer of 1939, but were canceled due to the continued hostilities of World War II, 1939–45.

1948 LONDON, ENGLAND

The 14th Summer Games were staged in London, England from July 29–August 14, 1948, with 59 countries participating. England was still in the grip of postwar rationing, and the facilities reflected the grim conditions. However, the Games had been successfully revived, and that was a major accomplishment given the postwar situation.

General records Sprinter/hurdler Fanny Blankers-Koen (Netherlands) became the first woman to win four gold medals at one Games, still a record for track and field competition.

FLYING DUTCHWOMAN ■ FANNY BLANKERS-KOEN (NETHERLANDS) WON FOUR GOLD MEDALS AT THE 1948 GAMES, A RECORD UNSURPASSED IN TRACK AND FIELD EVENTS.

Most gold medals The United States won 38 gold medals in 1948.

Most medals The United States won 84 medals in 1948: 38 gold, 27 silver and 19 bronze.

1952 HELSINKI, FINLAND

The 15th Summer Games were staged in Helsinki, Finland from July 19–August 3, 1952, with 69 countries participating. The Helsinki Games marked the entry of the Soviet Union into the Olympic Games. Emil Zatopek (Czechoslovakia) notched the most memorable performance of the Games, winning a unique distance-running triple: 5,000 meters, 10,000 meters, and marathon.

General records Gymnast Maria Gorokhovskaya (USSR) won seven medals (two gold and five silver), the most by any female athlete at one Games.

Most gold medals The United States won 40 gold medals in 1952.

Most medals The United States won 76 medals in 1952: 40 gold, 19 silver and 17 bronze.

1956 MELBOURNE, AUSTRALIA

The 16th Summer Games were held in Melbourne, Australia from November 22–December 8, 1956, with 67 countries participating. Because of the strict Australian quarantine regulations, the equestrian events were held in Stockholm, Sweden from June 10–17, 1956. A tense world political climate loomed over these Games, as it had in 1936. The Soviet crushing of the Hungarian uprising, and the Suez Crisis, caused several countries to withdraw from the Games. The 1956 Games saw the introduction of another Olympic tradition, the mingling of athletes at the closing ceremony parade.

Most gold medals The Soviet Union won 37 gold medals in 1956.

Most medals The Soviet Union won 98 medals in 1956: 37 gold, 29 silver and 32 bronze.

United States U.S. athletes won 74 medals in 1956: 32 gold, 25 silver and 17 bronze.

1960 ROME, ITALY

The 17th Summer Games were held in Rome, Italy from August 5–September 11, 1960, with 83 countries participating. These Games were noted for high standards of performance: in swimming, Olympic records were set in every event; in track

and field, Herb Elliott (Australia) set a world record in the 1,500 meters, finishing 2.8 seconds ahead of the second place finisher; in gymnastics, Boris Shakhlin (USSR) won seven medals: four gold, two silver and one bronze.

General records Fencer Aladar Gerevich (Hungary) was a member of the winning team in the sabre event for the sixth consecutive Olympic Games, a record unsurpassed in Olympic history. Yachtsman Paul Elvstrom (Denmark) won a fourth consecutive yachting title, a record for successive wins in individual events.

Most gold medals The Soviet Union won 43 gold medals in 1960.

Most medals The Soviet Union won 103 medals in 1960: 43 gold, 29 silver and 31 bronze.

United States U.S. athletes won 71 medals in 1960: 34 gold, 21 silver and 16 bronze.

1964 Tokyo, Japan

The 18th Summer Games were staged in Tokyo, Japan from October 10–24, 1964, with 93 countries participating. The Tokyo Games are known as "the happy Games," with little outside political interference and few on-site officiating complaints. A reported $3 billion was spent on athletic and transport facilities, and these Games have been hailed as the best-organized in Olympic history.

General records Gymnast Larissa Latynina (USSR) completed the most successful career in Olympic history. She won six medals in Tokyo, bringing her career total to 18 (a women's record nine gold, five silver and four bronze), the most by any athlete in Olympic history. Swimmer Dawn Fraser (Australia) won her third consecutive 100-meter freestyle gold medal, equaling the mark for most consecutive titles won by a female athlete in Olympic history.

Most gold medals The United States won 36 gold medals in 1964.

Most medals The United States won 90 medals in 1964: 36 gold, 26 silver and 28 bronze.

1968 Mexico City, Mexico

The 19th Summer Games were held in Mexico City, Mexico from October 12–27, 1968, with 112 countries participating. The Mexico City Games were awash in controversy from the moment the city was selected as the 1968 host. The rarefied air at the city's altitude of 2,240 meters worried medical experts, who feared for the safety of athletes competing in the long-distance running events. These fears were not realized, but performances in the endurance events were affected. The opposite reaction occurred in the "explosive" events, where the thin air helped the athletes, contributing to some astounding performances—highlighted by the 29 foot 2½ inch long jump record set by Bob Beamon (U.S.), which surpassed the previous mark by 1 foot 9¾ inches. Controversy was not limited to the field of play: student riots in Mexico City, the aftermath of the crushing of the "Prague Spring," and the black power demonstration atop the medal podium by Tommie Smith and John Carlos (both U.S.) heralded the beginning of a new era for the Games as they became a major forum for international political protests.

General records Discus thrower Al Oerter (U.S.) won his fourth consecutive discus title, a record for most consecutive titles at the same event. Fencer Janice Romary competed in her sixth consecutive Olympic Games, the most for any American woman athlete.

Most gold medals The United States won 45 gold medals in 1968.

Most medals The United States won 107 medals in 1968: 45 gold, 28 silver and 34 bronze.

1972 MUNICH, WEST GERMANY

The 20th Summer Games were held in Munich, West Germany from August 26–September 10, 1972, with 122 countries participating. The Munich Games were stained by tragedy, when Palestinian terrorists killed two Israeli athletes and seized nine other Israelis as hostages in the Olympic village. An unsuccessful attempt to rescue them at the airport resulted in the deaths of the nine Israelis, along with five of their captors. The Games were then suspended, but with the agreement of Israeli officials, the IOC decided to complete the Games. Munich not only witnessed the Games' greatest tragedy, but also its greatest performance: swimmer Mark Spitz (U.S.) winning a record seven gold medals (see below).

General records Mark Spitz (U.S.) won seven gold medals at the Munich Games, the most by any athlete at one Games. The narrowest margin of victory in Olympic history happened at the 1972 Games: Gunnar Larsson (Sweden) defeated Tim McKee (U.S.) by two one-thousands of a second, 4:31.981 to 4:31.983, to win the 400-meter individual medley swimming event.

Most gold medals The Soviet Union won 50 gold medals in 1972.

Most medals The Soviet Union won 99 medals in 1972: 50 gold, 27 silver and 22 bronze.

United States U.S. athletes won 94 medals in 1972: 33 gold, 31 silver and 30 bronze.

1976 MONTREAL, CANADA

The 21st Summer Games were held in Montreal, Canada from July 17–August 1, 1976, with 92 countries participating. Once again, the Games were marred by off-field events: construction strikes, inefficient budget planning, and alleged corruption led to the largest financial disaster in the history of the Games. The boycott of the Games by 22 countries protesting the inclusion of New Zealand, whose rugby team had toured South Africa, diluted the quality of the field in many of the track and boxing events.

General records Gymnast Nadia Comaneci (Romania) captivated the world with her artistry, becoming the first gymnast in Olympic history to be awarded a perfect score of 10.00 for her performance on the uneven bars during the team competition. Show jumper Raimondo D'Inzeo (Italy) competed in his eighth Olympic Games, a record that was later equaled by two other men at the 1988 Games.

Most gold medals The Soviet Union won 49 gold medals in 1976.

Most medals The Soviet Union won 125 medals in 1976: 49 gold, 41 silver and 35 bronze.

United States U.S. athletes won 94 medals in 1976: 34 gold, 35 silver and 25 bronze.

MAGNIFICENT SEVEN ■ IN 1972, SWIMMER MARK SPITZ WON A RECORD SEVEN GOLD MEDALS AT ONE GAMES.

1980 Moscow, USSR

The 22nd Olympic Games were held in Moscow, USSR from July 19–August 1, 1980, with 81 countries participating. Following the Soviet invasion of Afghanistan in December 1979, the United States proposed a boycott of the Moscow Games, which was eventually supported by 45 to 50 other countries, including West Germany, Japan and Canada. The effect of the boycott was to create a virtual Eastern bloc sports festival, with occasional outstanding performances from Western athletes such as Britain's track triumvirate of Seb Coe, Steve Ovett and Daley Thompson.

General records Gymnast Aleksandr Dityatin (USSR) won an unprecedented eight medals in Moscow: three gold, four silver and one bronze. Gymnast Nikolai Andrianov (USSR) completed his magnificent Olympic career by winning five medals, to increase his collection to 15 medals, the most won by any male athlete in the history of the Games.

Most gold medals The Soviet Union won 80 gold medals in 1980.

Most medals The Soviet Union won 195 medals in 1980: 80 gold, 69 silver and 46 bronze.

SUMMER OLYMPIC GAMES MEDAL WINNERS (1896–1988)

Country	Gold	Silver	Bronze	Total	Country	Gold	Silver	Bronze	Total
United States	746	560	475	1,781	Yugoslavia	26	29	28	83
USSR	395	323	299	1,017	Austria	19	26	34	79
Great Britain	174	223	207	604	South Korea	19	22	29	70
Germany*	157	207	207	571	China	20	19	21	60
France	153	167	177	497	Cuba	23	21	15	59
Sweden	131	139	169	439	New Zealand	26	6	23	55
East Germany**	153	129	127	409	South Africa	16	15	21	52
Italy	147	121	124	392	Turkey	24	13	10	47
Hungary	124	112	136	372	Argentina	13	18	13	44
Finland	97	75	110	282	Mexico	9	12	18	39
Japan	87	75	82	244	Brazil	7	9	20	36
Australia	71	67	87	225	Kenya	11	9	11	31
Romania	55	64	82	201	Iran	4	11	15	30
Poland	40	56	95	191	Spain	4	12	8	24
Canada	39	62	73	174	Jamaica	4	10	8	22
Switzerland	40	66	57	163	Estonia††	6	6	9	21
Netherlands	43	47	63	153	Egypt	6	6	6	18
Bulgaria	37	62	52	151	India	8	3	3	14
Denmark	33	58	53	144	Ireland	4	4	5	13
Czechoslovakia	45	48	49	142	Portugal	2	4	7	13
Belgium	35	48	42	125	North Korea†	2	5	5	12
Norway	42	33	33	108	Mongolia	0	5	6	11
Greece	22	39	39	100	Ethiopia	5	1	4	10

* Germany 1896–1964, West Germany from 1968   † North Korea from 1964   (Table continues on next page)

** East Germany from 1968   †† Estonia and Latvia up to 1936

United States The United States boycotted the 1980 Games as a protest against the 1979 Soviet invasion of Afghanistan.

1984 LOS ANGELES, CALIF.

The 23rd Olympic Games were held in Los Angeles, Calif. from July 28–August 12, 1984, with 140 countries participating. The Soviet Union and its Eastern bloc partners, with the exception of Romania, boycotted the Games in protest against what they perceived as the inadequate security arrangements. Without Soviet competition, U.S. athletes dominated the Games, with Carl Lewis duplicating Jesse Owens's four-gold-medal performance in 1936.

Most gold medals The United States won 83 gold medals in 1984.

Most medals The United States won 174 medals in 1984: 83 gold, 61 silver and 30 bronze.

1988 SEOUL, SOUTH KOREA

The 24th Olympic Games were held in Seoul, South Korea from September 17–October 2, 1988, with 159 countries participating. For the first time since 1972 there was no major boycott of the Games. The facilities in Seoul were magnificent, and the only black mark on the Games was the disqualification of 100-meter winner Ben Johnson (Canada) for violating drug rules.

General records Swimmer Kristin Otto (East Germany) won six gold medals, the most by any woman athlete in any sport at one Games. Yachtsmen Paul Elvstrom (Denmark) and Durward

---

SUMMER OLYMPIC GAMES MEDAL WINNERS (1896–1988)

Country	Gold	Silver	Bronze	Total	Country	Gold	Silver	Bronze	Total
Pakistan	3	3	3	9	Haiti	0	1	1	2
Uruguay	2	1	6	9	Iceland	0	1	1	2
Venezuela	1	2	5	8	Algeria	0	0	2	2
Chile	0	6	2	8	Panama	0	0	2	2
Trinidad	1	2	4	7	Surinam	1	0	0	1
Philippines	0	1	6	7	Zimbabwe	1	0	0	1
Morocco	3	1	2	6	Costa Rica	0	1	0	1
Uganda	1	3	1	5	Indonesia	0	1	0	1
Tunisia	1	2	2	5	Ivory Coast	0	1	0	1
Colombia	0	2	3	5	Netherlands Antilles	0	1	0	1
Lebanon	0	2	2	4	Senegal	0	1	0	1
Nigeria	0	1	3	4	Singapore	0	1	0	1
Puerto Rico	0	1	3	4	Sri Lanka	0	1	0	1
Peru	1	2	0	3	Syria	0	1	0	1
Latvia††	0	2	1	3	Virgin Islands	0	1	0	1
Taipei (Taiwan)	0	1	2	3	Bermuda	0	0	1	1
Ghana	0	1	2	3	Djibouti	0	0	1	1
Thailand	0	1	2	3	Dominican Republic	0	0	1	1
Luxembourg	1	1	0	2	Guyana	0	0	1	1
Bahamas	1	0	1	2	Iraq	0	0	1	1
Tanzania	0	2	0	2	Niger	0	0	1	1
Cameroon	0	1	1	2	Zambia	0	0	1	1

†† Estonia and Latvia up to 1936

CLEAN SWEEP ■ SWIMMER KRISTIN OTTO (EAST GERMANY) (LEFT) WON SIX GOLD MEDALS AT THE 1988 GAMES, A RECORD FOR A WOMAN ATHLETE AT ONE GAMES.

Knowles (Bahamas) both competed in their eighth Games, matching Raimondo D'Inzeo's mark. Cyclist Christa Rothenburger-Luding (East Germany) became the first athlete to win medals at the Winter and Summer Games in the same year. Rothenburger-Luding won a silver medal in Seoul to go with the gold and silver she had won in Calgary in speed skating earlier in the year.

Most gold medals The Soviet Union won 55 gold medals in 1988.

Most medals The Soviet Union won 132 medals in 1988: 55 gold, 31 silver and 46 bronze.

United States U.S. athletes won 94 medals in 1988: 36 gold, 31 silver and 27 bronze.

1992 BARCELONA, SPAIN

The 25th Olympic Games are scheduled to be held in Barcelona, Spain from July 25–August 9, 1992.

1996 ATLANTA, GA.

The 26th Olympic Games are scheduled to be held in Atlanta, Ga. from July 20–August 4, 1996.

WINTER GAMES CHRONOLOGY (1924–1998)

1924 CHAMONIX, FRANCE

The first Winter Olympic Games were held in Chamonix, France from January 25–February 4, 1924. Figure skating events had been held at the 1908 and 1920 Summer Games, and a hockey tournament had been included in 1920. The original 16 countries competing in the Winter Games were Austria, Belgium, Canada, Czechoslovakia, Finland, France, Great Britain, Hungary, Italy,

Latvia, Norway, Poland, Sweden, Switzerland, the United States and Yugoslavia. They competed in six sports: bobsled, figure skating, hockey, Nordic skiing, ski jumping, and speed skating. Curling and military patrol were staged as demonstration sports.

General records The first gold medal was won by Charles Jewtraw (U.S.) in the 500-meter speed skating event. Speed skaters Clas Thunberg (Finland) and Roald Larsen (Norway) both won five medals at these Games, a single Games record matched only by Eric Heiden (U.S.) in 1980. Thunberg won three gold, one silver and one bronze; Larsen won three silver and two bronze.

Most gold medals Norway and Finland each won four gold medals in 1924.

Most medals Norway won 17 medals in 1924: four gold, seven silver and six bronze.

United States U.S. athletes won four medals in 1924: one gold, two silver and one bronze.

1928 ST. MORITZ, SWITZERLAND

The second Winter Games were held in St. Moritz, Switzerland from February 11–19, 1928, with 25 countries participating. St. Moritz experienced some severe weather during the Games, causing the bobsled event to be reduced from four to two runs, and the cancellation of some speed skating events.

General records Speed skater Clas Thunberg (Finland) won two gold medals, extending his career total to a record five gold medals at the Winter Games. Figure skater Gillis Grafstrom (Sweden) won his third consecutive men's title, a record for Winter Olympic competition. Bobsled racer William Fiske (U.S.) became the youngest gold medalist in Winter Games history, when he drove the U.S. team to victory in the five-man bobsled event at age 16 years 260 days.

Most gold medals Norway won six gold medals in 1928.

Most medals Norway won 15 medals in 1928: six gold, four silver and five bronze.

United States U.S. athletes won six medals in 1928: two gold, two silver and two bronze.

1932 LAKE PLACID, N.Y.

The third Winter Games were held in Lake Placid, N.Y. from February 4–15, 1932, with 17 countries participating. Again the weather dogged the Games, but this time it was warm weather, resulting in the organizers' having to ship in snow from

Canada and from other parts of the United States. The thaw was so prolonged that the four-man bobsled event was held after the closing ceremony.

General records Bobsled racer Eddie Eagan (U.S.) was a member of the winning four-man bobsled team, and thus became the only athlete to win gold medals in both the Summer and Winter Games, having won the 1920 light-heavyweight boxing title. The four-man bobsled event provided further Olympic history when Eagan's teammate Jay O'Brien became the oldest gold medalist in the Winter Games at age 48 years 359 days.

Most gold medals The United States won six gold medals in 1932.

Most medals The United States won 12 medals in 1932: six gold, four silver and two bronze.

1936 GARMISCH–PARTENKIRCHEN, GERMANY

The fourth Winter Games were held in Garmisch–Partenkirchen, Germany from February 6–16, 1936, with 28 countries participating. Alpine skiing was introduced to the Winter Games for the first time.

General records Figure skater Sonja Henie (Norway) won her third consecutive women's title, a record for consecutive victories by a female athlete, which was to be tied in later Games by swimmer Dawn Fraser (Australia) and figure skater Irina Rodnina (USSR).

Most gold medals Norway won seven gold medals in 1936.

Most medals Norway won 15 medals in 1936: seven gold, five silver and three bronze.

United States U.S. athletes won four medals in 1936: one gold and three bronze.

1940

The fifth Winter Games were originally scheduled to be held in Sapporo, Japan, but were relocated to St. Moritz, Switzerland with the outbreak of war between Japan and China in 1938. Later the Games were rescheduled a second time, to Garmisch–Partenkirchen, Germany, but because of the outbreak of World War II, the Games were canceled.

1944

Following the outbreak of World War II, the IOC rescheduled the fifth Winter Games to take place in Cortina d'Ampezzo, Italy in 1944. However, the continuation of the war forced the cancellation of these Games as well.

1948 ST. MORITZ, SWITZERLAND

The fifth Winter Games were finally staged at St. Moritz, Switzerland, from January 30–February 8, 1948, with 28 countries participating. Unlike the Summer Games, the canceled Winter Games of World War II are not included in the numeric sequence, and thus St. Moritz is the fifth Winter Games, not the seventh.

Most gold medals Norway and Sweden each won four gold medals in 1948.

Most medals Norway, Sweden and Switzerland each won 10 medals in 1948: Norway and Sweden both won four gold, three silver and three bronze; Switzerland won three gold, four silver and three bronze.

United States U.S. athletes won nine medals in 1948: three gold, four silver and two bronze.

1952 OSLO, NORWAY

The sixth Winter Games were held in Oslo, Norway from February 14–25, 1952, with 22 countries participating. Bad weather again plagued the Winter Games, but this did not deter the Norwegian fans; there were enormous crowds at all the events, including an estimated 150,000 for the ski jumping event.

Most gold medals Norway won seven gold medals in 1952.

Most medals Norway won 16 medals in 1952: seven gold, three silver and six bronze.

United States U.S. athletes won 11 medals in 1952: four gold, six silver and one bronze.

1956 CORTINA D'AMPEZZO, ITALY

The seventh Winter Games were held in Cortina d'Ampezzo, Italy from January 26–February 5, 1956, with 32 countries participating. The weather conditions again proved difficult, with snow having to be shipped in from other parts of the country. The Soviet Union entered a team for the first time at any Olympic Games, and started a trend by winning the most medals.

General records Skier Toni Sailer (Austria) became the first athlete to sweep all the Alpine skiing events, a feat matched by Jean-Claude Killy (France) in 1968.

Most gold medals The Soviet Union won seven gold medals in 1956.

Most medals The Soviet Union won 16 medals in 1956: seven gold, three silver and six bronze.

United States U.S. athletes won seven medals in 1956: two gold, three silver and two bronze.

1960 SQUAW VALLEY, CALIF.

The eighth Winter Games were held in Squaw Valley, Calif., from February 18–28, 1960, with 30 countries participating. Squaw Valley was a controversial selection as host, as there were no facilities and the area had no tradition of winter sports. Bobsled was dropped from the program, since the organizers didn't feel it was worth the cost to construct a track.

Most gold medals The Soviet Union won seven gold medals in 1960.

Most medals The Soviet Union won 21 medals in 1960: seven gold, five silver and nine bronze.

United States U.S. athletes won 10 medals in 1960: three gold, four silver and three bronze.

1964 INNSBRUCK, AUSTRIA

The ninth Winter Games were held in Innsbruck, Austria from January 29–February 9, 1964, with 36 countries participating. For the only time, traditional winter-sports powerhouse Switzerland failed to win a medal at the Winter Games.

General records Nordic skier Sixten Jernberg (Sweden) won three medals to complete his remarkable Olympic career with a tally of nine medals (four gold, three silver and two bronze), the most of any athlete in Winter Games history. Speed skater Lydia Skoblikova (USSR) won four gold medals, the most by any female athlete at one Winter Games. Skoblikova extended her Olympic gold medal haul to six golds, the most of any woman athlete in Winter Games history.

Most gold medals The Soviet Union won 11 gold medals in 1964.

Most medals The Soviet Union won 25 medals in 1964: 11 gold, eight silver and six bronze.

United States U.S. athletes won seven medals in 1964: one gold, two silver and four bronze.

1968 GRENOBLE, FRANCE

The 10th Winter Games were held in Grenoble, France from February 6–18, 1968, with 37 countries participating. The facilities at Grenoble drew complaints, mainly because the events were so widespread and transportation was so limited; also, the bobsled run was poorly designed, which made the track extremely dangerous. However, the host nation rejoiced in the success of Frenchman Jean-Claude Killy, who swept the men's Alpine events (see next page).

ALLEZ KILLY ■ IN 1968, JEAN-CLAUDE KILLY (FRANCE) SWEPT ALL THE MEN'S ALPINE EVENTS, MATCHING TONI SAILER'S FEAT OF 1956. IN 1992 KILLY PERFORMED ANOTHER OLYMPIC FEAT, SERVING AS CO-PRESIDENT OF THE ALBERTVILLE GAMES.

General records Skier Jean-Claude Killy (France) won all three Alpine events to emulate Toni Sailer's feat of 1956.

Most gold medals Norway won six gold medals in 1968.

Most medals Norway won 14 medals in 1968: six gold, six silver and two bronze.

United States U.S. athletes won seven medals in 1968: one gold, five silver and one bronze.

1972 SAPPORO, JAPAN

The 11th Winter Games were held in Sapporo, Japan from February 3–13, 1972, with 35 countries participating. The Sapporo Games were well organized, with superb facilities. The only real controversy at these Games was sparked by disputes regarding the amateur status of the competitors. Skier Karl Schranz (Austria) was declared a professional and expelled from the Games, but the Soviet hockey team was allowed to participate. This prompted Canada to withdraw from the tournament, protesting that state-sponsored athletes were professionals.

Most gold medals The Soviet Union won eight gold medals in 1972.

Most medals The Soviet Union won 16 medals in 1972: eight gold, five silver and three bronze.

United States U.S. athletes won eight medals in 1972: three gold, two silver and three bronze.

1976 INNSBRUCK, AUSTRIA

The 12th Winter Games were held in Innsbruck, Austria from February 4–15, 1976, with 37 countries participating. This was the first time that a city had repeated as host of the Winter Games, Innsbruck having staged the 1964 Games. The highlight of the Games was the victory of Austrian national hero Franz Klammer in the men's downhill ski race.

General records Speed skater Tatyana Averina (USSR) won four gold medals, which tied the mark for most gold medals won by a woman athlete at the Winter Games.

Most gold medals The Soviet Union won 13 gold medals in 1976.

Most medals The Soviet Union won 27 medals in 1976: 13 gold, six silver and eight bronze.

United States U.S. athletes won 10 medals in 1976: three gold, three silver and four bronze.

GOLDEN GLIDE ■ ERIC HEIDEN WON ALL FIVE MEN'S SPEED SKATING EVENTS AT THE 1980 GAMES, SETTING A RECORD FOR THE MOST GOLD MEDALS WON AT ONE WINTER GAMES.

1980 LAKE PLACID, N.Y.

The 13th Winter Games were held in Lake Placid, N.Y. from February 13–24, 1980, with 37 countries participating. Lake Placid had previously hosted the 1932 Games, but all-new facilities were constructed for the 1980 Games. Transportation was the biggest headache of these Games, with fans and media personnel often either unable to reach the site of an event, or stranded when they arrived. The highlights of the Games were Eric Heiden's five-gold-medal performance (see below), and the victory of the U.S. hockey team, whose 4–3 win over the Soviet Union in the medal round sent the host country into a frenzy.

General records Speed skater Eric Heiden (U.S.) swept all the men's speed skating events to win five gold medals, the most by any athlete at the Winter Games. Figure skater Irina Rodnina (USSR) won her third consecutive pairs title, tying the women's mark for most consecutive gold medals at one event.

Most gold medals The Soviet Union won 10 gold medals in 1980.

Most medals The Soviet Union won 22 medals in 1980: 10 gold, six silver and six bronze.

United States U.S. athletes won 12 medals in 1980: six gold, four silver and two bronze.

1984 SARAJEVO, YUGOSLAVIA

The 14th Winter Games were held in Sarajevo, Yugoslavia from February 8–19, 1984, with 49 countries participating. The amateur/professional controversy raged again when defending Alpine ski champions Ingemar Stenmark (Sweden) and Hanni Wenzel (Liechtenstein) were declared professionals and expelled from the Games.

General records Speed skater Karin Enke (East Germany) and Nordic skier Marja-Liisa Hamalainen (Finland) both won four gold medals, to tie the mark for most gold medals won by a female athlete at the Winter Games. Skier Michaela Figini (Switzerland) became the youngest athlete to win a gold medal at the Winter Olympics when she won the women's downhill race at age 17 years 314 days.

Most gold medals East Germany won nine gold medals in 1984.

Most medals The Soviet Union won 25 medals in 1984: six gold, ten silver and nine bronze.

United States U.S. athletes won eight medals in 1984: four gold and four silver.

1988 CALGARY, CANADA

The 15th Winter Games were held in Calgary, Canada from February 13–28, 1988, with 57 countries participating. Unseasonably warm weather caused by the early arrival of the "Chinook winds" caused problems at the bobsled and ski jumping venues. Speed skating events were held indoors for the first time. The conditions were ideal, and seven world records were set in nine events.

General records Nordic skier Raisa Smetanina (USSR) won two medals, to raise her career total to nine medals (three gold, five silver and one bronze), tying the Winter Games record. Speed skater Monika Holzner (West Germany) competed in her fifth Games, a record for a female athlete at the Winter Games.

Most gold medals The Soviet Union won 11 gold medals in 1988.

Most medals The Soviet Union won 29 medals in 1988: 11 gold, nine silver and nine bronze.

United States U.S. athletes won six medals in 1988: two gold, one silver and three bronze.

1992 ALBERTVILLE, FRANCE

The 16th Winter Games were held in Albertville, France from February 8–23, 1992. For a complete listing of results and records, see pages 243–245.

1994 LILLEHAMMER, NORWAY

The 17th Winter Games are scheduled to be held in Lillehammer, Norway from February 20–March 6, 1994. This will be the first time that the Winter and Summer Games have not been held in the same year.

1998 NAGANO, JAPAN

On June 15, 1991, the IOC selected Nagano, Japan as the site of the 1998 Winter Games.

WINTER OLYMPIC GAMES MEDAL WINNERS (1924–1988)

Country	Gold	Silver	Bronze	Total
USSR	79	57	59	195
Norway	54	60	54	168
United States	42	47	34	123
East Germany*	39	36	35	110
Finland	33	43	34	110
Austria	28	38	32	98
Sweden	36	25	31	92
Germany**	26	26	23	75
Switzerland	23	25	25	73
Canada	14	13	17	44
Netherlands	13	17	12	42
France	13	10	16	39
Italy	14	10	9	33
Czechoslovakia	2	8	13	23
Great Britain	7	4	10	21
Liechtenstein	2	2	5	9
Japan	1	4	2	7
Hungary	0	2	4	6
Belgium	1	1	2	4
Poland	1	1	2	4
Yugoslavia	0	3	1	4
Spain	1	0	0	1
North Korea†	0	1	0	1
Bulgaria	0	0	1	1
Romania	0	0	1	1

* East Germany from 1968

** Germany 1924–64, West Germany from 1968

† North Korea from 1964

ORIENTEERING

Orienteering combines cross-country running with compass and map navigation. The object of the sport is for the competitor to navigate across a set course in the fastest time possible using a topographical map and a compass. The course contains designated locations called controls, identified by orange and white markers, which the runner must find and identify on a punch card that is handed to the official timer at the end of the race.

ORIGINS Orienteering can be traced to Scandinavia at the turn of the 20th century. Major Ernst Killander (Sweden) is regarded as the father of the sport, having organized the first large race in Saltsjobaden, Sweden in 1919. The Swedish federation, *Svenska Orienteringsforbundet*, was founded in 1936. The International Orienteering Federation was established in 1961.

United States Orienteering was introduced to the U.S. in the 1940s. The first U.S. Orienteering Championships were held on October 17, 1970. The U.S. Orienteering Federation (USOF) was founded on August 1, 1971.

WORLD CHAMPIONSHIPS The world championships were first held in 1966 in Fiskars, Finland, and are held biennially.

Most titles (relay) The men's relay has been won a record seven times by Norway—1970, 1978, 1981, 1983, 1985, 1987 and 1989. Sweden has won the women's relay nine times—1966, 1970, 1974, 1976, 1981, 1983, 1985, 1989 and 1991.

Most titles (individual) Three women's individual titles have been won by Annichen Kringstad (Sweden) in 1981, 1983 and 1985. The men's title has been won twice by three men: Age Hadler (Norway), in 1966 and 1972; by Egil Johansen (Norway), in 1976 and 1978; and by Oyvin Thon (Norway), in 1979 and 1981.

MAPPED OUT ■ OYVIN THON (NORWAY) (LEFT) IS ONE OF THREE MEN TO HAVE WON THE WORLD ORIENTEERING TITLE TWICE. ANNICHEN KRINGSTAD (SWEDEN) (RIGHT) HAS WON THE WOMEN'S TITLE A RECORD THREE TIMES.

UNITED STATES NATIONAL CHAMPIONSHIPS First held on October 17, 1970, the nationals are held annually.

Most titles Sharon Crawford, New England Orienteering Club, has won a record 11 overall women's titles: 1977–82, 1984–87, and 1989. The men's title has been won five times by two men: Peter Gagarin, New England Orienteering Club, 1976–79, 1983; Mikell Platt, New England Orienteering Club, 1986, 1988–91.

PAN AMERICAN GAMES

ORIGINS The Pan American Games were the brainchild of the Argentine Olympic Committee, which felt that a multisports event modeled after the Olympic Games would help countries of the Western Hemisphere in preparing for the Olympics, while also raising revenue and improving inter-American relations. The inaugural Pan American Games were set for 1942, but were postponed when World War II intervened. In 1948, delegates to the Pan American Congress voted to stage the inaugural Games in Buenos Aires, Argentina from February 25–March 8, 1951. The Games have been held quadrennially since, with the 11th Pan American Games being staged in Havana, Cuba from August 2–18, 1991. The Games were run by the Pan American Games Committee from 1951–67. In 1967 the Pan American Sports Organization (PASO) was formed and became the governing body for the Games.

INDIVIDUAL RECORDS

Most medals Fencer Peter Westbrook (U.S.) has won a record eight medals at the Pan American Games: one gold, individual sabre, 1983; six silver, individual sabre, 1979, 1983, team sabre, 1975, 1979, 1983, 1987; one bronze, individual sabre, 1975.

POLO

The playing field for polo is the largest of any sport, with a standard length of 300 yards and a width of 200 yards (without boards) or 160 yards (with boards). The object of the game is to score in the opponent's goals, the goalposts being eight yards

PAN AMERICAN GAMES MEDAL WINNERS (1951–1991)

Country	Gold	Silver	Bronze	Total	Country	Gold	Silver	Bronze	Total
United States	1,257	870	561	2,688	Ecuador	4	5	14	23
Cuba	468	349	294	1,111	N'lands Antilles	1	8	10	19
Canada	169	334	436	939	Guatemala	2	4	12	18
Argentina	166	179	201	546	Costa Rica	4	5	5	14
Mexico	85	130	281	496	Guyana	2	3	9	14
Brazil	116	144	199	459	Bahamas	2	6	5	13
Venezuela	29	90	120	239	Barbados	0	2	4	6
Colombia	20	49	79	148	U.S. Virgin Is.	0	1	5	6
Chile	26	45	72	143	Nicaragua	0	2	3	5
Puerto Rico	13	48	72	133	Surinam	1	2	1	4
Jamaica	10	20	41	71	Bermuda	0	1	2	3
Dominican Rep.	1	20	39	60	Haiti	0	1	2	3
Uruguay	8	15	29	52	Belize	0	0	2	2
Peru	4	18	30	52	El Salvador	0	0	2	2
Panama	2	17	23	42	Bolivia	0	1	0	1
Trinidad & Tobago	6	12	14	32					

wide, with the team scoring the most goals winning the game. Each side fields a team of four players; the game is played over six periods of seven minutes' duration each. A period is known as a chukker, and players must change their mount after each chukker. Polo players are assigned handicaps based on their skill, with a 10 handicap being the highest level of play.

ORIGINS Polo originated in Central Asia, possibly as early as 3100 B.C., in the state of Manipur. The name is derived from the Tibetan word *pulu*. The modern era began in India in the 1850s when British army officers were introduced to the game. The Cachar Club, Assam, India was founded in 1859, and is believed to be the first polo club of the modern era. The game was introduced in England in 1869. The world governing body, the Hurlingham Polo Association, was founded in London, England in 1874 and drew up the laws of the game in 1875.

United States Polo was introduced to the U.S. by James Gordon Bennett in 1876, when he arranged for the first indoor game at Dickel's Riding Academy, N.Y. The first game played outdoors was held on May 13, 1876 at the Jerome Park Racetrack in Westchester County, N.Y. The oldest existing polo club in the United States is Meadow Brook Polo Club, Jericho, N.Y., founded in 1879. The United States Polo Association was formed on March 21, 1890.

OLYMPIC GAMES Polo was an official Olympic sport in 1900, 1908, 1920, 1924 and 1936.

Most gold medals Great Britain won the gold medal three times, in 1900, 1908 and 1920.

United States U.S. teams have won two medals in polo competition, a silver in 1924, and a bronze in 1920.

WORLD CHAMPIONSHIPS The first world championships were held in Berlin, West Germany in 1989. The U.S. won the title, defeating Great Britain 7–6 in the final.

UNITED STATES OPEN POLO CHAMPIONSHIP The U.S. Open was first staged in 1904 and is an annual event.

Most wins The Meadow Brook Polo Club, Jericho, N.Y. has won the U.S. Open 28 times: 1916, 1920, 1923-41, 1946-51, and 1953.

Highest score The highest aggregate number of goals scored in an international match is 30, when Argentina beat the U.S. 21–9 at Meadowbrook, Long Island, N.Y. in September 1936.

POOL

ORIGINS Pool traces its ancestry to billiards, an English game introduced in Virginia in the late 17th century. During the 19th century the game evolved from one in which a mace was used to push balls around a table, to a game of precise skill using a cue, with the aim of pocketing numbered balls. The original form of pool in the United States was known as pyramid pool, with the object being to pocket eight out the 15 balls on the table. "61-pool" evolved from this game: each of the 15 balls was worth points equal to its numerical value; the first player to score 61 points was the winner. In 1878 the first world championship was staged under the rules of 61-pool. In 1910, Jerome Keogh suggested that the rules be adjusted to make the game faster and more attractive; he proposed that the last ball be left free on the table to be used as a target on the next rack; the result was 14.1 continuous pool (also known as American straight pool). 14.1 was adopted as the championship form of pool from 1912 onwards. In the last 20 years, nine-ball pool and eight-ball pool have surpassed 14.1 in popularity. In 1990 the World Pool Billiard Association inaugurated the nine-ball world championship.

14.1 CONTINUOUS POOL (ALSO KNOWN AS AMERICAN STRAIGHT POOL)

WORLD CHAMPIONSHIPS The first official world championship was held in April 1912 and was won by Edward Ralph (U.S.).

Most titles Two players have won the world title six times: Ralph Greenleaf (U.S.) and Willie Mosconi (U.S.). From 1919-37, Greenleaf won the title six times and defended it 13 times. Between 1941 and 1956, Mosconi also won the title six times and defended it 13 times.

Longest consecutive run The longest consecutive run in 14.1 recognized by the Billiard Congress of America (BCA) is 526 balls, by Willie Mosconi in March 1954 during an exhibition in Springfield, Ohio. Michael Eufemia is reported to

have pocketed 625 balls at Logan's Billiard Academy in Brooklyn, N.Y. on February 2, 1960; however, this run has never been ratified by the BCA.

NINE-BALL POOL

WORLD CHAMPIONSHIP In this competition, inaugurated in 1990, Earl Strickland (U.S.) has won the men's title in both 1990 and 1991. Robin Bell (U.S.) has won both women's events.

POWERBOAT RACING

ORIGINS A gasoline engine was first installed in a boat by Jean Lenoir on the River Seine, Paris, France in 1865. Organized powerboat races were first run at the turn of the 20th century. The first major international competition was the Harnsworth Trophy, launched in 1903. Modern powerboat racing is broken down into two main types: circuit racing in sheltered waterways, and offshore racing. Offshore events were initially for displacement (nonplaning) cruisers, but in 1958 the 170-mile Miami, Fla.-to-Nassau, Bahamas race was staged for planing cruisers.

United States The American Power Boat Association (APBA) was founded on April 22, 1903 in New York City. In 1913 the APBA issued the "Racing Commission" rules, which created its powers for governing the sport in North America. In 1924 the APBA set rules for boats propelled by outboard detachable motors and became the governing body for both inboard and outboard racing in North America. The APBA is currently based in East Detroit, Mich.

APBA GOLD CUP The APBA held its first Gold Cup race at the Columbia Yacht Club on the Hudson River, N.Y. in 1904, when the winner was *Standard*, piloted by C. C. Riotto at an average speed of 23.6 mph.

Most wins (pilot) The most wins by a pilot is eight, by Bill Muncey, 1956–57, 1961–62, 1972 and 1977–79.

Most wins (boat) The most successful boat has been *Atlas Van Lines*, piloted by Muncey to victory in 1972 and 1977–79, and by Chip Hanauer in 1982–84.

Consecutive wins Chip Hanauer has won a record seven successive victories, 1982–88.

Longest races The longest offshore race has been the London (England) to Monte Carlo (Monaco) Marathon Offshore international event. The race extended over 2,947 miles in 14 stages from June 10–25, 1972. It was won by *H.T.S.* (Great Britain), piloted by Mike Bellamy, Eddie Chater and Jim Brooker in 71 hours 35 minutes 56 seconds, for an average speed of 41.15 mph. The longest circuit race is the 24-hour race held annually since 1962 on the River Seine at Rouen, France.

FULL THROTTLE ■ BILL MUNCEY WON A RECORD EIGHT APBA GOLD CUP TITLES.

POWERBOAT SPEED RECORDS

The following is a selection of speed records recognized by the APBA as of January 1, 1992.

Distance: One Kilometer

Type	Class	Speed (mph)	Driver	Location	Year
Inboard	GP	170.024	Kent MacPhail	Decatur, Ill.	1989
Inboard	KRR	146.649	Gordon Jennings	Lincoln City, Ore.	1989
Offshore	Super Boat	148.238	Thomas Gentry	New Orleans, La.	1987
Offshore	Open	138.512	Al Copeland	New Orleans, La.	1987
PR Outboard	500ccH	121.940	Daniel Kirts	Moore Haven, Fla.	1987
PR Outboard	700ccH	116.504	George Andrews	Moore Haven, Fla.	1982
Performance	Champ Boat	131.963	Jim Merten	Kaukauna, Wis.	1978
Performance	Mod U	142.968	Bob Wartinger	Moore Haven, Fla.	1989
Special Event	Formula 1	165.338	Robert Hering	Parker, Ariz.	1986
Special Event	Jet	317.600	Ken Warby	Tumut, Australia	1976

Unlimited in Competition

Type	Distance	Speed (mph)	Driver	Location	Year
Qual. Lap	2 miles	160.122	Thomas D'Eath	Evansville, Ind.	1990
Lap	2 miles	147.722	Thomas D'Eath	Evansville, Ind.	1990
Qual. Lap	2.5 miles	168.128	Chip Hanauer	San Diego, Calif.	1990
Lap	2.5 miles	154.573	Chip Hanauer	San Diego, Calif.	1990
Lap	3 miles	155.682	Mark Tate	San Diego, Calif.	1991

Source: APBA

RACQUETBALL

ORIGINS Racquetball, using a 40-foot x 20-foot court, was invented in 1950 by Joe Sobek at the Greenwich YMCA, Greenwich, Conn. Sobek designed a "strung paddle racquet" and combined the rules of squash and handball to form the game of "paddle rackets." The International Racquetball Association (IRA) was founded in 1960 by Bob Kendler, and was renamed the American Amateur Racquetball Association (AARA) in 1979. The International Amateur Racquetball Federation (IARF) was founded in 1979 and staged its first world championship in 1981.

WORLD CHAMPIONSHIPS First held in 1981, the IARF world championships have been held biennially since 1984.

Most titles (team) The United States has won all five team titles, in 1981, 1984, 1986 (tie with Canada), 1988 and 1990.

OFF THE WALL ■ EGAN INOUE (LEFT) HAS WON THE MEN'S RACQUETBALL WORLD TITLE TWICE.

Most titles (men) Egan Inoue (U.S.) has won two singles titles, in 1986 and 1990.

Most titles (women) Two women have won two world titles: Cindy Baxter (U.S.), 1981 and 1986; and Heather Stupp (Canada), 1988 and 1990.

UNITED STATES NATIONAL CHAMPIONSHIPS The first championships were held in 1968.

Most titles A record four men's open titles have been won by Ed Andrews of California, 1980–81 and 1985–86, and a record four women's open titles by Cindy Baxter of Pennsylvania, 1981, 1983, 1985–86.

RODEO

ORIGINS Rodeo originated in Mexico, developing from 18th century fiestas, and moved north to the United States and Canada with the expansion of the North American cattle industry in the 18th and 19th centuries. There are several claims to the earliest organized rodeo. The Professional Rodeo Cowboys Association (PRCA) sanctions the West of the Pecos Rodeo, Pecos, Tex, as the oldest; it was first held in 1883. The development of rodeo as a regulated national sport can be traced to the formation of the Cowboys' Turtle Association in 1936. In 1945 the Turtles became the Rodeo Cowboy Association, which in 1975 was renamed the Professional Rodeo Cowboys Association (PRCA). The PRCA is recognized as the oldest and largest rodeo-governing body in the world.

Rodeo events are divided into two groups: roughstock and timed.

Roughstock The roughstock events are saddle bronc riding, bareback riding, and bull riding. In these events the cowboy is required to ride the mount for eight seconds to receive a score. The cowboy must use only one hand to grip the "rigging" (a handhold secured to the animal), and is disqualified if the free hand touches the animal or equipment during the round. The performance is judged on the cowboy's technique and the animal's bucking efforts.

Timed The timed events are calf roping, steer roping, team roping, and steer wrestling. In these events the cowboy chases the calf or steer, riding a registered quarter horse, catches up to the animal, and then captures the animal performing the required feat. The cowboy's performance is timed, with the fastest time winning the event.

WORLD CHAMPIONSHIPS The Rodeo Association of America organized the first world championships in 1929. The championship has been organized under several different formats and sponsored by several different groups throughout its existence. The current championship is a season-long competition based on PRCA earnings. The PRCA has organized the championship since 1945 (as the Rodeo Cowboy Association through 1976).

Most titles (overall) Jim Shoulders has won 16 rodeo world championship events: all-around, 1949, 1956–59; bareback riding, 1950, 1956–58; bull riding, 1951, 1954–59.

INDIVIDUAL EVENTS

All-around Two cowboys have won six all-around titles: Larry Mahan, 1966–70, 1973; Tom Ferguson, 1974–79.

Saddle bronc riding Casey Tibbs won six saddle bronc titles, in 1949, 1951–54 and 1959.

Bareback riding Two cowboys have won five titles: Joe Alexander, 1971–75; Bruce Ford, 1979–80, 1982–83, 1987.

Bull riding Don Gay has won eight bullriding titles: 1975–81 and 1984.

Calf roping Dean Oliver has won eight titles: 1955, 1958, 1960–64 and 1969.

Steer roping Everett Shaw has won six titles: 1945–46, 1948, 1951, 1959 and 1962.

Steer wrestling Homer Pettigrew has won six titles: 1940, 1942–45 and 1948.

Team roping The team of Jake Barnes and Clay O'Brien Cooper has won five titles, 1985–89.

Women's barrel racing Charmayne Rodman has won eight titles, 1984–91.

Oldest world champion Ike Rude won the 1953 steer roping title at age 59 to became the oldest rodeo titleholder.

Youngest world champion Jim Rodriguez Jr. won the 1959 team roping title at age 18 to become the youngest rodeo titleholder.

RIDING RECORDS

HIGHEST SCORES (MAXIMUM POSSIBLE: 100 POINTS)

Bull riding Wade Leslie scored 100 points riding Wolfman Skoal at Central Point, Ore. in 1991.

Saddle bronc riding Doug Vold scored 95 points riding Transport at Meadow Lake, Saskatchewan, Canada in 1979.

Bareback riding Joe Alexander scored 93 points riding Marlboro at Cheyenne, Wyo. in 1974.

FASTEST TIMES

Calf roping The fastest time in this event is 5.7 seconds, by Lee Phillips at Assinobia, Saskatchewan, Canada in 1978.

Steer wrestling Without a barrier, the fastest time is reported to have been 2.2 seconds by Oral Zumwalt in the 1930s. With a barrier, the record time is 2.4 seconds, achieved by three cowboys: Jim Bynum at Marietta, Okla. in 1955; Gene Melton at Pecatonia, Ill. in 1976; and Carl Deaton at Tulsa, Okla. in 1976.

Team roping The team of Bob Harris and Tee Woolman performed this feat in a record 3.7 seconds at Spanish Fork, Utah in 1986.

BULLISH ■ IN 1991, TY MURRAY EARNED $258,750 IN PRIZE MONEY, SURPASSING THE RODEO SEASON EARNINGS MARK HE HAD SET IN 1990.

Steer roping The fastest time in this event is 8.5 seconds, by Shaun Burchett at Fredonia, Kan. in 1987.

HIGHEST EARNINGS

Career Roy Cooper holds the career PRCA earnings mark at $1,282,874, 1976–91.

Season The single-season PRCA mark is $258,750 by Ty Murray in 1991.

ROLLER SKATING

ORIGINS Roller skates were invented by Joseph Merlin of Belgium. He demonstrated his new mode of transport at a masquerade party in London in 1760, with disastrous consequences—he was unable to stop and crashed into a large mirror, receiving near-fatal wounds. In 1863, James L. Plimpton of Medfield, Mass. patented the modern four-wheeled roller skate. In 1866, he opened the first public roller skating rink in the United States in Newport, R.I. *The Federation Internationale de Roller Skating* was founded in 1924 and is now headquartered in Spain. The Roller Skating Rink Operators' Association staged the first U.S. National Championship in 1937. Since 1973 the United States Amateur Confederation of Roller Skating has been the governing body of the sport in the United States. Three distinct sports have derived from roller skating: speed skating, artistic skating, and roller hockey.

SPEED SKATING

Speed skating events are divided into two categories: road racing and track racing. World championships are staged in alternate years for each discipline.

WORLD CHAMPIONSHIPS The first world championships were held in Monza, Italy in 1937. A women's championship was first staged in 1953.

Most titles Alberta Vianello (Italy) has won a record 19 world titles—eight track and 11 road—1953–65. Marco Cantarella (Italy) has won 15 men's titles—seven track and eight road—1964–80.

UNITED STATES NATIONAL CHAMPIONSHIPS The first U.S. championships were staged in 1937 for indoor competition, and contests have been held annually since. In 1985 a separate outdoor cham-

		Men	
Distance	**Time**	**Skater (Country)**	**Date**
300 m	0:24.99	Luca Anatoniel (Italy)	July 31, 1988*
1,500 m	2:07.77	Giuseppe de Persio (Italy)	August 1, 1980**
10,000 m	14:55.64	Giuseppe de Persio (Italy)	August 1, 1988*
		Women	
300 m	0:26.79	Marisa Canofogilia (Italy)	August 27, 1987*
1,500 m	2:14.12	Marisa Canofogilia (Italy)	August 28, 1987*
10,000 m	15:58.02	Marisa Canofogilia (Italy)	August 30, 1987**

* Record set on the road   **Record set on track
Source: U.S. Amateur Confederation of Roller Skating

pionship was initiated, and this is also staged annually.

Most titles Mary Merrell has won a record six overall champion titles, 1959–61, 1964, and 1966–67 (all indoors). Dante Muse has won four men's overall titles—two indoors, 1986 and 1990; two outdoors, 1987 and 1989.

ARTISTIC SKATING

WORLD CHAMPIONSHIPS The first world championships were held in Washington D.C. in 1947.

ON A ROLL ■ SCOTT COHEN WON HIS RECORD FIFTH MEN'S ROLLER SKATING WORLD TITLE IN 1991.

The championships have been held annually since 1970.

Most titles Scott Cohen (U.S.) has won five men's free-skating titles, 1985–86 and 1989–91. Astrid Bader (Germany) has won four women's free-skating titles, 1965–68.

UNTIED STATES NATIONAL CHAMPIONSHIPS The first U.S. championships were staged in 1939, and contests are now held annually.

Most titles Michael Jacques has won seven free-skating titles, 1966–72. Laurene Anselmi has won seven women's titles—three figure skating, 1951, 1953–54; four free-skating, 1951–54.

ROLLER HOCKEY

Roller hockey is played by two five-man teams over two twenty-minute periods.

WORLD CHAMPIONSHIPS First held in Stuttgart, Germany in 1936, the world championships have been held under several formats, both annual and biennial. Currently the tournament is an annual event.

Most titles Portugal has won 13 world titles: 1947–50, 1952, 1956, 1958, 1960, 1962, 1968, 1974, 1982 and 1991.

ROWING

ORIGINS Forms of rowing can be traced back to ancient Egypt; however, the modern sport of rowing dates to 1715, when the Doggett's Coat and

Badge scull race was established in London, England. Types of regattas are believed to have taken place in Venice, Italy in 1300, but the modern regatta can also be traced to England, where races were staged in 1775 on the River Thames at Ranleigh Gardens, Putney. The world governing body is the *Federation Internationale des Sociétés d'Aviron* (FISA), founded in 1892. Rowing has been part of the Olympic Games since 1900.

United States The first organized boat races in the United States were reportedly races staged between boatmen in New York harbor in the late 18th century. The first rowing club formed in the United States was the Castle Garden Amateur Boat Club Association, New York City, in 1834. The oldest active boat club is the Detroit Boat Club, founded in 1839. The first and oldest collegiate boat club was formed at Yale University in 1843. The National Association of Amateur Oarsmen (NAAO) was formed in 1872. The NAAO merged with the National Women's Rowing Association in 1982 to form the United States Rowing Association.

OLYMPIC GAMES Men's rowing events have been included in the Olympic Games since 1900. In 1976 women's events were included.

Most gold medals Six oarsmen have won three gold medals: John Kelly (U.S.), single sculls, 1920, double sculls, 1920 and 1924; Paul Costello (U.S.), double sculls, 1920, 1924 and 1928; Jack Beresford (Great Britain), single sculls, 1924, coxless fours, 1932, double sculls, 1936; Vyacheslav Ivanov (USSR), single sculls, 1956, 1960 and 1964; Siegfried Brietzke (East Germany), coxless pairs, 1972, coxless fours, 1976 and 1980; Pertti Karppinen (Finland), single sculls, 1976, 1980 and 1984.

Most medals Jack Beresford (Great Britain) won five medals in rowing competition: three gold (see above) and two silver (single sculls, 1920, and eights, 1928).

Most medals (country) The United States has won 65 medals in Olympic rowing competition: in men's events, 27 gold, 18 silver and 14 bronze; in women's competition, one gold, four silver and one bronze.

WORLD CHAMPIONSHIPS World rowing championships staged separately from the Olympic

Games were first held in 1962. Since 1974 the championships have been staged annually. In Olympic years the Games are considered the world championships, and results from the Olympics are included in this section.

Most titles Giuseppe and Carmine Abbagnale (both Italy) have won nine coxed pairs titles, 1981–82, 1984–85 and 1987–91. Jutta Behrendt (née Hampe; East Germany) has won six titles: three single sculls, 1983, 1986 and 1988; three quadruple sculls, 1985, 1987 and 1989.

Single sculls Two oarsmen have won five single sculls titles: Peter-Michael Kolbe (West Germany), 1975, 1978, 1981, 1983 and 1986; and Pertti Karppinen (Finland), 1976, 1979–80 and 1984–85. Christine Hahn (née Scheiblich; East Germany) has won five women's titles, 1974–78.

Eights Since 1962, East German crews have won seven men's eights titles—1970, 1975–80. In women's competition the USSR has won seven titles—1978–79, 1981–83, 1985–86.

COLLEGIATE CHAMPIONSHIPS Harvard and Yale staged the first intercollegiate boat race in 1852. The Intercollegiate Rowing Association was formed in 1895, and in 1898 inaugurated the Varsity Challenge Cup, which was recognized as the national championship. In 1979 the United States Rowing Association introduced the women's National Collegiate Championship, which was extended to men's competition in 1982, supplanting the Varsity Cup as the men's national title.

AWESOME OARSMAN ■ **PETER-MICHAEL KOLBE (WEST GERMANY) IS ONE OF TWO MEN TO HAVE WON FIVE SINGLE SCULLS WORLD TITLES.**

Most wins (men) Cornell has won 21 titles: 1901–03, 1905–07, 1909–12, 1915, 1930, 1955–58, 1962–63, 1971, 1977, and 1981. Since 1982, Harvard has won five titles, 1983, 1985, and 1987–89.

Most wins (women) Washington has won seven titles—1981–85, 1987–88.

Fastest speed The fastest recorded speed on nontidal water for 2,000 meters is by an American eight, in 5 minutes 27.14 seconds (13.68 mph) at Lucerne, Switzerland on June 17, 1984. A crew from Penn AC was timed in 5 minutes 18.8 seconds (14.03 mph) in the FISA Championships on the River Meuse, Liège, Belgium on August 17, 1930.

RUGBY

ORIGINS As with baseball in the United States, the origins of rugby are obscure—but a traditional "history" has become so embedded in the national psyche, in this case that of Great Britain, that any historical revision is either ignored or derided. The tradition is that the game began when William Webb Ellis picked up the ball during a soccer game at Rugby School in November 1823 and ran with it. Whether or not there is any truth to this legend, the "new" handling code of soccer developed, and the game was played at Cambridge University in 1839. The first rugby club was formed at Guy's Hospital, London, England in 1843, and the Rugby Football Union (RFU) was founded in January 1871. The International Rugby Football Board (IRFB) was founded in 1886.

OLYMPIC GAMES Rugby was played at four Games from 1900 to 1924. The only double gold medalist was the U.S., which won in 1920 and 1924.

WORLD CUP The World Cup is staged every four years and is the world championship for rugby. The first World Cup was hosted by Australia and New Zealand in 1987.

Most wins New Zealand won the first World Cup in 1987, and Australia won the second tournament in 1991.

WORLD CUP SCORING RECORDS (1987–91)

TEAM RECORDS

Most points (game) The most points in World Cup play is 74, scored by New Zealand against Fiji (13 points) at Christchurch, New Zealand on May 27, 1987.

Most points (game, aggregate score) The highest aggregate score in World Cup competition is 87 points, New Zealand defeating Fiji 74–13 (see above).

INDIVIDUAL RECORDS

Most points (game) Didier Camberabero (France) scored 30 points (three tries and nine conversions) v. Zimbabwe at Auckland, New Zealand on June 2, 1987.

Most points (tournament) Grant Fox (New Zealand) scored 126 points in 1987.

Most points (career) Grant Fox (New Zealand) scored 170 points in 1987 and 1991.

INTERNATIONAL RUGBY RECORDS

Highest score The highest score by a team in a full international game is 106 points, which has occurred twice: New Zealand 106, Japan 4, at Tokyo, Japan on November 1, 1987; France 106, Paraguay 12, at Asunción, Paraguay on June 28, 1988.

INDIVIDUAL RECORDS

Game

Most points Phil Bennett (Wales) scored 34 points (two tries, ten conversions, two penalty goals) v. Japan at Tokyo on September 24, 1975.

Most tries Patrice Lagisquet (France) scored seven tries v. Paraguay at Asunción, Paraguay on June 28, 1988.

Most penalty goals Mark Wyatt (Canada) kicked eight penalty goals v. Scotland at St. John, New Brunswick on May 25, 1991.

Career

Most points Michael Lynagh (Australia) has scored a record 689 points in international rugby competition, 1984–91.

Most tries David Campese (Australia) is the leading try scorer in international competition with 46 tries, 1982–91.

Most internationals Serge Blanco (France) has played a record 93 international matches, 1980–91.

Consecutive internationals Two players played in 53 consecutive games: Gareth Ed-

ON TOP DOWN UNDER ■ IN 1991, DAVID CAMPESE EXTENDED HIS RECORD FOR TRIES IN INTERNATIONAL RUGBY TO 46, AND SPEARHEADED AUSTRALIA'S FIRST WORLD CUP VICTORY.

wards (Wales), 1967–78; Willie John McBride (Ireland), 1962–75.

SHOOTING

The National Rifle Association recognizes four categories of shooting competition: conventional, international, silhouette, and action pistol. This section reports records only for international style shooting—the shooting discipline used at the Olympic Games.

ORIGINS The earliest recorded shooting club is the Lucerne Shooting Guild (Switzerland), formed *c*. 1466. The first known shooting competition was held at Zurich, Switzerland in 1472. The international governing body, the *Union International de Tir* (UIT), was formed in Zurich in 1907.

United States The National Rifle Association (NRA) was founded in 1871, and is designated as the national governing body for shooting sports in the United States by the U.S. Olympic Committee.

INTERNATIONAL STYLE SHOOTING

International or Olympic-style shooting is comprised of four disciplines: rifle, pistol, running target, and shotgun. Running target events are limited to male competitors. The targets for rifle, pistol, and running deer events are the same, but in running deer the target is moving. Shotgun shooting (also known as trap and skeet) requires the competitor to hit clay targets released from a skeet.

OLYMPIC GAMES Shooting has been part of the Olympic program since the first modern Games in 1896. Women were allowed to compete against men at the 1968 Games, and separate women's events were included in 1984.

Most gold medals Seven marksmen have won five gold medals: Konrad Staheli (Switzerland), 1900–1906; Louis Richardet (Switzerland), 1900–06; Alfred Lane (U.S.), 1912–20; Carl Osburn (U.S.), 1912–24; Ole Lilloe-Olsen (Norway), 1920–24; Morris Fisher (U.S.), 1920–24; and Willis Lee (U.S.), 1920. No woman competitor has won more than one gold medal.

Most medals Carl Osburn (U.S.) has won 11 medals: five gold, four silver and two bronze. Three women have won two medals: Wu Xiaoxuan (China), one gold, one bronze in 1984; Nino Saloukvadze (USSR), one gold, one silver in 1988; Silvia Sperber (West Germany), one gold, one silver in 1988.

Most medals (country) The United States has won 85 medals: in men's competition, 42 gold, 23 silver and 17 bronze; in women's competition, one gold, one silver and one bronze.

NCAA CHAMPIONSHIPS A combined NCAA rifle championship was inaugurated in 1980, and the contest is now held annually.

Most titles (team) West Virginia has won seven NCAA team titles, 1983–84, 1986, and 1988–91.

Most titles (individual) Six competitors have won two individual titles: Rod Fitz-Randolph, Tennessee Tech, smallbore and air rifle, 1980; Kurt Fitz-Randolph, Tennessee Tech, smallbore, 1981–82; John Rost, West Virginia, air rifle, 1981–82; Pat Spurgin, Murray State, air rifle, 1984, smallbore, 1985; Web Wright, West Virginia, smallbore, 1987–88; Michelle Scarborough, South Florida, air rifle, 1989, smallbore, 1990.

SHOOTING—INDIVIDUAL WORLD RECORDS

In 1986 the International Shooting Union introduced new regulations for determining major championships and world records. Now the leading competitors undertake an additional round with a target subdivided to tenths of a point for rifle and pistol shooting and an extra 25 shots for trap and skeet. The table below shows the world records for the 13 Olympic shooting disciplines, giving in parentheses the score for the number of shots specified plus the score in the additional round.

Men

Event	Points	Marksman (Country)	Date
Free rifle 50 m 3 x 40 shots	1,276.7 (1,179 + 97.7)	Rajmond Debevec (Yugoslavia)	June 2,1990
	1,276.7 (1,177 + 99.7)	Rajmond Debevec (Yugoslavia)	June 7,1991
Free rifle 50 m 60 shots prone	703.5 (599 + 104.5)	Jens Harskov (Denmark)	June 6, 1991
Air rifle 10 m 60 shots	699.4 (596 + 103.4)	Rajmond Debevec (Yugoslavia)	June 7, 1990
Free pistol 50 m 60 shots	671 (579 + 92)	Sergey Pyzhyanov (USSR)	May 30, 1990
	671 (577 + 94)	Spas Koprinkov (Bulgaria)	August 9, 1991
Rapid-fire pistol 25 m 60 shots	891 (594 +297)	Ralf Schumann (East Germany)	June 3, 1989
Air pistol 10 m 60 shots	695.1 (593 + 102.1)	Sergey Pyzhyanov (USSR)	October 3, 1989
Running target 10 m 30 + 30 shots	679 (582 + 97)	Lubos Racansky (Czechoslovakia)	May 30, 1991

Women

Event	Points	Markswoman (Country)	Date
Standard rifle 50 m 3 x 20 shots	684.9 (584 + 100.9)	Vessela Letcheva (Bulgaria)	August 29, 1991
Air rifle 10 m 40 shots	500.8 (399 + 101.8)	Valentina Cherkasova (USSR)	March 23, 1991
Sport pistol 25 m 60 shots	693 (593 + 100)	Nino Salukvadse (USSR)	July 13, 1989
Air pistol 10 m 40 shots	492.4 (392 + 100.4)	Lieselotte Breker (West Germany)	May 18, 1989

Open

Event	Points	Marksman (Country)	Date
Trap 200 targets	224 (200 + 24)	Jorg Damme (West Germany)	August 18, 1990
Skeet 200 targets	225 (200 + 25)	Axel Wegner (Germany)	August 31, 1991
	225 (200 + 25)	Hennie Dompeling (Netherlands)	August 31, 1991

The first world record by a woman at any sport for a category in direct and measurable competition with men was by Margaret Murdock (née Thompson; U.S.), who set a world record for smallbore rifle (kneeling position) of 391 in 1967.

SKIING

ORIGINS Skiing traces its history to Scandinavia; *ski* is the Norwegian word for snowshoe. A ski discovered in a peat bog in Hoting, Sweden dates to *c*. 2500 B.C., and records note the use of skis at the Battle of Isen, Norway in A.D. 1200. The first ski races were held in Norway and Australia in the 1850s and 1860s. Two men stand out as pioneers of the development of skiing in the 19th century: Sondre Nordheim, a Norwegian, who designed equipment and developed skiing techniques; and Mathias Zdarsky, an Austrian, who pioneered Alpine skiing. The first national governing body was that of Norway, formed in 1833. The International Ski Commission was founded in 1910 and was succeeded as the world governing body in 1924 by the International Ski Federation (FIS).

United States The first ski club in the United States was formed at Berlin, N.H. in January 1872. The United States Ski Association was originally founded as the National Ski Association in 1905; in 1962, it was renamed the United States Ski Association, and in 1990 it was renamed U.S. Skiing.

In the modern era, skiing has evolved into two main categories, Alpine and Nordic. Alpine skiing encompasses downhill and slalom racing. Nordic skiing covers ski jumping events and cross-country racing.

ALPINE SKIING

OLYMPIC GAMES Downhill and slalom events were first included at the 1936 Olympic Games.

Most gold medals In men's competition, the most gold medals won is three, by two skiers: Anton Sailer (Austria), who won all three events, downhill, slalom and giant slalom, in 1956; and Jean-Claude Killy (France), who matched Sailer's feat in 1968. For women the record is two golds, achieved by six skiers: Andrea Mead-Lawrence (U.S.), slalom, giant slalom, 1952; Marielle Goitschel (France), giant slalom 1964, slalom, 1968; Marie-Therese Nadig (Switzerland), downhill, giant slalom, 1972; Rosi Mittermaier (West Germany), downhill, slalom,

1976; Hanni Wenzel (Liechtenstein), giant slalom, slalom, 1980; and Vareni Schneider (Switzerland), giant slalom, slalom, 1988.

Most medals Hanni Wenzel (Liechtenstein) has won four Olympic medals: two gold, one silver and one bronze, 1976–80. The most medals won by a male skier is three, by six skiers: Anton Sailer and Jean-Claude Killy (see above), Henri Oreiller (France), two gold, one bronze, 1948; Josef Steigler (Austria), one gold, one silver and one bronze, 1960–64; Gustav Theoni (Italy), one gold, two silver, 1972–76; and Ingemar Stenmark (Sweden), two gold, one bronze, 1976–80.

Most medals (country) Austria has won 56 medals in Olympic competition: in men's events, 10 gold, 12 silver and 11 bronze; in women's events, seven gold, eight silver and eight bronze.

United States U.S. skiers have won 20 medals in Olympic competition: in men's events, two gold, three silver and one bronze; in women's events, five gold, five silver and four bronze.

WORLD CHAMPIONSHIPS This competition was inaugurated in 1931 at Murren, Switzerland. From 1931–39 the championships were held annually; from 1950 they were held biennially. Up to 1980, the Olympic Games were considered the world championships, except in 1936. In 1985, the championship schedule was changed so as not to coincide with an Olympic year.

Most gold medals Christel Cranz (Germany) won a record 12 titles: four slalom, 1934, 1937–39; three downhill, 1935, 1937, 1939; five combined, 1934–35, 1937–39. Anton Sailer (Austria) holds the men's record with seven titles: one slalom, 1956; two giant slalom, 1956, 1958; two downhill, 1956, 1958; two combined, 1956, 1958.

WORLD CUP Contested annually since 1967, the World Cup is a circuit of races where points are earned during the season, with the champion being the skier with the most points at the end of the season.

INDIVIDUAL RACING RECORDS

Most wins (men) Ingemar Stenmark (Sweden) won a record 86 races (46 giant slalom, 40 slalom) from 287 contested, 1974–89.

Most wins (women) Annemarie Moser-Pröll (Austria) won a record 62 races, 1970–79.

KINGS OF THE HILLS ■ PIRMIN ZURBRIGGEN (SWITZERLAND) (ABOVE) HAS WON A RECORD FOUR OVERALL WORLD CUP TITLES AND FOUR SUPER GIANT SLALOM TITLES. INGEMAR STENMARK (SWEDEN) (BELOW) HAS WON A RECORD 86 WORLD CUP RACES, AND EIGHT SLALOM AND SEVEN GIANT SLALOM TITLES.

Most wins (season) Ingemar Stenmark (Sweden) won 13 races in 1978–79 to set the men's mark. Vreni Schneider (Switzerland) won 13 races in 1988–89 to set the women's mark.

Consecutive wins Ingemar Stenmark (Sweden) won 14 successive giant slalom races from March 18, 1978 to January 21, 1980. The women's record is 11 wins by Annemarie Moser-Pröll (Austria) in the downhill from December 1972 to January 1974.

RECORD FILE: ANNEMARIE MOSER-PRÖLL

Born March 27, 1953, Salzburg, Austria

OLYMPIC GAMES CAREER STATISTICS
1972–80

Downhill Title	Slalom Title
1	0

WORLD CUP CAREER STATISTICS
1970–80

Overall Title	Downhill Title	Slalom Title	Total
6*	7*	3	16*

WORLD CHAMPIONSHIPS CAREER STATISTICS
1972–80

Downhill Title	Combination Title	Slalom Title	Total
3†	2	0	5

RECORD NOTES Moser-Pröll holds the women's record for most World Cup race wins at 62. She also holds the record for most consecutive downhill race wins at 11, December 1972 to January 1974.

* Indicates all-time record; † indicates shares record.

UNITED STATES NATIONAL CHAMPIONSHIPS

Most titles Tamara McKinney won seven slalom titles, 1982–84, 1986–89—the most by any skier in one discipline. Phil Mahre won five giant slalom titles, 1975, 1977–79, 1981—the most by a male skier in one event.

NCAA CHAMPIONSHIPS The NCAA skiing championship was introduced in 1954. Teams compete in both Alpine and cross-country events, with cumulative point totals determining the national champion. Teams are comprised of both men and women.

Most titles (team) Denver has won 14 titles, 1954–57, 1961–67, and 1969–71.

Most titles (individual) Chiharu Igaya of Dartmouth won a record six NCAA titles: Alpine, 1955–56; downhill, 1955; slalom, 1955–57.

Fastest speed The official world record, as recognized by the International Ski Federation, for a skier is 139.030 mph, by Michael Prufer (Monaco), and the fastest by a woman is 133.234 mph, by Tarja Mulari (Finland), both at Les Arcs, France on April 16, 1988.

NORDIC SKIING

CROSS-COUNTRY SKIING

OLYMPIC GAMES Cross-country racing has been included in every Winter Olympic Games.

Most gold medals In men's competition, three skiers have each won four gold medals: Sixten Jernberg (Sweden), 50 km, 1956, 30 km, 1960, 50 km and 4 x 10 km relay, 1964; Gunde Svan (Sweden), 15 km and 4 x 10 km relay, 1984, 50 km and 4 x 10 km relay, 1988; Thomas Wassberg (Sweden), 15 km, 1980, 50 km and 4 x 10 km relay, 1984, 4 x 10 km relay, 1988. The women's record is also four golds, won by Galina Kulakova (USSR), 5 km, 10 km and 3 x 5 km relay, 1972, 4 x 5 km relay, 1976.

Most medals The most medals won in Nordic events is nine for both men and women. Sixten Jernberg (Sweden) holds the men's record (four gold, three silver, two bronze, 1956–64), and Raise Smetanina (USSR) holds the women's record (three gold, five silver and one bronze, 1976–88).

WORLD CUP A season series of world cup races was instituted in 1981.

Most titles Gunde Svan (Sweden) has won five overall cross-country skiing titles, 1984–86 and

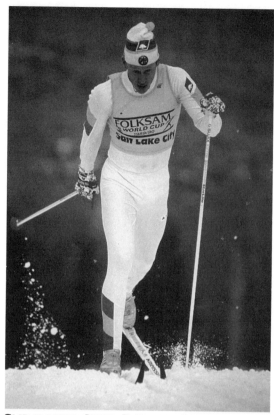

SLIP-SLIDING AWAY ■ GUNDE SVAN (SWEDEN) HAS WON A RECORD FIVE CROSS-COUNTRY WORLD CUP TITLES AND A RECORD-EQUALING FOUR OLYMPIC GOLD MEDALS.

1988–89. Marjo Matikainen (Finland) has won a record three women's overall titles.

UNITED STATES NATIONAL CHAMPIONSHIPS

Most titles Martha Rockwell has won a record 14 national titles, 1969–75. The record in men's competition is 12, by Audun Endestad, 1984–90.

Fastest speed—cross-country Bill Koch (U.S.) on March 26, 1981 skied 10 times around a 3.11 mile loop on Marlborough Pond, near Putney, Vt. He completed the course in 1 hour 59 minutes 47 seconds—an average speed of 15.57 mph.

SKI JUMPING

OLYMPIC GAMES Ski jumping has been included in every Winter Games.

Most gold medals Matti Nykanen (Finland) has won four gold medals: 70-meter hill, 1988; 90-meter hill, 1984 and 1988; 90-meter team, 1988.

Ski Lift ■ Finland's Matti Nykanen dominates ski jumping records, having won the most World Cup titles—four—and the most Olympic titles—four.

Most medals Matti Nykanen has won five medals in Olympic competition: four gold (see above) and one silver, 70-meter hill, 1984.

World Cup A season series of ski jumping events was instituted in 1981.

Most titles Matti Nykanen (Finland) has won four World Cup titles, 1983, 1985–86 and 1988.

United States National Championships

Most titles Lars Haugen has won seven ski jumping titles, 1912–28.

Longest ski jump The longest ski jump ever recorded is one of 636 feet, by Piotr Fijas (Poland) at Planica, Yugoslavia on March 14, 1987.

SLED DOG RACING

Origins Racing between harnessed dog teams (usually huskies) is believed to have been practiced by Inuits in North America, and also by the peoples of Scandinavia, long before the first recorded formal race, the All-America Sweepstakes, which took place in 1908. Sled dog racing was a demonstration sport at the 1932 Olympic Games. The best known race is the Iditarod Trail Sled Dog Race, first run in 1973.

IDITAROD TRAIL SLED DOG RACE

The annual 1,049-mile race from Anchorage to Nome, Alaska commemorates the 1925 midwinter emergency mission to get medical supplies to Nome during a diphtheria epidemic. Raced over alternate courses, the northern and southern trails, the Iditarod was first run in 1973.

IDITAROD WINNERS

Year	Musher	Elapsed Time
1973	Dick Wilmarth	20 days, 00:49:41
1974	Carl Huntington	20 days, 15:02:07
1975	Emmitt Peters	14 days, 14:43:45
1976	Gerald Riley	18 days, 22:58:17
1977	Rick Swenson	16 days, 16:27:13
1978	Rick Mackey	14 days, 18:52:24
1979	Rick Swenson	15 days, 10:37:47
1980	Joe May	14 days, 07:11:51
1981	Rick Swenson	12 days, 08:45:02
1982	Rick Swenson	16 days, 04:40:10
1983	Rick Mackey	12 days, 14:10:44
1984	Dean Osmar	12 days, 15:07:33
1985	Libby Riddles	18 days, 00:20:17
1986	Susan Butcher	11 days, 15:06:00
1987	Susan Butcher	11 days, 02:05:13
1988	Susan Butcher	11 days, 11:41:40
1989	Joe Runyan	11 days, 05:24:34
1990	Susan Butcher	11 days, 01:53:23
1991	Rick Swenson	12 days, 16:34:39

Most wins Rick Swenson has won the event five times: 1977, 1979, 1981–82, 1991.

Record time The fastest recorded time is 11 days, 1 hour 53 minutes 23 seconds by Susan Butcher in 1990.

TOUGH SLEDDING ■ SUSAN BUTCHER WON THE 1990 IDITAROD TRAIL SLED DOG RACE IN THE RECORD TIME OF 11 DAYS 1 HOUR 53 MINUTES 23 SECONDS.

SNOOKER

ORIGINS Neville Chamberlain, a British army officer, is credited with inventing the game in Jubbulpore, India in 1875. Snooker is a hybrid of pool and pyramids. Chamberlain added a set of colored balls to the 15 red ones used in pyramids and devised a scoring system based on pocketing the balls in sequence: red, color, red, color until all the reds have been cleared, leaving the colored balls to be pocketed in numerical order. The modern scoring system (a red ball is worth one point, yellow—2, green—3, brown—4, blue—5, pink—6 and black—7) was adopted in England in 1891. The sequence of pocketing the balls is called a break, the maximum possible being 147. The name *snooker* comes from the term coined for new recruits at the Woolwich Military Academy and was Chamberlain's label for anyone who lost at his game.

WORLD PROFESSIONAL CHAMPIONSHIPS This competition was first organized in 1927.

Most titles Joe Davis (England) won the title on the first 15 occasions it was contested, and this still stands as the all-time record for victories.

Maximum break The only 147 "maximum break" in world championship competition was compiled by Cliff Thorburn (Canada) on April 23, 1988.

SOARING

ORIGINS Research by Isadore William Deiches has shown evidence of the use of gliders in ancient Egypt *c.* 2500–1500 B.C. Emanuel Swedenborg of Sweden made sketches of gliders *c.* 1714. The earliest human-carrying glider was designed by Sir George Cayley and carried his coachman (possibly John Appleby) about 500 yards across a valley in Brompton Dale, North Yorkshire, England in the summer of 1853.

WORLD CHAMPIONSHIPS World championships were instituted in 1937.

Most individual titles The most individual titles won is four, by Ingo Renner (Australia) in 1976 (Standard class), 1983, 1985 and 1987 (Open).

United States The most titles won by an American pilot is two, by George Moffat, in the Open category, 1970 and 1974.

SOARING WORLD RECORDS (SINGLE-SEATERS)

DISTANCE AND HEIGHT

Straight distance 907.7 miles, Hans-Werner Grosse (Germany), Lubeck, Germany to Biarritz, France, April 25, 1972.

Declared goal distance 779.4 miles, by three pilots: Bruce Drake, David Speight and Dick Georgeson (all New Zealand), who each flew from Te Anau to Te Araroa, New Zealand, January 14, 1978.

Goal and return 1,023.2 miles, Tom Knauff (U.S.), Williamsport, Pa. to Knoxville, Tenn., April 25, 1983.

Absolute altitude 49,009 feet, Robert R. Harris (U.S.), over California, February 17, 1986. The women's record is 41,449 feet, by Sabrina Jackintell (U.S.) on February 14, 1979.

Height gain 42,303 feet, Paul Bikle (U.S.), Mojave, Calif., February 25, 1961. The women's record is 33,506 feet, by Yvonne Loader (New Zealand) at Omarama, New Zealand on January 12, 1988.

SPEED OVER TRIANGULAR COURSE

100 km 121.35 mph, Ingo Renner (Australia), December 14, 1982.

300 km 105.32 mph, Jean-Paul Castel (France), November 15, 1986.

500 km 105.67 mph, Beat Bunzli (Switzerland), January 9, 1988.

750 km 98.43 mph, Hans-Werner Grosse (Germany), January 8, 1985.

1,000 km 90.32 mph, Hans-Werner Grosse (Germany), January 3, 1979.

1,250 km 82.79 mph, Hans-Werner Grosse (Germany), January 9, 1980.

SOCCER

ORIGINS A game called *tsu chu* ("to kick a ball of stuffed leather") was played in China more than 2,500 years ago. However, the ancestry of the modern game is traced to England. In 1314, King Edward II prohibited the game because of excessive noise. Three subsequent monarchs also banned the game. Nevertheless, "football," the name by which soccer is known outside the United States, continued its development in England. In 1848, the first rules were drawn up at Cambridge University; in 1863, the Football Association (FA) was founded in England. The sport grew in popularity worldwide, and the *Fédération Internationale de Football Association* (FIFA), the world governing body, was formed in Paris, France in 1904. FIFA currently has more than 160 members.

WORLD CUP

The first World Cup for the Jules Rimet Trophy was held in Uruguay in 1930, and the contest has been staged quadrennially since, with a break from 1939–49 because of World War II. In 1970, Brazil won its third World Cup and was awarded permanent possession of the Jules Rimet Trophy. Countries now compete for the FIFA World Cup.

TEAM RECORDS

Most wins Three countries have won the World Cup on three occasions: Brazil (1958, 1962, 1970); Italy (1934, 1938, 1982); West Germany (1954, 1974, 1990).

Most appearances Brazil is the only country to qualify for all 14 World Cup tournaments.

Most goals The highest score by one team in a game is 10, by Hungary in a 10–1 defeat of El Salvador at Elche, Spain on June 15, 1982. The most goals in tournament history is 148 (from 66 games) by Brazil.

Highest-scoring game The highest-scoring game took place on June 26, 1954 when Austria defeated Switzerland 7–5.

INDIVIDUAL RECORDS

CHAMPIONSHIP GAME

Most wins Pelé (Brazil) is the only player to have played on three winning teams. Mario Zagalo (Brazil) was the first man to both play for (in 1958 and 1962) and be manager of (1970) a World Cup winning team. Franz Beckenbauer emulated Zagalo when he managed the West German team to victory in 1990. He had previously captained the 1974 winning team. Beckenbauer is the only man to have both captained and managed a winning side.

WORLD CUP FINALS (1930–1990)

Year	Winner	Loser	Score	Year	Winner	Loser	Score
1930	Uruguay	Argentina	4–2	1966	England	West Germany	4–2
1934	Italy	Czechoslovakia	2–1	1970	Brazil	Italy	4–1
1938	Italy	Hungary	4–2	1974	West Germany	Netherlands	2–1
1950	Uruguay	Brazil	2–1	1978	Argentina	Netherlands	3–1
1954	West Germany	Hungary	3–2	1982	Italy	West Germany	3–1
1958	Brazil	Sweden	5–2	1986	Argentina	West Germany	3–2
1962	Brazil	Czechoslovakia	3–1	1990	West Germany	Argentina	1–0

SOCCER'S BEST ■ PELÉ (BRAZIL) (LEFT) IS THE ONLY SOCCER PLAYER TO HAVE PLAYED ON THREE WORLD CUP WINNING TEAMS. HERE HE SCORES BRAZIL'S FIRST GOAL IN ITS 4–1 DEFEAT OF ITALY IN 1970.

Most goals The most goals scored in a final is three, by Geoff Hurst for England *v.* West Germany on July 30, 1966.

FINALS TOURNAMENT

Most games played Two players have appeared in 21 games in the finals tournament: Uwe Seeler (West Germany, 1958–70); Wladyslaw Zmuda (Poland, 1974–86).

Most goals scored The most goals scored by a player in a game is four; this has occurred nine times. The most goals scored in one tournament is 13, by Just Fontaine (France) in 1958, in six games. The most goals scored in a career is 14, by Gerd Muller (West Germany), 10 goals in 1970 and four in 1974.

OLYMPIC GAMES There is some dispute among Olympic historians as to whether soccer became an official Olympic sport in 1900 or in 1908. Since most Olympic histories do include the results from 1900, those results are included in the statistics in this section.

Most gold medals Two countries have won three Olympic titles: Great Britain, 1900, 1908 and 1912; Hungary, 1952, 1964 and 1968.

Most medals Four countries have won five medals: Hungary, three gold (see above), one silver, 1972, and one bronze, 1960; USSR, two gold, 1956 and 1988, three bronze, 1972, 1976 and 1980; Denmark, one gold, 1906, three silver, 1908, 1912 and 1960, one bronze, 1948; Yugoslavia, one gold, 1960, three silver, 1948, 1952 and 1956, one bronze, 1984.

United States U.S. teams have won two medals in Olympic competition, one silver and one bronze, both in 1904.

MAJOR SOCCER LEAGUE (MSL)

The Major Soccer League was founded in 1978 as the Major Indoor Soccer League (MISL), and was renamed for the 1990–91 season.

Most titles The San Diego Sockers have won seven MSL championships: 1983, 1985–86, 1988–91.

SCORING RECORDS (CAREER)

Most goals Steve Zungul (New York Arrows, 1978–83; Golden Bay Earthquakes, 1983; San

INSIDE FORWARD ■ STEVE ZUNGUL HOLDS MSL CAREER RECORDS FOR GOALS, ASSISTS AND POINTS SCORED.

Diego Sockers, 1984–86, 1989–90; Tacoma Stars, 1986–88) scored a record 652 goals in MSL games.

Most assists Steve Zungul holds the career assists mark at 471.

Most points Steve Zungul scored a record 1,123 points.

NCAA DIVISION I CHAMPIONSHIPS The NCAA Division I men's championship was first staged in 1959. A women's tournament was introduced in 1982.

Most titles (men) The University of St. Louis has won the most Division I titles with 10 victories, which includes one tie: 1959–60, 1962–63, 1965, 1967, 1969–70, 1972–73.

Most titles (women) The University of North Carolina has won a record nine Division I titles. Its victories came in 1982–84 and 1986–91.

SOFTBALL

ORIGINS Softball, a derivative of baseball, was invented by George Hancock at the Farragut Boat Club, Chicago, Ill. in 1887. Rules were first codified in Minneapolis, Minn. in 1895 under the name kitten ball. The name softball was introduced by Walter Hakanson at a meeting of the National Recreation Congress in 1926. The name was adopted throughout the United States in 1930. Rules were formalized in 1933 by the International Joint Rules Committee for Softball and adopted by the Amateur Softball Association of America. The International Softball Federation was formed in 1950 as governing body for both fast pitch and slow pitch.

FAST PITCH SOFTBALL

WORLD CHAMPIONSHIPS A women's fast pitch world championship was first staged in 1965, and a men's tournament in 1966. Both tournaments are held quadrennially.

Most titles (men) The United States has won five world titles: 1966, 1968, 1976 (tied), 1980 and 1988.

Most titles (women) The United States has won three world titles: 1974, 1978 and 1986.

AMATEUR SOFTBALL ASSOCIATION NATIONAL CHAMPIONSHIP The first ASA national championship was staged in 1933 for both men's and women's teams.

DYNASTY ■ IN 1991, THE RAYBESTOS BRAKETTES WON THEIR 21ST NATIONAL SOFTBALL TITLE.

Most titles (men) The Clearwater Bombers (Florida) won 10 championships between 1950 and 1973.

Most titles (women) The Raybestos Brakettes (Stratford, Conn.) have won 21 women's fast pitch titles from 1958 through 1991.

NCAA CHAMPIONSHIPS The first NCAA Division I women's championship was staged in 1982.

Most titles UCLA has won six titles: 1982, 1984–85, 1988–90.

SLOW PITCH SOFTBALL

WORLD CHAMPIONSHIPS A slow pitch world championship was staged for men's teams in 1987. The United States team won this event. So far a second tournament has not been scheduled. No world championship has been staged for women's teams.

AMATEUR SOFTBALL ASSOCIATION NATIONAL CHAMPIONSHIP The first men's ASA national championship was staged in 1953. The first women's event was staged in 1962.

Most titles (men—major slow pitch) Two teams have won three major slow pitch championships: Skip Hogan A.C. (Pittsburgh, Pa.), 1962, 1964–65; Joe Gatliff Auto Sales (Newport, Ky.), 1956–57, 1963.

Most titles (men—super slow pitch) Two teams have won three super slow pitch titles: Howard's Western Steer (Denver, Colo.), 1981, 1983–84; Steele's Silver Bullets (Grafton, Ohio), 1985–87.

Most titles (women) The Dots of Miami (Fla.) have won five major slow pitch titles, 1969, 1974–75, 1978–79.

SPEED SKATING

ORIGINS The world's longest skating race, the 124-mile "Elfstedentocht" ("Tour of the Eleven Towns"), is said to commemorate a similar race staged in the Netherlands in the 17th century. The first recorded skating race was staged in 1763, from Wisbech to Whittlesey, England. The International Skating Union (ISU) was founded at Scheveningen, Netherlands in 1892 and is the governing body for both speed skating and figure skating.

OLYMPIC GAMES Men's speed skating events have been included in the Olympic Games since 1924. Women's events were first staged in 1960.

Most gold medals Lidiya Skoblikova (USSR) has won six gold medals: 500-meter, 1964; 1,000-meter, 1964; 1,500-meter, 1960, 1964; 3,000-meter, 1960, 1964. The men's record is five, shared by two skaters: Clas Thunberg (Finland), 500-meter, 1928; 1,500-meter, 1924, 1928; 5,000-meter, 1924; all-around title, 1924; and Eric Heiden (U.S.), 500-meter, 1,000-meter, 1,500-meter, 5,000-meter, and 10,000-meter, all in 1980.

Most medals Karin Enke-Kania (East Germany) has won eight medals: three gold, four silver and one bronze, 1980–88. The men's record is seven, by two skaters: Clas Thunberg (Finland), five gold (see above), one silver and one bronze, 1924–28; and Ivar Ballangrud (Norway), four gold, two silver and one bronze, 1928–36.

Most medals (country) Norway has won 66 medals in Olympic competition: in men's events, 18 gold, 24 silver and 22 bronze; in women's events, one gold and one silver.

United States U.S. athletes have won 41 medals: in men's events, 13 gold, seven silver and three bronze; in women's events, four gold, eight silver and six bronze.

WORLD CHAMPIONSHIPS Speed skating world championships were first staged in 1893.

Most titles Oscar Mathisen (Norway) and Clas Thunberg (Finland) have won a record five overall world titles. Mathisen won titles in 1908–09 and

FASTEST SKATER ■ BONNIE BLAIR SET THE WOMEN'S 500-METER WORLD RECORD AT THE 1988 WINTER OLYMPIC GAMES.

1912–14; Thunberg won in 1923, 1925, 1928–29 and 1931. Karin Enke-Kania (East Germany) holds the women's mark, also at five. She won in 1982, 1984 and 1986–88.

UNITED STATES Eric Heiden won three overall world titles, 1977–79, the most by any U.S. skater. His sister Beth became the only American woman to win an overall championship in 1979.

SQUASH

ORIGINS Squash is an offshoot of rackets and is believed to have been first played at Harrow School, London, England in 1817. The International Squash Rackets Federation (ISRF) was founded in 1967. The Women's International Squash Rackets Federation was formed in 1976.

United States The U.S. Squash Racquets Association was formed in 1907, and staged the first U.S. amateur championships that year.

WORLD OPEN CHAMPIONSHIPS Both the men's and women's events were first held in 1976. The men's competition is an annual event, but the women's tournament was biennial until 1989, when it switched to the same system as the men's event. There was no championship in 1978.

Most titles Jahangir Khan (Pakistan) has won six titles, 1981–85 and 1988. Susan Devoy (New Zealand) holds the mark in the women's event with four victories, 1985, 1987, 1990 and 1991.

UNITED STATES AMATEUR CHAMPIONSHIPS The U.S. Amateur Championships were first held for men in 1907, and for women in 1928.

Most titles G. Diehl Mateer won 11 men's doubles titles between 1949 and 1966 with five different partners.

Most titles (singles) Alicia McConnell has won seven women's singles titles, 1982–88. Stanley Pearson won a record six men's titles, 1915–17, 1921–23.

SURFING

ORIGINS The Polynesian sport of surfing in a canoe (*ehorooe*) was first recorded by the British explorer Captain James Cook in December 1771 during his exploration of Tahiti. The modern sport developed in Hawaii, California and Australia in the mid-1950s. Although Hawaii is one of the 50 states, it is allowed to compete separately from the U.S. in international surfing competition.

WORLD AMATEUR CHAMPIONSHIP First held in May 1964 in Sydney, Australia, the open championship is the most prestigious event in both men's and women's competition.

Most titles In the women's division the title has been won twice by two surfers: Joyce Hoffman (U.S.), 1965–66; and Sharon Weber (Hawaii), 1970 and 1972. The men's title has been won by different surfers on each occasion.

WORLD PROFESSIONAL CHAMPIONSHIPS First held in 1970, the World Championship has been organized by the Association of Surfing Professionals (ASP) since 1976. The World Championship is a

LET 'EM RIP ■ FOUR-TIME PRO SURFING CHAMPION FRIEDA ZAMBA DEMONSTRATES HER RECORD-BREAKING TECHNIQUE.

circuit of events held throughout the year; the winning surfer is the one who gains the most points over the course of the year.

Most titles The most titles won by a professional surfer is five, by Mark Richards (Australia), 1975, 1979–82. The women's record is four, by Frieda Zamba (U.S.), 1984–86, 1988.

SWIMMING

ORIGINS The earliest references to swimming races were in Japan in 36 B.C. The first national swimming association, the Metropolitan Swimming Clubs Association, was founded in England in 1791. The international governing body for swimming, diving and water polo—the *Fédération Internationale de Natation Amateur* (FINA)—was founded in 1908.

OLYMPIC GAMES Swimming events were included in the first modern Games in 1896 and have been included in every Games since.

Most gold medals The greatest number of Olympic gold medals won is nine, by Mark Spitz (U.S.): 100-meter and 200-meter freestyle, 1972; 100-meter and 200-meter butterfly, 1972; 4 x 100-meter freestyle, 1968 and 1972; 4 x 200-meter freestyle, 1968 and 1972; 4 x 100-meter medley, 1972. The record number of gold medals won by a woman is six, by Kristin Otto (East Germany) at Seoul, South Korea in 1988: 100-meter freestyle, back-

SWIMMING—MEN'S WORLD RECORDS (set in 50-meter pools)
Freestyle

Event	Time	Swimmer (Country)	Date
50 meters	21.81	Tom Jager (U.S.)	March 24, 1990
100 meters	48.42	Matt Biondi (U.S.)	August 10, 1988
200 meters	1:46.69	Giorgio Lamberti (Italy)	August 15, 1989
400 meters	3:46.95	Uwe Dassler (East Germany)	September 23, 1988
800 meters	7:47.85	Kleren Perkins (Australia)	August 25, 1991
1,500 meters	14:50.36	Jorg Hoffman (Germany)	January 1, 1991
4 x 100-meter relay	3:16.53	U.S. (Chris Jacobs, Troy Dalbey, Tom Jager, Matt Biondi)	September 25, 1988
4 x 200-meter relay	7:12.51	U.S. (Troy Dalbey, Matt Cetlinski, Doug Gjertson, Matt Biondi)	September 21, 1988

Breaststroke

Event	Time	Swimmer (Country)	Date
100 meters	1:01.29	Norbert Kosza (Hungary)	August 20, 1991
200 meters	2:10.60	Michael Barrowman (U.S.)	August 13, 1991

Butterfly

Event	Time	Swimmer (Country)	Date
100 meters	52.84	Pablo Morales (U.S.) ·	June 23, 1986
200 meters	1:55.69	Melvin Stewart (U.S.)	January 12, 1991

Backstroke

Event	Time	Swimmer (Country)	Date
100 meters	53.93	Jeff Rouse (U.S.)	August 25, 1991
200 meters	1:57.30	Martin Zubero (Spain)	August 13, 1991

Individual Medley

Event	Time	Swimmer (Country)	Date
200 meters	1:59.36	Tamás Darnyi (Hungary)	January 13, 1991
400 meters	4:12.36	Tamás Darnyi (Hungary)	January 8, 1991
4 x 100-meter relay	3:36.93	U.S. (David Berkoff, Rich Schroeder, Matt Biondi, Chris Jacobs)	September 23, 1988

DIFFERENT STROKES ■ TAMÁS DARNYI (HUNGARY) HOLDS THE WORLD RECORDS FOR BOTH THE 200- AND 400-METER INDIVIDUAL MEDLEY EVENTS.

stroke and butterfly, 50-meter freestyle, 4 x 100-meter freestyle and 4 x 100-meter medley.

Most medals The most medals won by a swimmer is 11, by Mark Spitz (U.S.): nine gold (see above), one silver and one bronze, 1968–72. The most medals won by a woman is eight, by three swimmers: Dawn Fraser (Australia), four gold, four silver, 1956–64; Kornelia Ender (East Germany), four gold, four silver, 1972–76; Shirley Babashoff (U.S.), two gold, six silver, 1972–76.

Most medals (one Games) The most medals won at one Games is seven, by two swimmers: Mark Spitz (U.S.), seven golds in 1972; and Matt

SWIMMING—WOMEN'S WORLD RECORDS (set in 50-meter pools)

Freestyle

Event	Time	Swimmer (Country)	Date
50 meters	24.98	Yang Wenyi (China)	April 11, 1988
100 meters	54.73	Kristin Otto (East Germany)	August 19, 1986
200 meters	1:57.55	Heike Freidrich (East Germany)	June 18, 1986
400 meters	4:03.85	Janet Evans (U.S.)	September 22, 1988
800 meters	8:16.22	Janet Evans (U.S.)	August 20, 1989
1,500 meters	15:52.10	Janet Evans (U.S.)	March 26, 1988
4 x 100-meter relay	3:40.57	East Germany (Kristin Otto, Manuella Stellmach, Sabina Schulze, Heike Freidrich)	August 19, 1986
4 x 200-meter relay	7:55.47	East Germany (Manuella Stellmach, Astrid Strauss, Anke Möhring, Heike Freidrich)	August 18, 1987

Breaststroke

Event	Time	Swimmer (Country)	Date
100 meters	1:07.91	Silke Hörner (East Germany)	August 21, 1987
200 meters	2:26.71	Silke Hörner (East Germany)	September 21, 1988

Butterfly

Event	Time	Swimmer (Country)	Date
100 meters	57.93	Mary T. Meagher (U.S.)	August 16, 1981
200 meters	2:05.97	Mary T. Meagher (U.S.)	August 13, 1981

Backstroke

Event	Time	Swimmer (Country)	Date
100 meters	1:00.31	Kristina Egerszegi (Hungary)	August 20, 1991
200 meters	2:06.82	Kristina Egerszegi (Hungary)	August 26, 1991

Individual Medley

Event	Time	Swimmer (Country)	Date
200 meters	2:11.73	Ute Geweniger (East Germany)	July 4, 1981
400 meters	4:36.10	Petra Schneider (East Germany)	August 1, 1982
4 x 100-meter relay	4:03.69	East Germany (Ina Kleber, Sylvia Gerasch, Ines Geissler, Birgit Meineke)	August 24, 1984

Source: USA Swimming

MADAME BUTTERFLY ■ MARY T. MEAGHER HAS SET MARKS FOR THE 100-METER AND 200-METER BUTTERFLY THAT HAVE STOOD, INCREDIBLY, FOR OVER 10 YEARS.

Biondi (U.S.), five gold, one silver and one bronze in 1988. Kristin Otto (East Germany) won six gold medals at the 1988 Games, the most for a woman swimmer.

Most medals (country) The United States has won 348 medals in Olympic competition: in men's events, 91 gold, 69 silver and 48 bronze; in women's events, 63 gold, 41 silver and 36 bronze.

WORLD CHAMPIONSHIPS The first world swimming championships were held in Belgrade, Yugoslavia in 1973. The championships have been held quadrennially since 1978.

SWIMMING—MEN'S U.S. NATIONAL RECORDS (set in 50-meter pools)

Freestyle

Event	Time	Name	Date
50 meters	21.81	Tom Jager	March 24, 1990
100 meters	48.42	Matt Biondi	August 10, 1988
200 meters	1:47.72	Matt Biondi	August 8, 1988
400 meters	3:48.06	Matt Cetlinski	August 11, 1988
800 meters	7:52.45	Sean Killion	July 27, 1987
1,500 meters	15:01.51	George DiCarlo	June 30, 1984
4 x 100 meter relay	3:16.53	United States (Chris Jacobs, Troy Dalbey, Tom Jager, Matt Biondi)	September 23, 1988
4 x 200 meter relay	7:12.51	United States (Troy Dalbey, Matt Cetlinski, Doug Gjertsen, Matt Biondi)	September 21, 1988

Breaststroke

Event	Time	Name	Date
100 meters	1:01.65	Steve Lundquist	July 29, 1984
200 meters	2:10.60	Michael Barrowman	August 13, 1991

Butterfly

Event	Time	Name	Date
100 meters	52.84	Pablo Morales	June 23, 1986
200 meters	1:55.69	Melvin Stewart	January 12, 1991

Backstroke

Event	Time	Name	Date
100 meters	53.93	Jeff Rowe	August 25, 1991
200 meters	1:58.86	Rick Carey	June 27, 1984

Individual Medley

Event	Time	Name	Date
200 meters	2:00.11	David Wharton	August 20, 1989
400 meters	4:15.21	Eric Namesnick	January 8, 1991
4 x 100 meter relay	3:36.93	United States (David Berkoff, Rich Schroeder, Matt Biondi, Chris Jacobs)	September 25, 1988

Most gold medals Kornelia Ender (East Germany) won eight gold medals, 1973–75. Jim Montgomery (U.S.) won six gold medals, 1973–75, the most by a male swimmer.

Most medals Michael Gross (West Germany) has won 13 medals: five gold, five silver and three bronze, 1982–90. The most medals won by a female swimmer is 10, by Kornelia Ender, who won eight gold and two silver, 1973–75.

Most medals (one championship) Matt Biondi (U.S.) won seven medals—three gold, one silver and three bronze—in 1986 at Madrid, Spain.

UNITED STATES NATIONAL CHAMPIONSHIPS The first United States swimming championships were

SWIMMING—WOMEN'S U.S. NATIONAL RECORDS (set in 50-meter pools)

Freestyle

Event	Time	Name	Date
50 meters	25.50	Leigh Ann Fetter	August 13, 1988
	25.50	Leigh ann Fetter	January 13, 1991
100 meters	55.14	Angel Martino	August 23, 1991
200 meters	1:58.23	Cynthia Woodhead	September 3, 1979
400 meters	4:03.85	Janet Evans	September 22, 1988
800 meters	8:16.22	Janet Evans	August 20, 1989
1,500 meters	15:52.10	Janet Evans	March 26, 1988
4 x 100 meter relay	3:43.26	U.S. World Championship Team (Nicole Haislett, Julie Cooper, Whitney Hedgeperth, Jenny Thompson)	January 9, 1991
4 x 200 meter relay	8:02.12	U.S. World Championship Team (Betsy Mitchell, Mary T. Meagher, Kim Brown, Mary Alice Wayte)	August 22, 1986

Breastroke

100 meters	1:08.91	Tracey McFarlane	August 11, 1988
200 meters	2:27.08	Anita Nall	April 4, 1991

Butterfly

100 meters	57.93	Mary T. Meagher	August 16, 1981
200 meters	2:05.97	Mary T. Meagher	August 13, 1981

Backstroke

100 meters	1:01.00	Janie Wagstaff	August 22, 1991
200 meters	2:08.60	Betsy Mitchell	June 27, 1986

Individual Medley

200 meters	2:12.64	Tracy Caulkins	August 3, 1984
400 meters	4:37.75	Janel Evans	September 19, 1988
4 x 200 meter relay	4:05.98	U.S. Pan Pacific Team (Janie Wagstaff, Keli King, Crissy Ahmann-Leighton, Nicole Haislett)	August 25, 1991

Source: USA Swimming

staged by the Amateur Athletic Union on August 25, 1888.

Most titles Tracy Caulkins has won a record 48 national swimming titles, 1977–84. The most titles for a male swimmer is 36, by Johnny Weissmuller, 1921–28.

Fastest swimmer In a 25-yard pool, Tom Jager (U.S.) achieved an average speed of 5.37 mph, swimming 50 yards in 19.05 seconds at Nashville, Tenn. on March 23, 1990. The women's fastest time is 4.48 mph, by Yang Wenyi (China) in her 50-meter world record (see World Records table).

SYNCHRONIZED SWIMMING

In international competition, synchronized swimmers compete in two disciplines: solo and duet. In both disciplines the swimmers perform to music a series of moves that are judged for technical skills and musical interpretation. In solo events the swimmer has to be synchronized with the music; in duet events the swimmers have to be synchronized with each other as well as with the music.

ORIGINS Annette Kellerman and Kay Curtis are considered the pioneers of synchronized swimming in the United States. Kellerman's water ballet performances drew widespread attention throughout the U.S. at the beginning of the 20th century. Curtis was responsible for establishing synchronized swimming as part of the physical education program at the University of Wisconsin. In the 1940s, film star Esther Williams again drew attention to the sport, and in 1945 the Amateur Athletic Union recognized the sport. In 1973 the first world championship was staged, and in 1984 synchronized swimming was recognized as an official Olympic sport. The governing body for the sport in this country is United States Synchronized Swimming, formed in 1978.

OLYMPIC GAMES Synchronized swimming was first staged as an official sport at the 1984 Games.

Most gold medals Two swimmers have won two gold medals: Tracie Ruiz-Conforto (U.S.), solo and duet, 1984; CarolynWaldo (Canada), solo and duet, 1988.

Most medals Two swimmers have won three medals: Tracie Ruiz-Conforto (U.S.), two gold and one silver, 1984–88; Carolyn Waldo (Canada), two gold and one silver, 1984–88.

Most medals (country) Three countries have won four medals: Canada, two gold, two silver; United States, two gold, two silver; Japan, four bronze.

WORLD CHAMPIONSHIPS The world championships were first held in 1973, and have been held quadrennially since 1978.

Most titles The solo title has been won by a different swimmer on each occasion.

Most titles (team) The United States has won four team titles, 1973, 1975, 1978 and 1991.

AQUATIC GRACE ■ TRACIE RUIZ-CONFORTO (U.S.) DEMONSTRATES HER 1984 DOUBLE-OLYMPIC GOLD-MEDAL-WINNING TECHNIQUE.

UNITED STATES NATIONAL CHAMPIONSHIPS The first national championships were staged in 1946, and the competition is now an annual event.

Most titles Gail Johnson has won 11 national titles: six solo (two indoors, four outdoors), 1972–75; and five duet (two indoors, three outdoors), 1972–74.

Most titles (duet) The team of Karen and Sarah Josephson has won five national duet titles, 1985–88, and 1990.

TABLE TENNIS

ORIGINS The earliest evidence relating to a game resembling table tennis has been found in the catalogs of London sporting goods manufacturers in the 1880s. The International Table Tennis Federation (ITTF) was founded in 1926.

United States The United States Table Tennis Association was established in 1933. In 1971, a U.S. table tennis team was invited to play in the People's Republic of China, thereby initiating the first officially sanctioned Chinese-American cultural exchange in almost 20 years.

OLYMPIC GAMES Table tennis was included in the Olympic Games in 1988 for the first time.

Most medals Two players won two medals at the 1988 Games: Chin Jing (China), gold in the women's singles and silver in the doubles; Yoo Man-Kyu (South Korea), gold in the men's singles and bronze in the doubles.

Most medals (country) China won five medals at the 1988 Games: two gold, two silver and one bronze.

United States U.S. athletes did not win any medals at the 1988 Games.

WORLD CHAMPIONSHIPS The ITTF instituted European championships in 1926 and later designated this event the world championship. The tournament was staged annually until 1957, when the event became biennial.

SWAYTHLING CUP The men's team championship is named after Lady Swaythling, who donated the trophy in 1926.

Most titles The most wins is 12, by Hungary (1926, 1928–31, 1933 [two events were held that year, with Hungary winning both times], 1935, 1938, 1949, 1952, 1979).

CORBILLON CUP The women's team championship is named after M. Marcel Corbillon, president of the French Table Tennis Association, who donated the trophy in 1934.

Most titles China has won the most titles, with nine wins (1965, 1975, 1977, 1979, 1981, 1983, 1985, 1987, 1989).

Men's singles The most victories in singles is five, by Viktor Barna (Hungary), 1931, 1932–35.

Women's singles The most victories is six, by Angelica Rozeanu (Romania), 1950–55.

Men's doubles The most victories is eight, by Viktor Barna (Hungary), 1929–35 (twice in 1933), 1939. The partnership that has won the most titles is Viktor Barna and Miklos Szabados (Hungary), 1929–33, 1935.

TABLE TOPPER ■ LEAH NEUBERGER WON A RECORD 21 U.S. NATIONAL TABLE TENNIS TITLES BETWEEN 1941 AND 1961.

Women's doubles The most victories is seven, by Maria Mednyanszky (Hungary), 1928, 1930–35. The team that has won the most titles is Maria Mednyanszky and Anna Sipos (Hungary), 1930–35.

Mixed doubles Maria Mednyanszky (Hungary) has won a record six mixed doubles titles: 1927–28, 1930–31, 1933 (twice). The pairing of Miklos Szabados and Maria Mednyanszky (Hungary) won the title a record three times: 1930–31, 1933.

UNITED STATES NATIONAL CHAMPIONSHIPS U.S. national championships were first held in 1931.

Most titles Leah Neuberger (née Thall) won a record 21 titles between 1941 and 1961: nine women's singles, 12 women's doubles. Richard Mills won a record 10 men's singles titles between 1945 and 1962.

TAEKWONDO

ORIGINS Taekwondo is a martial art, with all activities based on defensive spirit, developed over 20 centuries in Korea. It was officially recognized as part of Korean tradition and culture on April 11, 1955. The first World Taekwondo Championships were organized by the Korean Taekwondo Association and were held at Seoul, South Korea in 1973. The World Taekwondo Federation was then formed and has organized biennial championships.

United States The United States Taekwondo Union was founded in 1974.

OLYMPIC GAMES Taekwondo was included as a demonstration sport at the 1988 Games, and will be included as a demonstration sport at the 1992 Games in Barcelona, Spain.

WORLD CHAMPIONSHIPS These biennial championships were first held in Seoul, South Korea in 1973, when they were staged by the Korean Taekwondo Association. Women's events were first staged unofficially in 1983 and have been officially recognized since 1987.

Most titles Chung Kook-hyun (South Korea) has won a record four world titles: light middleweight, 1982–83; welterweight 1985, 1987.

TEAM HANDBALL

ORIGINS Team handball developed around the turn of the 20th century. It evolved from a game devised by soccer players in northern Germany and Denmark designed to keep them fit during the winter months. An outdoors version of the game was included in the 1936 Olympic Games as a demonstration sport. In 1946 the International Handball Federation (IHF) was formed. The growth of team handball has been rapid since its reintroduction into the Olympic Games in 1972 as an indoor game with seven players on each side. The IHF claims 4.2 million members from 88 countries, second only to soccer in terms of worldwide membership.

United States Team handball was first introduced to the United States in the 1920s, and a national team entered the 1936 Olympic demonstration competition. In 1959 the United States Team Handball Federation (USTHF) was formed, and it still governs the sport in this country.

OLYMPIC GAMES

Most wins In men's competition, two countries have won the Olympic gold medal twice: Yugosla-

via, 1972 and 1984; USSR, 1976 and 1988. In women's competition, introduced in 1976, the USSR has won the title twice, in 1976 and 1980.

United States The United States has never won a medal in team handball competition.

WORLD CHAMPIONSHIP This competition was instituted in 1938.

Most titles (country) Romania has won four men's and three women's titles (two outdoor, one indoor) from 1956 to 1974. East Germany has also won three women's titles, in 1971, 1975 and 1978.

TENNIS

ORIGINS The modern game evolved from the indoor sport of real tennis. There is an account of a game called "field tennis" in an English sports periodical dated September 29, 1793; however, the "father" of lawn tennis is regarded as Major Walter Wingfield, who patented a type of tennis called "sphairistike" in 1874. The Marylebone Cricket Club, England revised Wingfield's initial rules in 1877, and the famed All-England Croquet Club (home of the Wimbledon Championships) added the name Lawn Tennis to its title in 1877. The "open" era of tennis, when amateurs were permitted to play with and against professionals, was introduced in 1968.

GRAND SLAM

The modern grand slam is achieved by winning all four grand slam events—the Australian Open, French Open, Wimbledon and U.S. Open—in succession. The traditional slam is winning the four events in one calendar year.

GRAND SLAM WINNERS

Singles Don Budge (U.S.) was the first player to hold all four championships simultaneously, when he won the last two events of 1937 and the first two of 1938. He was also the first to win all four in the same year, 1938. The only player to have won the grand slam twice is Rod Laver (Australia), who accomplished this in 1962 and 1969. Four women have completed the grand slam: Maureen Connolly (U.S.), in 1953; Margaret Court (née Smith; Australia), in 1970; Martina Navratilova (U.S.), in 1983–84 (last three slams of

1983 and first of 1984); and Steffi Graf (West Germany), in 1988.

Doubles The only men to win the grand slam for doubles were Frank Sedgman and Ken McGregor (Australia) in 1951. Four women have won the grand slam: Louise Brough (U.S.) in 1949–50 (last three of 1949 and first of 1950); Maria Bueno (Brazil) in 1960; Martina Navratilova and Pam Shriver (U.S.) in 1984. Navratilova and Shriver won eight consecutive doubles titles from 1983–85.

Mixed doubles Ken Fletcher and Margaret Court (Australia) won all four legs of the grand slam in 1963. Owen Davidson (Australia) won all four events, with two partners, in 1967.

MOST GRAND SLAM TITLES

Singles The most singles championships won in grand slam tournaments is 24, by Margaret Court (née Smith; Australia): 11 Australian, five French, three Wimbledon, five U.S. Open between 1960 and 1973. The men's record is 12, by Roy Emerson (Australia): six Australian, two French, two Wimbledon, two U.S. Open between 1961 and 1967.

Doubles The most wins by a doubles partnership is 20, by two teams: Louise Brough (U.S.) and Margaret Du Pont (U.S.), who won three French, five Wimbledon and 12 U.S. Opens, 1942–57; and by Martina Navratilova (U.S.) and Pam Shriver (U.S.). They won seven Australian, four French, five Wimbledon, four U.S. Opens, 1981–89.

WIMBLEDON CHAMPIONSHIPS

The "Lawn Tennis Championships" at the All-England Club, Wimbledon are generally regarded as the most prestigious in tennis and currently form the third leg of the grand slam events. They were first held in 1877 and, until 1922, were organized on a challenge round system (the defending champion automatically qualifies for the following year's final and plays the winner of the challenger event). Wimbledon became an open championship (professionals could compete) in 1968.

Most titles (men) Overall, the most titles is seven, by William Renshaw (Great Britain), 1881–86, 1889. Since the abolition of the Challenge Round in 1922, the most wins is five, by Bjorn Borg (Sweden), 1976–80.

Most titles (women) Martina Navratilova has won a record nine titles: 1978–79, 1982–87, 1990.

RECORD FILE: MARTINA NAVRATILOVA

BORN October 18, 1956, Prague, Czechoslovakia

GRAND SLAM TITLES
1973–91

Event	Singles	Doubles	Mixed Doubles	Total
Australian Open	3	8	0	11
French Open	2	7	2	11
Wimbledon	9*	7	1	17
U.S. Open	4	9	2	15
Totals	18	31*	5	54

TOUR CAREER STATISTICS
1973–91

	Matches					
Wins	Losses	Total	Percentage	Tour Wins	Earnings
1,321*	182	1,503*	.879	157†	$17,661,593*

RECORD NOTES In singles, Navratilova holds the tour record for consecutive victories at 74 matches, January 15 to December 6, 1984. She is one of four women to win the Grand Slam—she won the last three titles of 1983 and the first of 1984. In doubles, Navratilova, with partner Pam Shriver, holds the record for consecutive doubles wins at 109 matches from April 24, 1983 to July 6, 1985. Navratilova and Shriver share the record for most doubles Grand Slam titles at 20, 1982–89, and are the only team to win the doubles Grand Slam three times.

* Indicates all-time record; † indicates tied record.

Men's doubles Lawrence and Reginald Doherty (Great Britain) won the doubles title a record eight times: 1897–1901, 1903–05.

Women's doubles Suzanne Lenglen (France) and Elizabeth Ryan (U.S.) won the doubles a rec-

ord six times: 1919–23, 1925. Elizabeth Ryan was a winning partner on a record 12 occasions: 1914, 1919–23, 1925–27, 1930, 1933–34.

Mixed doubles The team of Ken Fletcher and Margaret Court (née Smith), both of Australia,

WIMBLEDON CHAMPIONS (1877–1932)

Men's Singles				Women's Singles			
Year	Player	Year	Player	Year	Player	Year	Player
1877	Spencer Gore	1905	Lawrence Doherty	1877	no event	1905	May Sutton
1878	Frank Hadlow	1906	Lawrence Doherty	1878	no event	1906	Dorothea Douglass
1879	Rev. John Hartley	1907	Norman Brookes	1879	no event	1907	May Sutton
1880	Rev. John Hartley	1908	Arthur Gore	1880	no event	1908	Charlotte Sterry[2]
1881	William Renshaw	1909	Arthur Gore	1881	no event	1909	Dora Boothby
1882	William Renshaw	1910	Tony Wilding	1882	no event	1910	Dorothea Lambert-Chambers[3]
1883	William Renshaw	1911	Tony Wilding	1883	no event	1911	Dorothea Lambert-Chambers[3]
1884	William Renshaw	1912	Tony Wilding	1884	Maud Watson	1912	Ethel Larcombe
1885	William Renshaw	1913	Tony Wilding	1885	Maud Watson	1913	Dorothea Lambert-Chambers[3]
1886	William Renshaw	1914	Norman Brookes	1886	Blanche Bingley	1914	Dorothea Lambert-Chambers[3]
1887	Herbert Lawford	1915	not held	1887	Lottie Dod	1915	not held
1888	Ernest Renshaw	1916	not held	1888	Lottie Dod	1916	not held
1889	William Renshaw	1917	not held	1889	Blanche Hillyard[1]	1917	not held
1890	Willoughby Hamilton	1918	not held	1890	Helene Rice	1918	not held
1891	Wilfred Baddeley	1919	Gerald Patterson	1891	Lottie Dod	1919	Suzanne Lenglen
1892	Wilfred Baddeley	1920	Bill Tilden	1892	Lottie Dod	1920	Suzanne Lenglen
1893	Joshua Pim	1921	Bill Tilden	1893	Lottie Dod	1921	Suzanne Lenglen
1894	Joshua Pim	1922	Gerald Patterson	1894	Blanche Hillyard[1]	1922	Suzanne Lenglen
1895	Wilfred Baddeley	1923	William Johnston	1895	Charlotte Cooper	1923	Suzanne Lenglen
1896	Harold Mahoney	1924	Jean Borotra	1896	Charlotte Cooper	1924	Kathleen McKane
1897	Reginald Doherty	1925	Rene Lacoste	1897	Blanche Hillyard[1]	1925	Suzanne Lenglen
1898	Reginald Doherty	1926	Jean Borotra	1898	Charlotte Cooper	1926	Kathleen Godfree[4]
1899	Reginald Doherty	1927	Henri Cochet	1899	Blanche Hillyard[1]	1927	Helen Wills
1900	Reginald Doherty	1928	Rene Lacoste	1900	Blanche Hillyard[1]	1928	Helen Wills
1901	Arthur Gore	1929	Henri Cochet	1901	Charlotte Sterry[2]	1929	Helen Wills
1902	Lawrence Doherty	1930	Bill Tilden	1902	Muriel Robb	1930	Helen Moody[5]
1903	Lawrence Doherty	1931	Sidney Wood	1903	Dorothea Douglass	1931	Cilly Aussem
1904	Lawrence Doherty	1932	Ellsworth Vines	1904	Dorothea Douglass	1932	Helen Moody[5]

1–Blanche Hillyard (née Bingley) 2–Charlotte Sterry (née Cooper) 3–Dorothea Lambert-Chambers (née Douglass) 4–Kathleen Godfree (née McKane)
5–Helen Moody (née Wills)

won the mixed doubles a record four times: 1963, 1965–66, 1968. Fletcher's four victories tie him for the men's record for wins, which is shared by two other players: Vic Seixas (U.S.), 1953–56; Owen Davidson (Australia), 1967, 1971, 1973–74. Elizabeth Ryan (U.S.) holds the women's record with seven wins: 1919, 1921, 1923, 1927–28, 1930, 1932.

WIMBLEDON CHAMPIONS (1933–1991)

Men's Singles

Year	Player	Year	Player
1933	Jack Crawford	1963	Chuck McKinley
1934	Fred Perry	1964	Roy Emerson
1935	Fred Perry	1965	Roy Emerson
1936	Fred Perry	1966	Manuel Santana
1937	Don Budge	1967	John Newcombe
1938	Don Budge	1968	Rod Laver
1939	Bobby Riggs	1969	Rod Laver
1940	not held	1970	John Newcombe
1941	not held	1971	John Newcombe
1942	not held	1972	Stan Smith
1943	not held	1973	Jan Kodes
1944	not held	1974	Jimmy Connors
1945	not held	1975	Arthur Ashe
1946	Yvon Petra	1976	Bjorn Borg
1947	Jack Kramer	1977	Bjorn Borg
1948	Bob Falkenburg	1978	Bjorn Borg
1949	Ted Schroeder	1979	Bjorn Borg
1950	Budge Patty	1980	Bjorn Borg
1951	Dick Savitt	1981	John McEnroe
1952	Frank Sedgman	1982	Jimmy Connors
1953	Vic Seixas	1983	John McEnroe
1954	Jaroslav Drobny	1984	John McEnroe
1955	Tony Trabert	1985	Boris Becker
1956	Lew Hoad	1986	Boris Becker
1957	Lew Hoad	1987	Pat Cash
1958	Ashley Cooper	1988	Stefan Edberg
1959	Alex Olmedo	1989	Boris Becker
1960	Neale Fraser	1990	Stefan Edberg
1961	Rod Laver	1991	Michael Stich
1962	Rod Laver		

Women's Singles

Year	Player	Year	Player
1933	Helen Moody [5]	1963	Margaret Smith
1934	Dorothy Round	1964	Maria Bueno
1935	Helen Moody [5]	1965	Margaret Smith
1936	Helen Jacobs	1966	Billie Jean King
1937	Dorothy Round	1967	Billie Jean King
1938	Helen Moody [5]	1968	Billie Jean King
1939	Alice Marble	1969	Ann Jones
1940	not held	1970	Margaret Court [6]
1941	not held	1971	Evonne Goolagong
1942	not held	1972	Billie Jean King
1943	not held	1973	Billie Jean King
1944	not held	1974	Chris Evert
1945	not held	1975	Billie Jean King
1946	Pauline Betz	1976	Chris Evert
1947	Margaret Osborne	1977	Virginia Wade
1948	Louise Brough	1978	Martina Navratilova
1949	Louise Brough	1979	Martina Navratilova
1950	Louise Brough	1980	Evonne Cawley [7]
1951	Doris Hart	1981	Chris Evert
1952	Maureen Connolly	1982	Martina Navratilova
1953	Maureen Connolly	1983	Martina Navratilova
1954	Maureen Connolly	1984	Martina Navratilova
1955	Louise Brough	1985	Martina Navratilova
1956	Shirley Fry	1986	Martina Navratilova
1957	Althea Gibson	1987	Martina Navratilova
1958	Althea Gibson	1988	Steffi Graf
1959	Maria Bueno	1989	Steffi Graf
1960	Maria Bueno	1990	Martina Navratilova
1961	Angela Mortimer	1991	Steffi Graf
1962	Karen Susman		

5 – Helen Moody (née Wills)   6 – Margaret Court (née Smith)   7 – Evonne Cawley (née Goolagong)

Most titles (overall) Billie Jean King (U.S.) won a record 20 Wimbledon titles from 1961–79: six singles, 10 doubles and four mixed doubles.

Youngest champions The youngest champion was Lottie Dod (Great Britain), who was 15 years 285 days when she won in 1887. The youngest men's champion was Boris Becker (Germany), who was 17 years 227 days when he won in 1985.

UNITED STATES OPEN CHAMPIONSHIPS

The first official U.S. championships were staged in 1881. From 1884 to 1911, the contest was based

U.S. OPEN CHAMPIONS (1881–1938)

Men's Singles				Women's Singles			
Year	Player	Year	Player	Year	Player	Year	Player
1881	Richard Sears	1910	William Larned	1881	no event	1910	Hazel Hotchkiss
1882	Richard Sears	1911	William Larned	1882	no event	1911	Hazel Hotchkiss
1883	Richard Sears	1912	Maurice McLoughlin	1883	no event	1912	Mary Browne
1884	Richard Sears	1913	Maurice McLoughlin	1884	no event	1913	Mary Browne
1885	Richard Sears	1914	Norris Williams	1885	no event	1914	Mary Browne
1886	Richard Sears	1915	William Johnston	1886	no event	1915	Molla Bjurstedt
1887	Richard Sears	1916	Norris Williams	1887	Ellen Hansell	1916	Molla Bjurstedt
1888	Henry Slocum Jr.	1917	Lindley Murray	1888	Bertha Townsend	1917	Molla Bjurstedt
1889	Henry Slocum Jr.	1918	Lindley Murray	1889	Bertha Townsend	1918	Molla Bjurstedt
1890	Oliver Campbell	1919	William Johnston	1890	Ellen Roosevelt	1919	Hazel Wightman [1]
1891	Oliver Campbell	1920	Bill Tilden	1891	Mabel Cahill	1920	Molla Mallory [2]
1892	Oliver Campbell	1921	Bill Tilden	1892	Mabel Cahill	1921	Molla Mallory [2]
1893	Robert Wrenn	1922	Bill Tilden	1893	Aline Terry	1922	Molla Mallory [2]
1894	Robert Wrenn	1923	Bill Tilden	1894	Helen Helwig	1923	Helen Wills
1895	Fred Hovey	1924	Bill Tilden	1895	Juliette Atkinson	1924	Helen Wills
1896	Robert Wrenn	1925	Bill Tilden	1896	Elisabeth Moore	1925	Helen Wills
1897	Robert Wrenn	1926	Rene Lacoste	1897	Juliette Atkinson	1926	Molla Mallory [2]
1898	Malcolm Whitman	1927	Rene Lacoste	1898	Juliette Atkinson	1927	Helen Wills
1899	Malcolm Whitman	1928	Henri Cochet	1899	Marion Jones	1928	Helen Wills
1900	Malcolm Whitman	1929	Bill Tilden	1900	Myrtle McAteer	1929	Helen Wills
1901	William Larned	1930	John Doeg	1901	Elisabeth Moore	1930	Betty Nuthall
1902	William Larned	1931	Ellsworth Vines	1902	Marion Jones	1931	Helen Moody [3]
1903	Lawrence Doherty	1932	Ellsworth Vines	1903	Elisabeth Moore	1932	Helen Jacobs
1904	Holcombe Ward	1933	Fred Perry	1904	May Sutton	1933	Helen Jacobs
1905	Beals Wright	1934	Fred Perry	1905	Elisabeth Moore	1934	Helen Jacobs
1906	William Clothier	1935	Wilmer Allison	1906	Helen Homans	1935	Helen Jacobs
1907	William Larned	1936	Fred Perry	1907	Evelyn Sears	1936	Alice Marble
1908	William Larned	1937	Don Budge	1908	Maud Bargar-Wallach	1937	Anita Lizana
1909	William Larned	1938	Don Budge	1909	Hazel Hotchkiss	1938	Alice Marble

1 – Hazel Wightman (née Hotchkiss)   2 – Molla Mallory (née Bjurstedt)   3 – Helen Moody (née Wills)

on a challenger format. In 1968 and 1969, separate amateur and professional events were held. Since 1970, there has been only an Open competition. On the current schedule the U.S. Open is the fourth and final leg of the grand slam and is played at the U.S. National Tennis Center, Flushing Meadows, N.Y.

Most titles (men) The most wins is seven, by three players: Richard Sears (U.S.), 1881–87; William Larned (U.S.), 1901–02, 1907–11; Bill Tilden (U.S.), 1920–25, 1929.

Most titles (women) Molla Mallory (née Bjurstedt; U.S.) won a record eight titles: 1915–18, 1920–22, 1926.

U.S. OPEN CHAMPIONS (1939–1991)

Men's Singles

Year	Player	Year	Player
1939	Bobby Riggs	1967	John Newcombe
1940	Donald McNeil	1968	Arthur Ashe
1941	Bobby Riggs	1968	Arthur Ashe
1942	Ted Schroeder	1969	Stan Smith
1943	Joseph Hunt	1969	Rod Laver
1944	Frank Parker	1970	Ken Rosewall
1945	Frank Parker	1971	Stan Smith
1946	Jack Kramer	1972	Ilie Nastase
1947	Jack Kramer	1973	John Newcombe
1948	Pancho Gonzalez	1974	Jimmy Connors
1949	Pancho Gonzalez	1975	Manuel Orantes
1950	Arthur Larsen	1976	Jimmy Connors
1951	Frank Sedgman	1977	Guillermo Vilas
1952	Frank Sedgman	1978	Jimmy Connors
1953	Tony Trabert	1979	John McEnroe
1954	Vic Seixas	1980	John McEnroe
1955	Tony Trabert	1981	John McEnroe
1956	Ken Rosewall	1982	Jimmy Connors
1957	Malcolm Anderson	1983	Jimmy Connors
1958	Ashley Cooper	1984	John McEnroe
1959	Neale Fraser	1985	Ivan Lendl
1960	Neale Fraser	1986	Ivan Lendl
1961	Roy Emerson	1987	Ivan Lendl
1962	Rod Laver	1988	Mats Wilander
1963	Raphael Osuna	1989	Boris Becker
1964	Roy Emerson	1990	Pete Sampras
1965	Manuel Santana	1991	Stefan Edberg
1966	Fred Stolle		

Women's Singles

Year	Player	Year	Player
1939	Alice Marble	1967	Billie Jean King
1940	Alice Marble	1968	Margaret Court [4]
1941	Sarah Cooke	1968	Virginia Wade
1942	Pauline Betz	1969	Margaret Court [4]
1943	Pauline Betz	1969	Margaret Court [4]
1944	Pauline Betz	1970	Margaret Court [4]
1945	Sarah Cooke	1971	Billie Jean King
1946	Pauline Betz	1972	Billie Jean King
1947	Louise Brough	1973	Margaret Court [4]
1948	Margaret Du Pont	1974	Billie Jean King
1949	Margaret Du Pont	1975	Chris Evert
1950	Margaret Du Pont	1976	Chris Evert
1951	Maureen Connolly	1977	Chris Evert
1952	Maureen Connolly	1978	Chris Evert
1953	Maureen Connolly	1979	Tracy Austin
1954	Doris Hart	1980	Chris Evert
1955	Doris Hart	1981	Tracy Austin
1956	Shirley Fry	1982	Chris Evert
1957	Althea Gibson	1983	Martina Navratilova
1958	Althea Gibson	1984	Martina Navratilova
1959	Maria Bueno	1985	Hanna Mandlikova
1960	Darlene Hard	1986	Martina Navratilova
1961	Darlene Hard	1987	Martina Navratilova
1962	Margaret Smith	1988	Steffi Graf
1963	Maria Bueno	1989	Steffi Graf
1964	Maria Bueno	1990	Gabriela Sabatini
1965	Margaret Smith	1991	Monica Seles
1966	Maria Bueno		

4– Margaret Court (née Smith)

RECORD FILE: JIMMY CONNORS

Born September 2, 1952, Belleville, Ill.

GRAND SLAM TITLES
1970–91

Event	Singles	Doubles	Mixed Doubles	Total
Australian Open	1	0	0	1
French Open	0	0	0	0
Wimbledon	2	1	0	3
U.S. Open	5	1	0	6
Totals	8	2	0	10

TOUR CAREER STATISTICS
1970–91

		Matches*			
Wins	Losses	Total	Percentage	Tour Wins	Earnings
931	200	1,131	.823	109†	$8,323,004

RECORD NOTES Connors held the number-one ranking for a record 159 weeks, from July 29, 1974 to August 16, 1977. He shares the record for most singles titles in a season at 15, a record he established in 1977. Connors is the only man to win the U.S. Open on three different surfaces: grass, clay, and hardcourt. Connors has both played in and won the most singles matches at the U.S. Open and Wimbledon; his record at the U.S. Open is 97–16; at Wimbledon, 84–17.

* The ATP Tour has kept match statistics since 1978. These figures include estimated numbers for Connors' career prior to 1978.

† Indicates all-time record.

Men's doubles The most wins by one pair is five, by Richard Sears and James Dwight (U.S.), 1882–84, 1886–87. The most wins by an individual player is six, by two players: Richard Sears, 1882–84, 1886–87 (with Dwight) and 1885 (with Joseph Clark); Holcombe Ward, 1899–1901 (with Dwight Davis), 1904–06 (with Beals Wright).

Women's doubles The most wins by a pair is 12, by Louise Brough and Margaret Du Pont (née Osborne), both of the U.S.. They won in 1942–50 and in 1955–57. Margaret Du Pont holds the record for an individual player with 13 wins; adding to her victories with Brough was the 1941 title with Sarah Cooke.

Mixed doubles The most wins by one pair is four, by William Talbert and Margaret Osborne (U.S.), who won in 1943–46. The most titles won by any individual is nine, by Margaret Du Pont (née Osborne). She won in 1943–46, 1950, 1956, 1958–60. The most titles won by a man is four, accomplished by six players: Edwin Fischer (U.S.), 1894–96, 1898; Wallace Johnson (U.S.), 1907, 1909, 1911, 1920; Bill Tilden (U.S.), 1913–14, 1922–23; William Talbert (U.S.), 1943–46; Owen Davidson (Australia), 1966–67, 1971, 1973; and Marty Riessen (U.S.), 1969–70, 1972, 1980.

Most titles (overall) Margaret Du Pont (née Osborne) won a record 25 U.S. Open titles from 1941–60—three singles, 13 doubles, and nine mixed doubles.

Youngest champions The youngest singles champion was Tracy Austin (U.S.), who was 16 years 271 days when she won the women's singles in 1979. The youngest men's champion was Pete Sampras (U.S.), who was 19 years 28 days when he won the 1990 title.

FRENCH OPEN CHAMPIONSHIPS

The first French championships were held in 1891; however, entry was restricted to members of French clubs until 1925. Grand Slam records include the French Open only from 1925. This event has been staged at the Stade Roland Garros since 1928 and currently is the second leg of the grand slam.

Most wins (men) Bjorn Borg (Sweden) has won the French title a record six times: 1974–75, 1978–81.

FRENCH OPEN CHAMPIONS (1925–1991)

Men's Singles

Year	Player	Year	Player
1925	Rene Lacoste	1959	Nicola Pietrangeli
1926	Henri Cochet	1960	Nicola Pietrangeli
1927	Rene Lacoste	1961	Manuel Santana
1928	Henri Cochet	1962	Rod Laver
1929	Rene Lacoste	1963	Roy Emerson
1930	Henri Cochet	1964	Manuel Santana
1931	Jean Borotra	1965	Fred Stolle
1932	Henri Cochet	1966	Tony Roche
1933	Jack Crawford	1967	Roy Emerson
1934	Gottfried Von Cramm	1968	Ken Rosewall
1935	Fred Perry	1969	Rod Laver
1936	Gottfried Von Cramm	1970	Jan Kodes
1937	Henner Henkel	1971	Jan Kodes
1938	Don Budge	1972	Andres Gimeno
1939	Donald McNeil	1973	Ilie Nastase
1940	not held	1974	Bjorn Borg
1941	not held	1975	Bjorn Borg
1942	not held	1976	Adriano Panatta
1943	not held	1977	Guillermo Vilas
1944	not held	1978	Bjorn Borg
1945	not held	1979	Bjorn Borg
1946	Marcel Bernard	1980	Bjorn Borg
1947	Jozsef Asboth	1981	Bjorn Borg
1948	Frank Parker	1982	Mats Wilander
1949	Frank Parker	1983	Yannick Noah
1950	Budge Patty	1984	Ivan Lendl
1951	Jaroslav Drobny	1985	Mats Wilander
1952	Jaroslav Drobny	1986	Ivan Lendl
1953	Ken Rosewall	1987	Ivan Lendl
1954	Tony Trabert	1988	Mats Wilander
1955	Tony Trabert	1989	Michael Chang
1956	Lew Hoad	1990	Andres Gomez
1957	Sven Davidson	1991	Jim Courier
1958	Mervyn Rose		

Women's Singles

Year	Player	Year	Player
1925	Suzanne Lenglen	1959	Christine Truman
1926	Suzanne Lenglen	1960	Darlene Hard
1927	Kea Bouman	1961	Ann Haydon
1928	Helen Moody[1]	1962	Margaret Smith
1929	Helen Moody[1]	1963	Lesley Turner
1930	Helen Moody[1]	1964	Margaret Smith
1931	Cilly Aussem	1965	Lesley Turner
1932	Helen Moody[1]	1966	Ann Jones[3]
1933	Margaret Scriven	1967	Francoise Durr
1934	Margaret Scriven	1968	Nancy Richey
1935	Hilde Sperling	1969	Margaret Court[4]
1936	Hilde Sperling	1970	Margaret Court[4]
1937	Hilde Sperling	1971	Evonne Goolagong
1938	Simone Mathieu	1972	Billie Jean King
1939	Simone Mathieu	1973	Margaret Court[4]
1940	not held	1974	Chris Evert
1941	not held	1975	Chris Evert
1942	not held	1976	Sue Barker
1943	not held	1977	Mimi Jausovec
1944	not held	1978	Virginia Ruzici
1945	not held	1979	Chris Evert
1946	Margaret Osborne	1980	Chris Evert
1947	Pat Todd	1981	Hana Mandlikova
1948	Nelly Landry	1982	Martina Navratilova
1949	Margaret Du Pont[2]	1983	Chris Evert
1950	Doris Hart	1984	Martina Navratilova
1951	Shirley Fry	1985	Chris Evert
1952	Doris Hart	1986	Chris Evert
1953	Maureen Connolly	1987	Steffi Graf
1954	Maureen Connolly	1988	Steffi Graf
1955	Angela Mortimer	1989	Aranxta Sanchez Vicario
1956	Althea Gibson		
1957	Shirley Bloomer	1990	Monica Seles
1958	Zsuzsi Kormoczy	1991	Monica Seles

1 – Helen Moody (née Wills)   2 – Margaret Du Pont (née Osborne)   3 – Ann Jones (née Haydon)   4 – Margaret Court (née Smith)

Most wins (women) Chris Evert has won a record seven French titles: 1974–75, 1979–80, 1983, 1985–86.

Men's doubles Roy Emerson (Australia) has won the men's doubles a record six times, 1960–65, with five different partners.

Women's doubles The pair of Martina Navratilova and Pam Shriver (both U.S.) have won the doubles title a record four times, 1984–85, 1987–88. The most wins by an individual player is seven, by Martina Navratilova—four times with Pam Shriver, 1984–85, 1987–88; and with three other players, in 1975, 1982 and 1986.

Mixed doubles Two teams have won the mixed title three times: Ken Fletcher and Margaret Smith (Australia), 1963–65; Jean-Claude Barclay and Francoise Durr (France), 1968, 1971, 1973. Margaret Court (née Smith) has won the title the most times with four wins, winning with Marty Riessen (U.S.) in 1969, in addition to her three wins with Fletcher. Fletcher and Barclay share the men's record of three wins.

Most titles (overall) Margaret Court (née Smith) has won a record 13 French Open titles, 1962–73: five singles, four doubles and four mixed doubles.

Youngest champions The youngest singles champion at the French Open was Monica Seles (Yugoslavia) in 1990, at 16 years 169 days. The youngest men's winner is Michael Chang (U.S.), who was 17 years 109 days when he won the 1989 title.

AUSTRALIAN OPEN CHAMPIONSHIPS

The first Australasian championships were held in 1905, with New Zealand hosting the event in 1906 and 1912. A women's championship was not introduced until 1922. The tournament was changed to the Australian Open in 1925 and is counted as a grand slam event from that year. There were two championships in 1977 because the event was moved from early season (January) to December. It reverted to a January date in 1987, which meant there was no championship in 1986. Currently the tournament is held at the Australian Tennis Center in Melbourne and is the first leg of the grand slam.

Most wins (men) The most wins is six, by Roy Emerson (Australia), 1961, 1963–67.

Most wins (women) The most wins is 11, by Margaret Court (née Smith) of Australia, 1960–66, 1969–71, 1973.

Men's doubles The most wins by one pair is eight, by John Bromwich and Adrian Quist (Australia), 1938–40, 1946–50. In addition, Quist holds the record for most wins by one player with 10, winning in 1936–37 with Don Turnbull, to add to his triumphs with Bromwich.

Women's doubles The most wins by one pair is 10, by Nancye Bolton (née Wynne) and Thelma Long (née Coyne), both Australian. Their victories came in 1936–40, 1947–49, 1951–52. Long also holds the record for most wins

PHENOM! ■ MONICA SELES (YUGOSLAVIA) BEGAN 1991 BY BECOMING THE YOUNGEST AUSTRALIAN OPEN LADIES' CHAMPION, AND FINISHED THE YEAR WITH A SINGLE-SEASON EARNINGS RECORD OF $2,457,758.

with 12, winning in 1956 and 1958 with Mary Hawton.

Mixed doubles The most wins by one pair is four, by two teams: Harry Hopman and Nell Hopman (née Hall; Australia), 1930, 1936–37, 1939; Colin Long and Nancye Bolton (née Wynne; Australia), 1940, 1946–48.

Most titles (overall) Margaret Court (née Smith) has won a record 21 Australian Open titles between 1960 and 1973—11 singles, eight doubles and two mixed doubles.

Youngest champions The youngest women's singles champion was Monica Seles, Yugoslavia, who won the 1991 event at age 17 years 55 days.

OLYMPIC GAMES Tennis was reintroduced to the Olympic Games in 1988, having originally been included at the Games from 1896 to 1924. It was also a demonstration sport in 1968 and 1984.

Most gold medals Max Decugis (France) won four gold medals: men's singles, 1906; men's doubles, 1906; mixed doubles, 1906 and 1920.

AUSTRALIAN OPEN CHAMPIONS (1905–1952)

Men's Singles				Women's Singles			
Year	Player	Year	Player	Year	Player	Year	Player
1905	Rodney Heath	1929	John Gregory	1905	no event	1929	Daphne Akhurst
1906	Tony Wilding	1930	Gar Moon	1906	no event	1930	Daphne Akhurst
1907	Horace Rice	1931	Jack Crawford	1907	no event	1931	Coral Buttsworth
1908	Fred Alexander	1932	Jack Crawford	1908	no event	1932	Coral Buttsworth
1909	Tony Wilding	1933	Jack Crawford	1909	no event	1933	Joan Hartigan
1910	Rodney Heath	1934	Fred Perry	1910	no event	1934	Joan Hartigan
1911	Norman Brookes	1935	Jack Crawford	1911	no event	1935	Dorothy Round
1912	J. Cecil Parke	1936	Adrian Quist	1912	no event	1936	Joan Hartigan
1913	E. F. Parker	1937	V. B. McGrath	1913	no event	1937	Nancye Wynne
1914	Pat O'Hara Wood	1938	Don Budge	1914	no event	1938	Dorothy M. Bundy
1915	Francis Lowe	1939	John Bromwich	1915	no event	1939	Emily Westacott
1916	not held	1940	Adrian Quist	1916	not held	1940	Nancye Wynne
1917	not held	1941	not held	1917	not held	1941	not held
1918	not held	1942	not held	1918	not held	1942	not held
1919	A. Kingscote	1943	not held	1919	no event	1943	not held
1920	Pat O'Hara Wood	1944	not held	1920	no event	1944	not held
1921	Rhys Gemmell	1945	not held	1921	no event	1945	not held
1922	Pat O'Hara Wood	1946	John Bromwich	1922	Margaret Molesworth	1946	Nancye Bolton[1]
1923	Pat O'Hara Wood	1947	Dinny Pails	1923	Margaret Molesworth	1947	Nancye Bolton[1]
1924	James Anderson	1948	Adrian Quist	1924	Sylvia Lance	1948	Nancye Bolton[1]
1925	James Anderson	1949	Frank Sedgman	1925	Daphne Akhurst	1949	Doris Hart
1926	John Hawkes	1950	Frank Sedgman	1926	Daphne Akhurst	1950	Louise Brough
1927	Gerald Patterson	1951	Dick Savitt	1927	Esna Boyd	1951	Nancye Bolton[1]
1928	Jean Borotra	1952	Ken McGregor	1928	Daphne Akhurst	1952	Thelma Long

1– Nancye Bolton (née Wynne)

Most medals Max Decugis (France) won a record six medals in Olympic competition: four gold (see above), one silver and one bronze, 1900–1920. Kitty McKane (Great Britain) won a women's record five medals: one gold, two silver and two bronze, 1920–24.

Most medals (country) Great Britain has won 44 medals in Olympic competition: 16 gold, 13 silver and 15 bronze.

United States U.S. athletes have won 20 medals in Olympic competition: nine gold, five silver and six bronze.

DAVIS CUP The Davis Cup, the men's international team championship, was first held in 1900, and is held annually.

Most wins The U.S. team has won the Davis Cup a record 29 times.

Most matches (career) Nicola Pietrangeli (Italy) played a record 163 matches (66 ties), 1954 to 1972, winning 120. He played 109 singles (winning 78) and 54 doubles (winning 42).

Most matches (season) Ilie Nastase (Romania) set a singles season mark of 18 wins (with 2 losses) in 1971.

UNITED STATES TEAM RECORDS

Most selections John McEnroe has played for the U.S. team on 27 occasions, 1978 through Feb. 1, 1992.

Most wins John McEnroe has won 57 matches in Davis Cup competition—41 singles and 16 doubles.

AUSTRALIAN OPEN CHAMPIONS (1953–1992)

Men's Singles

Year	Player	Year	Player
1953	Ken Rosewall	1974	Jimmy Connors
1954	Mervyn Rose	1975	John Newcombe
1955	Ken Rosewall	1976	Mark Edmondson
1956	Lew Hoad	1977	Roscoe Tanner
1957	Ashley Cooper	1977	Vitas Gerulaitis
1958	Ashley Cooper	1978	Guillermo Vilas
1959	Alex Olmedo	1979	Guillermo Vilas
1960	Rod Laver	1980	Brian Teacher
1961	Roy Emerson	1981	Johan Kriek
1962	Rod Laver	1982	Johan Kriek
1963	Roy Emerson	1983	Mats Wilander
1964	Roy Emerson	1984	Mats Wilander
1965	Roy Emerson	1985	Stefan Edberg
1966	Roy Emerson	1986	not held
1967	Roy Emerson	1987	Stefan Edberg
1968	Bill Bowrey	1988	Mats Wilander
1969	Rod Laver	1989	Ivan Lendl
1970	Arthur Ashe	1990	Ivan Lendl
1971	Ken Rosewall	1991	Boris Becker
1972	Ken Rosewall	1992	Jim Courier
1973	John Newcombe		

Women's Singles

Year	Player	Year	Player
1953	Maureen Connolly	1974	Evonne Goolagong
1954	Thelma Long	1975	Evonne Goolagong
1955	Beryl Penrose	1976	Evonne Cawley [4]
1956	Mary Carter	1977	Kerry Reid
1957	Shirley Fry	1977	Evonne Cawley [4]
1958	Angela Mortimer	1978	Christine O'Neill
1959	Mary Reitano [2]	1979	Barbara Jordan
1960	Margaret Smith	1980	Hana Mandlikova
1961	Margaret Smith	1981	Martina Navratilova
1962	Margaret Smith	1982	Chris Evert
1963	Margaret Smith	1983	Martina Navratilova
1964	Margaret Smith	1984	Chris Evert
1965	Margaret Smith	1985	Martina Navratilova
1966	Margaret Smith	1986	not held
1967	Nancy Richey	1987	Hana Mandlikova
1968	Billie Jean King	1988	Steffi Graf
1969	Margaret Court [3]	1989	Steffi Graf
1970	Margaret Court [3]	1990	Steffi Graf
1971	Margaret Court [3]	1991	Monica Seles
1972	Virginia Wade	1992	Monica Seles
1973	Margaret Court [3]		

2 – Mary Reitano (née Carter)   3 – Margaret Court (née Smith)   4 – Evonne Cawley (née Goolagong)

TEAM MAN ■ JOHN MCENROE HAS WON A U.S. TEAM RECORD 57 DAVIS CUP MATCHES, 41 SINGLES AND 16 DOUBLES.

FEDERATION CUP The Federation Cup, the women's international team championship, was first held in 1963 and is an annual event.

Most wins The United States has won the Federation Cup a record 14 times.

MEN'S PROFESSIONAL TOUR RECORDS (1968–91)

Most singles titles (career) Jimmy Connors (U.S.) has won 109 singles titles, 1972–89.

Most singles titles (season) Three players have won 15 titles in one season: Jimmy Connors (U.S.), 1977; Guillermo Vilas (Argentina), 1977; Ivan Lendl (Czechoslovakia), 1982.

Most doubles titles (career) Tom Okker (Netherlands) has won 78 doubles titles, 1968–79.

Most doubles titles (season) John McEnroe (U.S.) won 17 doubles titles in 1979.

Most consecutive match wins Guillermo Vilas (Argentina) won 46 consecutive matches, 1977–78.

Most weeks ranked number one Jimmy Connors (U.S.) held the number one ranking on the ATP computer from July 29, 1974 to August 16, 1977, a total of 159 weeks—the longest streak in tour history.

Highest earnings (career) Ivan Lendl (Czechoslovakia) has won a career record $18,211,061, 1978–91.

Highest earnings (season) Stefan Edberg (Sweden) earned a season record $2,363,575 in 1991.

WOMEN'S PROFESSIONAL TOUR RECORDS (1968–91)

Most singles titles (career) Two players have won 157 titles: Chris Evert (U.S.), 1972–88; Martina Navratilova (U.S.), 1975–91.

Most singles titles (season) Martina Navratilova won 13 titles in 1984.

Most consecutive matches won Martina Navratilova won 74 consecutive matches in 1984.

Most consecutive weeks ranked number one Steffi Graf (Germany) held the number one computer ranking from August 17, 1987 to March 11, 1991, a total of 186 weeks.

Highest earnings (career) Martina Navratilova (U.S.) has won a career record $17,661,593 in prize money.

Highest earnings (season) Monica Seles (Yugoslavia) won a season record $2,457,758 in 1991.

TRACK AND FIELD

ORIGINS Competition in running, jumping and throwing must have occurred from the earliest days of humankind. The earliest evidence of organized running is from 3800 B.C. in Egypt. The ancient Olympic Games were cultural festivals that highlighted the ancient Greek ideal of perfection of mind and body. The first modern Olympic Games, staged in 1896, focused on athletic achievement and the spirit of competition, and the Games have provided the focus for track and field as a sport ever since. In 1983, a separate world championship was introduced.

OLYMPIC GAMES The first modern Olympic Games were staged in Athens, Greece, April 6–15, 1896. Fifty-nine athletes from 10 nations competed; women's events were not added until 1928.

WORLD RECORDS—MEN

World records are for the men's events scheduled by the International Amateur Athletic Federation. Full automatic electronic timing is mandatory for events up to 400 meters.

Event	Time	Athlete (Country)	Place	Date
100 meters	9.86	Carl Lewis (U.S.)	Tokyo, Japan	August 25, 1991
200 meters	19.72	Pietro Mennea (Italy)	Mexico City, Mexico	September 12, 1979
400 meters	43.29	Butch Reynolds (U.S.)	Zürich, Switzerland	August 17, 1988
800 meters	1:41.73	Sebastian Coe (Great Britain)	Florence, Italy	June 10, 1981
1,500 meters	3:29.46	Saïd Aouita (Morocco)	Berlin, Germany	August 23, 1985
1 mile	3:46.32	Steve Cram (Great Britain)	Oslo, Norway	July 27, 1985
5,000 meters	12:58.39	Saïd Aouita (Morocco)	Rome, Italy	July 22, 1987
10,000 meters	27:08.23	Arturo Barrios (Mexico)	Berlin, Germany	August 18, 1989
110 meters	12.92	Roger Kingdom (U.S.)	Zürich, Switzerland	August 16, 1989
400 meters	47.02	Edwin Moses (U.S.)	Koblenz, Germany	August 31, 1983
3,000-meter steeplechase	8:05.35	Peter Koech (Kenya)	Stockholm, Sweden	July 4, 1989
4 x 100 meters	37.50	United States (Andre Cason, Leroy Burrell, Dennis Mitchell, Carl Lewis)	Tokyo, Japan	September 1, 1991
4 x 400 meters	2:56.16	United States (Vince Matthews, Ron Freeman, Larry James, Lee Evans)	Mexico City, Mexico	October 20, 1968
	2:56.16	United States (Danny Everett, Steve Lewis, Kevin Robinzine, Butch Reynolds)	Seoul, South Korea	October 1, 1988

Event	Distance	Athlete (Country)	Place	Date
High jump	8' 0"	Javier Sotomayor (Cuba)	San Juan, Puerto Rico	July 29, 1989
Pole vault	20' 0"	Sergey Bubka (USSR)	Malmo, Sweden	August 5, 1991
Long jump	29' 4½"	Mike Powell (U.S.)	Tokyo, Japan	August 30, 1991
Triple jump	58' 11½"	Willie Banks (U.S.)	Indianapolis, Ind.	June 16, 1985
Shot	75' 10¼"	Randy Barnes (U.S.)	Los Angeles, Calif.	May 20, 1990
Discus	243' 0"	Jürgen Schult (East Germany)	Neubrandenburg, Germany	June 6, 1986
Hammer	284' 7"	Yuriy Sedykh (USSR)	Stuttgart, Germany	August 30, 1986
Javelin	300' 0"	Steve Backley (Great Britain)	Auckland, New Zealand	January 25, 1992

Decathlon

8,847 points   Daley Thompson (Great Britian) (1st day: 100m 10.44 sec, Long jump 26' 3½", Shot put 51' 7", High jump 6' 8", 400 m 46.97 sec), (2nd day: 110 m hurdles 14.33 sec, discus 152' 9", Pole vault 16' 4¾, Javelin 214' 0", 1,500 m 4:35.00 sec), Los Angeles, Calif., August 8–9, 1984

	Time	Walking		
20 km	1:18.40.0	Ernesto Canto (Mexico)	Bergen, Norway	May 5, 1984
50 km	3:41.38.4	Raul Gonzales (Mexico)	Bergen, Norway	May 27, 1979

FASTEST HUMANS ■ FLORENCE GRIFFITH-JOYNER (LEFT) HOLDS THE WOMEN'S WORLD RECORDS FOR 100-METER AND 200-METER SPRINTS. CARL LEWIS (RIGHT) CELEBRATES HIS 100-METER WORLD RECORD RUN AT THE 1991 WORLD CHAMPIONSHIPS, A RACE IN WHICH FOUR MEN RAN UNDER 10 SECONDS.

Most gold medals Ray Ewry (U.S.) holds the all-time record for most appearances atop the winners' podium, with 10 gold medals: standing high jump (1900, 1904, 1906, 1908); standing long jump (1900, 1904, 1906, 1908); standing triple jump (1900, 1904). The women's record is four, shared by three athletes: Fanny Blankers-Koen (Netherlands): 100 m, 200 m, 80 m hurdles and 4 x 100 m relay in 1948; Betty Cuthbert (Australia): 100 m, 200 m, 4 x 100 m relay in 1956, and 400 m in 1964; Barbel Wockel (née Eckert; East Germany): 200 m and 4 x 100 m relay in both 1976 and 1980.

Most gold medals (one Games) Paavo Nurmi (Finland) won five gold medals at the 1924 Games. His victories came in the 1,500 m, 5,000 m, 10,000 m cross-country, 3,000 m team, and cross-country team. The most wins at individual events (not including relay or other team races) is four, by Alvin Kraenzlein (U.S.) in 1900 at 60 m, 110 m hurdles, 200 m hurdles and the long jump.

Most medals won Paavo Nurmi (Finland) won a record 12 medals (nine gold, three silver) in the Games of 1920, 1924 and 1928. The women's record is seven, shared by two athletes: Shirley de la Hunty (Australia), three gold, one silver, three bronze in the 1948, 1952 and 1956 Games; Irena Szewinska (Poland), three gold, two silver, two bronze in the 1964, 1968, 1972 and 1976 Games.

Most medals (country) The United States has won 645 medals in Olympic competition: in men's events, 244 gold, 186 silver and 151 bronze; in women's events, 32 gold, 21 silver and 11 bronze. The United States has won the most medals in men's events, 581 (see above); the USSR has won the most medals in women's events, 84: 30 gold, 20 silver and 34 bronze.

WORLD RECORDS—WOMEN

World records are for the women's events scheduled by the International Amateur Athletic Federation. The same stipulation about automatically timed events applies in the six events up to 400 meters as in the men's list.

Event	Time	Athlete (Country)	Place	Date
100 meters	10.49	Florence Griffith-Joyner (U.S.)	Indianapolis, Ind.	July 16, 1988
200 meters	21.34	Florence Griffith-Joyner (U.S.)	Seoul, South Korea	September 29, 1988
400 meters	47.60	Marita Koch (East Germany)	Canberra, Australia	October 6, 1985
800 meters	1:53.28	Jarmila Kratochvilová (Czechoslovakia)	Münich, Germany	July 26, 1983
1,500 meters	3:52.47	Tatyana Kazankina (USSR)	Zürich, Switzerland	August 13, 1980
1 mile	4:15.61	Paula Ivan (Romania)	Nice, France	July 10, 1989
3,000 meters	8:22.62	Tatyana Kazankina (USSR)	Leningrad, USSR	August 26, 1984
5,000 meters	14:37.33	Ingrid Kristiansen (Norway)	Stockholm, Sweden	August 5, 1986
10,000 meters	30:13.74	Ingrid Kristiansen (Norway)	Oslo, Norway	July 5, 1986
100 meters	12.21	Yordanka Donkova (Bulgaria)	Stara Zagora, Bulgaria	August 20, 1988
400 meters	52.94	Marina Styepanova (USSR)	Tashkent, USSR	September 17, 1986
4 x 100 meters	41.37	East Germany (Silke Gladisch, Sabine Rieger, Ingrid Auerswald, Marlies Göhr)	Canberra, Australia	October 6, 1985
4 x 400 meters	3:15.17	USSR (Tatyana Ledovskaya, Olga Nazarova, Maria Pinigina, Olga Bryzgina)	Seoul, South Korea	October 1, 1988

Event	Distance	Athlete (Country)	Place	Date
High jump	6' 10¼"	Stefka Kostadinova (Bulgaria)	Rome, Italy	August 30, 1987
Long jump	24' 8¼"	Galina Chistyakova (USSR)	Leningrad, USSR	June 11, 1988
Triple jump	49' ¾"	Inessa Kravets (USSR)	Moscow, USSR	June 10, 1991
Shot	74' 3"	Natalya Lisovskaya (USSR)	Moscow, USSR	June 7, 1987
Discus	252' 0"	Gabriele Reinsch (East Germany)	Neubrandenburg, Germany	July 9, 1988
Javelin	262' 5"	Petra Felke (East Germany)	Potsdam, Germany	September 9, 1988

Heptathlon

7,291 points Jacqueline Joyner-Kersee (U.S.) (100 m hurdles 12.69 sec; High jump 6' 1¼"; Shot 51' 10"; 200 m 22.56 sec; Long jump 23' 10 "; Javelin 149' 9"; 800 m 2:08.51 sec), Seoul, South Korea, September 23–24, 1988

Walking

	Time	Athlete (Country)	Place	Date
5 km	20:07.52	Beate Anders (East Germany)	Rostock, Germany	June 23, 1990
10 km	41:46.21	Nadezhda Ryashkina (USSR)	Seattle, Wash.	July 24, 1990

INDIVIDUAL RECORDS (U.S. ATHLETES)

Most medals Ray Ewry's 10 gold medals are the most won by any U.S. athlete (see above). Florence Griffith-Joyner has won a women's record five medals in track and field—three golds, two silver in the 1984 and 1988 Games.

Most gold medals Ray Ewry holds the Olympic mark for most golds (see above). The women's record for gold medals is three, set by four athletes: Wilma Rudolph, 100 m, 200 m and 4 x 100 m relay in 1960; Wyomia Tyus, 100 m in 1964, 100 m and 4 x 100 m relay in 1968; Valerie Brisco, 200 m, 400 m and 4 x 400 m relay in 1984; Florence Griffith-Joyner, 100 m, 200 m and 4 x 100 m relay in 1988.

Most gold medals (one Games) The most gold medals won at one Olympics is four, by three men: Alvin Kraenzlein (see page 205); Jesse Owens, 100 m, 200 m, long jump and 4 x 100 m relay in 1936; Carl Lewis, 100 m, 200 m, long jump and 4 x 100 m relay in 1984. The women's record is three golds, held by Wilma Rudolph, Valerie Brisco and Florence Griffith-Joyner (see above).

WORLD CHAMPIONSHIPS Quadrennial world championships distinct from the Olympic Games were first held in 1983 at Helsinki, Finland.

Most medals The most medals won is nine: seven gold, two silver by Carl Lewis (U.S.), 1983–91. The most medals won by a woman is five, by Heike Drechsler (East Germany/Germany): two silver, three bronze, 1983–91.

UNITED STATES NATIONAL CHAMPIONSHIPS

Most titles The most American national titles won at all events, indoors and out, is 65, by Ronald Owen Laird at various walking events between 1958 and 1976. Excluding the walks, the record is 41, by Stella Walsh (née Walasiewicz), who won 41 women's events between 1930 and 1954: 33 outdoors and eight indoors.

UNITED STATES NATIONAL RECORDS—MEN

Event	Time	Athlete	Place	Date
100 meters	9.86	Carl Lewis	Tokyo, Japan	August 25, 1991
200 meters	19.75	Carl Lewis	Indianapolis, Ind.	June 19, 1983
	19.75	Joe DeLoach	Seoul, South Korea	September 28, 1988
400 meters	43.29	Butch Reynolds	Zürich, Switzerland	August 17, 1988
800 meters	1:42.60	Johnny Gray	Koblenz, Germany	August 28, 1985
1,500 meters	3:29.77	Sydney Maree	Cologne, Germany	August 25, 1985
1 mile	3:47.69	Steve Scott	Oslo, Norway	July 7, 1982
5,000 meters	13:01.50	Sydney Maree	Oslo, Norway	July 27, 1985
10,000 meters	27:20.56	Marcus Nenow	Brussels, Belgium	September 5, 1986
110 meters	12.92	Roger Kingdom	Zürich, Switzerland	August 16, 1989
400 meters	47.02	Edwin Moses	Koblenz, Germany	August 31, 1983
3,000-meter steeplechase	8:09.17	Henry Marsh	Koblenz, Germany	August 28, 1985
4 x 100 meters	37.50	National Team (Andre Cason, Leroy Burrell, Dennis Mitchell, Carl Lewis)	Tokyo, Japan	September 1, 1991
4 x 400 meters	2:56.16	National Team (Vince Matthews, Ron Freeman, Larry James, Lee Evans)	Mexico City, Mexico	October 20, 1968
	2:56.16	National Team (Danny Everett, Steve Lewis, Kevin Robinzine, Butch Reynolds)	Seoul, South Korea	October 1, 1988

	Distance			
High jump	7' 10½"	Charles Austin	Zürich, Switzerland	August 7, 1991
Pole vault	19' 6½"	Joe Dial	Norman, Okla.	June 18, 1987
Long jump	29" 4½"	Mike Powell	Tokyo, Japan	August 30, 1991
Triple jump	58' 11½"	Willie Banks	Indianapolis, Ind.	June 16, 1985
Shot	75' 10¼"	Randy Barnes	Los Angeles, Calif.	May 20, 1990
Discus	237' 4"	Ben Plunknett	Stockholm, Sweden	July 7, 1981
Hammer	268' 8"	Jud Logan	University Park, Pa.	April 22, 1988
Javelin	280' 1"	Tom Petranoff	Helsinki, Finland	July 7, 1986

Decathlon

8,812 points Dan O'Brien (1st day: 100 m 10.41 sec, Long jump 25' 11", Shot put 50" 3½", High jump 6" 3¼", 400 m 46.53 sec), (2nd day: 110 m hurdles 13.94 sec, Discus 154' 10", Pole vault 17' ¾", Javelin 199' 0", 1,500 m 4:37.50 sec), Tokyo, Japan, August 29–30, 1991

Walking

	Time			
20 km	1:24:50.00	Tim Lewis	Seattle, Wash.	May 7, 1988
50 km	3:56:55.00	Marco Evoniuk	Seoul, South Korea	September 30, 1988

UNITED STATES NATIONAL RECORDS—WOMEN

Event	Time	Athlete	Place	Date
100 meters	10.49	Florence Griffith-Joyner	Indianapolis, Ind.	July 16, 1988
200 meters	21.34	Florence Griffith-Joyner	Seoul, South Korea	September 29, 1988
400 meters	48.83	Valerie Brisco	Los Angeles, Calif.	August 6, 1984
800 meters	1:56.90	Mary Slaney	Berne, Switzerland	August 16, 1985
1,500 meters	3:57.12	Mary Slaney	Stockholm, Sweden	July 26, 1983
1 mile	4:16.71	Mary Slaney	Zürich, Switzerland	August 21, 1985
3,000 meters	8:25.83	Mary Slaney	Rome, Italy	September 7, 1985
5,000 meters	15:00.00	Patti-Sue Plumer	Stockholm, Sweden	July 3, 1989
10,000 meters	31:28.92	Francie Larrieu-Smith	Austin, Tex.	April 4, 1991
100 meters	12.48	Gail Devers-Roberts	Berlin, Germany	September 10, 1991
400 meters	53.37	Sandra Farmer-Patrick	New York, N.Y.	July 23, 1989
4 x 100 meters	41.55	National Team (Alice Brown, Diane Williams, Florence Griffith, Pam Marshall)	Berlin, Germany	August 21, 1987
4 x 400 meters	3:15.51	National Team (Denean Howard, Diane Dixon, Valerie Brisco, Florence Griffith-Joyner)	Seoul, South Korea	October 1, 1988

Event	Distance	Athlete	Place	Date
High jump	6' 8"	Louise Ritter	Austin, Tex.	July 8, 1988
	6' 8"	Louise Ritter	Seoul, South Korea	September 30, 1988
Long jump	24' 5½"	Jacqueline Joyner-Kersee	Indianapolis, Ind.	August 13, 1987
Triple jump	46' 0¾"	Sheila Hudson	Durham, N.C.	June 2, 1990
Shot	66' 2½"	Ramona Pagel	San Diego, Calif.	June 25, 1988
Discus	216' 10"	Carol Cady	San Jose, Calif.	May 31, 1986
Javelin	227' 5"	Kate Schmidt	Fürth, Germany	September 11, 1977

Heptathlon

7,291 points — Jacqueline Joyner-Kersee (100 m hurdles 12.69 sec; High jump 6' 1¼"; Shot 51' 10"; 200 m 22.56 sec; Long jump 23' 10"; Javelin 149' 9"; 800 m 2:08.51 sec), Seoul, South Korea, September 23–24, 1988

Walking

	Time	Athlete	Place	Date
10 km	45:28.40	Debbi Lawrence	Los Angeles, Calif.	July 19, 1991

Longest winning sequence Iolanda Balas (Romania) won a record 140 consecutive competitions at high jump from 1956 to 1967. The record at a track event was 122, at 400 meter hurdles, by Edwin Moses (U.S.) between his loss to Harald Schmid (West Germany) at Berlin, Germany on August 26, 1977 and that to Danny Harris (U.S.) at Madrid, Spain on June 4, 1987.

ROAD RUNNING

MARATHON

The marathon is run over a distance of 26 miles 385 yards. This distance was the one used for the race at the 1908 Olympic Games, run from Windsor to the White City stadium, London, England, and it became standard from 1924 on. The mara-

BOSTON MARATHON

Known for its historic course and its amateur traditions (the race did not accept commercial sponsorship until 1986), the Boston Marathon is the world's oldest annual running race. First run on April 19, 1897, the race was originally staged to commemorate the famed ride of Paul Revere in 1775. Fifteen men competed in the first race, run over a distance of 24 miles 1,232 yards; the race was won by John J. McDermott. The official marathon distance of 26 miles 385 yards was first run in 1927. The marathon attracted controversy in 1967, when Kathy Switzer became the first woman to enter the race. Switzer had entered the race disguised as a man, thus evading the ban on women runners, but race director Jock Semple attempted to push her off the course when her identity was revealed. It wasn't until 1972 that women were allowed to enter the marathon. Currently the race starts in Hopkinton, Mass. and finishes in Copley Square, Boston.

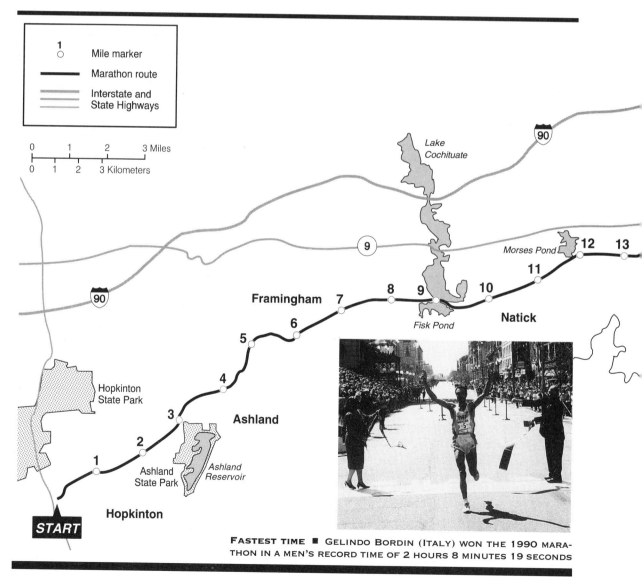

FASTEST TIME ■ GELINDO BORDIN (ITALY) WON THE 1990 MARATHON IN A MEN'S RECORD TIME OF 2 HOURS 8 MINUTES 19 SECONDS

BOSTON MARATHON RECORDS (1897–1991)

MEN'S DIVISION

Most wins: 7, Clarence De Mar (U.S.), 1911, 1922–24, 1927–28, 1930

Fastest time: 2 hours 8 minutes 19 seconds, Gelindo Bordin (Italy), 1990

WOMEN'S DIVISION

Most wins: 3, Rosa Mota (Portugal), 1987–88, 1990

Fastest time: 2 hours 22 minutes 43 seconds, Joan Benoit (now Samuelson) (U.S.), 1983

Note: The 1990 marathon set records for the most starters, 9,412, and the most finishers, 7,950.

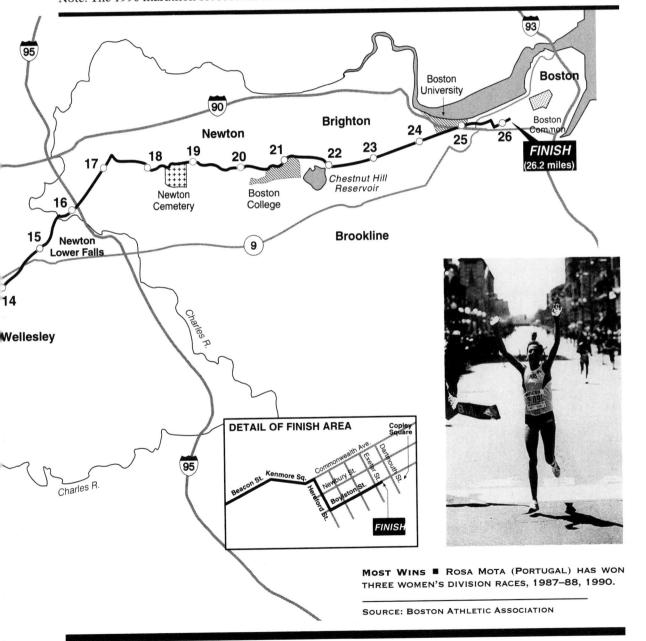

MOST WINS ■ ROSA MOTA (PORTUGAL) HAS WON THREE WOMEN'S DIVISION RACES, 1987–88, 1990.

SOURCE: BOSTON ATHLETIC ASSOCIATION

thon was introduced at the 1896 Olympic Games to commemorate the legendary run of Pheidippides (or Philippides) from the battlefield of Marathon to Athens in 490 B.C. The 1896 Olympic marathon was preceded by trial races that year. The first Boston Marathon, the world's oldest annual marathon race, was held on April 19, 1897 at 24 miles 1,232 yards, and the first national marathon championship was that of Norway in 1897.

The first championship marathon for women was organized by the Road Runners Club of America on September 27, 1970.

WORLD RECORDS There are as yet no official records for the marathon, and it should be noted that courses may vary in severity. The following are the best times recorded, all on courses with verified distances: for men, 2 hours 6 minutes 50 seconds, by Belayneh Dinsamo (Ethiopia) at Rotterdam, Netherlands on April 17, 1988; for women, 2 hours 21 minutes 6 seconds, by Ingrid Kristiansen (née Christensen; Norway) at London, England on April 21, 1985.

United States The Athletics Congress recognizes the following U.S. records: for men, Pat Peterson, 2 hours 10 minutes 4 seconds, at London, England on April 23, 1989; for women, Joan Benoit Samuelson, 2 hours 21 minutes 21 seconds, at Chicago, Ill., on October 20, 1985.

OLYMPIC GAMES The marathon has been run at every Olympic Games of the modern era; however, a women's race wasn't included in the Games until 1984.

Most gold medals The record for most wins in the men's race is two, by two marathoners: Abebe Bikila (Ethiopia), 1960 and 1964; Waldemar Cierpinski (East Germany), 1976 and 1980. The women's event has been run twice, with different winners.

NEW YORK CITY MARATHON The race was run in Central Park each year from 1970 to 1976, when, to celebrate the U.S. Bicentennial, the course was changed to a route through all five boroughs of the city. From that year, when there were 2,090 runners, the race has become one of the world's great sporting occasions; in 1991 there were a record 25,797 finishers.

Most wins Grete Waitz (Norway) has won nine times—1978–80, 1982–86 and 1988. Bill Rodgers has a men's record four wins—1976–79.

Fastest time The course record for men is 2 hours 8 minutes 1 second, by Juma Ikangaa (Tanzania), and for women, 2 hours 25 minutes 30 seconds, by Ingrid Kristiansen (Norway) in 1989.

On a course subsequently remeasured as about 170 yards short, Grete Waitz was the 1981 women's winner in 2 hours 25 minutes 29 seconds.

LONG-DISTANCE RUNNING RECORDS

Longest race (distance) The longest races ever staged were the 1928 (3,422 miles) and 1929 (3,665 miles) transcontinental races from New York City to Los Angeles, Calif. Johnny Salo (U.S.) was the winner in 1929 in 79 days, from March 31 to June 18. His elapsed time of 525 hours 57 minutes 20 seconds (averaging 6.97 mph) left him only 2 minutes 47 seconds ahead of Englishman Peter Gavuzzi.

The longest race staged annually is Australia's Westfield Run from Paramatta, New South Wales to Doncaster, Victoria (Sydney to Melbourne). The distance run has varied slightly, but the record is by Yiannis Kouros (Greece) in 5 days 2 hours 27 minutes 27 seconds in 1989, when the distance was 658 miles.

Longest runs The longest run by an individual is one of 11,134 miles around the United States, by Sarah Covington-Fulcher (U.S.), starting and fin-

LONG DISTANCE ■ SARAH COVINGTON-FULCHER COMPLETED THE LONGEST-KNOWN RUN BY ANY RUNNER ON OCTOBER 2, 1988, HAVING RUN 11,134 MILES AROUND THE U.S., FROM AND TO LOS ANGELES, CALIF.

ishing in Los Angeles, Calif., between July 21, 1987 and October 2, 1988. Robert J. Sweetgall (U.S.) ran 10,608 miles around the perimeter of the United States, starting and finishing in Washington D.C., between October 1982 and July 15, 1983.

WALKING

OLYMPIC GAMES Walking races have been included in the Olympic events since 1906.

Most gold medals The only walker to win three gold medals has been Ugo Frigerio (Italy), with the 3,000 meter in 1920, and the 10,000 meter in 1920 and 1924.

Most medals The record for most medals is four, by two walkers: Ugo Frigerio (Italy), three gold, one bronze, 1920–32; Vladimir Golubnichiy (USSR), two gold medals, one silver and one bronze, 1960–68.

TRAMPOLINING

ORIGINS Trampolining has been part of circus acts for many years. The sport of trampolining dates from 1936, when the prototype "T" model trampoline was designed by George Nissen of the United States. The first official tournament took place in 1947.

WORLD CHAMPIONSHIPS Instituted in 1964, championships have been staged biennially since 1968. The world championships recognize champions, both men and women, in four events: individual, synchronized pairs, tumbling, and double mini trampoline.

Most titles Judy Wills (U.S.) has won a record five individual world titles, 1964–68. The men's record is two, shared by five trampolinists: Wayne Miller (U.S.), 1966 and 1970; Dave Jacobs (U.S.), 1967–68; Richard Tisson (France), 1974 and 1976; Yevgeniy Yanes (USSR), 1976 and 1978; and Lionel Pioline (France), 1984 and 1986.

UNITED STATES NATIONAL CHAMPIONSHIPS The American Trampoline & Tumbling Association staged the first national championship in 1947. The inaugural event was open only to men; a women's event was introduced in 1961.

Most titles Stuart Ransom has won a record 12 national titles: six individual, 1975–76, 1978–80,

1982; three synchronized, 1975, 1979–80; three double mini-tramp, 1979–80, 1982. Leigh Hennessy has won a record ten women's titles: one individual, 1978; eight synchronized, 1972–73, 1976–78, 1980–82; one double mini-tramp, 1978.

TRIATHLON

ORIGINS The triathlon combines long distance swimming, cycling, and running. The sport was developed by a group of dedicated athletes who founded the Hawaii "Ironman" in 1974. After a series of unsuccessful attempts to create a world governing body, *L'Union Internationale de Triathlon* (UIT) was founded in Avignon, France in 1989. The UIT staged the first official world championships in Avignon on August 6, 1989.

WORLD CHAMPIONSHIPS An unofficial world championship has been held in Nice, France since 1982. The three legs comprise a 3,200 meter swim (4,000 meter since 1988), 120 kilometer bike ride, and 32 kilometer run.

Most titles Mark Allen (U.S.) has won a record eight times, 1982–86, 1989–91. Paula Newby-Fraser (Zimbabwe) has won a record three women's titles, 1989–91.

Fastest times The men's record is 5 hours 46 minutes 10 seconds, by Mark Allen (U.S.) in 1988. The women's record is 6 hours 27 minutes 6 seconds, by Erin Baker (New Zealand) in 1988.

HAWAII IRONMAN This is the first, and best known, of the triathlons. Instituted on February 18, 1978, the first race was contested by 15 athletes. The Ironman grew rapidly in popularity, and 1,000 athletes entered the 1984 race. Contestants must first swim 2.4 miles, then cycle 112 miles, and finally run a full marathon of 26 miles 385 yards.

Most titles Dave Scott (U.S.) has won the Ironman a record six times, 1980, 1982–84, 1986–87. The women's event has been won a record three times by Paula Newby-Fraser (Zimbabwe) in 1986, 1988–89.

Fastest times Mark Allen (U.S.) holds the course record at 8 hours 9 minutes 16 seconds in 1989. Paula Newby-Fraser holds the women's record at 9 hours 56 seconds.

THREE-EVENT COURSE ■ SWIMMING, CYCLING AND RUNNING ARE THE THREE TRIATHLON DISCIPLINES. PAULA NEWBY-FRASER (ZIMBABWE) (LOWER LEFT AND RIGHT) IS A THREE-TIME HAWAII IRONMAN WOMEN'S CHAMPION.

Fastest time The fastest time ever recorded over the Ironman distances is 8 hours 1 minute 32 seconds by Dave Scott (U.S.) at Lake Biwas, Japan on July 30, 1989.

Largest field The most competitors to finish a triathlon race were the 3,888 who completed the 1987 Bud Lite U.S. Triathlon in Chicago, Ill.

VOLLEYBALL

ORIGINS The game was invented as *mintonette* in 1895 by William G. Morgan at the YMCA gymnasium at Holyoke, Mass. The International Volleyball Association (IVA) was formed in Paris, France in April 1947. The United States Volleyball Association was founded in 1922 and is the governing body for the sport in this country. The United States National Championships were inaugurated for men in 1928, and for women in 1949.

OLYMPIC GAMES Volleyball became an official Olympic sport in 1964, when both men's and women's tournaments were staged in Tokyo, Japan.

Most gold medals (country) The USSR has won three men's titles, 1964, 1968 and 1980; and four women's titles, 1968, 1972, 1980 and 1988.

Most medals (individual) Inna Ryskal (USSR) has won four medals in Olympic competition: two gold, 1968, 1972; and two silver, 1964, 1976. The men's record is three, won by two players: Yuriy Poyarkov (USSR), two golds, 1964 and 1968, one bronze, 1972; Katsutoshi Nekoda (Japan), one gold, 1972, one silver, 1968, and one bronze, 1964.

Most medals (country) The USSR has won 12 medals in Olympic competition: in men's events, three gold, two silver and one bronze; in women's events, four gold and two silver.

United States U.S. teams have won three medals: in men's events, two golds, 1984 and 1988; in women's events, one silver in 1984.

WORLD CHAMPIONSHIPS World championships were instituted in 1949 for men and in 1952 for women.

Most titles The USSR has won six men's titles, 1949, 1952, 1960, 1962, 1978 and 1982, and five women's titles, 1952, 1956, 1960, 1970 and 1990.

BEACH VOLLEYBALL

In professional beach volleyball the court dimensions are the same as in the indoor game: 30 feet x 60 feet, or 30 feet x 30 feet on each side, with the net set at a height of eight feet. In beach volleyball, teams play two-a-side, as opposed to six-a-side for the indoor game.

ORIGINS Beach volleyball originated in California in the 1940s. The sport grew rapidly in the 1960s, and the first world championships were staged in 1976. In 1981 the Association of Volleyball Professionals was founded, and the AVP/Miller Lite Tour was formed that year.

AVP/MILLER LITE TOUR RECORDS (1977–91)

Most tour wins Sinjin Smith has won 125 tour events, 1977–91.

LIFE'S A BEACH ■ SINJIN SMITH HAS WON A CAREER RECORD 125 TITLES ON THE PRO BEACH VOLLEYBALL TOUR.

Highest earnings Randy Stoklos has a earned a career record $993,267, 1982–91.

WATER POLO

ORIGINS This game was originally played in England as "water soccer" in 1869. The first rules were drafted in 1876. Water polo has been an Olympic event since 1900. In 1908, FINA (see Swimming) became the governing body for water polo. The first world championships were held in 1973.

OLYMPIC GAMES Water polo was first included at the 1900 Games, and has been included in every Games since.

Most gold medals (country) Hungary has won six Olympic titles, 1932, 1936, 1952, 1956, 1964 and 1976.

Most gold medals (players) Five players have won three gold medals: George Wilkinson (Great Britain), 1900, 1908, 1912; Paul Radmilovic (Great Britain), 1908, 1912, 1920; Charles Smith (Great Britain), 1908, 1912, 1920; Deszo Gyarmati (Hungary), 1952, 1956, 1964; Gyorgy Karpati (Hungary), 1952, 1956, 1964.

Most medals (player) Deszo Gyarmati (Hungary) has won five medals: three gold (see above), one silver, 1948, and one bronze, 1960.

Most medals (country) Hungary has won 12 medals in Olympic competition: six gold, three silver and three bronze.

United States U.S. teams have won eight medals in Olympic competition: one gold, three silver and four bronze.

WORLD CHAMPIONSHIPS A competition was first held at the World Swimming Championships in 1973. A women's event was included from 1986.

Most titles Two countries have won two men's titles: USSR, 1975 and 1982; Yugoslavia, 1986 and 1991. The women's competition was won by Australia in 1986, and by the Netherlands in 1991.

UNITED STATES NATIONAL CHAMPIONSHIPS The first men's national championship was held in 1891. A women's tournament was first held in 1926.

Most titles The New York Athletic Club has won 24 men's titles: 1892–96, 1903–08, 1922, 1929–31,

1933–35, 1937–39, 1954, 1961 and 1971. The Industry Hills Athletic Club (Calif.) has won seven women's titles: 1980–81 and 1984–88.

WATERSKIING

ORIGINS Modern waterskiing was pioneered in the 1920s. Ralph Samuelson, who skied on Lake Pepin, Minn. in 1922 using two curved pine boards, is generally credited as being the father of the sport. Forms of skiing on water can be traced back centuries to people attempting to walk on water with planks. The development of the motorboat to tow skiers was the largest factor in the sport's growth. The world governing body is the World Water Ski Union (WWSU), which succeeded the *Union Internationale de Ski Nautique* that had been formed in Geneva, Switzerland in 1946. The American Water Ski Association was founded in 1939 and held the first national championships that year.

WORLD CHAMPIONSHIPS The first world chamionships were held in 1949.

Most titles Sammy Duvall (U.S.) has won four overall titles, in 1981, 1983, 1985 and 1987. Two women have won three overall titles: Willa McGuire (née Worthington; U.S.), 1949–50 and 1955; Liz Allan-Shetter (U.S.), 1965, 1969 and 1975.

Most individual titles Liz Allan-Shetter has won a record eight individual championship events and is the only person to win all four titles—slalom, jumping, tricks, and overall in one year, at Copenhagen, Denmark in 1969.

UNITED STATES NATIONAL CHAMPIONSHIPS National championships were first held at Marine Stadium, Jones Beach State Park, Long Island, N.Y. on July 22, 1939.

Most titles The most overall titles is eight, by Willa Worthington McGuire, 1946–51 and 1954–55, and by Liz Allan-Shetter, 1968–75. The men's record is six titles, by Chuck Stearns, 1957–58, 1960, 1962, 1965 and 1967.

Fastest speed The fastest waterskiing speed recorded is 143.08 mph, by Christopher Massey (Australia) on the Hawkesbury River, Windsor, Australia on March 6, 1983. His drag boat driver was Stanley Sainty. Donna Patterson Brice set a women's record of 111.11 mph at Long Beach, Calif. on August 21, 1977.

WEIGHTLIFTING

There are two standard lifts in weightlifting: the "snatch" and the "clean and jerk." Totals of the two lifts determine competition results. The "press," which had been a standard lift, was abolished in 1972.

ORIGINS Competitions for lifting weights of stone were held at the ancient Olympic Games. In the 19th century, weightlifting consisted of professional exhibitions in which some of the advertised poundages were open to doubt. The *Fédération Internationale Haltérophile et Culturiste*, now the International Weightlifting Federation (IWF), was established in 1905, and its first official championships were held in Tallinn, Estonia on April 29–30, 1922.

OLYMPIC GAMES Weightlifting events were included in the first modern Games in 1896.

Most gold medals Three lifters have won two gold medals: John Davis Jr. (U.S.), heavyweight, 1942 and 1952; Tommy Kono (U.S.), lightweight, 1952, light heavyweight, 1956; and Chuck Vinci Jr. (U.S.), bantamweight, 1956 and 1960.

Most medals Norbert Schemansky (U.S.) has won four medals: one gold, one silver and two bronze, 1960–64.

Most medals (country) The USSR has won 63 medals in Olympic competition: 39 gold, 21 silver and three bronze.

United States U.S. lifters have won 41 medals in Olympic competition: 15 gold, 16 silver and 10 bronze.

WORLD CHAMPIONSHIPS The IWF held its first world championships at Tallinn, Estonia in 1922, but has subsequently recognized 18 championships held in Vienna, Austria between 1898 and 1920. The championships have been held annually since 1946, with the Olympic Games recognized as world championships in the year of the Games until 1988, when a championship separate from the Olympics was staged. A women's championship was introduced in 1987.

WORLD WEIGHTLIFTING RECORDS (MEN)
Bantamweight 56 kg (123¼ lb)

Event	Weight	Lifter (Country)	Date
Snatch	135.0 kg	Liu Shoubin (China)	September 28, 1991
Jerk	171.0 kg	Neno Terziiski (Bulgaria)	September 6, 1987
Total	300.0 kg	Naim Suleimanov (Bulgaria)	May 11, 1984

Featherweight 60 kg (132¼ lb)

Snatch	152.5 kg	Naim Suleymanoglü (Turkey)*	September 20, 1988
Jerk	190.0 kg	Naim Suleymanoglü (Turkey)*	September 20, 1988
Total	342.5 kg	Naim Suleymanoglü (Turkey)*	September 20, 1988

Lightweight 67.5 kg (148¾ lb)

Snatch	160.0 kg	Israil Militosyan (USSR)	September 18, 1989
Jerk	200.5 kg	Mikhail Petrov (Bulgaria)	September 8, 1987
Total	355.0 kg	Mikhail Petrov (Bulgaria)	December 5, 1987

Middleweight 75 kg (165¼ lb)

Snatch	170.0 kg	Angel Guenchev (Bulgaria)	December 11, 1987
Jerk	215.5 kg	Aleksandr Varbanov (Bulgaria)	December 5, 1987
Total	382.5 kg	Aleksandr Varbanov (Bulgaria)	February 20, 1988

Light-Heavyweight 82.5 kg (181¾ lb)

Snatch	183.0 kg	Asen Zlatev (Bulgaria)	December 7, 1986
Jerk	225.0 kg	Asen Zlatev (Bulgaria)	November 12, 1986
Total	405.0 kg	Yuri Vardanyan (USSR)	September 14, 1984

Middle-Heavyweight 90 kg (198¼ lb)

Snatch	195.5 kg	Blagoi Blagoyev (Bulgaria)	May 1, 1983
Jerk	235.0 kg	Anatoliy Khrapatliy (USSR)	April 29, 1988
Total	422.5 kg	Viktor Solodov (USSR)	September 15, 1984

First-Heavyweight 100 kg (220¼ lb)

Snatch	200.5 kg	Nicu Vlad (Romania)	November 14, 1986
Jerk	242.5 kg	Aleksandr Popov (USSR)	March 5, 1988
Total	440.0 kg	Yuriy Zakharevich (USSR)	March 4, 1983

Heavyweight 110 kg (242½ lb)

Snatch	210.0 kg	Yuriy Zakharevich (USSR)	September 27, 1988
Jerk	250.5 kg	Yuriy Zakharevich (USSR)	April 30, 1988
Total	455.0 kg	Yuriy Zakharevich (USSR)	September 27, 1988

Super-Heavyweight—over 110 kg (242½ lb)

Snatch	216.0 kg	Antonio Krastev (Bulgaria)	September 13, 1987
Jerk	266.0 kg	Leonid Taranenko (USSR)	November 26, 1988
Total	475.0 kg	Leonid Taranenko (USSR)	November 26, 1988

* Formerly Naim Suleimanov or Neum Shalamanov of Bulgaria

POWER PLAY ■ SOVIET WEIGHTLIFTER VASILIY ALEKSEYEV IS ONE OF THREE MEN TO HAVE WON EIGHT WORLD CHAMPIONSHIPS.

Most titles The record for most titles is eight, held by three lifters: John Davis (U.S.), 1938, 1946–52; Tommy Kono (U.S.), 1952–59; Vasiliy Alekseyev (USSR), 1970–77.

UNITED STATES NATIONAL CHAMPIONSHIPS

Most titles The most titles won is 13, by Anthony Terlazzo at 137 pounds, 1932 and 1936, and at 148 pounds, 1933, 1935, 1937–45.

WRESTLING

ORIGINS Wrestling was the most popular sport in the ancient Olympic Games; wall drawings dating to c. 2600 B.C. show that the sport was popular long before the Greeks. Wrestling was included in the first modern Games. The International Amateur Wrestling Association (FILA) was founded in 1912. There are two forms of wrestling at international level: freestyle and Greco-Roman. The use of the legs and holds below the waist are prohibited in Greco-Roman.

OLYMPIC GAMES Wrestling events have been included in all the Games since 1896.

Most gold medals Three wrestlers have won three Olympic titles: Carl Westergren (Sweden) in 1920, 1924 and 1932; Ivar Johansson (Sweden) in

1932 (two) and 1936; and Aleksandr Medved (USSR) in 1964, 1968 and 1972.

Most medals (individual) Wilfried Dietrich (Germany) has won five medals in Olympic competition: one gold, two silver and two bronze, 1956–68.

Most medals (country) The USSR has won 119 medals in Olympic competition: 62 gold, 34 silver and 23 bronze.

United States U.S. wrestlers have won 93 medals in Olympic competition: 40 gold, 31 silver and 22 bronze.

WORLD CHAMPIONSHIPS

Most titles The freestyler Aleksandr Medved (USSR) won a record 10 world championships, 1962–64 and 1966–72, in three weight categories.

NCAA DIVISION I CHAMPIONSHIP Oklahoma State University was the first unofficial national champion, in 1928.

Most titles Including five unofficial titles, Oklahoma State has won a record 29 NCAA titles, in 1928–31, 1933–35, 1937–42, 1946, 1948–49, 1954–56, 1958–59, 1961–62, 1964, 1968, 1971, 1989–90.

Consecutive titles The University of Iowa has won the most consecutive titles, with nine championships from 1978–86.

SUMO WRESTLING

Sumo bouts are fought between two wrestlers (*rikishi*) inside a 14.9-foot-diameter earthen circle (*dohyo*), covered by a roof, symbolizing a Shinto shrine. The wrestlers try to knock each other out of the ring or to the ground. The wrestler who steps out of the dohyo or touches the ground with any part of his body except the soles of his feet loses the contest. Sumo wrestlers are ranked according to their skills; the highest rank is *Yokozuma* (Grand Champion).

ORIGINS Sumo wrestling traces its origins to the development of the Shinto religion in Japan in the eighth century A.D. Sumo matches were staged at Shinto shrines to honor the divine spirits (known as *kami*) during planting and harvesting ceremonies. During the Edo era (1600–1868) sumo wrestling became a professional sport. Currently, sumo wrestling is governed by Nihon Sumo Kyokai (Japan Sumo Association), which stages six 15-day tournaments (*basho*) throughout the year.

SUMO WALTZ ■ IN WESTERN EYES, SUMO WRESTLING IS ONE OF THE MOST MYSTERIOUS, BUT POSSIBLY THE MOST REVEALING, OF ALL SPORTS. KONISHIKI (RIGHT), A SAMOAN-BORN WRESTLER, IS REPORTED TO BE THE HEAVIEST RIKISHI EVER, AT 556 POUNDS.

Most wins (bouts) Kenji Hatano, known as Oshio, won a record 1,107 bouts in 1,891 contests, 1962–88.

Highest winning percentage Tameemon Torokichi, known as Raiden, compiled a .961 winning percentage—244 wins in 254 bouts—1789 to 1810.

YACHTING

ORIGINS Sailing as a sport dates from the 17th century. Originating in the Netherlands, it was introduced to England by Charles II, who participated in a 23 mile race along the River Thames in 1661. The oldest yacht club in the world is the Royal Cork Yacht Club, which claims descent from the Cork Harbor Water Club, founded in Ireland in 1720. The oldest continuously existing yacht club in the United States is the New York Yacht Club, founded in 1844.

AMERICA'S CUP The America's Cup was originally won as an outright prize by the schooner *America* on August 22, 1851 at Cowes, England and was later offered by the New York Yacht Club as a challenge trophy. On August 8, 1870, J. Ashbury's

MAST...ERPIECE ■ THE LARGEST YACHT TO HAVE COMPETED IN THE AMERICA'S CUP WAS THE 1903 DEFENDER, RELIANCE. THE 1903 CHAMPION WAS 144 FEET LONG, WITH A SAIL AREA OF 16,160 SQUARE FEET, ON A RIG 175 FEET HIGH.

Cambria (Great Britain) failed to capture the trophy from *Magic*, owned by F. Osgood (U.S.). The Cup has been challenged 27 times. The U.S. was undefeated until 1983, when *Australia II*, skippered by John Bertrand and owned by a Perth syndicate headed by Alan Bond, beat *Liberty* 4–3, the narrowest series victory, at Newport, R.I.

Most wins (skipper) Three skippers have won the cup three times: Charlie Barr (U.S.), who defended in 1899, 1901 and 1903; Harold S. Vanderbilt (U.S.), who defended in 1930, 1934 and 1937; and Dennis Conner (U.S.), who defended in 1980, challenged in 1987, and defended in 1988.

Largest yacht The largest yacht to have competed in the America's Cup was the 1903 defender, the gaff rigged cutter *Reliance*, with an overall length of 144 feet, a record sail area of 16,160 square feet and a rig 175 feet high.

OLYMPIC GAMES Bad weather caused the abandonment of yachting events at the first modern Games in 1896. However, the weather has stayed "fair" ever since, and yachting has been part of every Games.

Most gold medals Paul Elvstrom (Denmark) won a record four gold medals in yachting, and in the process became the first competitor in Olympics history to win individual gold medals in four successive Games. Elvstrom's titles came in the Firefly class in 1948, and in the Finn class in 1952, 1956 and 1960.

AMERICA'S CUP WINNERS (1851–1988)

Year	Cup Winner	Skipper	Challenger	Series
1851	America	Richard Brown	—	—
1870	Magic	Andrew Comstock	Cambria (England)	—
1871	Columbia	Nelson Comstock	Livonia (England)	4–1
1876	Madeleine	Josephus Williams	Countess of Dufferin (Canada)	2–0
1881	Mischief	Nathaniel Cook	Atalanta (Canada)	2–0
1885	Puritan	Aubrey Crocker	Genesta (England)	2–0
1886	Mayflower	Martin Stone	Galatea (England)	2–0
1887	Volunteer	Henry Haff	Thistle (Scotland)	2–0
1893	Vigilant	William Hansen	Valkyrie II (England)	3–0
1895	Defender	Henry Haff	Valkyrie III (England)	3–0
1899	Columbia	Charlie Barr	Shamrock I (England)	3–0
1901	Columbia	Charlie Barr	Shamrock II (England)	3–0
1903	Reliance	Charlie Barr	Shamrock III (England)	3–0
1920	Resolute	Charles Adams	Shamrock IV (England)	3–2
1930	Enterprise	Harold Vanderbilt	Shamrock V (England)	4–0
1934	Rainbow	Harold Vanderbilt	Endeavour (England)	4–2
1937	Ranger	Harold Vanderbilt	Endeavour II (England)	4–0
1958	Columbia	Briggs Cunningham	Sceptre (England)	4–0
1962	Weatherly	Emil Mosbacher Jr.	Gretel (Australia)	4–1
1964	Constellation	Bob Bavier Jr.	Sovereign (England)	4–0
1967	Intrepid	Emil Mosbacher Jr.	Dame Pattie (Australia)	4–0
1970	Intrepid	Bill Fricker	Gretel II (Australia)	4–1
1974	Courageous	Ted Hood	Southern Cross (Australia)	4–0
1977	Courageous	Ted Turner	Australia (Australia)	4–0
1980	Freedom	Dennis Conner	Australia (Australia)	4–1
1983	Australia II	John Bertrand	Liberty (U.S.)	4–3
1987	Stars & Stripes	Dennis Conner	Kookaburra III (Australia)	4–0
1988	Stars & Stripes	Dennis Conner	New Zealand (New Zealand)	2–0

Most medals Paul Elvstrom's four gold medals are also the most medals won by any Olympic yachtsman.

Most medals (country) The United States has won 39 medals in Olympic competition: 15 gold, 13 silver and 11 bronze.

ROUND-THE-WORLD RACING

Longest race (nonstop) The world's longest nonstop sailing race is the Vendée Globe Challenge, the first of which started from Les Sables d'Olonne, France on November 26, 1989. The distance circumnavigated without stopping was 22,500 nautical miles. The race is for boats between 50–60 feet, sailed single-handed. The record time on the course is 109 days 8 hours 48 minutes 50 seconds, by Titouan Lamazou (France) in the sloop *Ecureuil d'Aquitaine*, which finished at Les Sables on March 19, 1990.

Longest race (total distance) The longest and oldest regular sailing race around the world is the quadrennial Whitbread Round the World race (instituted August 1973), organized by the Royal Naval Sailing Association (Great Britain). It starts in England, and the course around the world and the number of legs with stops at specified ports are varied from race to race. The distance for 1989–90 was 32,000 nautical miles from Southampton, England and return, with stops and restarts at Punta del Este, Uruguay; Fremantle, Australia; Auckland, New Zealand; Punta del Este, Uruguay, and Fort Lauderdale, Fla.

A listing of world champions, national champions, tournament winners and leading money winners of the 1991 sports season.

Country abbreviation codes:

ALG	Algeria	KEN	Kenya
AUS	Australia	LUX	Luxembourg
AUT	Austria	MEX	Mexico
BEL	Belgium	MOR	Morocco
BRA	Brazil	NL	Netherlands
BUL	Bulgaria	NOR	Norway
CAN	Canada	PAN	Panama
CHI	China	PAR	Paraguay
CHL	Chile	POL	Poland
COL	Colombia	PR	Puerto Rico
CUB	Cuba	ROM	Romania
CZE	Czechoslovakia	SAF	South Africa
DEN	Denmark	SK	South Korea
ENG	England	SPA	Spain
FIN	Finland	SUR	Surinam
FRA	France	SWE	Sweden
GB	Great Britian	SWI	Switzerland
GER	Germany	THA	Thailand
GHA	Ghana	U.S.	United States
HUN	Hungary		of America
IRA	Iran	USSR	Soviet Union
IRE	Ireland	VEN	Venezuela
ITA	Italy	VI	Virgin Islands
JAP	Japan	ZAM	Zambia

ARCHERY

WORLD TARGET CHAMPIONSHIPS (AT CRAKOW, POLAND)

Men's Results

Individual Simon Fairweather (AUS)

Team South Korea

Women's Results

Individual Soo-Nyung Kim (SK)

Team South Korea

UNITED STATES NATIONAL CHAMPIONSHIPS (AT OXFORD, OHIO)

Men Ed Eliason

Women Denise Parker

AUTO RACING

CART PPG–INDY CAR WORLD SERIES

Champion Michael Andretti, K-mart/Havoline L91 Chevrolet, 234 points

NASCAR WINSTON CUP CHAMPIONSHIP

Champion Dale Earnhardt, 4,287 points

FORMULA ONE DRIVERS CHAMPIONSHIP

Champion Ayrton Senna (BRA), McLaren, 96 points

NHRA WINSTON CUP CHAMPIONSHIP

Top Fuel Champion Joe Amato, Valvoline dragster, 14,388 points

Funny Car Champion John Force, Castrol GTX Olds Cutlass, 15,538 points

Pro Stock Champion Darrell Alderman, Wayne County Speed Shop, Dodge Daytona, 18,280 points

BADMINTON

WORLD CHAMPIONSHIPS (AT COPENHAGEN, DENMARK)

Men's Singles Jianhua Zhao (CHI)

Women's Singles Jiuhong Tang (CHI)

Men's Doubles Joo Bong Park/Moon Soo Kim (SK)

Women's Doubles Weizhen Guan/Qunhua Nong (CHI)

Mixed Doubles Joo Bong Park/Myeong Hee Chung (SK)

UNITED STATES NATIONAL CHAMPIONSHIPS (AT COLORADO SPRINGS, COLO.)

Men's Singles Chris Jogis

Women's Singles Liz Aronsohn

Men's Doubles Tom Reidy/John Britton

Women's Doubles Ann French/Joy Kitzmiller

Mixed Doubles Tariq Wadood/Traci Britton

BASEBALL

MAJOR LEAGUES

1991 FINAL STANDINGS

American League East

Team	W	L	Pct.	GB
Toronto	91	71	.562	—
Boston	84	78	.519	7
Detroit	84	78	.519	7
Milwaukee	83	79	.512	8
New York	71	91	.438	20
Baltimore	67	95	.414	24
Cleveland	57	105	.352	34

American League West

Team	W	L	Pct.	GB
Minnesota	95	67	.586	—
Chicago	87	75	.537	8
Texas	85	77	.525	10
Oakland	84	78	.519	11
Seattle	83	79	.512	12
Kansas City	82	80	.506	13
California	81	81	.500	14

National League East

Team	W	L	Pct.	GB
Pittsburgh	98	64	.605	—
St. Louis	84	78	.519	14
Philadelphia	78	84	.481	20
Chicago	77	83	.481	20
New York	77	84	.478	20½
Montreal	71	90	.441	26½

National League West

Team	W	L	Pct.	GB
Atlanta	94	68	.580	—
Los Angeles	93	69	.574	1
San Diego	84	78	.519	10
San Francisco	75	87	.463	19
Cincinnati	74	88	.457	20
Houston	65	97	.401	29

1991 STATISTICAL LEADERS

American League

Batting Average	.341	Julio Franco, Texas
Runs Batted In	133	Cecil Fielder, Detroit
Home Runs	44	Cecil Fielder, Detroit Jose Canseco, Oakland
Triples	13	Lance Johnson, Chicago Paul Molitor, Milwaukee
Doubles	49	Rafael Palmeiro, Texas
Hits	216	Paul Molitor, Milwaukee
Runs	133	Paul Molitor, Milwaukee
Stolen Bases	58	Rickey Henderson, Oakland
Earned Run Average	2.62	Roger Clemens, Boston
Victories	20	Scott Erickson, Minnesota (20–8) Mark Langston, California (20–9)
Strikeouts	241	Roger Clemens, Boston
Saves	46	Bryan Harvey, California

National League

Batting Average	.319	Terry Pendleton, Atlanta
Runs Batted In	117	Howard Johnson, New York
Home Runs	38	Howard Johnson, New York
Triples	15	Ray Lankford, St. Louis
Doubles	44	Bobby Bonilla, Pittsburgh
Hits	187	Terry Pendleton, Atlanta
Runs	112	Brett Butler, Los Angeles
Stolen Bases	76	Marquis Grissom, Montreal
Earned Run Averaage	2.39	Dennis Martinez, Montreal
Victories	20	John Smiley, Pittsburgh (20–11) Tommy Glavine, Atlanta (20–11)
Strikeouts	241	David Cone, New York
Saves	47	Lee Smith, St. Louis

AWARDS

American League

Most Valuable Player Cal Ripken Jr., Baltimore
Cy Young Award Roger Clemens, Boston
Rookie of the Year Chuck Knoblauch, Minnesota
Manager of the Year Tom Kelly, Minnesota

National League

Most Valuable Player Terry Pendleton, Atlanta
Cy Young Award Tommy Glavine, Atlanta
Rookie of the Year Jeff Bagwell, Houston
Manager of the Year Bobby Cox, Atlanta

1991 PLAYOFFS

American League Championship Series
Minnesota Twins 4, Toronto Blue Jays 1

Game 1 (at Minnesota) Minnesota 5, Toronto 4
Game 2 (at Minnesota) Toronto 5, Minnesota 2
Game 3 (at Toronto) Minnesota 3, Toronto 2[*]

---

[*] 10-inning game

Game 4 (at Toronto) Minnesota 9, Toronto 3
Game 5 (at Toronto) Minnesota 8, Toronto 5

Most Valuable Player Kirby Puckett, Minnesota

National League Championship Series
Atlanta Braves 4, Pittsburgh Pirates 3

Game 1 (at Pittsburgh) Pittsburgh 5, Atlanta 1
Game 2 (at Pittsburgh) Atlanta 1, Pittsburgh 0
Game 3 (at Atlanta) Atlanta 10, Pittsburgh 3
Game 4 (at Atlanta) Pittsburgh 3, Atlanta 2[*]
Game 5 (at Atlanta) Pittsburgh 1, Atlanta 0
Game 6 (at Pittsburgh) Atlanta 1, Pittsburgh 0
Game 7 (at Pittsburgh) Atlanta 4, Pittsburgh 0

[*] 10-inning game

Most Valuable Player Steve Avery, Atlanta

WORLD SERIES
Minnesota Twins 4, Atlanta Braves 3

Game 1 (at Minnesota) Minnesota 5, Atlanta 2
Game 2 (at Minnesota) Minnesota 3, Atlanta 2
Game 3 (at Atlanta) Atlanta 5, Minnesota 4[*]
Game 4 (at Atlanta) Atlanta 3, Minnesota 2
Game 5 (at Atlanta) Atlanta 14, Minnesota 5
Game 6 (at Minnesota) Minnesota 4, Atlanta 3[*]
Game 7 (at Minnesota) Minnesota 1, Atlanta 0[*]

[*] Game 3, 12 innings; Game 6, 11 innings; Game 7, 10 innings

Most Valuable Player Jack Morris, Minnesota

ALL-STAR GAME (at SkyDome, Toronto, Canada)
American League 4, National League 2

Most Valuable Player Cal Ripken Jr. American League

COLLEGE BASEBALL

COLLEGE WORLD SERIES
(at Rosenblatt Stadium, Omaha, Neb.)
Louisiana State 6, Wichita State 3

NCAA DIVISION II CHAMPIONSHIP TOURNAMENT
(at Paterson Stadium, Montgomery, Ala.)
Jacksonville State 20, Missouri Southern State 4

NCAA DIVISION III CHAMPIONSHIP TOURNAMENT
(at Battle Creek, Mich.)
Southern Maine 9, Trenton State 0

LITTLE LEAGUE
LITTLE LEAGUE WORLD SERIES (at Williamsport, Pa.)
Taiwan 11, Danville (Calif.) 0

BASKETBALL

NATIONAL BASKETBALL ASSOCIATION (NBA)

1990–91 FINAL STANDINGS

EASTERN CONFERENCE
Atlantic Division

Team	W	L	Pct.	GB
Boston	56	26	.683	—
Philadelphia	44	38	.537	12
New York	39	43	.476	17
Washington	30	52	.366	26
New Jersey	26	56	.317	30
Miami	24	58	.293	32

Central Division

Team	W	L	Pct.	GB
Chicago	61	21	.744	—
Detroit	50	32	.610	11
Milwaukee	48	34	.585	13
Atlanta	43	39	.524	18
Indiana	41	41	.500	20
Cleveland	33	49	.402	28
Charlotte	26	56	.317	35

WESTERN CONFERENCE
Midwest Division

Team	W	L	Pct.	GB
San Antonio	55	27	.671	—
Utah	54	28	.659	1
Houston	52	30	.634	3
Orlando	31	51	.378	24
Minnesota	29	53	.354	26
Dallas	28	54	.341	27
Denver	20	62	.244	35

Pacific Division

Team	W	L	Pct.	GB
Portland	63	19	.768	—
L A Lakers	58	24	.707	5
Phoenix	55	27	.671	8
Golden State	44	38	.537	19
Seattle	41	41	.500	22
L A Clippers	31	51	.378	32
Sacramento	25	57	.305	38

1990–91 Statistical Leaders

	Total	Avg.	
Scoring	2,580 pts	31.5 pts	Michael Jordan, Chicago
Assists	1,164	14.2	John Stockton, Utah
Rebounds	1,063	13.0	David Robinson, San Antonio
Steals	246	3.04	Alvin Robertson, Milwaukee
Blocked Shots	221*	3.95	Hakeem Olajuwon, Houston

* David Robinson, San Antonio, had a league-leading 320 blocked shots.

Awards

Most Valuable Player Michael Jordan, Chicago
Coach of the Year Don Chaney, Houston
Rookie of the Year Derrick Coleman, New Jersey

1991 Playoffs

Eastern Conference (series score)

First Round

Chicago Bulls 3, New York Knicks 0
Philadelphia 76ers 3, Milwaukee Bucks 0
Boston Celtics 3, Indiana Pacers 2
Detroit Pistons 3, Atlanta Hawks 2

Semifinals

Chicago Bulls 4, Philadelphia 76ers 1
Detroit Pistons 4, Boston Celtics 2

Finals

Chicago Bulls 4, Detroit Pistons 0

Western Conference (series score)

First Round

Portland Trail Blazers 3, Seattle Supersonics 2
Utah Jazz 3, Phoenix Suns 1
Golden State Warriors 3, San Antonio Spurs 1
Los Angeles Lakers 3, Houston Rockets 0

Semifinals

Portland Trail Blazers 4, Utah Jazz 1
Los Angeles Lakers 4, Golden State Warriors 1

Finals

Los Angeles Lakers 4, Portland Trail Blazers 2

NBA Championship Finals

Chicago Bulls 4, Los Angeles Lakers 1

Game 1 (at Chicago) LA Lakers 93, Chicago 91
Game 2 (at Chicago) Chicago 107, LA Lakers 86
Game 3 (at Los Angeles) Chicago 104, LA Lakers 96 (OT)
Game 4 (at Los Angeles) Chicago 97, LA Lakers 82
Game 5 (at Los Angeles) Chicago 108, LA Lakers 101

NBA Finals MVP Michael Jordan, Chicago

COLLEGE BASKETBALL (MEN)

NCAA Division I

1990–91 Conference Winners

Conference	Reg. Season	Tournament
American South	New Orleans	Lousiana Tech
Assoc. of Mid-Continent	North Illinois	Wisconsin–Green Bay
Atlantic Coast	Duke	North Carolina
Atlantic 10	Rutgers	Penn St.
Big East	Syracuse	Seton Hall
Big Eight	Oklahoma St.* Kansas*	Missouri
Big Sky	Montana	Montana
Big South	Coastal Carolina	Coastal Carolina
Big Ten	Ohio St.	N/A
Big West	UNLV	UNLV
Colonial Athletic Assoc.	James Madison	Richmond
East Coast	Towson St.	Towson St.
Ivy League	Princeton	N/A
Metro	Southern Miss.	Florida St.
Metro Atlantic	Sienna	St. Peter's
Mid-American	Eastern Michigan	Eastern Michigan
Mid-Eastern Athletic	Coppin St.	Florida A&M
Midwestern Collegiate	Xavier	Xavier
Missouri Valley	Creighton	Creighton
North Atlantic	Northeastern	Northeastern
Northeast	St. Francis (Pa)	St. Francis (Pa)
Ohio Valley	Murray St.	Murray St.
Pacific-10	Arizona	N/A
Patriot	Fordham	Fordham
Southeastern	Mississippi St.* Louisiana St.*	Alabama
Southern	Furman	E Tennessee St.
Southland	NE Louisiana	NE Louisiana
Southwest	Arkansas	Arkansas
Southwestern Athletic	Jackson St.	Jackson St.
Sun Belt	South Alabama	South Alabama
Trans-America	Tex–San Antonio	Georgia St.
West Coast	Pepperdine	Pepperdine
Western Athletic	Utah	BYU

* Tied

NCAA Division I Tournament

East Regional
First Round
North Carolina 101, Northeastern 66
Villanova 50, Princeton 48
Eastern Michigan 76, Mississippi St. 56
Penn St. 74, UCLA 69
N.C. St. 114, So. Miss. 85
Oklahoma St. 67, New Mexico 54
Temple 80, Purdue 63
Richmond 73, Syracuse 69

Second Round
North Carolina 84, Villanova 69
Eastern Michigan 71, Penn St. 68 (OT)
Oklahoma St. 73, N.C. St. 64
Temple 77, Richmond 64

Regionals
North Carolina 93, Eastern Michigan 67
Temple 72, Oklahoma St. 63 (OT)

Semifinals
North Carolina 75, Temple 72

East Regional Final Four Qualifier   North Carolina

Southeast Regional
First Round
Arkansas 117, Georgia St. 76
Arizona St. 79, Rutgers 76
Wake Forest 71, Louisiana Tech. 65
Alabama 89, Murray St. 79
Pittsburgh 76, Georgia 68 (OT)
Kansas 55, New Orleans 49
Florida St. 75, Southern Cal. 72
Indiana 79, Coastal Carolina 69

Second Round
Arkansas 97, Arizona St. 90
Alabama 96, Wake Forest 88
Kansas 77, Pittsburgh 66
Indiana 82, Florida St. 60

Regionals
Arkansas 93, Alabama 70
Kansas 83, Indiana 65

Semifinals
Kansas 93, Arkansas 81

Southeast Regional Final Four Qualifier   Kansas

West Regional
First Round
UNLV 99, Montana 65
Georgetown 70, Vanderbilt 60
Michigan St. 60, Wisconsin–Green Bay 58
Utah 82, So. Alabama 72
Creighton 64, New Mexico St. 56
Seton Hall 71, Pepperdine 51
BYU 61, Virginia 48
Arizona 93, St. Francis (Pa) 80

Second Round
UNLV 62, Georgetown 54
Utah 85, Michigan St. 84 (OT)
Seton Hall 81, Creighton 69
Arizona 76, BYU 61

Regionals
UNLV 83, Utah 66
Seton Hall 81, Arizona 77

Semifinals
UNLV 77, Seton Hall 65

West Regional Final Four Qualifier   UNLV

Midwest Regional
First Round
Ohio St. 97, Towson St. 86
Georgia Tech. 87, DePaul 70
Texas 73, St. Peter's 65
St. John's 75, No. Illinois 68
Connecticut 79, LSU 62
Xavier 89, Nebraska 84
Iowa 76, E. Tennessee St. 73
Duke 102, NE Louisiana 73

Second Round
Ohio St. 65, Georgia Tech. 61
St. John's 84, Texas 76
Connecticut 66, Xavier 50
Duke 85, Iowa 70

Regionals
St. John's 91, Ohio St. 74
Duke 81, Connecticut 67

Semifinals
Duke 78, St. John's 61

Midwest Final Four Regional Qualifier   Duke

FINAL FOUR
(at Market Square Arena, Indianapolis, Ind.) _____

Semifinals
Duke 79, UNLV 77
Kansas 79, North Carolina 73

Championship Game
Duke 72, Kansas 65

Final Four MVP Christian Laettner, Duke

FINAL ONE ■ CHRISTIAN LAETTNER LED DUKE TO ITS FIRST NCAA TITLE, AND WAS VOTED THE FINAL FOUR MVP.

NCAA DIVISION II CHAMPIONSHIP _____
North Alabama 79, Bridgeport 72

NCAA DIVISION III CHAMPIONSHIP _____
Wisconsin Platteville 81, Franklin & Marshall 74

COLLEGE BASKETBALL (WOMEN)

NCAA DIVISION I TOURNAMENT _____

First Round
Southwest Missouri St. 94, Tennessee Tech. 64
Florida St. 96, Appalachian St. 57
Holy Cross 81, Maryland 74
Vanderbilt 73, South Carolina 64
UNLV 70, Texas Tech 65
Southern Cal. 63, Utah 52
Iowa 64, Montana 53
Cal. St. Fullerton 84, Louisiana Tech 80
James Madison 70, Kentucky 62
Providence 88, Fairfield 87
Toledo 83, Rutgers 65
George Washington 73, Richmond 62
Stephen F. Austin 72, Mississippi 62
Oklahoma St. 81, DePaul 80
Northwestern 82, Washington St. 62
Lamar 77, Texas 63

Second Round
Tennessee 55, Southwest Missouri St. 47
Western Kentucky 72, Florida St. 69
Auburn 84, Holy Cross 58
Vanderbilt 69, Purdue 63
Georgia 86, UNLV 62
Long Beach St. 83, Southern Cal. 58
Washington 70, Iowa 53
Stanford 91, Cal. St. Fullerton 67
James Madison 73, Penn St. 71
Clemson 103, Providence 91
Connecticut 81, Toledo 80
N.C. State 94, George Washington 83
Virginia 74, Stephen F. Austin 72
Oklahoma St. 96, Michigan St. 94 (3 OT)
Arkansas 105, Northwestern 68
Lamar 93, Louisiana St. 73

Regional Semifinals
Tennessee 68, Western Kentucky 61
Auburn 58, Vanderbilt 45
Georgia 87, Long Beach St. 77
Stanford 73, Washington 47
Clemson 57, James Madison 55
Connecticut 82, N.C. State 71
Virginia 76, Oklahoma St. 61
Lamar 91, Arkansas 75

Regional Championships
Tennessee 69, Auburn 65
Stanford 75, Georgia 67
Connecticut 60, Clemson 57
Virginia 85, Lamar 70

FINAL FOUR (at New Orleans, La.) _____
Virginia 61, Connecticut 55
Tennessee 68, Stanford 60

CHAMPIONSHIP GAME _____
Tennessee 70, Virginia 67 (OT)

Final Four MVP   Dawn Staley, Virginia

NCAA DIVISION II CHAMPIONSHIP_____
North Dakota St. 81, Southeast Missouri St. 74

NCAA DIVISION III CHAMPIONSHIP_____
St. Thomas (Minn.) 73, Muskingum 55

BIATHLON

1991 WORLD CHAMPIONSHIPS (AT LAHTI, FINLAND)

Men's Results
10 km   Mark Kirchner (GER)
20 km   Mark Kirchner (GER)
Relay (4 x 7.5 km)   Germany

Women's Results
7.5 km   Grete Ingegorb Nykkelmo (NOR)
15 km   Petra Schaff (GER)
Relay (3 x 7.5 km)   USSR

BOBSLED AND LUGE

BOSLED WORLD CHAMPIONSHIPS (AT ALTEMBERG/SACHSEN, GERMANY)

2-man   Rudy Lochner/Marcus Zimmerman (SWI)
4-man   Germany I (driver, Wolfgang Hoppe)

LUGE WORLD CHAMPIONSHIPS (AT WINTERBERG, GERMANY)

Single (men)   Arnold Huber (ITA)
Single (women)   Susi Erdman (GER)
Doubles (men)   Stefan Krausse/Jan Behrendt (GER)

BOWLING

PROFESSIONAL BOWLERS' ASSOCIATION TOUR

Leading Money Winner   David Ozio, $225,585
P.B.A. Player of the Year   David Ozio

LADIES' PROFESSIONAL BOWLING TOUR

Leading Money Winner   Leanne Barrette, $87,618
L.P.B.T. Player of the Year   Leanne Barrette

AMERICAN BOWLING CONGRESS

A.B.C. Championships Tournament Results

Event	Winner
Singles	Ed Deines
Doubles	Jimmy Johnson and Dan Nadeau
All Events	Tom Howery
Regular team	Tri-State Lane No. 1, Chattanooga, Tenn.
Booster team	Lewis Marine Supply Inc., Ft. Lauderdale, Fla.
Team All Events	Nadeau's Pro Shop, Las Vegas, Nev.

WOMEN'S INTERNATIONAL BOWLING CONGRESS

W.I.B.C. Championship Tournament Results

Event	Winner
Open singles	Debbie Kuhn
Open doubles	Lucy Giovinco and Cindy Coburn-Carroll
Open team event	Clear-Vu Window Cleaning, Milwaukee, Wis.
Open All Events	Debbie Kuhn

BOXING

WORLD CHAMPIONS (AS OF DECEMER 30, 1991)

Division	Boxer	Recognition
Heavyweight	Evander Holyfield (U.S.)	W.B.A, W.B.C., I.B.F.
Cruiserweight	Bobby Czyz (U.S.)	W.B.A.
	Anaclet Wamba (FRA)	W.B.C.
	James Warring (U.S.)	I.B.F.
Light-heavyweight	Thomas Hearns (U.S.)	W.B.A.
	Jeff Harding (AUS)	W.B.C.
	Charles Williams (U.S.)	I.B.F.
Super-middleweight	Victor Cordova (PAN)	W.B.A.
	Mauro Galvano (ITA)	W.B.C.
	Darren Van Horn (U.S.)	I.B.F.
Middleweight	vacant	W.B.A.
	Julian Jackson (VI)	W.B.C.
	James Toney (U.S.)	I.B.F.

Jr. middleweight	Vinny Pazienza (U.S.)	W.B.A.
	Terry Norris (U.S.)	W.B.C.
	Gianfranco Rossi (ITA)	I.B.F.
Welterweight	Meldrick Taylor (U.S.)	W.B.A.
	James McGirt (U.S.)	W.B.C.
	Maurice Blocker (U.S.)	I.B.F.
Jr. welterweight	Edwin Rosario (PR)	W.B.A.
	Julio César Chavez (MEX)	W.B.C.
	Rafael Pineda (COL)	I.B.F.
Lightweight	Pernell Whitaker (U.S.)	W.B.A., W.B.C., I.B.F.
Jr. lightweight	Ganaro Hernandez (U.S.)	W.B.A.
	Azumah Nelson (GHA)	W.B.C.
	Brian Mitchell (SAF)	I.B.F.
Featherweight	Yung-kyun Park (SK)	W.B.A.
	Paul Hodkinson (GB)	W.B.C.
	Manuel Medina (MEX)	I.B.F.
Jr. featherweight	Raul Perez (MEX)	W.B.A.
	Daniel Zaragoza (MEX)	W.B.C.
	Welcome Ncita (SAF)	I.B.F.
Bantamweight	Israel Contreras (VEN)	W.B.A.
	Joichiro Tatsuyoshi (JAP)	W.B.C.
	Orlando Canizales (U.S.)	I.B.F.
Jr. bantamweight	Khaosai Galaxy (THA)	W.B.A.
	Sung-kil Moon (SK)	W.B.C.
	Robert Quiroga (U.S.)	I.B.F.
Flyweight	Yong-kang Kim (SK)	W.B.A.
	Muangchai Kittikasem (THA)	W.B.C.
	Dave McCauley (GB)	I.B.F.
Jr. flyweight	Myung-Woo Yuh (SK)	W.B.A.
	Humberto Gonzalez (MEX)	W.B.C.
	Michael Carbajal (U.S.)	I.B.F.
Mini-flyweight	Hi-yong Choi (SK)	W.B.A.
	Ricardo Lopez (MEX)	W.B.C.
	Fah-Lan Lookmingkwan (THA)	I.B.F.

Notes: W.B.A. = World Boxing Association; W.B.C. = World Boxing Council; I.B.F. = International Boxing Federation

WORLD AMATEUR CHAMPIONSHIPS (AT SYDNEY, AUSTRALIA)

106 pounds	Eric Griffin (U.S.)
112 pounds	Istvan Kovacs (HUN)
119 pounds	Serafin Todorov (BUL)
125 pounds	Kirkor Kirkorov (BUL)
132 pounds	Marco Rudolph (GER)
139 pounds	Konstantin Tzyu (USSR)
147 pounds	Juan Hernandez (CUB)
156 pounds	Juan Lemus (CUB)
165 pounds	Tommaso Russo (ITA)
178 pounds	Torsten May (GER)
201 pounds	Felix Savon (CUB)
+201 pounds	Roberto Balado (CUB)

CANOEING

CANOE AND KAYAK WORLD CHAMPIONSHIPS (AT MARNE LA VALLEE, FRANCE)

Men's Results

Canadian Singles
500 m Mikhail Slivinski (USSR)
1,000 m Ivan Klementiev (USSR)
10,000 m Zsolt Bohacs (HUN)

Canadian Pairs
500 m Hungary
1,000 m Germany
10,000 m Hungary

Canadian Fours
500 m USSR
1,000 m USSR

Kayak Singles
500 m Renn Crichlow (CAN)
1,000 m Knut Holmann (NOR)
10,000 m Greg Barton (U.S.)

Kayak Pairs
500 m Spain
1,000 m Germany
10,000 m France

Kayak Fours
500 m Germany
1,000 m Hungary
10,000 m Germany

Women's Results

Kayak Singles
500 m Katrin Borchert (GER)
5,000 m Josefa Idem (ITA)

Kayak Pairs
500 m Germany
5,000 m Germany

Kayak Fours
500 m Germany

CROQUET

WORLD CROQUET CHAMPIONSHIPS (AT HURLINGHAM, ENGLAND)

Singles John Walters (ENG)

CROSS-COUNTRY RUNNING

WORLD CHAMPIONSHIPS (AT ANTWERP, BELGIUM)

Men's Results

Individual Khalid Skah (MOR)
Team Kenya

Women's Results

Individual Lynn Jennings (U.S.)
Team Kenya

CURLING

WORLD CHAMPIONSHIPS (AT WINNIPEG, CANADA)

Men's team Scotland, David Smith (skip)
Women's team Norway, Djordi Nordby (skip)

CYCLING

PROFESSIONAL EVENTS

TOUR DE FRANCE (2,445 miles) _____
Miguel Indurain (SPA) 101 hours 1 minute 20.2 seconds

OTHER MAJOR TOUR RACE RESULTS _____
Tour Du Pount Erik Breukink (NL)
Italy Franco Chioccioli (ITA)
Switzerland Luc Roosen (BEL)
Great Britain Phil Anderson (AUS)
Netherlands Frans Maassen (NL)
Ireland Sean Kelly (IRE)

WORLD CHAMPIONSHIPS (AT STUTTGART, GERMANY)

Men's Results
Sprint Void[*]
Pursuit Francis Moreau (FRA)
Road Race Gianni Bugno (ITA)

Women's Results
Sprint Ingrid Haringa (NL)
Pursuit Petra Rossner (GER)
Road Race Leontien van Moorsel (NL)

[*] Carey Hall (AUS) won the race but was disqualified after failing a drug test.

DIVING

WORLD CHAMPIONSHIPS (AT PERTH, AUSTRALIA)

Men's Results
1 m Springboard Edwin Jongejans (NL)
3 m Springboard Kent Ferguson (U.S.)
Platform Shun Shuwei (CHI)

Women's Results
1 m Springboard Gao Min (CHI)
3 m Springboard Gao Min (CHI)
Platform Fu Mingxia (CHI)

YOUNGEST CHAMPION ■ CHINA'S FU MINGXIA BECAME THE YOUNGEST WOMEN'S WORLD CHAMPION IN ANY SPORT WHEN SHE WON THE PLATFORM DIVING TITLE AT AGE 12, IN 1991.

FENCING

WORLD CHAMPIONSHIPS (AT BUDAPEST, HUNGARY)

Men's Results
Foil Ingo Weissenborn (GER)

Foil (Team) Cuba
Épée Andrei Chouvalov (USSR)
Épée (Team) USSR
Sabre Gregory Kirienko (USSR)
Sabre (Team) Hungary

Women's Results

Foil Giovanna Trillini (ITA)
Foil (Team) Italy
Épée Marianne Horvath (HUN)
Épée (Team) Hungary

FIGURE SKATING

WORLD CHAMPIONSHIPS (AT MUNICH, GERMANY)

Men Kurt Browning (CAN)
Women Kristi Yamaguchi (U.S.)
Pairs Natalia Mishkuteniok/Artur Dmitriev (USSR)
Dance Isabelle Duchesnay/Paul Duchesnay (FRA)

UNITED STATES CHAMPIONSHIPS (AT MINNEAPOLIS, MINN.)

Men Todd Eldredge
Women Tonya Harding
Pairs Natasha Kuchiki/Todd Sand
Dance Elizabeth Punsalan/Jerod Swallow

FOOTBALL

NATIONAL FOOTBALL LEAGUE (NFL)

1991 NFL FINAL STANDINGS

AMERICAN CONFERENCE
Eastern Division

Team	W	L	Pct.
Buffalo	13	3	.813
NY Jets	8	8	.500
Miami	8	8	.500
New England	6	10	.375
Indianapolis	1	15	.063

Central Division

Houston	11	5	.688
Pittsburgh	7	9	.438
Cleveland	6	10	.375
Cincinnati	3	13	.188

Western Division

Denver	12	4	.750
Kansas City	10	6	.625
LA Raiders	9	7	.563
Seattle	7	9	.438
San Diego	4	12	.250

NATIONAL CONFERENCE
Eastern Division

Team	W	L	Pct.
Washington	14	2	.875
Dallas	11	5	.688
Philadelphia	10	6	.625
NY Giants	8	8	.500
Phoenix	4	12	.250

Central Division

Detroit	12	4	.750
Chicago	11	5	.688
Minnesota	8	8	.500
Green Bay	4	12	.250
Tampa Bay	3	13	.188

Western Division

New Orleans	11	5	.688
Atlanta	10	6	.625
San Francisco	10	6	.625
LA Rams	3	13	.188

NFL 1991 STATISTICAL LEADERS

Passing yardage	4,690 yds	Warren Moon, Houston
Rushing yardage	1,563 yds	Emmitt Smith, Dallas
Total yardage	2,038 yds	Thurman Thomas, Buffalo
Points scored	149	Chip Lohmiller, Washington
Touchdowns scored	17	Barry Sanders, Detroit
Touchdowns thrown	33	Jim Kelly, Buffalo
Quarterback rating	101.8 pts	Steve Young, San Francisco
Receptions	100	Haywood Jeffries, Houston
Sacks	17	Pat Swilling, New Orleans
Interceptions	8	Ronnie Lott, LA Raiders

SUPER BOWL XXVI PLAYOFFS

American Conference

Wildcard Games
Houston Oilers 17, New York Jets, 10
Kansas City Chief 10, Los Angeles Raiders 6

Second Round
Buffalo Bills 37, Kansas City Chiefs, 14
Denver Broncos 26, Houston Oilers 24

A.F.C. Championship Game (at Buffalo)
Buffalo Bills 10, Denver Broncos 7

National Conference

Wildcard Games
Atlanta Falcons 27, New Orleans Saints 20
Dallas Cowboys 17, Chicago Bears 13

Second Round
Washington Redskins 24, Atlanta Falcons 7
Detroit Lions 38, Dallas Cowboys 6

N.F.C. Championship Game (at Washington)
Washington Redskins 41, Detroit Lions 10

SUPER BOWL XXVI (at Hubert H. Humphrey
Metrodome, Minneapolis, Minn.) _____
Washington Redskins 37, Buffalo Bills 24

Super Bowl MVP Mark Rypien, Washington

COLLEGE FOOTBALL

NCAA DIVISION I-A

1991 Final National Polls

Poll	No. 1 Ranked	Record
A.P.	Miami, Fla.	12–0–0
U.P.I.	Washington	12–0–0
USA Today/CNN	Washington	12–0–0

BOWL GAME RESULTS (1991 season)

Big Four
Orange Miami, Fla. 22, Nebraska 0
Rose Washington 34, Michigan 14
Sugar Notre Dame 39, Florida 28
Cotton Florida St. 10, Texas A&M 2

Other Bowl Results
Aloha Georgia Tech 18, Stanford 17
Blockbuster Alabama 30, Colorado 25
California Bowling Green 28, Fresno St. 21
Citrus California 37, Clemson 13
Copper Indiana 24, Baylor 0
Fiesta Penn St. 42, Tennessee 17
Freedom Tulsa 28, San Diego St. 17

Gator Oklahoma 48, Virginia 14
Hall of Fame Syracuse 24, Ohio St. 17
John Hancock UCLA 6, Illinois 3
Heritage Alabama St. 36, N. Carolina A&T 13
Holiday Iowa 13, BYU 13
Independence Georgia 24, Arkansas 15
Liberty Air Force 38, Mississippi St. 15

AWARDS

Heisman Trophy Desmond Howard, Michigan
Outland Trophy Steve Emtman, Washington

HEISMAN WINNER ■ MICHIGAN FLANKER DESMOND HOWARD WON THE 1991 HEISMAN TROPHY

NCAA DIVISION I-AA CHAMPIONSHIP GAME
(at Statesboro, Ga.)_____
Youngstown State 25, Marshall 17

NCAA DIVISION II CHAMPIONSHIP GAME
(at Florence, Ala.) _____
Pittsburg State (Kan.) 23, Jacksonville St. (Ala.) 6

NCAA Division III Championship Game

(at Bradenton, Fla.)

Ithaca 34, Dayton 20

Canadian Football League (CFL)

1991 CFL Final Standings
Eastern Division

Team	W	L	Pct.
Toronto	13	5	.722
Winnipeg	9	9	.500
Ottawa	7	11	.389
Hamilton	3	15	.167

Western Division

Edmonton	12	6	.667
Calgary	11	7	.611
B.C. Lions	11	7	.611
Saskatchewan	6	12	.333

Grey Cup Playoffs

Eastern Division

Semifinal

Winnipeg Blue Bombers 26, Ottawa Rough Riders 8

Final

Toronto Argonauts 42, Winnipeg Blue Bombers 3

Western Division

Semifinal

Calgary Stampeders 43, B.C. Lions 41

Final

Calgary Stampeders 38, Edmonton Eskimos 36

Grey Cup Final (at Winnipeg)

Toronto Argonauts 36, Calgary Stampeders 21

Grey Cup MVP Raghib Ismail, Toronto

GOLF

PGA Tour

Grand Slam Results

The Masters Ian Woosnam (GB)

U.S. Open Payne Stewart

British Open Ian Baker-Finch (AUS)

PGA Championship John Daly

Awards

1991 Leading Money Winner Corey Pavin, $979,430

PGA Player of the Year Fred Couples

Rookie of the Year John Daly

Ryder Cup (at Kiawah Island, S. C.)

United States 14½, Europe 13½

Senior PGA Tour

Grand Slam Events

The Tradition Jack Nicklaus

PGA Seniors Championship Jack Nicklaus

Sr. Players Championship Jim Albus

U.S. Senior Open Jack Nicklaus

Awards

1991 Leading Money Winner Mike Hill, $1,065,657

Senior Player of the Year Mike Hill and George Archer

Senior Rookie of the Year Jim Colbert

L.P.G.A. Tour

Grand Slam Results

Nabisco Dinah Shore Amy Alcott

LPGA Championship Meg Mallon

U.S. Open Meg Mallon

du Maurier Ltd. Classic Nancy Scranton

Awards

1991 Leading Money Winner Pat Bradley, $763,118

Player of the Year Pat Bradley

Rookie of the Year Brandie Burton

Amateur Golf

Results of Leading Events

U.S. Amateur (men) Mitch Voges

U.S. Amateur (women) Amy Fruhwirth

NCAA (individual, men) Warren Schutte, UNLV

NCAA (team, men) Oklahoma State

NCAA (individual, women) Annika Sorenstam, Arizona

NCAA (team, women) UCLA

Walker Cup United States

GYMNASTICS

WORLD CHAMPIONSHIPS (AT INDIANAPOLIS, IND.)

Men's Results

Team USSR
All-Around Grigori Misutin (USSR)
Floor Exercise Igor Korobchinski(USSR)
Pommel Horse Valeri Belenki(USSR)
Still Rings Grigori Misutin(USSR)
Vault Ok Youl You (SK)
Parallel Bars Jing Li (CHI)
High Bar Chun-yang Li (CHI)[*]
Ralf Buechner (GER)[*]

Women's Results

Team USSR
All-Around Kim Zmeskal (U.S.)
Floor Exercise Christina Bontas (ROM) [*]
Oksana Tchusovitina (USSR) [*]
Vault Lavinia Milosovici (ROM)
Uneven Bars Gwang Suk Kim (SK)
Beam Svetlana Boguinskaia (USSR)

[*] Tie

HARNESS RACING

TRIPLE CROWN RACE WINNERS

Trotters

Race	Winner
Yonkers Trot	Crown's Invitation
Hambletonian	Giant Victory
Kentucky Futurity	Whiteland Janice

Pacers

Cane Pace	Silky Stallone
Little Brown Jug	Precious Bunny
Messenger Stakes	Die Laughing

Leading Money Winners

Trotter Giant Victory, $1,130,488
Pacer Precious Bunny, $2,217,222

HOCKEY

NATIONAL HOCKEY LEAGUE (NHL)

1990–91 FINAL STANDINGS

Wales Conference
Adams Division

Team	W	L	T	Pts.
Boston	44	22	12	100
Montreal	39	30	11	89
Buffalo	31	30	19	81
Hartford	31	38	11	73
Quebec	16	50	14	46

Patrick Division

Pittsburgh	41	33	6	88
NY Rangers	36	31	13	85
Washington	37	36	7	81
New Jersey	32	33	15	79
Philadelphia	33	37	10	76
NY Islanders	25	45	10	60

Campbell Conference
Norris Division

Chicago	49	23	8	106
St. Louis	47	22	11	105
Detroit	34	38	8	76
Minnesota	27	39	14	68
Toronto	23	46	11	56

Smythe Division

Los Angeles	46	24	10	102
Calgary	46	26	8	100
Edmonton	37	37	6	80
Vancouver	28	43	9	65
Winnipeg	26	43	11	63

NHL 1990–91 STATISTICAL LEADERS

Points	163	Wayne Gretzky, Los Angeles
Goals	86	Brett Hull, St. Louis
Assists	122	Wayne Gretzky, Los Angeles
Wins	43	Ed Belfour, Chicago
Shutouts	5	Don Beaupre, Washington

AWARDS

Hart Trophy (MVP) Brett Hull, St. Louis
Art Ross Trophy (scoring champion) Wayne Gretzky, Los Angeles

Vezina Trophy (top goalie) Ed Belfour, Chicago
Calder Trophy (top rookie) Ed Belfour, Chicago

STANLEY CUP PLAYOFFS 1991

Wales Conference *(series score)*

Adams Division

First Round
Boston Bruins 4, Hartford Whalers 2
Montreal Canadiens 4, Buffalo Sabres 2

Semifinals
Boston Bruins 4, Montreal Canadiens 3

Adams Division Champion Boston Bruins

Patrick Division

First Round
Pittsburgh Penguins 4, New Jersey Devils 3
Washington Capitals 4, New York Rangers 2

Semifinals
Pittsburgh Penguins 4, Washington Capitals 1

Patrick Division Champion Pittsburgh Penguins

Wales Conference Final
Pittsburgh Penguins 4, Boston Bruins 3

Campbell Conference *(series score)*

Norris Division

First Round
Minnesota North Stars 4, Chicago Blackhawks 2
St. Louis Blues 4, Detroit Red Wings 3

Semifinals
Minnesota North Stars 4, St. Louis Blues 2

Norris Division Champion Minnesota North Stars

Smythe Division

First Round
Los Angeles Kings 4, Vancouver Canucks 2
Edmonton Oilers 4, Calgary Flames 3

Semifinals
Edmonton Oilers 4, Los Angeles Kings 2

Smythe Division Champion Edmonton Oilers

Campbell Conference Final
Minnesota North Stars 4, Edmonton Oilers 1

STANLEY CUP FINAL
Pittsburgh Penguins 4, Minnesota North Stars 2

Game 1 (at Pittsburgh) Minnesota 5, Pittsburgh 4
Game 2 (at Pittsburgh) Pittsburgh 4, Minnesota 1
Game 3 (at Bloomington) Minnesota 3, Pittsburgh 1
Game 4 (at Bloomington) Pittsburgh 5, Minnesota 3
Game 5 (at Pittsburgh) Pittsburgh 6, Minnesota 4
Game 6 (at Bloomington) Pittsburgh 8, Minnesota 0

Conn Smythe Trophy (Playoffs MVP) Mario Lemieux, Pittsburgh Penguins

WORLD CHAMPIONSHIPS (AT HELSINKI, FINLAND)
Winner Sweden

NCAA DIVISION I CHAMPIONSHIP
Northern Michigan 8, Boston U. 7 (3 OT)

NCAA DIVISION III CHAMPIONSHIP
Wisconsin–Stevens Point 6, Mankato St. 2

HORSE RACING

TRIPLE CROWN WINNERS
Kentucky Derby Strike the Gold
Preakness Stakes Hansel
Belmont Stakes Hansel

BREEDERS' CUP WINNERS
Sprint Sheikh Albadou
Juvenile Fillies Pleasant Stage
Distaff Dance Smartly
Mile Opening Verse
Juvenile Arazi
Turf Miss Alleged
Classic Black Tie Affair

INTERNATIONAL RACES
Prix de l'Arc de Triomphe, France Suave Dancer
Epson Derbe, England Generous
Irish Derby, Ireland Generous
Grand National, England Seagram

AWARDS
Horse of the Year Black Tie Affair
Jockey of the Year Pat Day
Felix DeCheval Memorial Trophy George P. Slaney

JUDO

WORLD CHAMPIONSHIPS (AT BARCELONA, SPAIN)

Men's Results

60 kg   Tadanori Koshino (JAP)

71 kg   Udo Quellmalz (GER)

78 kg   Daniel Lascau (GER)

86 kg   Hirotaka Okada (JAP)

95 kg   Stephane Traineau (FRA)

95 kg+   Sergei Kosorotov (USSR)

open   Naoya Agawa (JAP)

Women's Results

48 kg   Cecile Nowak (FRA)

52 kg   Alessandra Giungi (ITA)

56 kg   Miriam Blasco (SPA)

61 kg   Frauke Eickhoff (GER)

66 kg   Emanuela Pierantozzi (ITA)

72 kg   Mo-Jung Kim (SK)

72 kg+   Ji-Yoon Moon (SK)

open   Yiaoyan Zhuang (CHI)

LACROSSE

NCAA DIVISION I (men) _____

North Carolina 18, Towson St. 13

NCAA DIVISION III (men) _____

Hobart 12, Salisbury St. 11

NCAA DIVISION I (women)_____

Virginia 8, Maryland 6

NCAA DIVISION III (women) _____

Trenton St. 7, Ursinus 6

MODERN PENTATHLON

MEN'S WORLD CHAMPIONSHIPS (AT SAN ANTONIO, TEX.)

Team USSR

Individual Arkad Skrzypaszek (Poland)

WOMEN'S WORLD CHAMPIONSHIPS (AT SYDNEY, AUSTRALIA)

Team Poland

Individual Eva Fjellerup (DEN)

MOTORCYCLE RACING

WORLD CHAMPIONS

125 cc Loris Capirossi (ITA)

250 cc Luca Cadalora (ITA)

500 cc Wayne Rainey (U.S.)

ORIENTEERING

WORLD CHAMPIONSHIPS (AT MARIANSKE LAZNE, CZECHOSLOVAKIA)

Men's Results

Classic (15 km) Jorgen Martensson (SWE)

Short (5 km) Petr Kozak (CZE)

Relay Switzerland

Women's Results

Classic (9 km) Katalin Olah (HUN)

Short (4 km) Jana Cieslarova (CZE)

Relay Sweden

PAN AMERICAN GAMES (AT HAVANA, CUBA)

Final Medal Winners				
Country	G	S	B	Total
United States	130	125	97	352
Cuba	140	62	63	265
Canada	22	46	59	127
Brazil	21	21	37	79
Mexico	14	23	38	75
Argentina	11	15	29	55
Colombia	5	15	21	41
Venezuela	4	14	20	38
Puerto Rico	3	13	11	27
Chile	2	1	7	10
Dominican Rep.	0	5	4	9
Jamaica	2	1	5	8
Guatemala	0	1	5	6
Surinam	1	2	1	4
Nicaragua	0	1	2	3
Peru	0	0	3	3
Trinidad	1	1	0	2
Costa Rica	1	0	1	2
Bahamas	0	1	1	2
Ecuador	0	1	1	2

(cont. on next page)

Pan American Games Final Medal Winners (cont'd)

Country	G	S	B	Total
Guyana	0	0	2	2
U.S. Virgin Is.	0	0	2	2
Bolivia	0	1	0	1
Panama	0	1	0	1
Uruguay	0	1	0	1
Haiti	0	0	1	1

POLO

U.S. OPEN CHAMPIONSHIP (AT LEXINGTON, KY.)

Grants Farm Manor 9, Michelob Dry 8 (OT)

RODEO

PRCA All-Around Champion Ty Murray (U.S.)

ROWING

WORLD CHAMPIONSHIPS (AT VIENNA, AUSTRIA)

Men's Results
Single Sculls Thomas Lange (GER)
Double Sculls Netherlands
Quadruple Sculls USSR
Coxless Pairs Great Britain
Coxed Pairs Italy
Coxless Fours Australia
Coxed Fours Germany
Eights Germany

Women's Results
Single Sculls Silken Laumann (CAN)
Double Sculls Germany
Quadruple Sculls Germany
Coxless Pairs Canada
Coxless Fours Canada
Eights Canada

RUGBY

WORLD CUP FINAL (AT TWICKENHAM, ENGLAND)

Australia 12, England 6

SKIING

WORLD ALPINE CHAMPIONSHIPS (AT SAALBACH-HINTERGLEMM, AUSTRIA)

Men's Results
Downhill Franz Heinzer (SWI)
Slalom Marc Giradelli (LUX)
Giant Slalom Rudolf Nierlich (AUT)
Super G Stefan Eberharter (AUT)
Combined Stefan Eberharter (AUT)

Women's Results
Downhill Petra Kronberger (AUT)
Slalom Vreni Schneider (SWI)
Giant Slalom Pernilla Wiberg (SWE)
Super G Ulrike Maier (AUT)
Combined Chantal Bournissen (SWI)

WORLD NORDIC CHAMPIONSHIPS (AT VAL DI FLEMME, ITALY)

Men's Results
30 km Classic Gunde Svan (SWE)
15 km Freestyle Bjorn Dahlie (NOR)
10 km Classic Terje Langli (NOR)
50 km Freestyle Torgny Mogren (SWE)
70 m ski jump Heinz Kuttin (AUT)
90 m ski jump Franci Petek (YUG)
90 m team Austria

Women's Results
30 km Freestyle Jyubov Egorova (USSR)
15 km Classic Elena Valbe (USSR)
10 km Freestyle Elena Valbe (USSR)
5 km Classic Trude Dybendahl (NOR)
20 km relay USSR

SLED DOG RACING

THE IDITAROD (ANCHORAGE TO NOME, ALASKA)

Rick Swenson, 12 days 16 hours 34 minutes 39 seconds

SOCCER

INTERNATIONAL TOURNAMENTS

FIFA WOMEN'S WORLD CUP

Championship Game (at Guangzhou, China)
United States 2, Norway 1

COPA AMERICA (South American Championship, at Santiago, Chile) _____

Winner Argentina

NORTH AMERICAN GOLD CUP _____

Championship Game (at Los Angeles, Calif.)

United States 0, Honduras 0 (U.S. won penalty kick shootout 4–3)

INTERNATIONAL CLUB COMPETITIONS

TOYOTA WORLD CUP CHAMPIONSHIP (at Tokyo, Japan) _____

Red Star Belgrade (YUG) 3, Colo Colo (CHL) 0

EUROPEAN CUP FINAL (at Bari, Italy)_____

Red Star Belgrade (YUG) 0, Olympique Marseille (FRA) 0 (OT) (Red Star won penalty kick shootout 5–3)

EUROPEAN CUP WINNERS' CUP FINAL
(at Rotterdam, Netherlands) _____

Manchester United (ENG) 2, Barcelona (SPA) 1

UEFA CUP (2-game/aggregate goals series) _____

Internazionale of Milan (ITA) 2, A.S. Roma (ITA) 0

A.S. Roma 1, Internazionale 0 (Internazionale win 2–1)

LIBERTADORES CUP (2-game/aggregate goals series) _

Olimpia (PAR) 0, Colo Colo (Chile) 0

Colo Colo 3, Olimpia 0 (Colo Colo win 3–0)

MAJOR SOCCER LEAGUE

Championship Series

San Diego 4, Cleveland 2

Game 1 (at San Diego) San Diego 8, Cleveland 4
Game 2 (at San Diego) Cleveland 4, San Diego 3
Game 3 (at Cleveland) San Diego 6, Cleveland 5
Game 4 (at Cleveland) Cleveland 7, San Diego 5
Game 5 (at Cleveland) San Diego 6, Cleveland 1
Game 6 (at San Diego) San Diego 8, Cleveland 6

NCAA DIVISION I MEN'S FINAL (at Tampa, Fla.)____

Virginia 0, Santa Clara 0 (Virginia won penalty kick shootout 3–1)

NCAA DIVISION I WOMEN'S FINAL
(at Chapel Hill, N.C.)_____

North Carolina 3, Wisconsin 1

SOFTBALL

AMERICAN SOFTBALL ASSOCIATION CHAMPIONSHIPS

Men's Super Slow Pitch Worth/Sunbelt, Centerville, Ga.
Men's Major Slow Pitch Riverside Paving, Louisville, Ky.
Women's Major Slow Pitch Cannan's Illusion, San Antonio, Tex.
Men's Major Fast Pitch Guanella Brothers, Rohnert Park, Calif.
Women's Major Fast Pitch Raybestos Brakettes, Stratford, Conn.

SWIMMING

WORLD CHAMPIONSHIPS (AT PERTH, AUSTRALIA)

Men's Results

50 m freestyle Tom Jager (U.S.)
100 m freestyle Matt Biondi (U.S.)
200 m freestyle Giorgio Lamberti (ITA)
400 m freestyle Joerg Hoffman (GER)
1,500 m freestyle Joerg Hoffman (GER)
50 m butterfly Thilo Hasse (GER)
100 m butterfly Anthony Nesty (SUR)
200 m butterfly Melvin Stewart (U.S.)
50 m breaststroke Chen Jianhong (CHI)
100 m breaststroke Norbert Rozsa (HUN)
200 m breaststroke Mike Barrowman (U.S.)
50 m backstroke Dirk Richter (GER)
100 m backstroke Jeff Rouse (U.S.)
200 m backstroke Martin Lopez Zubero (SPA)
200 m medley Tamás Darnyi (HUN)
400 m medley Tamás Darnyi (HUN)
200 m relay (freestyle) Germany
400 m relay (freestyle) United States
800 m relay (freestyle) Germany
400 m relay (medley) United States

Women's Results

50 m freestyle Zhuang Yong (CHI)
100 m freestyle Nicole Haislett (U.S.)
200 m freestyle Hayley Lewis (AUS)
400 m freestyle Janet Evans (U.S.)
800 m freestyle Janet Evans (U.S.)
50 m butterfly Qian Hong (CHI)
100 m butterfly Qian Hong (CHI)
200 m butterfly Summer Sanders (U.S.)

50 m breaststroke Iulia Landik (USSR)

100 m breaststroke Linley Frame (AUS)

200 m breaststroke Elena Volkova (USSR)

50 m backstroke Yang Wenyi (CHI)

100 m backstroke Krisztina Egerszegi (HUN)

200 m backstroke Krisztina Egerszegi (HUN)

200 m medley Lin Li (CHI)

400 m medley Lin Li (CHI)

200 m relay (freestyle) Germany

400 m relay (freestyle) United States

800 m relay (freestyle) Germany

400 m relay (medley) United States

SYNCHRONIZED SWIMMING

WORLD CHAMPIONSHIPS (AT PERTH, AUSTRALIA)

Solo Sylvie Frechette (CAN)

Duet Karen Josephson/Sarah Josephson (U.S.)

Team United States

TENNIS

GRAND SLAM EVENTS

AUSTRALIAN OPEN

Men's Singles Boris Becker (GER)

Women's Singles Monica Seles (YUG)

Men's Doubles Scott Davis/David Pate (U.S.)

Women's Doubles Patty Fendick/Mary Joe Fernandez (U.S.)

Mixed Doubles Jeremy Bates/Jo Durie (GB)

FRENCH OPEN

Men's Singles Jim Courier (U.S.)

Women's Singles Monica Seles (YUG)

Men's Doubles John Fitzgerald (AUS)/Anders Jarryd (SWE)

Women's Doubles Gigi Fernandez (U.S.)/Jana Novotna (CZE)

Mixed Doubles Cyril Suk/Helena Sukova (CZE)

WIMBLEDON

Men's Singles Michael Stich (GER)

Women's Singles Steffi Graff (GER)

Men's Doubles John Fitzgerald (AUS)/Anders Jarryd (SWE)

Women's Doubles Larisa Savchenko/Natalya Zvereva (USSR)

Mixed Doubles John Fitzgerald/Elizabeth Smylie (AUS)

U.S. OPEN

Men's Singles Stefan Edberg (SWE)

Women's Singles Monica Seles (YUG)

Men's Doubles John Fitzgerald (AUS)/Anders Jarryd (SWE)

Women's Doubles Pam Shriver (U.S.)/Natalya Zvereva (USSR)

Mixed Doubles Manon Bollegraf/Tom Nijssen (NL)

I.B.M./APT TOUR

Leading Money Winner Stefan Edberg (SWE), $2,363,575

KRAFT GENERAL FOODS WORLD TOUR

Leading Money Winner Monica Seles (YUG), $2,457,758

TEAM COMPETITIONS

DAVIS CUP FINAL (at Lyon, France)

France 3, United States 1

FEDERATION CUP FINAL (at Nottingham, England)

Spain 2, United States 1

TRACK AND FIELD

WORLD CHAMPIONSHIPS (AT TOKYO, JAPAN)

Men's Results

100 meters Carl Lewis (U.S.)

200 meters Michael Johnson (U.S.)

400 meters Antonio Pettigrew (U.S.)

800 meters Billy Konchellah (KEN)

1,500 meters Noureddine Morceli (ALG)

Steeplechase Moses Kiptanui (KEN)

5,000 meters Yobes Ondieki (KEN)

10,000 meters Moses Tanui (KEN)

Marathon Hiromi Taniguchi (JAP)

110 meter hurdles Greg Foster (U.S.)

400 meter hurdles Samuel Matete (ZAM)

20 km walk Maurizio Damilano (ITA)

50 km walk Aleksandr Potashov (USSR)

High jump Charles Austin (U.S.)

Long jump Mike Powell (U.S.)

ONE GIANT LEAP ■ THE OUTSTANDING ATHLETIC PERFORMANCE OF 1991 WAS MIKE POWELL'S WORLD RECORD LONG JUMP LEAP OF 29 FEET 4½ INCHES.

Pole vault Sergey Bubka (USSR)

Triple jump Kenny Harrison (U.S.)

Javelin Kimmo Kinnunen (FIN)

Discus Lars Reidel (GER)

Shot put Werner Guenthor (SWI)

Hammer Yuri Sedykh (USSR)

Decathlon Dan O'Brien (U.S.)

4 x 100 m relay United States

4 x 400 m relay United States

Women's Results

100 meters Katrin Krabbe (GER)

200 meters Katrin Krabbe (GER)

400 meters Marie-Josee Perec (FRA)

800 meters Lilia Nurutdinova (USSR)

1,500 meters Hassiba Boulmerka (ALG)

3,000 meters Tatynana Dorovskikh (USSR)

10,000 meters Liz McColgan (GB)

Marathon Wanda Panfil (POL)

10 km walk Alina Ivanova (USSR)

100 meter hurdles Lyudmila Narozhilenko (USSR)

400 meter hurdles Tatyana Ledovskaya (USSR)

Long jump Jackie Joyner-Kersee (U.S.)

High jump Heike Henkel (GER)

Discus Tsvetanka Khristova (BUL)

Shot put Huang Zhihong (CHI)

Javelin Xu Demei (CHI)

Heptathlon Sabine Braun (GER)

4 x 100 m relay Jamaica

4 x 400 m relay USSR

WRESTLING

WORLD FREESTYLE CHAMPIONSHIPS (AT VARNA, BULGARIA)

105.5 lbs Vugar Orudzhev (USSR)

114.5 lbs Zeke Jones (U.S.)

125.5 lbs Sergei Smith (USSR)

136.5 lbs John Smith (U.S.)

149.5 lbs Arsen Fadzaev (USSR)

163 lbs Amir Khadem (IRA)

180.5 lbs Kevin Jackson (U.S.)

198 lbs Maharbek Khadartsev (USSR)

220 lbs Leri Khabelov (USSR)

286 lbs Andreas Schroder (GER)

Team Soviet Union

WORLD GRECO-ROMAN CHAMPIONSHIPS (AT VARNA, BULGARIA)

105.5 lbs Duk-Yong Gooun (SK)

114.5 lbs Raul Martinez (CUB)

125.5 lbs Rifat Yildiz (GER)

136.5 lbs Sergei Martynov (USSR)

149.5 lbs Islam Duguchiev (USSR)

163 lbs Mnatsakan Iskandarian (USSR)

180.5 lbs Peter Farkus (HUN)

198 lbs Maik Bullman (GER)

220 lbs Hector Millian (CUB)

286 lbs Alexander Karelin (USSR)

Team USSR

1992 WINTER GAMES RESULTS

(STAGED AT ALBERTVILLE, FRANCE, FEB. 8–23, 1992)

Country Abbreviation Codes: AUT, Austria; CAN, Canada; CHI, China; CZE, Czechoslovakia; FIN, Finland; FRA, France; GER, Germany; ITA, Italy; JAP, Japan; LUX, Luxembourg; NK, North Korea; NL, Netherlands; NOR, Norway; NZ, New Zealand; SK, South Korea; SPA, Spain SWE, Sweden; SWI, Switzerland; U.S., United States of America; U.T., Unified Team.

EVENTS	GOLD	SILVER	BRONZE
ALPINE SKIING (Men)			
Downhill	Patrick Ortlieb (AUT)	Franck Piccard (FRA)	Guenther Mader (AUT)
Slalom	Finn Christian Jagge (NOR)	Alberto Tomba (ITA)	Michael Tritscher (AUT)
Giant Slalom	Alberto Tomba (ITA)	Marc Girardelli (LUX)	Kjetil Andre Aamodt (NOR)
Super Giant Slalom	Kjetil Andre Aamodt (NOR)	Marc Girardelli (LUX)	Jan Einar Thorsen (NOR)
Combined	Josef Polig (ITA)	Gianfranco Martin (ITA)	Steve Locher (SWI)
ALPINE SKIING (Women)			
Downhill	Kerrin Lee-Gartner (CAN)	Hilary Lindh (U.S.)	Veronika Wallinger (AUT)
Slalom	Petra Kronberger (AUT)	Annelise Coberger (NZ)	Blanca Fernandez Ochoa (SPA)
Giant Slalom	Pernilla Wiberg (SWE)	Diann Roffe (U.S.)*[Tie] Anita Wachter (AUT)*[Tie]	
Super Giant Slalom	Deborah Compagnoni (ITA)	Carole Merle (FRA)	Katja Seizinger (GER)
Combined	Petra Kronberger (AUT)	Anita Wachter (AUT)	Florence Masnada (FRA)
BIATHON (Men)			
10 km	Mark Kirchner (GER)	Ricco Gross (GER)	Harri Eloranta (FIN)
20 km	Yevgeny Redkine (U.T.)	Mark Kirchner (GER)	Mikael Lofgren (SWE)
4 x7.5 km relay	Germany	Unified Team	Sweden
BIATHON (Women)			
7.5 km	Anfissa Restzova (U.T.)	Antje Misersky (GER)	Elena Belova (U.T.)
15 km	Antje Misersky (GER)	Svetlana Pecherskaia (U.T.)	Myriam Bedard (CAN)
3 x7.5 km relay	France	Germany	Unified Team
BOBSLED			
2–man	Gustav Weder/Donat Acklin (SWI)	Rudi Lochner/Markus Zimmerman (GER)	Christoph Langen/Gunther Eger (GER)
4–man	Austria I	Germany I	Switzerland I
CROSS-COUNTRY SKIING (Men)			
10 km	Vegard Ulvang (NOR)	Marco Alvarello (ITA)	Christer Majback (SWE)
15 km	Bjorn Dahlie (NOR)	Vegard Ulvang (NOR)	Giorgio Vanzetta (ITA)
30 km	Vegard Ulvang (NOR)	Bjorn Dahlie (NOR)	Terje Langli (NOR)
50 km	Bjorn Dahlie (NOR)	Maurilio De Zolt (ITA)	Giorgio Vanzetta (ITA)
4 x 10 km relay	Norway	Italy	Finland
CROSS-COUNTRY SKIING (Women)			
5 km	Marjut Lukkarinen (FIN)	Lyubov Egorova (U.T.)	Elena Valbe (U.T.)
10 km	Lyubov Egorova (U.T.)	Stefania Belmondo (ITA)	Elena Valbe (U.T.)
15 km	Lyubov Egorova (U.T.)	Marjut Lukkarinen (FIN)	Elena Valbe (U.T.)
30 km	Stefania Belmondo (ITA)	Lyubov Egorova (U.T.)	Elena Valbe (U.T.)
4 x 5 km relay	Unified Team	Norway	Italy

EVENTS	GOLD	SILVER	BRONZE
FIGURE SKATING			
Men	Viktor Petrenko (U.T.)	Paul Wylie (U.S.)	Petr Barna (CZE)
Women	Kristi Yamaguchi (U.S.)	Midori Ito (JAP)	Nancy Kerrigan (U.S.)
Pairs	Natalya Mishkutienok & Artur Dmitriev (U.T.)	Elena Bechke & Denis Petrov (U.T.)	Isabelle Brasseur & Lloyd Eisler (CAN)
Ice Dance	Marina Klimova & Sergei Ponomarenko (U.T.)	Isabelle & Paul Duchesnay (FRA)	Maia Usova & Aleksandr Zhulin (U.T.)
FREESTYLE SKIING (Moguls)			
Men	Edgar Grospiron (FRA)	Olivier Allamand (FRA)	Nelson Carmichael (U.S.)
Women	Donna Weinbrecht (U.S.)	Elizaveta Kojevnikova (U.T.)	Stine Hattestad (NOR)
HOCKEY			
	Unified Team	Canada	Czechoslovakia
LUGE (Men)			
Singles	Georg Hackl (GER)	Markus Prock (AUT)	Markus Schmidt (AUT)
2–man	Stefan Krausse & Jan Behrendt (GER)	Yves Mankel & Thomas Rudolph (GER)	Hansjorg Raffi & Norbert Huber (ITA)
LUGE (Women)			
Singles	Doris Neuner (AUT)	Angelika Neuner (AUT)	Susi Erdmann (GER)
NORDIC COMBINED			
Individual	Fabrice Guy (FRA)	Sylvain Guillaume (FRA)	Klaus Sulzenbacher (AUT)
Combined-team	Japan	Norway	Austria
SHORT TRACK SPEEDSKATING (Men)			
1,000 m	Kim Ki-Hoon (SK)	Frederic Blackburn (CAN)	Lee Yoon-Ho (SK)
5,000 m relay	South Korea	Canada	Japan
SHORT TRACK SPEEDSKATING (Women)			
500 m	Cathy Turner (U.S.)	Li Yan (CHI)	Hwang Ok Sil (NK)
3,000 m relay	Canada	United States	Unified Team
SKI JUMPING			
Normal Hill	Ernst Vettori (AUT)	Martin Hollwarth (AUT)	Toni Nieminen (FIN)
Large Hill	Toni Nieminen (FIN)	Martin Hollwarth (AUT)	Heinz Kuttin (AUT)
Team	Finland	Austria	Czechoslovakia
SPEED SKATING (Men)			
500 m	Uwe-Jens Mey (GER)	Toshiyuki Kuroiwa (JAP)	Junichi Inoue (JAP)
1,000 m	Olaf Zinke (GER)	Kim Yoon-Man (SK)	Yukinori Miyabe (JAP)
1,500 m	Johann Olav Koss (NOR)	Adne Sondral (NOR)	Leo Visser (NL)
5,000 m	Geir Karlstad (NOR)	Falco Zandstra (NL)	Leo Visser (NL)
10,000 m	Bart Veldkamp (NL)	Johann Olav Koss (NOR)	Geir Karlstad (NOR)

EVENTS	GOLD	SILVER	BRONZE
		SPEED SKATING (Women)	
500 m	Bonnie Blair (U.S.)	Ye Qiaobo (CHI)	Christa Luding (GER)
1,000 m	Bonnie Blair (U.S.)	Ye Qiaobo (CHI)	Monique Gatbrecht (GER)
1,500 m	Jacqueline Boerner (GER)	Gunda Niemann (GER)	Seiko Hashimoto (JAP)
3,000 m	Gunda Niemann (GER)	Heiko Warnicke (GER)	Emese Hunyady (AUT)
5,000 m	Gunda Niemann (GER)	Heiko Warnicke (GER)	Claudia Pechstein (GER)

1992 WINTER GAMES MEDAL TABLE

COUNTRY	GOLD	SILVER	BRONZE	TOTAL
Germany	10	10	6	26
Unified Team*	9	6	8	23
Austria	6	7	8	21
Norway	9	6	5	20
Italy	4	6	4	14
United States	5	4	2	11
France	3	5	1	9
Finland	3	1	3	7
Canada	2	3	2	7
Japan	1	2	4	7
South Korea	2	1	1	4
Netherlands	1	1	2	4
Sweden	1	0	3	4
Switzerland	1	0	2	3
China	0	3	0	3
Czechoslovakia	0	0	3	3
Luxembourg	0	2	0	2
New Zealand	0	1	0	1
North Korea	0	0	1	1
Spain	0	0	1	1

* Representing the former Soviet republics of Russia, Belarus, Ukraine, Kazakhistan and Uzbekistan.

OLYMPIC RECORDS SET AT ALBERTVILLE

Most medals Cross-country skier Raisa Smetanina (Unified Team) became the most successful competitor in Winter Games history. Her team's victory in the relay event increased her career medal haul to 10 medals, breaking the mark she had previously held with Sixten Jernberg (Sweden). Smetanina's record medal tally comprises four gold, five silver and one bronze. She had previously competed for the USSR, 1976–88.

Oldest gold medalist At age 39 years 352 days, Raisa Smetanina (Unified Team) became the oldest woman to win a Winter Games gold medal as a member of the winning 4 x 5 km cross-country relay team.

Youngest gold medalist At 16 years 259 days, Toni Nieminen (Finland) became the youngest gold medalist in Winter Games history, winning the ski jump team event. Nieminen was one day younger than the previous record holder, William Fiske (U.S.).

United States

Most gold medals (woman) Speed skater Bonnie Blair won two gold medals in Albertville, increasing her career tally to three, the most gold medals won by any American woman in Winter Games competition.

With the exception of names listed under "record files," names of sports figures appear only in the main body of the text.